CADOGANguides

tak *the kids*
Paris and
Disneyland® Resort Paris

HELEN TRUSZKOWSKI

About the series

take the kids guides are written specifically for parents, grandparents and carers. Each guide not only draws on what is of particular interest to kids, but also takes into account the realities of childcare – from tired legs to low boredom thresholds – enabling both grown-ups and their charges to have a great day out or a fabulous holiday.

Cadogan Guides
Highlands House, 165 The Broadway, Wimbledon,
London SW19 1NE
info@cadoganguides.co.uk
www.cadoganguides.com

The Globe Pequot Press
PO Box 480, Guilford,
Connecticut 06437–0480

Copyright © Helen Truszkowski 2000, 2002, 2003, 2004
Maps © Cadogan Guides, drawn by Kingston Presentation Graphics

Art direction and book design: Sarah Gardner
Layout: Tracey Ridgewell
All photography © Moritz Steiger, except for pp.193–224 © Disneyland® Resort Paris and p.104 © Parc Astérix

Managing Editor: Antonia Cunningham
Series Editor: Melanie Dakin
Editor: Anna Amari-Parker

Proofreading: Susannah Wight
Indexing: Isobel McLean
Production: Navigator Guides Ltd.
Printed in Italy by Printer Trento srl.
A catalogue record for this book is available from the British Library
ISBN 1-86011-146-7

About the author

Helen Truszkowski

Helen Truszkowski is an established travel writer and photographer. Over the past decade her journeys have taken her around the globe, including six months working in South Africa. She contributes to a range of magazines, newspapers and broadcast media worldwide. Helen's eight-year-old son, George, has accompanied her on her travels since he was a few weeks old, patiently awaiting his dream position as her research assistant for Disneyland® Paris. Helen is series consultant for Cadogan's *take the kids* series, and author of *take the kids Travelling*.

Acknowledgements

Thanks go to Nikki Palmas, Clare Fine, Lisa Baker and the Disneyland® Paris Press Office and PR teams; to Roger Harrison at Eurostar; to Moritz Steiger for a lively eye and being especially helpful; to the Davidsons for their updates and to George for his unbridled enthusiasm.

In memory of Rose, our exceptional Mum and Granny

Contributing authors

Joseph Fullman is a professional travel writer who fell in love with Paris as an awe-struck six-year-old and has been returning regularly ever since. For Cadogan, he is the author of *take the kids London*, *take the kids Short Breaks*, *take the kids England*, Navigator Guides and *Britain's Top Tourist Attractions*, and he has also contributed articles to newspapers and websites.

Derek Mackenzie-Hook is a single parent living in Scotland. During the last 10 years he has travelled widely with his two young sons who have acted as researchers, emergency photographers and sometimes guinea pigs on many assignments around the world. Derek specializes in writing family travel guides and features, focusing on providing information that will help parents to have a stress-free holiday by locating child-friendly destinations where children are genuinely welcomed, not just tolerated.

Series editor

Melanie Dakin is series editor of Cadogan's *take the kids* series, having previously acted as consultant editor on the Time Out *London for Children* guide and editor of *Kids Out* magazine. As a mother of two, Melanie has spent a great deal of time navigating cities with children, pushchairs, toys and luggage. To date only a couple of baby bottles and a small coolbag have been left behind.

Contents

4

You may think of Paris as a city just for grown-ups or couples. No surprises there. However, it's also great for kids. There are parks where they can take pony rides, sail model boats or have a picnic; funfairs with rides, games and candyfloss galore; and a vast array of museums from immense institutions to little gems, stuffed full of weird and wonderful things. La Villette, alone, is pretty close to every kid's dream – a sort of science theme park, crammed with interactive exhibits. In summer, you can even even take a trip to the beach without leaving the city limits because in July a stretch of the Seine riverbank is turned into a replica Mediterranean resort complete with sand, deck chairs and palm trees. When the sun goes down, make time for an evening trip on a *bateau mouche* (fly boat) to take in the riverside monuments picked out by spotlights. Day or night, there are spectacular views to enjoy – from the Eiffel Tower or the Arc de Triomphe, by the Sacré Coeur, and from the heights of the top level of the Grande Arche de la Défense.

In spite of all this, of course, you may find that your kids' greatest pleasure comes not from rides or sights or views, but just from seeing the little quirks of everyday living that make Paris such a special place: cast-iron drinking fountains on cobbled pavements; traders selling crêpes or roasted sweetcorn on street corners; and accordion-players performing outside crowded cafés.

Plus, a very big attraction, just 32km (20 miles) east of the city, is Disneyland® Resort Paris, a fun-filled, child-centred palace of pleasure. Here kids of every age can loop-the-loop at blood-chilling speed, hurtle past stars and planets, spin round in gigantic tea cups, race through kooky mazes, clamber across swaying rope bridges, stare into the jaws of foul-smelling dragons, and get up close and personal with the world's most famous mouse – yep, that's Mickey.

Guide to the Guide

Finding your way around this guide is easy.

Travel Gives you information on every aspect of journeying to, from and around the city of Paris and environs including how to get into the city from the airport, and local trains and buses.

Ideas Ideas These opening sections contain hints and tips to help you get to know Paris including what you can do for free, handy tickets and passes that will help you to see the city without a hitch, and themes to follow for a memorable day out.

See It Do It The heart of the book covers the sights of Paris with the low-down on stress-free, enjoyable tours and a Paris calendar. The guide to the city is divided into seven area chapters. In each, we have identified the main sights, the best local places to eat, and distinctive shops, walks and other engaging attractions for kids local to a specific area. For every attraction, there is up-to-date information on how to get there, opening times, admission prices and activities specifically for kids. Some indication of appropriate age ranges is also given, plus how long you might allow for each attraction. 'Kids in' details Paris' best indoor attractions and entertainment for tots (cinemas, circuses, unusual museums), while 'Kids out' covers the city's multipurpose parks. 'Sports and activities' points to the best places to watch and participate in different sports. In 'Days Out', we provide details of day trips within an hour's journey of the Paris city limits.

Need To Know This section contains a chapter on all kinds of practical information – post offices, banks, the police, babysitters, insurance, and so on – to make your stay in Paris as hassle-free and as safe as possible. Separate chapters list the best child-friendly places to stay, eat and shop in detail.

Disneyland® Resort Paris This final section is dedicated 100 per cent to Europe's première theme park, with advice on how to book, what to expect and tips on making the most of your visit: from which rides are suitable for younger children to the best places to stay at or around the Park.

Throughout, the text is sprinkled with questions and challenges to help you and your children get the most from your stay as well as stories to keep them entertained as you travel from A to B. The answers can be found in the guide, but are also listed separately on p.250.

Enjoy!

TRAVEL

Paris is not a difficult city to get to. It's one of the world's most popular destinations served by all the major air carriers and intense competition on transatlantic routes means there are always lots of cheap deals around from North America. Road and rail links with the rest of mainland Europe are good. For Brits, in particular, it's never been easier to get to Paris with the French capital just 3 hours away from London by train via the Eurotunnel.

For travel details to Disneyland® Resort Paris, *see* **Getting There** p.183.

Flights

Children under the age of 2 usually travel for just 10% of the adult fare although they will not be entitled to either a seat or baggage allowance. Between the ages of 3 and 11, children cost between a half and two-thirds of the adult fare. Children over 12 years old are regarded as adults and must pay the full fare.

From the UK

Once you've taken into account check-in times and transfers from the airport, flying from London to Paris isn't much quicker than taking the train. It's really only worth considering if you can get a substantially better fare than you would with Eurostar. Scour websites and weekend newspapers for bargains or, in London, check the listings in *Time Out* and the *Evening Standard*.

Of the scheduled airlines, British Airways and Air France offer competitive packages that include accommodation and long-haul carriers may offer cheap stop-off deals to Paris en route to some far-flung destination. As well as from Heathrow, British Airways operates flights from several other UK airports, while BMI–British Midland flies to Paris from Heathrow, Leeds–Bradford and East Midlands airport as well.

The biggest discounts are offered by the no-frills budget airlines. Easyjet (which flies from Luton Airport), BMI Baby (British Midland's budget sibling which flies from Heathrow) and Ryanair (which flies from Glasgow to Beauvais, 56km (35 miles) northeast of Paris) all run promotions throughout the year when you may be able to pick up a flight for as little as £19.99. Book these well in advance because Easyjet, in particular, operates an escalating fare policy. The first customers to enquire about a particular flight will get the cheapest deal but, as the service fills up, so the prices will rise until they are more or less compatible with those of the major carriers.

Discounts are available to anyone under 26 and students aged 32 or under. There's a multitude of cheap flight sites on the web. Check out:
www.lowestfare.com
www.cheapflights.co.uk
www.farebase.net
www.lastminute.com

Discount agents
STA 86 Old Brompton Rd, London SW7
t UK 0870 160 0599
www.statravel.co.uk
Branches across the UK.
Trailfinders 42–50 Earl's Court Road, London SW5
t UK 020 7938 3366
www.trailfinders.co.uk

Major airlines
Air France t UK 0845 345 1000
www.airfrance.com/uk
British Airways t UK 0870 850 9850
www.britishairways.com
British Midland t UK 0870 607 0555
www.flybmi.co.uk
Fly Bet UK 0870 567 6676
www.flybe.com

Budget airlines
BMI Baby t UK 0870 264 2229
www.bmibaby.com
Easyjet t UK 0871 750 0100
www.easyjet.com
Ryanair t UK 0871 246 0000
www.ryanair.com

From North America

Competition on transatlantic routes is fierce and there are many cheap deals to be found. The best value tickets offered by the major airlines are Apex and Super Apex, which must be booked 14–21 days before departure and involve a stay of at least seven nights. Charter flights are usually the cheapest: visit budget flight websites, especially those of consolidators, companies that buy blocks of unsold tickets from major airlines and sell them on at a discounted price.

Flight times to Paris from North America
New York 7–8 hours
Miami 5–6 hours
Los Angeles 10–11 hours
Hawaii 19 hours
Montreal 7 hours
Toronto 8 hours

Many of the larger airlines provide special on-board services for families such as designated flight attendants, children's TV channels, play packs and seat-back computer games.

Major airlines
Air Canada toll free **t** US/Canada 888 247 2262
www.aircanada.com
American Airlines toll free **t** US 800 433 7300
www.americanair.com
British Airways toll free **t** US 800 airways
www.britishairways.com
Delta Airlines
toll free **t** US 800 241 4141
www.delta.com
United Airlines toll free **t** US 800 538 2929
www.ual.com
Virgin Atlantic Airways
t US 800 862 8621
www.virgin-atlantic.com

Consolidators in North America
Air Brokers Travel toll free **t** US 800 883 3273
www.airbrokers.com
ELT Express t US 201 541 3867
www.eltexpress.com
UniTravel toll free **t** US 800 325 2222
www.unitravel.com

Arriving by air

Roissy–Charles de Gaulle
23km (14 miles) north of central Paris
t 01 48 62 22 80
www.adp.fr

Which of the transport services from Roissy best suits you may well depend on which part of Paris you are staying in, so check the map first.

RER: Line B3 or 'Roissyrail'
Every 8 mins, 5.44am–12.11pm

Child fares
On nearly all public transport in Paris, children aged between 4 and 11 pay a reduced fare (around half the adult one), while children younger than 4 go free, so long as they don't take up a seat.

Fares Adult single €7.60, child single €5.30
Journey time About 25mins to Gare du Nord
Line B runs to **m** Gare du Nord, Châtelet Les Halles, St Michel Nôtre Dame and Denfert Rochereau
RER is the fastest way to get to the centre of town. Your RER ticket is valid on the métro to complete your journey within Paris.

Air France bus
To the Arc de Triomphe via Porte Maillot
Every 12 mins, 5.50am–11pm
Fares Adult single €9.15, child single €4.58
Journey time 45mins to the Arc de Triomphe

To the Gare de Lyon and Gare Montparnasse
Every 30 minutes, 7am–9pm
Fares Adult single €10.67, child single €5.34
Journey time About 1 hour
Buy your tickets from the Cars Air France office at the airport before boarding the bus.

Roissybus
To Rue Scribe (by the Opéra Garnier)
Every 15 mins, 6am–11pm
Fares €8.08 (for adults or children)
Journey time About 45mins

RATP local buses
Line 350
Every 20 mins, 6.30am–8.30pm
Fares The journey will use up 6 single tickets (*see* Tickets and passes, p.13)
Journey time 50mins
To Gare du Nord and Gare de l'Est
Line 351
Every 30 mins, 6.30am–8.30pm
Fares The journey will use up 6 single tickets
Journey time 55mins
To Porte de Bagnolet, Porte de Vincennes, Nation

Orly
14km (9 miles) south of Paris
t 01 49 75 15 15
www.adp.fr

RER: Line C8 or 'Orlyrail'

Every 15–30 mins, 5.45am–11.30pm
Fares Adult single €5.15, child single €3.55
Journey time 40mins
To Gare d'Austerlitz, St Michel Nôtre Dame, Champ de Mars–Tour Eiffel

To use this line, you must take a free RATP shuttle bus from the Orly terminals to Pont de Rungis-Aéroport d'Orly station.

Orlyval

Every 5–8 minutes, 6.30am–11pm (Mon–Sat), 7am–10.55pm (Sun)
Fares Adult single to central Paris €8.65, child single €4.30
Journey time 35mins

An automatic, driverless mini-métro that connects with RER line B at Antony station – a faster route than line C to Châtelet and Right Bank Paris.

Air France Bus

Every 12 mins, 6am–11pm
Fares Adult single €8, child single €4
Journey time 30mins (to Invalides)
Stops at Gare Montparnasse and Invalides

Buy your tickets from the Cars Air France office at the airport before boarding the bus.

Orlybus

Every 12 mins, 6am–11.30pm
Fares €5.50 (for adults or children)
Journey time 30mins
Connects with RER Line B at Denfert Rochereau

Jetbus

Every 15 minutes, 6am–11pm
Fares Adult single €3.80
Journey time 12mins
Connects with Ⓜ Villejuif–Louis Aragon

Beauvais

56km (35 miles) northeast of Paris
t 01 58 05 08 95
www.aeroportbeauvais.com

Beauvais Airport Bus

20 mins after each arrival
Fares Adult single €10, child single €3.55
Journey time 1hr 10mins
Connects with Ⓜ Porte Maillot

Taxi
By far the least stressful way of getting into the city centre from the airports, but also the most expensive. Supplements will be added on if more than three people are travelling or if you have lots of luggage with you.
Fare from Roissy €30–40
Fare from Orly €23–30
Fare from Beauvais €65–75

By rail

Eurostar

t 0870 600 0782
t 0870 167 6767 (to request a brochure)
www.eurostar.com
20 trains daily from London Waterloo
Fares Vary. A Leisure Return, which must be booked 14 days ahead of departure, can be bought for as little as adults £59, children £50, under-4s free. The later you book, the more expensive the fare will be.
No baggage weight limit
Wheelchair users need to inform Eurostar staff of their requirements when booking

Eurostar trains arrive at the **Gare du Nord**, which has connections to two RER and two métro lines. It's a large station with several levels: taxis are parked on the level below the main platforms, but the rank is well signposted and they're not expensive. If you're continuing your journey by métro and don't have tickets already, it's a good idea to send the speediest member of your party sprinting off to buy them at the métro *guichet* (ticket office), before the rest of the train passengers get there.

Paris has five other main stations: **Gare de l'Est** (for services from northeast France, Switzerland, Austria, southern Germany), **Gare de Lyon** (southeast France, Switzerland and Italy), **Gare d'Austerlitz** (southwest France, most of Spain and Portugal), **Gare Montparnasse** (western France and Spain) and **Gare St Lazare** (Normandy). All have connections to the métro network. From Britain,

---

Don't miss the train!
Eurostar's service adheres to strict security codes. Much the same as when taking an airline flight, you are expected to check in at least 30 minutes before the train is due to depart. Otherwise the gates are closed and your ticket will be useless.

call **Rail Europe** on **t** UK 0870 584 8848 or log on to www.raileurope.co.uk for information on rail services (other than Eurostar) in France.

By ferry

The completion of the Eurotunnel transformed the cross-Channel travel industry. Ferry companies had to make fares more competitive and now offer a range of deals to draw custom away from the Chunnel – especially for 3- or 5-day returns, so it's always worth checking prices. Many lines offer perks for families – under-4s usually travel free, there are discounts for under-14s and most ferries boast family facilities (restaurants, baby-changing rooms, play areas, video rooms).

Dover–Calais
P&O Ferries, t UK 0870 520 2020
www.posl.com
35 sailings a day in High Season
Fares A family of four in a medium-sized car should expect to pay from about £260, depending on the time of year, but about £120 for a short-term return. Usual journey time is 1 hour 15 minutes.
Sea France, t UK 0870 571 1711
www.seafrance.co.uk
Around 25 sailings a day in High Season
Fares French-owned Sea France has some of the most competitive rates across the Channel with frequent special offers. It also operates the largest, fastest craft on the Dover–Calais route. Three-day returns start at £75 while standard returns begin at around £110
Hoverspeed, t UK 0870 240 8070
www.hoverspeed.com
Fares The Super Seacat usually crosses from Dover to Calais in 45 minutes (but is more affected than the larger ferries by bad weather). Fares for a family of four in a standard car range from £125 for a maximum of 5 days' stay and rise to around £270 for a longer trip.

Other ferry routes
Dover–Boulogne
Speed Ferries t UK 0130 420 3000
www.speedferries.com
Not yet operational at the time of going to press, the brand new Speed Ferry service is due to commence on 31 March 2004. The crossing time is expected to be just 50mins. As yet, no fare details have been made available.
Transmanche Ferries t UK 0800 817 1201
www.transmancheferries.com

Newhaven–Dieppe
Hoverspeed t UK 0870 240 8070
www.hoverspeed.com
Transmanche Ferries t UK 0800 817 1201
www.transmancheferries.com

Portsmouth–Caen, Poole–Cherbourg
Brittany Ferries t UK 0870 536 0360
www.brittany-ferries.com

Portsmouth–Le Havre, Portsmouth–Cherbourg
P&O European Ferries t 0870 242 4999
www.poportsmouth.com

By car via the Eurotunnel

Eurotunnel–Folkestone–Calais
t 0870 535 3535
www.eurotunnel.com
Three departures in an hour at most times
Fares Flexible returns start at around £130 if you stay for up to 5 days; fares for over 5 days begin at around £260 but, as is often the case with the ferries, there are frequent short-term offers. The fare is for car space only regardless of the number of passengers travelling.
Journey time 35mins
Check in at least 25 minutes but no more than 2 hours before departure.
British terminal: off junction 11a of the M20
French terminal: off junction 13 of the A16
No baggage weight limit
Wheelchair users need to inform Eurotunnel staff of their requirements when booking

Eurotunnel transports vehicles in purpose-built carriers between Folkestone and Calais. Most people choose to stay in their cars, although you can get out to stretch your legs and use the facilities in the compartment (toilets, drinks machines). It is advisable to book in advance although it is possible just to turn up and wait. You will be put on a standby list and given space on a first-come, first-served basis.

The A1/A16 motorway (*autoroute*) is toll free from Calais to Boulogne, after which there is a toll charge. The drive from Calais to Paris should cost around €16 in tolls and takes approximately 3 hours. Alternatively, you can opt for a scenic (and free) cruise along less congested N roads or the green-signed *flèches vertes* (holiday routes), which will take a good deal longer. Michelin Map 911 details both motorways and *flèches vertes*.

Any car entering France must have its registration and insurance papers with it and also a hazard warning triangle, which must be displayed 50m behind the vehicle in the event of an accident or breakdown. If you're coming from the UK or Ireland, remember to use headlamp adjusters for driving on the right. Seatbelts must be worn in the front seats of cars and in the back where fitted.

Drivers who hold a valid licence from an EU country, North America or Australia do not need an international licence in France. If you're thinking of hiring a car, bear in mind that rates are among the highest in Europe. If possible, try to arrange a fly-drive or holiday package before you go. For more details, *see* p.16.

By bus

National Express/Eurolines
52 Grosvenor Gardens, London SW1
t 0870 580 8080
www.nationalexpress.com
Fares A 30-day advance return costs £32; standard adult fares begin at £50. Discounts are available for under-25s, while under-16s pay half the adult fare and under-5s travel **free**.
Journey time About 8hrs (London–Paris)
Paris' international coach station, the Gare Routière International Paris–Gallieni, is on the eastern edge of the city in the suburb of Bagnolet, Ⓜ Gallieni.

The cheapest, but also the least comfortable, way of getting to Paris.

Border formalities

From Europe
Visitors from the European Union can enter France for up to 90 days with just a passport or national identity card. If you plan to stay longer, you'll have to apply for a *carte de séjour* or residency card.

From other parts of the world
Visitors from North America can enter France for up to 90 days without a visa. If you plan to stay longer, you must apply for a *carte de séjour*. Other nationals should check on their particular entry requirements with their respective embassies.

Customs
EU nationals over the age of 17 are no longer required to make a customs declaration upon entry into another EU country and can import a limitless amount of goods for personal use. Quantities defined as being for personal use are: 800 cigarettes, 400 small cigars, 200 cigars, 10 litres of spirits, 90 litres of wine and 110 litres of beer. For non-EU nationals, the limits are 200 cigarettes, 1 litre of spirits, 2 litres of wine and 50g of perfume. Visitors can carry up to €7,600 in currency.

Détaxe refund scheme
If you are from a non-EU country and have spent more than €180 in any one shop, you can claim a refund on any VAT (value-added tax) paid (VAT currently stands at 20.6 per cent) when you leave the country – so long as you don't stay longer than 90 days. Pick up a *détaxe* form at the shop, fill in the details, get the form stamped by customs when you leave France and then send it back to the shop, who will refund the money direct to your bank account or credit card. *See also* p. 235.

Paris has one of the best public transport systems of any European city. The **métro**, in particular, is a godsend – fast, efficient and reliable – and kids who have never travelled on an underground train before will appreciate the novelty. On the newest line, the automatic *Méteor* between Madeleine and Bibliothèque François Mitterand (line 14), they can even sit at the front pretending to drive the train. There's also an extensive **bus** network and a local train system, the **RER**, which you can use to zip quickly across town or take longer trips out to destinations in the suburbs (such as Versailles, *see* p.128) and the Île de France. Driving in Paris doesn't make much sense (too much congestion, too little parking), but walking does: Paris is a flat, safe, not to mention beautiful, city, best appreciated on foot. Do be aware, though, that pavements in many older parts of town, such as the Marais and the Latin Quarter, are quite narrow (many with cobblestones) and can be tricky for buggies and wheelchairs.

The **Office de Tourisme** (*see* p.144) provides an excellent free map of Paris (*Plan de Paris*), which includes a street plan and bus and métro/RER routes. Street maps (known as *Paris par Arrondissements*) that show all the individual bus routes can also be bought at most street kiosks and *papeteries*.

For all sightseeing tours of Paris – open-topped buses, *bateaux mouches* boat trips along the Seine or the canals, walking tours and bike tours – *see* **Seeing Paris**, pp.30–34.

By RATP

The Régie Autonome des Transports Parisiens controls Paris' buses and the métro system. For information in English, call **t** 08 36 68 41 14 (calls are charged at €0.34/minute), or check out their website **www**.ratp.fr.

Lost Property
t 01 40 06 75 27

By bus

Buses aren't nearly as speedy as métro trains – Paris' ongoing congestion problems see to that – but they do provide a more pleasant way of getting about the city, with the chance to do some sight-

Tickets and passes
▶ The same tickets are valid for the métro, city buses and RER local trains within the city.
▶ All ticket types can be bought at all métro stations and at tourist offices, the airports and RATP offices. Ten-journey **Carnets** can also be bought in tobacco shops (*tabacs*), but only single tickets can be bought on board buses. Children aged 4–10 pay 50 per cent of adult fares; under-4s travel for **free** so long as they don't take up a seat. Hold on to your ticket until the end of your journey: failure to show your ticket to an inspector could result in a spot fine of between €13 and €35.
▶ Paris and its suburbs are divided into **five concentric fare zones**. Virtually the whole of the city proper (within the *périphérique* ring road) is in zones 1–2. With an ordinary single ticket (adult €1.30, child €0.65) you can travel as far as you like on the whole métro system and the RER within zones 1–2, changing lines as many times as you need within a single journey. On buses, though, you have to buy/use a new ticket each time you change bus or cross into a new fare zone. Note also that buying tickets each time you travel will waste time and money: a much better-value option is to get a **Carnet** of 10 single tickets sold together (adults €10, child €5, a saving of over 30 per cent).
▶ On **RER** lines, maps and signs on the trains indicate the point at which you cross over into zone 3 and so you need an extra ticket. With some places at the end of métro lines that are served by métro and RER (La Défense, St Denis), you can go all the way there on the same métro ticket, but on the (faster) RER you will need to pay a little extra. **Disneyland® Paris** is at the end of RER line A4 in zone 5, and single tickets from central Paris will cost €5.95 for adults, €2.95 for children (*see also* pp. 182, 184).
▶ If you're planning to use public transport a lot (more than 10 separate trips a day) it's worth getting a **Paris Visite** card, which gives you unlimited travel on métro, buses, RER and SNCF trains within Paris for from 1 to 5 days and also entitles you to discounts at some attractions. For zones 1–3 (the minimum), the cost of a 1-day card is adult €8.35/child €4.55; 2 days adult €13.70/child €6.85; 3 days adult €18.25/child €9.15; 5 days adult €26.65/child €13.70.

seeing en route (*see* below). Métro tickets are also valid on the city buses although, unlike on the métro, your ticket is valid only for one trip; each time you change buses, or cross into a new fare zone, you have to use a new ticket. You must stamp (*oblitérer*) your ticket in the machine next to the driver as you enter. Drivers also sell individual tickets, which can only be used on that bus.

Most bus routes run from Monday to Saturday between 6.30am and 12.30am, at which point the Noctambus night bus network (*see* below) takes over. Most routes also operate on Sundays but with a less frequent service. When the number displayed on the front of a bus has a slash through

it, the bus will only run half its usual route. To get a bus to stop, press the red *arrêt demandé* button.

Night buses

The Noctambus night bus network operates between 12.30am and 5.30am. There are 16 lines, most of which leave from the Châtelet–Hôtel de Ville area. The standard fare is €2.60, double the daytime rate.

Trams

Two modern tramlines operate in the suburbs, Tramway T-1 on the north side of Paris (St Denis–Bobigny) and T-2 in the south (La Défense–Issy Val de Seine). They connect at the ends of each line with the métro or RER. Fares are the same as for city buses.

Bus routes to remember

All these city bus routes pass interesting places and engaging parts of town and, outside of the morning and evening rush hours, can provide you with pleasant, relaxed, bargain trips around Paris. Remember, though, that your ticket is only valid for one trip and not the entire journey, so if you wish to stop off at places along the way, use the métro instead.

29 From Gare St Lazare (Mon–Sat only)
Passes the Opéra Garnier, Pompidou Centre, the Marais and Bastille on the way to Gare de Lyon
38 From Gare du Nord
Passes the Pompidou Centre and Place du Châtelet, and then goes via the Sainte Chapelle (in one direction, and Nôtre Dame going north), to St Michel, the Sorbonne, the Luxembourg and the Catacombs
42 From Gare du Nord (Mon–Sat only)
Via Opéra Garnier, Madeleine, Concorde, the Champs Élysées, and then across the Seine and past the Eiffel Tower to Quai André Citroën
67 From Pigalle
Via the Louvre, Île St Louis, the Latin Quarter and Place d'Italie to Porte de Gentilly
69 From Gambetta (Mon–Sat only)
Via Bastille, Hôtel de Ville and Châtelet, then along the *quais* to the Musée d'Orsay, the Invalides and the Champ de Mars
73 From La Défense (Mon–Sat only)
Runs into central Paris past the Arc de Triomphe and along the Champs Élysées to Place de la Concorde, then over the Seine to Musée d'Orsay
86 From the Zoo in the Bois de Vincennes (Mon–Sat only)
Via Nation and Bastille to St Germain des Prés

By métro

The Paris underground system, the métro, is easily the most convenient way of moving around the city. Trains are fast, the service reliable, and the fares economical. With over 300 stations dotted throughout the capital, you're rarely more than 500 metres from a métro stop.

However, finding your way around the métro can be extremely confusing, as train directions are given by naming the station at the end of the line rather than the direction in which the trains are travelling. For instance, if you're travelling northwards on Line 4, which runs between Porte d'Orléans in the south of Paris and Porte de Clignancourt in the north via the city centre, you should look for signs saying *Direction Porte de Clignancourt*. If travelling south on the same line, look for signs saying *Direction Porte d'Orléans*. At big interchanges, a good tip is to follow signs for the number of the line that you wish to travel on: you will then come to a route map near your platform listing all the stations on the line in both directions. Many métro and RER lines meet in central Paris at **Châtelet Les Halles**, an unlovely but giant station where you'll often find yourself changing trains. Throughout the métro, direction signs are white, transfer (*correspondance*) signs are orange and exit signs (*sortie*) are blue. On the platform of every major métro station you'll also find a map of the local neigbourhood (*a plan du quartier*).

Question 1

In New York it's the subway, in London it's called the tube. What is it in Paris?

answer also on p.250

Métro trains run on each line from 5.30am to 12.50am every 3 to 10 minutes, depending on the time of day. There are now 14 métro lines with a few short 'offshoot lines' (3 bis, 7 bis) to bridge some of the gaps between the main lines. Line 14, known as La Météor, is the pride and joy of the RATP: an automatic, electronically driven, rubber-wheeled state-of-the-art service between Bibliothèque F. Mitterrand and Madeleine. Try to get a seat in the front carriage with its head-on views of the on-rushing tunnel.

If you're travelling with very small children, be aware that there are many stairs and only a few escalators in métro stations, while the heavy doors and tricky turnstiles require expert manoeuvring of pushchairs and buggies. If you can get hold of a baby backpack or quick-folding buggy, your life will be much easier.

By RER

The high-speed RER (Réseau Express Régional) city-suburb rail network is run jointly by the national rail company SNCF (Société Nationale des Chemins de Fer Français) and the Paris transport authority RATP (see above), and is best used for covering large stretches of town quickly and for day trips to places like Versailles, St Germain en Laye and (of course) Disneyland® Resort Paris (see p. 184). For nipping about the city centre, stick to the métro.

There are five RER lines (A, B, C, D and E), each of which divides at either end into branch lines (numbered A1, A2, and so on, so check carefully that you're getting o the right one as indicated on boards on the platform and on the front of each train). Trains run on all routes approximately every 12 minutes between 5.30am and 12.30am. All trains stop at all central Paris stations and other destinations are indicated on a board on the platform; there are several connecting points for changing to the métro network. Métro tickets are valid on the RER within the confines of the city (fare zones 1–2, see p.13).

By taxi

Paris' 15,000 licensed taxis are, on the whole, reliable, efficient and reasonably good value. In principle, drivers are obliged by law to stop when hailed, if they're free, to take you wherever you want to go (including the two airports), and to follow whatever route you choose although it doesn't follow that they always will.

Be aware, too, that drivers start their meters from the moment they set out to collect a fare so, if you call a cab from a distant rank, don't be surprised to see €3–5 already on the clock when it arrives. If you intend to use a lot of taxis, it will be worth finding out the number of the taxi stand closest to where you're staying.

A system of lights on the taxi's roof will tell you whether it's in service, driving to pick up a fare or available. When the taxi sign is lit, it's free. The minimum charge is €5 and rates are higher at night (10pm–6.30am). There are surcharges for luggage and for taking more than three passengers (drivers are within their rights to refuse a fourth passenger, but should take a couple and two children). Most journeys within central Paris cost €6–12. Taking a taxi to the suburbs can be quite expensive because as soon as the taxi crosses the périphérique (the Paris ring road), the driver will switch the meter over to a higher rate.

Taxi Companies

Alpha t 01 45 85 85 85
Artaxi t 01 42 03 50 50
G7 t 01 47 39 47 39
Taxi Bleus t 01 49 36 10 10

By car

Paris – at least the part of it that most people most want to see – is a small city and has such a good public transport system that using a car makes little sense. Parking is expensive and nigh on impossible as few hotels have garages, congestion is chronic and rising and, following the privatization of the tow firms, there's an increased risk of being towed away if you happen to be parked in the wrong place.

If you drive to Paris, it's best to choose a hotel with a car park (or maybe in the outskirts) and leave your vehicle there while you make any trips into the city. The speed limit in the centre of Paris is 50kph (around 30mph), on the Paris ring road 80kph (50mph), on country roads 90kph (55mph, but 80kph when wet) and on motorways (*autoroutes*) 130kph (80mph, but 110kph/70mph when wet). At intersections without signals, the car approaching to your right has the right of way. Seatbelts must be worn in the front seats of cars and in the back where fitted. Children under 10 are not allowed to travel in the front except in special rear-facing baby seats.

Car rental rates in France are among the highest in Europe, so if you want to explore the countryside it's worth investigating fly-drive or holiday packages before you arrive. Local firms offer the best rates; most car rental companies can also supply children's safety seats for a nominal cost.

Autorent
98 Rue de la Convention, 15th
t 01 45 54 22 45
Ⓜ Boucicaut

Valem
88 Rue de la Roquette, 11th
t 08 92 69 76 97
www.valem.fr
Ⓜ Voltaire

Rent-a-Car
23 Rue du Départ, 14th
t 01 43 21 56 50
www.rentacar.fr
Ⓜ Montparnasse–Bienvenüe

A good-value local agency with a wide range of vehicles and several offices around Paris. A Fiat Panda will cost about €30 a day with unlimited mileage and insurance.

24-hour emergency repair service
SOS Dépannage **t** 01 47 07 99 99

A general emergency breakdown service. If you take a car to France, it is advisable to have breakdown cover via the AA or RAC (there is no equivalent organization in France, but they offer Europe-wide cover with private services), your home insurance company, or specialist services such as Europ Assistance (**t** 01 44 44 22 11, **www**.europ-assistance.co.uk).

By bike

The RATP transport authority is working on a project called *Roue Libre*, centred around the Maison Roue Libre bike hire shop, to promote cycle use in the city, which includes an excellent range of **bike tours** (in English and other languages) in groups or with 'Talking Bicycles', with recorded commentaries attached to the bike. For details of these and other cycle tours, *see* pp.32–33.

For rollerskate and rollerblade hire shops, *see* p.125.

IDEAS IDEAS

TOP TIPS

The best of kids' Paris

This is the pick of the best things to see, eat, visit, shop, ride in and play with in France's capital city.

Best animal attraction
Zoo de Paris in the Bois de Vincennes, *see* p.120.

Best annual jamboree
Paris Plage, *see* p.37.

Best café
The tearoom in the Paris Mosque, *see* pp.96, 159.

Best Christmas experience
Going skating on the outdoor ice rink by the Hôtel de Ville, *see* p.38.

Best church
Gothic and glass: Sainte Chapelle, *see* p.80.

Best cinema
Sci-fi dome: the Géode, *see* pp.109, 112.

Best firework display
The biggest in town: Bastille Day, *see* p.36.

Best funfair
Summer in the Jardin des Tuileries, *see* p.36.

Best for gruesomeness
The dungeons of the Conciergerie, *see* p.79, or the skulls and bones of the Catacombes, *see* p.94.

Best interactive fun
Paris hi-tech science park, the Cité des Sciences et de l'Industrie, *see* pp.108–109.

Best market
For piles and piles of great junk: the St Ouen flea market, *see* p.103.

Best museum
Musée National d'Histoire Naturelle, for animal oddities, *see* pp.88–89, or Musée de la Curiosité et de la Magie, for just plain magic, *see* p.69.

Best park
The Jardin d'Acclimatation, a great kids' preserve right in the Bois de Boulogne, *see* p.118.

Best restaurant
Altitude 95, where you can eat right up on the Eiffel Tower, *see* pp.62, 154.

Best shop
Au Nain Bleu, *see* pp.47, 174, or Nature et Découvertes, *see* p.166–167.

Best sightseeing tour
Sailing down the Seine on the *bateaux mouches*, *see* pp.31–32.

Best sports event
The Tour de France (*see* p.37) or the Course des Garçons et Serveuses de Café (*see* p.36).

Best statue
The bizarre Stravinsky Fountain, *see* pp.67, 73.

Best view
The third floor of the Eiffel Tower (*see* p.56), the Tour Montparnasse (*see* p.95), or the Sacré Coeur (*see* p.100).

Tips for getting around

A few essentials can go a long way in helping you to get about Paris as painlessly (and cheaply) as possible. Probably around 80 per cent of the places you're likely to want to see are concentrated in central Paris, quite a small area, so it's possible to cover a lot of ground fairly quickly. For full details of tickets and all local transport, *see* pp.13–16.

► Paris has one of the best public transport systems in the world – fast and safe – so use it. Getting around in your own car is too painful (the traffic's awful and you'll spend half your time trying to park), while taxis soon get expensive (and you'll often be stuck in the same traffic).

► Children (4 to 11) travel for about half the full fare and under-4s travel for free, so long as they do not take up a seat, on nearly all local transport.

► The same tickets are used for the métro (underground/subway), city buses, and the RER local rail system within central Paris.

► **Don't** buy tickets every time you use the métro, buses or RER: if you're sightseeing, you're bound to make at least 10 trips on local transport in any visit of more than a day. Buy a **Carnet**, or block of 10 tickets, which works out cheaper than single tickets and you won't have to line up at the ticket booths every time you want to travel.

Know your arrondissements and the magic number 75

The city of Paris – historic Paris, within the périphérique ring road – is divided into 20 arrondissements (administrative districts), which spiral out in a clockwise direction more or less in the shape of a snail's shell from the first arrondissement in the very centre of the city around the Louvre. For all residents, arrondissement numbers are an essential shorthand for getting an idea of where things are and they can be just as helpful to new arrivals once you get an idea of the system (which is very logical being French) in your head. Different arrondissements are also naturally associated with certain features (the 1st, 7th and 8th suggest monuments and luxury, the 5th, students and bohemia, the 4th, history and old mansions and so on). In this guide, arrondissement numbers are given in English alongside all the addresses (1st, 3rd, 16th, etc.). The French equivalents are 1e, 3e, 16e and so on.

In addition, each one of the administrative départements into which France is divided has a specific number. For Paris, it's 75, and this number crops up in all sorts of things related to the city (in the rest of France, Parisians are even sometimes referred to as 75s). The five-digit postal codes for all addresses within the city begin with 75 and end with the number of the arrondissement (75001 to 75020). This system provides another way of working out the area within which an address is located. Also, all registered car number plates in Paris end in 75.

▶ If you're going to be making seven or more trips a day (per person, not for the whole family), then it pays to get **Paris Visite** cards, which give unlimited travel on all local transport within certain fare zones (the basic card, zones 1–3, covers all of central Paris), for from 1 to 5 days. This will save you time and money, and Paris Visite holders are entitled to discounts for a range of tours and attractions.

▶ **Sightseeing tours** are a greatly enjoyable way of getting an idea of the city. As this often involves sitting down and looking from a boat or bus, they provide a breather from too much traipsing the streets. The classic bateaux mouches boat trips on the Seine are among Paris' don't-miss attractions

that you have to try once. But don't pass over less well-known rides, like the open-top bus tours or the boats that run along the tranquil old canals of eastern Paris, for the energetic, guided walks or bike tours. For details, see pp.30–34.

Paris for free (almost)

Be under no illusions, Paris is not cheap. However, if you know where to look, there are savings to be made. Many museums don't charge for under-18s (see p.20), and the city's beautiful parks and churches are always free. Also, if you come at the right time of year, you may be able to catch a major free event such as the Marathon, the Bastille Day celebrations or the climax of the Tour de France.

Churches

Admission to all Paris' churches is free although you'll have to pay if you want to see the views from the top of either **Nôtre Dame** or the **Sacré Coeur**.

Parks

Parks, gardens and woods are all free, although you will have to pay a little for specific attractions such as the **Jardin d'Acclimatation** amusement park in the Bois de Boulogne, the flower garden (**Parc Floral**) in the Bois de Vincennes and the annual funfair at the **Jardin des Tuileries**. Around them, though, there are beautiful areas of parkland and elegant French-style gardens where you can take your time for zero outlay. See pp.118–122.

Events and festivals

A big range of free events is put on during the year for Parisians and you can join in, too. Bastille

Visit a park on Tuesday and a museum on Wednesday

If you can't decide between wanting to go to a museum or a park, remember that most of the city's museums are closed on Tuesdays (apart from the science museums which are closed on Wednesdays), while the parks tend to be much more crowded on Wednesday afternoons when French school children are let out of classes early.

Day and Christmas are naturally the big ones, but there are plenty of smaller-scale things going on. See pp.34–38, for more details of the Paris calendar.

Annual free events

January
La Grande Parade de Paris
New Year's Day Parade on the *Grands Boulevards*.
Nouvel An Chinois (Chinese New Year)

April
Poisson d'Avril (April Fool's Day)
Marathon de Paris

May
May Day
La Course au Ralenti
Vintage car race up Montmartre's steep *butte*.

June
Fête de la Musique
Great, city-wide music festival with free concerts.
Feux de la St Jean
Firework display over the Seine for the Feast of St John the Baptist.
Course des Garçons et Serveuses de Café
500 waiters and waitresses race over a 5-mile course, starting and finishing at the Hôtel de Ville.

July
Bastille Day
Big-scale organized fun and fireworks.
Tour de France
Watch the climax of the world-famous cycle race on the Champs Élysées.
Paris Plage
A section of the Seine riverbank becomes a Mediterranean beach resort for 1 month.

September
Fêtes de la Seine
Fireworks, power boats and water skiing.

December
Patinoire de l'Hôtel de Ville
An ice rink (*patinoire*) is erected yearly outside the Hôtel de Ville. You'll only pay for skate hire.
Christmas Lights and Carousels
Check out the Champs Élysées, Avenue Montaigne and Boulevard Haussmann. Carousels throughout the city are free to children during the Christmas period.

New Year's Eve
Most Paris' New Year celebrations take place on the Champs Élysées.

Museums for free
Foreign visitors sometimes aren't quite sure whether it is true that many of Paris' museums and monuments are free for youngsters at different ages. In addition, nearly all museums have a reduced price for those aged 18–25.

Free for all
Musée Carnavalet, *see* p.68
Musée de la Chasse et de la Nature, *see* p.68
Musée Cognacq-Jay, *see* p.69
Musée Fragonard, *see* p.47
Musée de la Préfecture, see p.91
Palais de Tokyo, see p.61

Free for under-18s
Arc de Triomphe, *see* p.49
Centre Pompidou, *see* p.66
Château de Vincennes, *see* p.119
Musée de l'Air et de l'Espace, *see* p.114
Musée de la Mode et du Costume, *see* p.60
Musée des Arts et Métiers, *see* p.114
Musée de l'Histoire de France, *see* p.69
Musée du Louvre, *see* pp.42–44
Musée de la Monnaie, *see* p.82
Musée des Arts d'Afrique et d'Oceanie, *see* p.114
Musée Nationale des Arts Asiatiques – Guimet, *see* p.60
Musée National du Moyen Âge – Thermes de Cluny, *see* p.91
Musée Nissim de Camondo, *see* p.115
Musée d'Orsay, *see* p.81
Musée Picasso, *see* pp.69–70
Musée Rodin, *see* p.59

Free for under-12s
Les Catacombes, *see* p.94
Centre de la Mer, *see* p.90
La Conciergerie, *see* p.79
Hôtel des Invalides (with Musée de l'Armée and Napoleon's Tomb), *see* p.58
Jeu de Paume, *see* p.45
Musée de l'Assistance Publique, *see* p.91
Musée de la Poste, *see* p.95

Aid for sightseers:
the Carte Musées et Monuments

Many of Paris' museums and monuments may be free for kids but for the accompanying adults it's advisable to buy a **Carte Musées et Monuments**, available from tourist offices, participating museums, some of the larger métro and RER stations, or by logging on to **www**.intermusees.com. This card grants unlimited admission to around 70 museums and monuments in Paris and the Île de France and you only need to visit two sights a day to break even. Better still, you skip the queues.

The cards currently cost €15 for 1 day, €30 for 3 days and €45 for 5 days. Among the venues to which they give free entry are the following:

Arc de Triomphe, see p.49
Centre Pompidou, see p.66
Cité des Sciences et de l'Industrie, see p.108
(not including La Géode or the Cité des Enfants)
La Conciergerie, see p.79
Les Égouts de Paris (Sewer Museum), see p.61
Hôtel des Invalides (Musée de l'Armée and Napoleon's Tomb), see p.58
Musée Cognacq-Jay, see p.69

Musée de la Mode et du Costume, see p.60
Musée de l'Assistance Publique, see p.91
Musée Carnavalet, see p.68
Musée du Louvre, see pp.42–44
Musée de la Marine, see p.60
Musée de la Monnaie, see p.82
Musée de la Musique, see p.110
Musée des Arts d'Afrique et d'Oceanie, see p.114
Musée National des Arts Asiatiques – Guimet, see p.60
Musée National des Arts et Traditions Populaires, see p.119
Musée National du Moyen Âge – Thermes de Cluny, see p.91
Musée Nissim de Camondo, see p.115
Musée d'Orsay, see p.81
Musée Picasso, see p.69
Musée Rodin, see p.59
Nôtre Dame bell towers, see p.78
Panthéon, see p.91
Sainte Chapelle, see p.80
Musée Condé – Château de Chantilly, see p.129
Châteaux de Versailles, see p.128
Château de Vincennes, see p.119

What to bring

The weather can catch you out in Paris so it's always a good idea to bring a few well-chosen games from home to pass the time.

▶ Any large, snap-together plastic construction bricks such as stickle bricks, Duplo or Mega Blocks.
▶ Hand puppets: guaranteed mood-lifters.
▶ Non-stain, washable colouring pens.
▶ A disposable, automatic camera.
▶ Classic travel toys Etch-a-Sketch and Magna Doodle. Pocket versions are now available.
▶ GameBoy and hand-held video games. For over-3s, they're top of the diversion list. The compact GameBoy Pocket is ideal for travel being 50 per cent lighter and 30 per cent smaller than its chunkier brother.
▶ Interactive learning games. Award-winners **Vtech** make the best range. Contact them on **t** UK (0123) 555 5545 or **t** US (212) 206 0890.
▶ Travel versions of classic board games Cluedo, Monopoly, Scrabble and Battleships.

▶ A deck of cards and peg-board versions of games such as chess.
▶ Have plenty of mobile, foldaway diversions to keep your baby amused while developing motor skills. They will allow you to concentrate on the task at hand. An early favourite consists of eye-catching cards that can be slotted into transparent pockets and attached by Velcro to the back of your travel seat. Wrist or sock rattles and colourful multisensory play mats are ideal distractions for babies finding their hands and feet. Portable versions have a useful clamp that attaches easily to your baby carrier, pushchair, cot, bouncer-seat, or table – in fact, just about anywhere.

Can you spot?
How many vehicles can you see with the number 75 on the registration plate?

Paris has so many wonders, so many great places to visit, that it's sometimes difficult to know where to start. Often your best bet can be to plan your family's sightseeing route according to a single theme or topic. Below are a few suggestions for itineraries following particular lines of interest, although there are always plenty of opportunities to be side-tracked.

Lions, tigers and bears

Morning Take the métro or RER to the Gare d'Austerlitz to visit the **Ménagerie** in the Jardin des Plantes, Paris' oldest zoo, founded in 1790. It is, as you might expect, a rather small, old-fashioned, but charming zoo, where you can see llamas, monkeys, deer and bears. Take a quick tour of the Grande Galerie de l'Evolution in the **Musée National d'Histoire Naturelle** to find out more about the evolution of the world's species.

Lunch Having seen some exotic beasts (dead and alive), continue the faraway theme with some delicious Moroccan snacks and mint tea in the café of Paris' principal mosque.
See p.159

Afternoon Head to Ⓜ Porte Dorée to reach the **Bois de Vincennes** and the modern **Parc Zoologique de Paris**, one of Europe's largest zoos, home to lions, tigers and elephants. Kids can help feed the sea lions. Then, if you've all had enough of that, there's plenty more to explore in the Bois, Paris' largest stretch of park and woodland (*see* p.119).

La Ménagerie
Jardin des Plantes, entrances on Place Valhubert, Rue Buffon and Rue Cuvier, 5th
t 01 40 79 30 00
See p.89

The Musée National d'Histoire Naturelle
57 Rue Cuvier, 5th
t 01 40 79 56 01
See pp.88–89

Salon de Thé de la Mosquée de Paris
1 Place du Puits de l'Ermite, 5th
t 01 43 31 38 20

Parc Zoologique de Paris
53 Avenue de St Maurice, 12th
t 01 44 75 20 10
See p.120

On the trail of the French Revolution

Morning To begin at the very beginning, start the day at the **Place de la Bastille** (Ⓜ Bastille), where the French Revolution erupted on 14 July 1789, when a mob of 8,000 people stormed and destroyed the notorious royal Bastille prison that stood on this spot. You can still see the outline of the fortress set into the pavement of the square.

From here, take the métro to Ⓜ Cité to visit the dark old fortress of the **Conciergerie** on the Île de la Cité, where King Louis XVI and his queen Marie Antoinette were both held prisoner by the revolutionaries before their execution in 1793. You can visit Marie Antoinette's reconstructed cell and the *Salle des Gardes* or guardroom, once packed full of prisoners awaiting their trip to the *guillotine*.

Lunch Enjoy tea and snacks in Cafés et Thés Verlet, a tranquil, family-friendly teashop with a slightly *ancien régime* air. Alternatively, nearby there's McDonald's.

Afternoon Walk around the Louvre along the Rue de Rivoli, past the **Palais Royal**. In front of one of the café's garden courtyards a young agitator called Camille Desmoulins made a fiery speech on 13 July 1789 standing on a table. It played a major part in spurring on the Paris crowds to attack the Bastille the next day, and so setting the whole thing off. From there, walk through the **Jardin des Tuileries** to the **Place de la Concorde**, where a couple of years later the *guillotine* was set up and the Egyptian obelisk now stands. Both Louis XVI and Marie Antoinette were executed here; so, too, was their arch-enemy Robespierre when the political winds turned against him in 1794.

Take the métro to Ⓜ Grands Boulevards for the **Musée Grevin**, where you can see waxwork reconstructions of various scenes from the Revolution, including the death of revolutionary leader Jean Paul Marat (he was stabbed while in his bathtub).

Alternately, take the métro to Ⓜ St Paul for the **Musée Carnavalet**, Paris' own history museum, to find out more about France's most celebrated event and see a whole range of revolutionary memorabilia that include a model *guillotine* carved from bone by French prisoners of war in England, Louis XVI's shaving kit and Napoleon's toothbrush.

La Conciergerie
Palais de la Cité, 2 Bd du Palais, 1st
t 01 53 40 60 97
See p.79

Cafés et Thés Verlet
256 Rue St Honoré, 1st
t 01 42 60 67 39
See p.158

McDonald's
184 Rue de Rivoli
Ⓜ Tuileries

Jardin des Tuileries
Rue de Rivoli, 1st
Entrances on Rue de Rivoli, Place de la Concorde and Avenue du Gal. Lemonnier
See p.45

Musée Carnavalet
23 Rue de Sévigné, 3rd
t 01 44 59 58 58
See p.68

Musée Grévin
10 Bd Montmartre, 9th
t 01 47 70 85 05
As well as Marat in his bath, the Grévin's favourite displays from French history include Josephine counselling Napoleon and Marie Antoinette in prison.
See pp.114–115

On the toy trail

Learning about history is all very well, but most kids want to spend some of their time chasing after more material concerns.

Morning Head down to the **Carrousel du Louvre**, the gleaming shopping and exhibition mall beneath the Louvre (Ⓜ Palais Royal–Musée du Louvre), where you will find a big branch of **Nature et Découvertes**, which has an excellent toy section on the first floor, and **Le Ciel est à tout le Monde**, which has a large selection of traditional toys. Around the corner is the miniature mecca, **Gault**, on the Rue de Rivoli.

From there, head back eastwards around the Louvre to the **Samaritaine**, the department store with the best toys of any big store in Paris, as well as a carousel and all sorts of other things to keep kids engrossed.

Lunch If you can tear them away – and since you'll all be in need of a rest – you're very conveniently placed to head upstairs to the top floor café and have an enjoyable lunch while taking in the wonderful view.

Afternoon Walk or take the métro to Ⓜ Concorde to reach **Au Nain Bleu**, Paris' largest toy store, on the Rue St Honoré, and spend the rest of the afternoon trying to get your kids to leave. You might be able to entice them outside with the promise of some window-shopping of a different kind, in front of the extraordinary cake and chocolate displays at Hédiard and Fauchon on the **Place de la Madeleine**.

Nature et Découvertes
Carrousel du Louvre, 1st
t 01 47 03 47 43
See pp.166–167

La Ciel est à tout la Monde
Carrousel du Louvre, 99 Rue de Rivoli, 1st
t 01 49 27 93 03
See p.174

Gault
206 Rue de Rivoli, 1st
t 01 42 60 51 17
See p.174

La Samaritaine
19 Rue de la Monnaie, 1st
t 01 40 41 20 20
See pp.47, 172–173

McDonald's
184 Rue de Rivoli
Ⓜ Tuileries
Keep your eyes open for their Disney tie-ins and toy promotions.

Au Nain Bleu
406–410 Rue St Honoré, 8th
t 01 42 60 39 01
See pp.47, 174

Paris just for fun

Paris can seem to some a rather stiff and smart city, where you need to watch your ps and qs, but it has plenty of places where children can just have a wild, kid's-idea-of-fun time with no consideration for fashion at all. The biggest all-fun facility of all in the area is Disneyland® Resort Paris, but within the city there are many more attractions that have long been loved by Parisian children, one and all. If you really want to wear your offspring out, here's a possible route with several alternative detours.

Morning Take the métro westwards out to Ⓜ/RER Porte Maillot. If it's running, which it is only in summer and at weekends, take the *Petit Train* mock-train or have a pleasant walk into the **Bois de Boulogne** to the **Jardin d'Acclimatation**, Paris' biggest children's amusement park and general entertainment zone. As well as a funfair with rollercoasters, dodgem cars , there are boat rides, a mini-zoo, mini-golf and lots more. If you feel like a break from funfair-ing, there are lovely park areas in the Bois all around.

Lunch There are several food outlets of a fast-foodish kind at the Jardin d'Acclimatation but, for something a bit more memorable, head back along métro line 1 into town and stop off at Ⓜ Franklin D. Roosevelt for a choice between branches of Paris' two leading family-friendly restaurant chains, **Bistro Romain** and **Hippopotamus**. Big, bright and friendly, both offer food that's tasty with ample kid-appeal (but distinctively French). Both establishments provide colouring books and games to keep the atmosphere lively.

Afternoon How you follow this up in the afternoon should probably vary depending on what time of the year you're in Paris and the weather. If you're here between April and June, head straight across to the opposite side of the city to Ⓜ Porte Dorée and the **Foire du Trône**, the giant funfair that takes over much of the Bois de Vincennes for 3 months

each year. If you want some variety, head off to another part of the Bois to the **Zoo de Paris** (*see* p.120). From June to August, you won't have far to travel as for the whole of the summer, a slightly smaller, but still buzzing, funfair sets up right in the middle of town amid the neat pathways of the **Jardin des Tuileries**.

Alternatively, during darker times of year, head to Ⓜ St Paul in the Marais and the **Musée de la Curiosité et de la Magie**, a unique, performance-based 'magic museum' that never fails to fascinate kids (but check its eccentric opening times before you go). Afterwards, little children who are not yet too blasé, might like to try out the charming old carousel that's permanently installed by the St Paul métro station.

Jardin d'Acclimatation
Bois de Boulogne, 16th
t 01 40 67 90 82
See p.118

Bistro Romain
73 Av des Champs Élysées, 8th
t 01 43 59 67 85
See p.154

Hippopotamus
42 Av des Champs Élysées, 8th
t 01 53 83 94 50
See p.154

Foire du Trône
4 April–1 June
Bois de Vincennes, Pelouse de Reuilly, 12th
t 01 46 27 52 29
See p.34

Funfair at the Jardin des Tuileries
Mid June–end of August
Jardin des Tuileries
See p.36

Musée de la Curiosité et de la Magie (Museum of Curiosities and Magic)
11 Rue St Paul, 4th
t 01 42 72 13 26
See p.69

Paris from below

There's a whole underground world beneath Paris and it's not only in the métro. There are no longer thousands of people living in tunnels beneath the city as there were in the 19th century but, for a mole's-eye-view of Paris (so long as you're not too squeamish), you can still spend a whole day almost entirely below ground.

Morning Take the métro to Ⓜ Denfert Rochereau in Montparnasse for a visit to the Catacombs, or 'Empire of the Dead', dark stone tunnels filled with 6 million skeletons stacked in neatly arranged piles, all of them moved here from the city's cemeteries after the leases on their original graves ran out. If your kids take to the macabre, just above the tunnels there is the huge Montparnasse cemetery.

Lunch Take the métro back into town to Ⓜ Palais Royal–Musée du Louvre, for a meal at one of the **Carrousel du Louvre**'s subterranean cafés. Elegant, but still underground.

Afternoon Take the métro to Ⓜ Alma Marceau and go back into the dark underworld of the Paris Sewers, *Les Égouts*, where you can get a very direct, warts-and-all view of the 'underside' of Paris – a smelly but very popular attraction.

Les Catacombes
1 Place Denfert Rochereau, 14th
t 01 43 22 47 63
See p.94

Les Égouts de Paris (Sewer Museum)
Entrance opposite 93 Quai d'Orsay by Pont de l'Alma, 7th
t 01 53 68 27 81
See p.61

Paris from above

Paris is a city of a thousand views from accidental to natural and deliberately created vantage points. Some have to be paid for but many of the best are free.

In the north
Sacré Coeur
Parvis du Sacré Coeur, 18th
t 01 53 41 89 00
From the steps of Montmartre's basilica you can see the entire city stretched out before you.
See p.100

In the centre
Pompidou Centre
Place Georges Pompidou, 4th
t 01 44 78 12 33
You can take in superb views of central Paris from the escalators (no admission) and particularly from the top floor and the café.
See p.66

La Samaritaine
19 Rue de la Monnaie, 1st
t 01 40 41 20 20
One of the most spectacular views of all in Paris is the one from the store's top-floor terrace and café.
See pp.47, 172–173

Nôtre Dame
6 Place du Parvis Nôtre Dame, 4th
t 01 42 34 56 10
The view from the bell tower – Quasimodo's viewpoint – is a timeless Paris classic, especially with one gargoyle in the corner of each eye.
See pp.78–79

In the south
Tour Montparnasse
33 Avenue du Maine, 15th
t 01 45 38 52 56
The modern competitor to the Eiffel Tower: from the top floor on a good day you can see all of Paris.
See p.95

In the west
Arc de Triomphe
Place Charles de Gaulle-Étoile, 8th
t 01 55 37 73 77
Scarcely anyone at any age fails to gasp at the spectacular geometry of Paris as seen from the top of the arch, looking down the Champs Élysées towards the Place de la Concorde, or up the Avenue de la Grande Armée towards la Défense.
See pp.49–50

Eiffel Tower

Champ de Mars, 7th

t 01 44 11 23 45

Paris' most must-see viewing point. Back at ground level, you can complement the view from the Tower by walking across the river to the **Jardins du Trocadéro** for one of the best views of the Eiffel Tower and the Champ de Mars.

See pp.56–57

Grande Arche de la Défense

1 Parvis de la Défense, 4th

t 01 49 07 27 57

Remarkable views for miles along the *Grand Axe* to compare against those from the Arc de Triomphe.

See p.51

Painters' Paris

Morning Take the métro to Ⓜ Abbesses for the **Dalí Espace Monmartre** and spend the morning looking at the bizarre creations of the Spanish surrealist: melted clocks, elephants standing on stilts, lip-shaped sofas and giant bronze snails. Alternatively, take the métro to Ⓜ Chemin Vert or St Paul for the Picasso Museum, which contains the most extensive collection by the great Spanish painter.

Lunch Have lunch nearby at the family-friendly Café de la Halle St Pierre and visit the Gallery of Naive Art and its bright pictures afterwards.

Afternoon Take a stroll through the pavement artists of the **Place du Tertre** and watch art being created first-hand. For €25 you could commission someone to paint you or your kids' portrait. Head to the **Musée du Montmartre** to see the collection of paintings of the area made the famous artists who lived here.

Dalí Espace Montmartre

11 Rue Poulbot, 18th

t 01 42 64 40 10

See p.100

Musée Picasso

Hôtel Salé, 5 Rue De Thorigny, 3rd

t 01 42 71 25 21

See pp.69–70

Café de la Halle St Pierre

2 Rue Ronsard, 18th

t 01 42 58 72 89

See p.158

Halle St Pierre/Musée d'Art Naif

2 Rue Ronsard, 18th

t 01 42 58 72 89

See p.101

Musée de Montmartre

12 Rue Cortot, 18th

t 01 46 06 61 11

See p.102

Applying science

Morning Begin the day with a quick whizz around the **Palais de la Découverte** (Ⓜ Franklin D. Roosevelt) and its vast assortment of hands-on gizmos, games and gadgets takes your fancy.

Lunch Have lunch on the terrace of **Bistro Romain on the Champs Elysées** (Ⓜ Franklin D. Roosevelt).

Afternoon take the métro to Ⓜ Porte de la Villette for the **Cité des Enfants**, where your kids can enjoy a 90-minute session making badges, experimenting with pumps, gears and robots, building giant foam houses and other science-related fun.

Palais de la Découverte

Av Franklin D. Roosevelt, 8th

t 01 40 74 00 00

See pp.48–49

Bistro Romain

26 Av des Champs Élysées, 8th

t 01 43 59 67 85

See pp.52, 154

Cité des Enfants

Parc de la Villette, 30 Av Corentin Cariou, 19th

t 01 40 05 12 12

See p.109

SEE IT DO IT

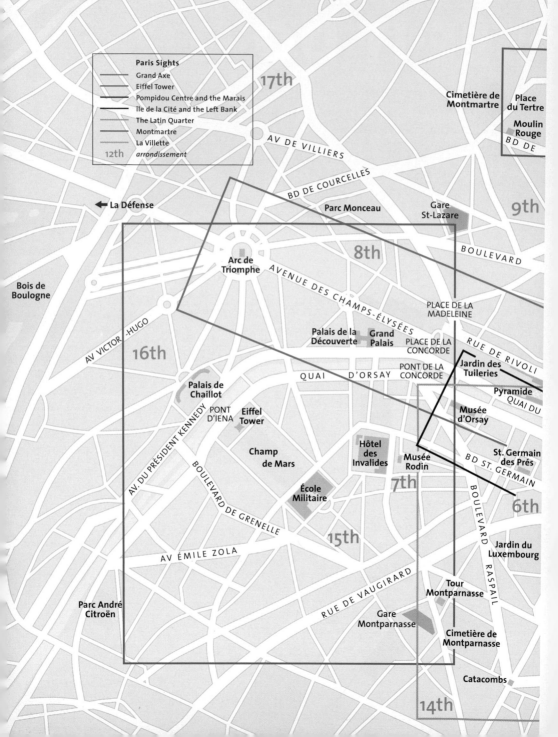

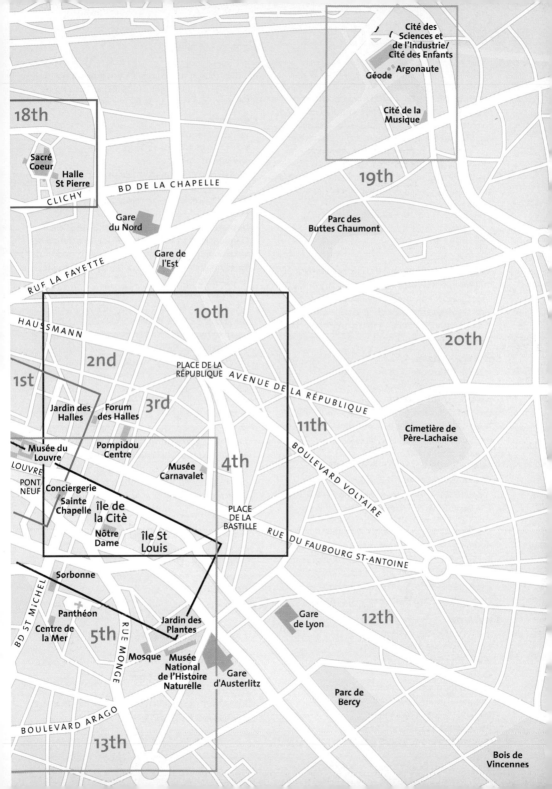

When you first arrive in Paris, you need to get things into perspective because Paris offers a great many ways to see the city, its magnificent monuments and unique old streets, beautiful vistas and odd little corners, by bus, boat, bike or just by wearing out the shoe leather. Of course, you can also sightsee with ordinary public transport – for some especially good routes, see p.14.

Full information and tickets for many of the tours are available from Paris' **tourist offices** (see p.144).

By bus

Bus tours are one of the most long-established, minimum-hassle ways of seeing any city but, in the last few years, the range available in Paris has incorporated some interesting variety with rides like **L'Opentour**, combining the convenience of the traditional tour with at-your-own-pace flexibility.

Les Cars Rouges

17 Quai de Grenelle, 15th
t 01 53 95 39 53 **f** 01 53 95 39 52
www.lescarsrouges.com
Ⓜ/RER Bir Hakeim, Champ de Mars–Tour Eiffel
Tours Daily every 10mins, 10am–6pm (April–Oct); every 20mins, 10am–6pm (Nov–Mar)
Departs Eiffel Tower
Fares Adults €21, 4–11s €10, under-4s **free**
Recorded commentary in English

'Panoramic tours' on double-decker buses around a circular route that begins at the Eiffel Tower and stops at nine points en route, including the Louvre, Nôtre Dame, Arc de Triomphe and other major monuments. Full tours last about 2 hours, tickets are valid for 2 days, and you can break your journey at any scheduled stop and get back on the bus later. Tickets can be purchased on board the buses. Discounts for **Paris Visite** (see p.13) card holders.

Cityrama

4 Place des Pyramides, 1st
t 01 44 55 61 30 **f** 01 42 60 33 71
www.cityrama.com
Ⓜ Tuileries
Tours Daily 9.30am–4.30pm (April–Oct) ; 9.30am–1.30pm (Nov–Mar)
Departs Place des Pyramides
Fares Adults €24, under-12s **free**
Recorded commentary in English

Bus tours with recorded commentary, around all the most famous sights. Trips last about 2 hours. Excursions in Paris, Île de France and the provinces.

L'Opentour

13 Rue Auber, 9th
t 01 42 66 56 56 **f** 01 42 66 56 57
www.paris-opentour.com
Ⓜ/RER Havre–Coumartin, Opéra, Auber
Tours Daily every 10–15 mins, 9am–8pm (April–Oct); every 25–30 mins, 9am–6pm (Nov–Mar)
Departs Routes 1 and 2 (Rue Auber by the Opéra Garnier); Route 3 (Nôtre Dame); Route 4 (Jardin du Luxembourg)
Fares Adults 1-day ticket €24 (2-day ticket €26), 4–11s €12, under-4s **free**
Recorded commentary in French and English

Run by the Paris transport authority, the RATP, these open-topped, double-decker buses run all week on four different daily itinerary circuits around the city: the 'Grand Tour' runs from the company office in Rue Auber (up the street from the old Paris Opéra) around the great sights of central and west Paris – the Arc de Triomphe, the Eiffel Tower, the Invalides, the Louvre; the 'Montmartre Tour' runs from Rue Auber around Montmartre and back; the 'Bastille-Bercy Tour' runs from Nôtre Dame through the Marais to the Bastille and the Parc de Bercy in eastern Paris; and the 'Montparnasse–St Germain Tour' explores much of the Left Bank including the Jardin du Luxembourg, Tour Montparnasse and Hôtel des Invalides. All four routes intersect at certain points so you can change buses. Tickets are valid for one or two days and you can get on and off the buses on all four routes as often as you like during that time – excellent value for money and a way of enjoying a more relaxing journey. Discounts for **Paris Visite** (see p.13) card holders.

Paris Vision

214 Rue de Rivoli, 1st
t 01 42 60 30 01 **f** 01 42 86 95 36
www.parisvision.com
Ⓜ Louvre Rivoli
Tours Daily 9.30am–3.30pm
Departs Rue de Rivoli
Fares Adults €24, under-12s €12, under-4s **free**
Multilingual commentary

Traditional bus tours of the main sights. The company also offers helicopter tours over the city for €240 per person.

By river and canal

Paris would be nowhere without the Seine and the river and elegant *quais* along its banks make up one of the essential attractions of the city. Most kids love being either in or on water, too, and a trip aboard one of the famous **bateaux mouches** glass-topped sightseeing boats is one of the best ways to see the sights of Paris, especially on a hot summer day. A wide variety of cruises are available along the Seine (including lunch and dinner options). If you want to stop off along the way and do some sightseeing on foot, go for the **batobus**.

Much less well known than the Seine cruises, but just as enjoyable (in a more low-key way), are trips along the canals of eastern Paris, particularly the **Canal St Martin**, which runs from a basin just off the Seine by the Bastille up to Parc de La Villette, from where the **Canal de l'Ourcq** and **Canal St Denis** continue out into the countryside. The boats here are much smaller than the *bateaux mouches* on the Seine, and the lazy-paced cruises along the canal give you a unique vantage point on the city. Kids will love going through the eerily lit tunnel which passes directly under the Place de la Bastille, followed by 19th-century locks and some enchanting areas of old Paris (it gets cool in the tunnel, even in summer, so take a sweater). Longer cruises offer lunch and dinner for around €45–80.

Bateaux Mouches

Pont de l'Alma, 7th
t 01 42 25 96 10/01 40 76 99 99 (infoline)
f 01 42 25 96 10
www.bateaux-mouches.fr
Ⓜ/RER Alma Marceau, Pont de l'Alma
Sailing times Daily every 30mins, 10am–8pm, every 20mins, 8am–11pm (April–Oct); 11am, 2.30pm, 4pm, 6pm, 9pm (Nov–Mar)
Departs Pont de l'Alma
Fares Adults €7, under-12s €4, under-4s **free**
Lunch from €50, dinner from €85
Wheelchair access
Suitable for all ages

Floating down the Seine aboard a sightseeing boat on a one-hour tour is a delightful way to see Paris, particularly at night when many monuments are illuminated. The *bateaux mouches* ('fly boats') take you upriver from the Pont de l'Alma bridge, east of the Eiffel Tower, as far as the Île St Louis, and then back again, past the Eiffel Tower, turning at the Pont de Grenelle (look out for Paris' own mini version of the Statue of Liberty) before returning to the Pont de l'Alma. A recorded commentary is played through loudspeakers in four languages – French, English, Spanish and German (in that order). Choose from lunch/dinner cruises and fancy dress cruises in summer for c. €80.

Bateaux Parisiens

Port de la Bourdonnais, 7th
t 01 44 11 33 44 **f** 01 45 56 07 88
www.bateauxparisiens.com
Ⓜ/RER Bir Hakeim, Trocadéro, St Michel Nôtre Dame
Sailing times Daily every 30mins, 10am–11pm (April–Oct); every 30mins, 11am–5pm and 8am–10pm; every hour, 10am–1pm and 5pm–8pm (Nov–Mar)
Departs Eiffel Tower: Pont Iéna
Fares Adults €9, *Croisière Enchantée* €9.50 per person, €8 (for groups larger than 4)
Wheelchair access
Suitable for all ages

Large, glass-topped *bateaux mouches*-style boats, with a similar range of cruises. At weekends, and daily from July to September, the company also offers a special variation for kids, **La Croisière Enchantée** ('The Enchanted Cruise'): your 3–10-year-olds are taken by a pair of elves on a one-hour enchanted boat journey up the Seine with songs and games along the way (in French).

Batobus

Port de la Bourdonnais, 7th
t 01 44 11 33 99 **f** 01 45 56 07 88
www.batobus.com
Ⓜ Bir Hakeim/Iéna
Sailing times Daily every 25mins, 10am–7pm (May, Oct–early Nov); every 25mins, 10am–9pm (June–Sept)
Departs Port de la Bourdonnais, 7th
Fares Adult 1-day pass €10, 4–11s €5.50; adult 2-day pass €12.50, 4–11s €6.50, under-4s **free**

Run in association with the RATP transport authority, batobuses provide a more flexible way of exploring the Seine than other cruise operators. The open-topped boats call at eight set stops en route (the Eiffel Tower, Champs Élysées, Musée d'Orsay, Louvre, St Germain des Prés, Nôtre Dame, Hôtel de Ville and Jardin des Plantes). As with l'Opentour buses, you can get on and off the boats as often as you like within your ticket period. When you board, you will be given a guidebook informing you of the walking time from each stop to a range of Paris attractions. Discounts for **Paris Visite** (*see* p.13) card holders.

Canauxrama

Bassin de la Villette, 13 Quai de la Loire, 19th
t 01 42 39 15 00 **f** 01 42 39 11 24
www.canauxrama.com
Ⓜ Bastille (Port de l'Arsenal)/ Jaurès, Stalingrad (Bassin de la Villette)
Sailing times Daily 9.45am and 2.45pm (from Bassin de la Villette) 9.45am and 2.30pm (from Port de l'Arsenal)
Departs Port de l'Arsenal, 12th; Bassin de la Villette, 19th
Fares Adults €13, 4–12s €8, under-6s **free**
Live commentary in English according to demand

Tours along the historic Canal St Martin, Canal de l'Ourcq, Canal St Denis and the banks of the Marne. The full trip lasts three hours. Shuttle boat service between Bassin de la Villette and Parc de la Villette.

Paris Canal

Bassin de la Villette, 19/21 Quai de la Loire, 19th
t 01 42 40 96 97 **f** 01 42 40 77 30
www.pariscanal.com
Ⓜ/RER Jaurès, Musée d'Orsay, Stalingrad (Bassin de la Villette)

Sailing times Daily 9.30am and 2.30pm (Mar–Sept); check the times for other routes
Departs Musée d'Orsay, Bassin de la Villette
Fares Adults €16, 12–25s €12, 4–11s €9, under-4s **free**
Live commentary in French or English

Paris Canal cruises combine mainly the Seine and the canals with a three-hour morning outing beginning on the river at the Musée d'Orsay, then turning onto the Canal St Martin by the Bastille to head up to La Villette before returning in the afternoon after lunch. Other routes include from the Musée d'Orsay around the loop of the Seine to La Défense, finishing at the Stade de France in St Dénis. Another cruise option is along the tranquil Canal de l'Ourcq out of the city to the River Marne.

Les Vedettes du Pont Neuf

Square du Vert Galant, 1st
t 01 46 33 98 38 **f** 01 43 29 86 19
www.pontneuf.net
Ⓜ Pont Neuf
Sailing times Daily every 30mins, 10am–10pm weekdays, 10am–11pm weekends (Apr–Oct); every 30mins, 11am–7pm weekdays, 11am–9pm weekends (Nov–Mar)
Departs Square du Vert Galant, Île de la Cité, 1st
Fares Adults €9, 4–12s €4.50, under-4s **free**

Open-topped *bateaux mouche* tours with a one-hour commentary.

By bike

No other country takes cycling as seriously as France. The world's première cycle race, the Tour de France, one of the country's great institutions, traditionally knocks just about anything else off the news in July. Paradoxically, Paris itself was rather lacking in cycle-friendly facilities until quite recently, and the city centre is still not a pleasant place to ride a bike, particularly during peak times. The Mairie de Paris (City Hall) has put in motion an energetic programme to encourage bike use and establish new cycle lanes through Paris.

The city now has over 200km (125 miles) of dedicated cycle lanes, while the *quais* along the Seine and the Canal St Martin are closed to cars on Sundays (9am–4pm Seine, 2pm–6pm Canal), providing lovely areas for cycling or watching rollerbladers. For rollerskate and rollerblade hire shops, see p.125.

Two major cycle tracks offer paths across the city away from the traffic although they are still criss-crossed by roads. One runs east–west between the Bois de Vincennes and Bois de Boulogne (the city's two great green open spaces). Another courses through eastern Paris between the Parc de Pantin and Porte de Vincennes. There is a permanent cycle path by the Canal de l'Ourcq, which runs north-eastwards out of the city from La Villette.

As part of this city programme, the RATP trans-port authority has introduced a scheme called Roue Libre, centred around the Maison Roue Libre (see below), which offers an imaginative range of easy guided bike tours (in French and English) and other ways to see the city by bike. Several private companies also offer good bike tours. Pick up a free Paris à Vélo map listing of the city's cycle routes at any district Mairie, tourist office or bike shop.

All hire shops require a deposit of around €150–300 when hiring a bicycle. Bikes are not allowed on the métro, but you can take a bicycle for free on some RER lines to the Paris suburbs (check with RATP or tourist offices).

Mike's Bike Tours Paris

24 Rue Edgar Faure, 15th
t 01 56 58 10 54 **f** 01 56 58 10 54
www.mikesbikestoursparis.com
Ⓜ Dupleix
Tours Twice daily 11am and 3pm; night-time tours 7.30pm Tues, Thurs, Sun (May–Oct)
Fares Adults €24

Enjoyable tours with English-speaking guides on both bikes and 'Segways' (a sort of stand-up motor-ized scooter). They also hire out bikes (including children's bikes, adult bikes fitted with child seats, tandems and trailers) for €2 per hour, €13 per day, €50 per week.

Maison Roue Libre

1 Passage Mondétour, 1st
t 01 53 46 43 77 **f** 01 40 28 01 00
www.ratp.fr
Ⓜ Forum Les Halles
Tours Daily Mar–Nov; Dec–Feb (Sat–Sun only)
Fares Adults €21, under–12s €14 (3 hour guided group tours)

The crown of the RATP's bike-promotion programme, this company offers varied group tours, bike hire, insurance, guides and hot drinks

and pastries on Sunday mornings. There is a choice of languages and child seats are available. Bike hire (€3 per hour, €8 per half day, €12 per day, €20 per weekend, €30 per week) comes with a free route guide. Their five 'Talking Bicycles Tours' allow you to stop at pre-set points and listen to recorded commentary from a box fitted to the bike. Additional Roue Libre bike hire points can be found at the Place de la Concorde, Forum des Halles, Porte d'Auteil, Hôtel de Ville, Bassin de la Villette, Bercy and Bois de Vincennes.

Paris Bike Tours

60 Rue de Saintonge, 3rd
t 01 43 90 80 80
www.parisbiketour.com
Ⓜ Sully Morland
Tours Daily at 9.30am and 2pm
Fares €29 per person

Two English language guided tours: one of the Right bank (Le Marais, Centre Pompidou, Musée du Louvre, Nôtre Dame etc.), the other of the Left Bank (Latin Quarter, St Germain des Prés, Jardin du Luxembourg etc.). Book 1 day in advance. Bikes can be hired for €13 (half day), €22 (1 day).

Paris à Vélo C'est Sympa

37 Boulevard Bourdon, 4th
t 01 48 87 60 01 **f** 01 48 87 61 01
www.parisvelosympa.com
Ⓜ Bastille
Fares Adults €30, under-26s €26, under-12s €16

Bikes and tandems for hire (€9.50 half day, €12.50 1 day or €45 1 week) and unusual guided theme tours of the city including 'Paris at Dawn', all-day-long tours and night visits.

On foot

Central Paris is still relatively easy to explore on foot but crossing Parisian roads can be tricky. It's worth remembering that to anybody moving around Paris on wheels (including cyclists and rollerbladers), pedestrians are a bit of a nuisance. French drivers are not obliged to stop at anything other than a red light, so only cross at the desig-nated zebra crossing points. British visitors, in particular, need to be aware that these do not signify a pedestrian's right of way, but only tell you that you cannot cross anywhere else.

There are many classic walks in Paris: along the *quais* of the Left Bank (*see* p.82), through the old streets of the Marais (*see* p.67), or following the Médaillons d'Arago, a series of metal plaques laid into the pavement between the Square Île de Seine in the south of the city and Avenue Pte de Montmartre in the north. Created in honour of the French astronomer and scientist Dominique Arago, and following the line of the now defunct Paris Meridian (a 19th-century rival of London's Greenwich Meridian), this route can turn your walk into a kind of treasure hunt with youngsters competing to be the first to 'find' the next plaque.

The following companies and city bodies are recommended for English-speaking guided tours.

Anne Hervé

t 01 47 90 52 16
www.parisidf.online.fr
Tickets €10

Scheduled group walks and private personalized tours around the city with an experienced guide.

Mairie de Paris (Paris City Hall)

29 Rue de Rivoli
t 01 42 76 43 43 (reception office)
Ⓜ Hotel de Ville
Open 9am–6pm, closed Sundays and public holidays
Tickets From €8

It runs an extensive programme of guided tours, mostly on Saturdays and many in English, which focus on some of the less obvious destinations, such as the Parc André Citroën, Père Lachaise cemetery and the Parc de Bercy. Information on the current tour programmes is available from the district town halls in each *arrondissement*, tourist offices, or by ringing them up.

Paris Contact

t 01 42 51 08 40
www.realfrance.com
Tickets From around €9

A variety of guided walks available 7 days a week.

Paris Walks

t 01 48 09 21 40
www.paris-walks.com
Tickets Adults €10, 12–25s €7, 4–11s €5

Well-planned, reliably enjoyable walks by Paris-based native English speakers with lots of fascinating stories and colourful details. Routes include the Marais, Montmartre, St Germain, Île de la Cité and the trail of the Revolution.

Events and entertainment suitable for the family take place all year round. From festivals and parades to firework displays, recreations of 17th-century glories and grand sporting occasions, there's always something going on. Summer is great for kids because the huge funfairs in the Bois de Vincennes and Jardin des Tuileries are open with their vast array of rides, games and stalls, and other open-air attractions are at their liveliest. For details on whether admission is free, *see* pp.19–21.

January

La Grande Parade de Paris (New Year's Day Parade)

1 January
Porte St Martin to the Madeleine by way of the Grands Boulevards
t 03 44 27 45 67
www.parisparade.com

A huge procession of decorated floats with bands, cheerleaders, vast floating balloon characters, jugglers, clowns and lots of music makes its way right through the heart of Paris.

Nouvel An Chinois (Chinese New Year)

22 January
Around Avenue d'Ivry and Avenue de Choisy, 13th
Ⓜ Porte d'Ivry, Porte de Choisy

Paris' Chinatown, in the southeast of the city, south of the Latin Quarter, celebrates Chinese New Year with firecrackers, paper lanterns and papier-mâché dragons that dance down the street.

April

Poisson d'Avril (April Fool's Day)

1 April

April Fool's Day is celebrated with a range of hoaxes and practical jokes, *poissons d'avril*, or 'April fishes'. The most popular involves sticking a paper fish to someone's back without them noticing.

Foire du Trône

4 April–1 June
Bois de Vincennes, Pelouse de Reuilly, 12th
t 01 46 27 52 29
www.foiredutrone.com
Ⓜ Porte Dorée
Open Daily from 2pm until late
Adm Rides cost €3–5, otherwise **free**

Paris' (and France's) biggest traditional funfair sets up the Bois de Vincennes (*see* p.119) every spring with a huge ferris wheel, rollercoasters, carousels, arcades and candyfloss *(barbe à papu)*. Great old-fashioned fun.

Marathon de Paris

6 April
Start 9am Avenue des Champs Élysées, finishes at Avenue Foch
t 01 41 33 15 68
www.parismarathon.com

On the day, 20,000 people run, jog or walk the nearly 42-km (26-mile) course between Place de la Concorde and the Hippodrome de Vincennes. Pick a vantage point along the *quais* and watch the seething mass go by.

Les Grandes Eaux Musicales

Every Sunday early April–early October
Parc du Château de Versailles
t 01 30 84 74 00
www.chateauversailles.fr
RER C5 to Versailles–Rive Gauche
Adm Adults €6, under-10s **free**

A little of the grandeur of the Sun King is revived each summer as Versailles' magnificent fountains are set in motion to the lush accompaniment of classical and baroque music *(see p.128)*.

May

Foire de Paris

Early May
Paris Expo, Place de la Porte de Versailles
t 01 49 09 60 00
www.foiredeparis.fr
Ⓜ Porte de Versailles
Adm €9

Similar to London's 'Ideal Home Exhibition', It celebrates its 100th anniversary in 2004. A giant lifestyle fair full of exhibition home interiors, model gardens and labour-saving devices, it has a special children's section where kids can try out the latest toys and gadgets.

Fête du Travail (May Day)

1 May
A party-like march snakes its way around eastern Paris, centring on the Bastille, and the streets are full of people selling lily of the valley *(muguet)* sprigs, the traditional lucky May Day flower.

Printemps des Rues

24–25 May
t 01 47 97 36 06
www.parisbienvenue.com

A weekend of street entertainment, exhibitions, and free concerts held around Bastille, Bercy, République, Nation and La Villette.

La Course au Ralenti

30 May
Montmartre (between Rue Lepic and Place du Tertre)
t 01 46 06 79 56

An annual, fairly crazy vintage car race down the slopes of Montmartre's steep hill *(butte)*.

French Open Tennis Championships

26 May–8 June
Stade Roland Garros, 2 Av Gordon Bennet, 16th
t 01 47 43 48 00
www.rolandgarros.com
Ⓜ Porte d'Auteuil
Tickets €27.50–52

A Grand Slam tennis tournament played on hard red clay courts which tends to produce a slow, tactical game. Hugely popular, you'll certainly have to queue to get tickets, so get there early for seats on the main courts. At the lovely southern end of the Bois de Boulogne, the Roland Garros stadium is open outside of competition times for guided tours and also has a new multimedia museum.

June

Fête de la Musique
21 June
All over Paris, particularly Palais Royal, Place de la République and Institut du Monde Arabe
t 01 40 03 94 70
www.fetedelamusique.culture.fr

On the longest day of the year, the city comes alive with the sound of music. Musicians give impromptu performances on street corners, in parks, outside cafés, to any audience, however small. More formal concerts are put on by classical orchestras at the Palais Royal, the Musée d'Orsay and the Place de la République, while Arab musicians perform at the Institut du Monde Arabe on the Left Bank by the Île St Louis.

Foire St Germain
Early June–early July
St Germain des Prés
t 01 40 46 75 12
www.foiresaintgermain.org
Ⓜ St Sulpice

An upscale antiques and culture fair held in Paris' most well-to-do district. Children are entertained with a small circus and a miniature steam train.

Feux de la St Jean
23 or 24 June
Quai St Bernard
Ⓜ Gare d'Austerlitz

The traditional feast of St John the Baptist is marked by a firework display over the Seine, seen at its best from the *quais* by the Latin Quarter.

Course des Garçons et Serveuses de Café
End of June
Start Hôtel de Ville via the Grands Boulevards, St Germain des Prés, and back again
t 01 42 96 60 75
Ⓜ Hôtel de Ville

The annual 'waiters' race' is one of Paris' sporting traditions. Over 500 waiters and waitresses in full serving uniform – long white aprons, waistcoats and bow ties – race along an 8-km (5-mile) course through the city's streets, starting and finishing at the Hôtel de Ville. They have to carry a tray with a cup all the way (drop the cup, and you're disqualified). A very popular and unique event.

Funfair at the Jardin des Tuileries
Mid June–end of August
Jardin des Tuileries
Ⓜ Tuileries, Concorde

As the Foire du Trône closes up in Vincennes (*see* p.34), another of Paris' most popular funfairs opens for business in the central, manicured Tuileries gardens (*see* p.45). There are wonderful views of the city from on top of the huge ferris wheel.

July

Fête Nationale du 14 Juillet (Bastille Day)
14 July

France's foremost national holiday, commemorating the storming of the Bastille in 1789, is celebrated throughout Paris with a whole range of events. The fun starts the night before on the evening of the 13th when the *Bals de Pompiers* (Fire Brigade Balls) are organized by the local fire stations in all the city's districts and a much bigger mass party gets going in Place de la Bastille. The festivities carry on the following day. The centre-piece official event is at 10am on the 14th, when the President inspects a military parade along the Champs Élysées. The evening finishes with more partying and a fabulous firework display at the Trocadéro, watched by thousands gathered around the Eiffel Tower in the Champ de Mars (*see* p.57). Be prepared for noisy, boisterous crowds.

Grands Fêtes de Nuit de Versailles
Selected weekends July–September
Parc du Château de Versailles
t 01 30 83 76 20
www.chateauversailles.fr
RER C5 to Versailles–Rive Gauche
Adm €12–42

These lavish and spectacular recreations of the royal pageants held for Louis XIV in Versailles' 17th-century heyday, combining dancing, extravagant costumes, music, fountains and fireworks, are a summer highlight at Versailles (*see* p.128). Tourist offices will have details of the performance dates.

Paris Plage (Paris Beach)

20 July–17 August
Banks of the Seine between Quai Henri IV and Quai des Tuileries
t 08 20 00 75 75
www.paris-touristoffice.com
Ⓜ Pont Neuf, Châtelet, Sully Morland

The popular brainchild of Paris Mayor Bertrand Delanoé who, in 2001, came up with a novel idea for encouraging Parisians to holiday in their own city instead of heading for the Mediterranean coast. For about four weeks, the riverbanks of the Seine are turned into a veritable beach complete with sand, deckchairs, palm trees and refreshment kiosks while a traffic ban is enforced. A whole host of events are laid on daily between 9.30am and 10.30pm including numerous children's activities.

Festival du Cinéma en Plein Air

14 July–20 August
Parc de la Villette, 19th
t 08 03 80 33 06
www.la-villette.com
Ⓜ Porte de la Villette

Settle back in a deck chair as night falls over La Villette park, and watch a classic movie projected (often in the original language, with French subtitles) onto the big screen in the Prairie du Triangle.

Tour de France

5–27 July
Avenue des Champs Élysées, 8th
t 01 41 33 15 00
www.letour.fr
Ⓜ Charles de Gaulle-Étolle, George V, Franklin D. Roosevelt, Champs Élysées–Clemenceau, Concorde

The world's greatest cycle race celebrates its centenary (1903–2003) finishing (as every year) on the Champs Élysées. Huge crowds line the route on the final day.

September

Fêtes de La Seine

Throughout September
Quais de la Seine

t 01 42 76 67 00

Fireworks, power boats, water-skiing, a *brocante* antiques market and other events are held beside the river.

October

Fête des Vendanges à Montmartre

First Saturday in October
14–18 Rue des Saules and around Montmartre, 18th
t 01 46 06 00 32
www.montmartrenet.com
Ⓜ Abbesses, Blanche, Lamarck Caulaincourt

The **Clos Montmartre** on Rue des Saules is Paris' most historic vineyard and the annual grape-picking makes for an enjoyable folklore festival. Celebrations include a street parade up Montmartre, marching bands, music, locals in traditional outfits and plenty of wine drinking.

Salon du Champignon

Mid–late October
Jardin des Plantes, 5th

t 01 40 79 36 00
www. mnhn. fr
Ⓜ Gare d'Austerlitz, Jussieu

To greet the wild mushroom-picking season, the Musée d'Histoire Naturelle puts on an exhibition of fungi of all shapes and sizes with lessons in distinguishing the deadly from the edible.

Salon Européen du Chocolat
October–November
Carrousel du Louvre, 99 Rue de Rivoli, 1st
t 01 45 03 21 26
www. chocoland.com
Ⓜ Alma Marceau
Adm Adults €10, under-12s €5, under-3s **free**

The chocolate festival will encourage both adults and children to stuff themselves silly with sticky treats. Look out for the chocolate sculptures.

Hallowe'en
31 October

Hallowe'en has caught on big time in Paris. Virtually unknown a few years ago, it's now one of the biggest nights for restaurants and costume stores, an excuse for everyone to dress up and decorate their houses. Trick or treating, however, is still unheard of.

December
Salon Nautique de Paris
6–15 December
Paris Expo, Porte de Versailles, 15th
t 08 36 68 00 51
www. salonnautiquesparis.com
Ⓜ Porte de Versailles
Adm €5–15

This international boat show hosts a Children's Beach Club for 3–12-year-olds featuring nautically themed workshops and games (in French).

Salon du Cheval, du Poney et de l'Ane
29 November–7 December
Paris Expo, Porte de Versailles, 15th
t 01 49 09 64 27
www. salon-cheval.com
Ⓜ Porte de Versailles
Adm Adults €11, under-12s €8, under-6s **free**

This equestrian festival allows children to watch and pet as many horses and ponies as they like.

Patinoire de l'Hôtel de Ville
Mid December–early March
Hôtel de Ville
t 08 20 00 75 75
Ⓜ Hôtel de Ville
Adm free except for skate hire (€4.50–8)

Grab your mittens, bobble hats and scarves for a skate on the open-air ice rink outside Hôtel de Ville. Surrounded by fir trees brought in for the occasion, it has a wonderful Christmas feel. There are mini-carousels on hand for non-skating children.

Noël (Christmas Lights and Carousels)

If you're in Paris around Christmas time, look out for the lights on the Champs Élysées, Avenue Montaigne and Boulevard Haussmann, while in front of the Hôtel de Ville a huge, lovingly assembled life-size Nativity scene is installed. A rich chocolate yule log (*bûche de Noël*) is the favourite Christmas treat and there's very special, very Parisian tradition: carousels throughout the city.

Fête de St Sylvestre (New Year's Eve)

Full of noisy crowds largely made up of teenagers and tourists, the Champs Élysées is the prime spot to be at midnight to usher in the New Year. Be aware that local kids have a tendency to celebrate by throwing around small banger-like fireworks.

Grand Axe

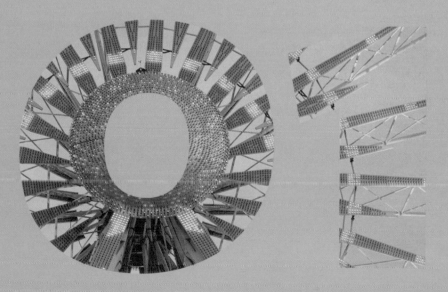

Running all the way through the northwest quarter of Paris is one great avenue – not always under the same name, but rolling on in a straight, unbroken line through streets, squares, palaces and parks – known as the *Grand Axe*, the 'Great Axis'. It provides a point of alignment for the whole Right Bank of the city, linking some of Paris' most famous, must-see attractions.

Because the Axe stretches for some 8km (5 miles), it's important to plan your day carefully to cater to your family's tastes (and stamina).

At one end, the base of the *Axe*, is the **Louvre**, one of the world's great museums, crammed with galleries of pots and sculptures, and all sorts of artefacts that kids will find fascinating: mummies, weapons, jewels and huge gory paintings. The *Axe* began life as a grand approach to the Louvre in the days when it was the principal palace of the Kings of France. The **Jardin des Tuileries** links the Louvre to the **Place de la Concorde**, from where Paris' most famous street, the **Champs Élysées**, stretches up to the **Arc de Triomphe**,

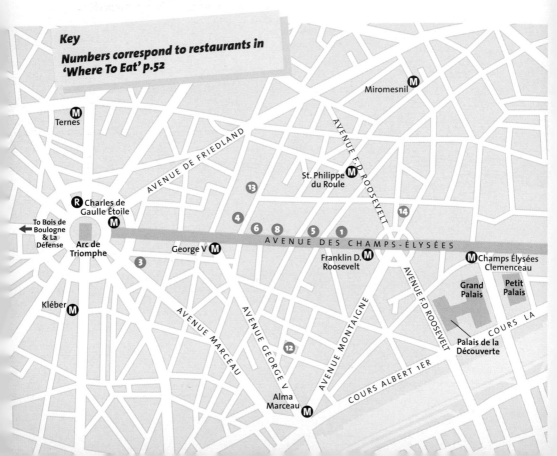

which offers fantastic views of the city. Along the way there are loads of shops and cafés, and attractions that give kids the chance to stretch their imaginations and their legs such as the **Palais de la Découverte** hands-on science museum and the Tuileries gardens themselves, where in summer there's a funfair with a ferris wheel.

Beyond the Arc de Triomphe, the avenue passes one corner of the **Bois de Boulogne**, Paris's largest green space (with its best amusement park, *see* p.118), before running on to the modern business area of **La Défense**, with its giant arch-shaped block, the **Grande Arche**. There are more great views from the top and, on a decent day, you can see the arch all the way from the Louvre, right at the other end of the *Axe*.

Highlights

Looking up through the giant glass pyramid in the courtyard of the Louvre

Climbing to the top of the Arc de Triomphe

Testing out the dazzling chocolate cabinets at Hédiard in the Place de la Madeleine

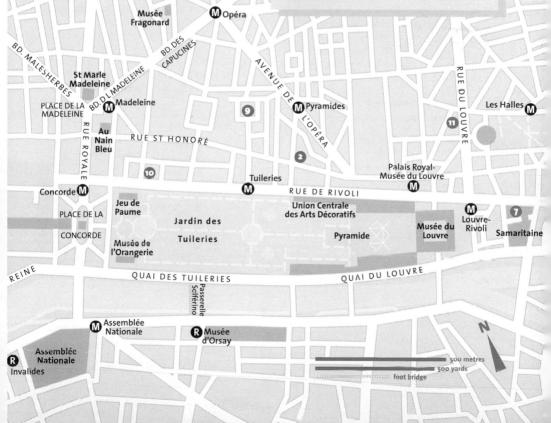

Musée du Louvre

Quai du Louvre, 1st
t 01 40 20 51 51 (infoline in 5 languages)
t 01 40 20 53 17 (infoline for disabled visitors)
www.louvre.fr
Ⓜ Palais Royal–Musée du Louvre, Louvre–Rivoli
Open 9am–6pm (Mon, Wed until 9.45pm); closed
Tuesday
Adm Adults €7.50, children **free** (reduced adult
rate of €5 applies after 3pm and all day Sunday);
free admission for everyone on first Sunday of
each month and on 14 July
Carte Musées et Monuments valid
Entrance via the pyramid in the main courtyard,
the Galerie du Carrousel (99 Rue de Rivoli), the
Porte des Lions, or the Passage Richelieu (for
groups and visitors with museum passes)
Wheelchair access and adapted toilets
Suitable for all ages, particularly older children
Allow at least 2 hours or more
*A wide range of activities is available for children
throughout the year, although these are primarily
aimed at French-speaking kids.*

This is one of the world's great museums, home
of the *Mona Lisa* and the *Venus de Milo*, as well as
countless other priceless historic artefacts and
works of art. But that doesn't mean it has imme-
diate appeal for children, and adults, too, are often
daunted by the sheer size and scope of the collec-

Top tips

▶ A *Carte Musées et Monuments* (*see* p.21) gives
access to the Louvre and some 70 other
museums in Paris and the Île de France, and
allows you to skip standing in line.
▶ Queues for the Louvre are always shorter at
the Rue de Rivoli entrance.
▶ If you are waiting in line outside the main
pyramid entrance, and have a pushchair or a
stroller, you are allowed to go to the head of the
queue. Simply ask the uniformed staff on duty.
▶ Avoid the long lines by purchasing your tickets
in advance either online or at the ticket outlets
at Fnac, Carrefour and Virgin stores.
▶ Tickets are valid for the whole day, allowing
you to leave and re-enter as often as you like.

tion. The Louvre is enormous, but don't be put off
by its labyrinthine confines; every visitor gets lost
at least once.

As with any major museum, it's best to treat your
visit as a sort of treasure hunt. Pick out a few
choice exhibits and plan your route accordingly –
kids love being the first one to find each exhibit.
The Louvre provides a good colour-coded map
which you can pick up from the front desk (get in
early before the English versions run out), along
with a 'First Visit' leaflet which takes you direct to
50 of the most famous works of art. Audioguides
(in English) are also available, as are guided tours;

the museum also organizes special storytelling tours for children, but in French only. Otherwise, just follow the hordes making their way towards the *Mona Lisa*, a glazed hypnotic look in their eyes.

The museum is divided into the **Richelieu**, **Denon** and **Sully** wings. A section of the massive keep of the original, medieval Louvre building, erected in the 1190s for King Philippe-Auguste, and later turned into a royal residence in the mid 14th century by Charles V, is also open to view in the complex beneath the pyramid entrance.

The **Richelieu Wing**, which has the smallest number of headline exhibits, houses galleries dedicated to French, German and Dutch painting; Middle Eastern Art; extraordinary sculptures from ancient Mesopotamia such as giant winged bulls with the heads of men; and the sumptuous, carefully preserved apartments of Napoleon III.

Italian Renaissance art is housed in the **Denon Wing**. For most people this means just one thing – the *Mona Lisa* (or, in French, *La Joconde*). Set behind bulletproof glass and permanently surrounded by furiously photographing tourists, it makes a peculiar spectacle. Should you manage to get a close look at it, you may find yourself wondering what all the fuss is about. It may be the world's most popular picture, but does it deserve to be hailed as 'the greatest picture ever painted'? Is it any better than the less famous canvases hanging around it?

Denon also contains the **Galerie d'Apollon**, a vast royal dining room decorated with zodiac-themed frescoes and lashings of gilt, which houses those of France's crown jewels that survived the Revolution. The centrepiece is a cabinet displaying Louis XV's lavish ceremonial crown: covered in red, green and

Tell me a story:
The Louvre: a long-term survivor

The Louvre has been around for a while. The first Louvre, built as a castle-fortress in 1190, was demolished and rebuilt in the mid-16th century to become an opulent royal palace. A century later, Louis XIV moved his court to Versailles (*see* p.128), but the Louvre remained the Paris home of France's Kings and Queens. Then, in 1793, following the Revolution, it was turned into a public museum to house the royal art collection.

President Mitterrand ordered its refurbishment in the 1980s as one of his *Grands Projets* for revamping and beautifying France's great buildings and monuments. He also commissioned the modern Louvre's most controversial feature, the huge glass and aluminium pyramid that now forms the main entrance to the museum. Designed by the Chinese–American architect I. M. Pei, the pyramid has divided French and world opinion down the middle: for everyone who considers it a futuristic masterpiece that neatly contrasts with the classical stone façade, there's someone else who sees it as a horrible modern monstrosity. It's perhaps best viewed from below, with light streaming through it, or at night when the whole complex is beautifully illuminated.

blue gems, and encrusted with diamonds, it could have been made by a small child unleashed on a jewel box with a pot of glue. This wing is also home to the Louvre's largest pictures – vast canvases featuring life-size, and sometimes larger, figures. Look out for Delacroix's *Liberty Leading the People*, one of France's most beloved paintings.

The **Sully Wing** has several galleries devoted to classical antiquity, where you'll find Greek statues, Roman mosaics and those perennial children's favourites, Egyptian mummies: there's an entire gallery stuffed full of ancient bandaged corpses – people, fish, birds and even cats. Sully's prized exhibit is, however, the *Venus de Milo*, a mysterious armless figure from Ancient Greece which is arguably the most famous statue in the world.

Outside, almost forming a boundary between the Louvre and the Tuileries gardens, there is the **Arc du Carrousel**, a 'mini-arch' commissioned by Napoleon almost as a prototype for his far grander Arc de Triomphe further down the *Grand Axe*. Whenever you feel yourself becoming over

Can you spot?
The Pharaohs on Place du Palais Royal? Forget buskers, accordion-players, jugglers and other such over-talented wannabes. The only skill needed to be the favourite street performer of the younger generation is the ability to stand still. Dressed as a soldier, Charlie Chaplin, the Statue of Liberty, or a bright gold Egyptian Pharaoh, these living statues are an endless source of fascination to kids, who will do anything in their power to make them move. A €1 coin usually does the trick.

Question 2
How is La Joconde *better known in English?*
answer also on p.250

whelmed by culture, you can also take refuge in the **Carrousel du Louvre**, a swish shopping and exhibition centre built under the museum in the 1980s. It can be accessed either from the Pyramid in the Louvre's central courtyard or from a less crowded street entrance on Rue de Rivoli. The Carrousel's shops may prove a bigger hit with the kids than the museum itself, particularly with younger ones. There are a few good toy shops, several cafés and restaurants as well as a major branch of **Nature et Découvertes**, a strange but very popular French chain which stocks an eclectic mix of goods – aromatherapy kits, turquoise jewellery, paper made from coffee beans – and has a whole floor dedicated to painted wooden toys, zoetrope lanterns, rocking horses, dinosaur model kits, mini-hammocks and mini-accordions (*see* pp.166–167). Look out, too, in the Carrousel for the wooden model of the entire Louvre complex, bisected to expose its subterranean levels.

Union Centrale des Arts Décoratifs

107 Rue de Rivoli, 1st
t 01 44 55 57 50
www.ucad.fr
Ⓜ Louvre, Palais–Royal
Open 11am–6pm (Tues–Fri), until 9pm (Wed), 10am–6pm (Sat–Sun)
Adm Adults €5.40, under-25s €3.90, under-8s **free** (each museum)
Wheelchair access
Suitable for all ages 10 and over; allow over 1 hour

The Marson wing of the Palais du Louvre on the Rue de Rivoli holds a further three small museums which, along with the Musée Nissim de Camondo on Rue de Monceau (*see* pp.115–116), make up the Union Centrale des Arts Décoratifs, bringing together creation and production, industry and culture. The pick of the bunch is the **Musée de la Mode et du Textile** (Museum of Fashion and Textiles) which should appeal to fashion-conscious teenagers with its constantly changing displays of vintage clothes with everything from extravagant 18th-century royal court dresses to the latest Yves Saint Laurent creations on display. Of the other two museums, the **Musée de la Publicité** (Museum of

Advertising) is perhaps the least accessible for younger visitors, but nonetheless holds a fascinating array of advertising materials – posters, packages, computer screens showing film and TV commercials – only a small part of which is ever on display at one time. The final museum, the **Musée des Arts Décoratifs** (Museum of Decorative Arts), is currently undergoing reorganization due for completion some time in late 2004. Until then, you can only visit the Medieval and Renaissance galleries and wander your way through a series of reconstructed period rooms filled with original artwoks showing how the Parisian population lived, worked and worshipped during the Middle Ages. Art and craft workshops (in French) for 4–12-year-olds are available during the holidays.

Around the Louvre

Filling a whole block between the Louvre and the Pont Neuf bridge is **La Samaritaine**, perhaps Paris's most attractive department store (*see* pp.47, 172–173). Flanking the north side of the museum is the **Rue de Rivoli**, built for Napoleon and one of Paris' grandest streets, lined with columned

Tell me a story: a tale of two obelisks
In the early 19th century, Muhammad Ali, the Viceroy of Egypt, presented the governments of France and Britain with an ancient Egyptian obelisk each. Around 3,300 years old, carved from pink Luxor granite, originally from the Temple of Ramses II in Thebes, and decorated from top to bottom with intricate hieroglyphics, these were priceless gifts, and the countries were suitably grateful. They were also a little overwhelmed at the prospect of getting these 50-ft, 225-tonne blocks of stone back home and deciding what to do with them once they got there. Britain spent the best part of 59 years blundering from mishap to mishap before the pillar – since known as Cleopatra's Needle – finally arrived in London. The journey of the French obelisk was, by contrast, serenity itself. Sailed up the Mediterranean in a specially designed open-decked boat, it was made the centrepiece of Paris' most beautiful square, Place de la Concorde. The contribution of M. Lelais, who organized its transportation, is commemorated at the foot of the monument. You can see a 3-D model of the hauling and despatch of the obelisk in the **Musée de la Marine** (*see* p.60).

arcades that shelter some of the city's best shops (and some pretty touristy places, too). Just across the street from the Louvre is a giant antiques market, the **Louvre des Antiquaires** and, a little further back, the **Palais Royal**. Begun for Cardinal Richelieu in the 1630s, this palace was turned into a public pleasure garden by the Duke of Orléans shortly before the Revolution in the 1780s. Today, most of the building is taken up by France's Culture Ministry but the gardens behind it are one of the most charming, tranquil spots to take a break in central Paris, ringed by arcades hosting an individual mix of cafés, restaurants and interesting old shops, many selling antiques and old prints. The Palais's main courtyard, meanwhile, has a 1980s sculpture of nearly 300 black-and-white striped columns, like lines of mints, and is a favourite place for watching street entertainers in action.

South of the Louvre on the Quai du Louvre, you'll find one of the embarcation points for the batobus sightseeing cruises (*see* pp.31–32).

Question 3
Why was the head-chopping device used during the French Revolution called a guillotine?
answer also on p.250

This was also the site of Paris' first public toilets, and its first newspaper kiosk, later marking the spot where the world's first gas airship took to the skies. More recently, the gardens underwent a good deal of restoration work as part of the *Grand Louvre* project.

Next to the Place de la Concorde are two charming buildings that were once part of the royal gardens. The **Jeu de Paume**, built as a court for playing real tennis, now hosts contemporary art exhibitions, while across in the southwest corner is the **Orangerie**, which houses a museum with an important collection of Post-impressionist paintings (currently undergoing renovation and due to reopen late in 2004). Work at the museum is unlikely to be finished before 2003 and the collection is on a world tour.

Galerie Nationale du Jeu de Paume

1 Place de la Concorde, 1st
t 01 47 03 12 50/01 47 03 12 52
Ⓜ Concorde, Tuileries
Open 12 noon–7pm (Wed–Fri), 10am–7pm (Sat–Sun), 12 noon–9.30pm (Tues), closed Mondays
Adm Adults €6, under-18s €4.50, under-13s **free**

Jardin des Tuileries

Rue de Rivoli, 1st
Ⓜ Tuileries, Concorde
Open 7am–9pm (April–Oct); 7.30am–7.30pm (Nov–Mar)
Adm Free
Entrances on Rue de Rivoli, Place de la Concorde and Av du Gal. Lemonnier
Suitable for all ages; allow at least 1 hour

These grand formal gardens between the Place de la Concorde and the Louvre have long been one of Paris' most popular attractions for children. There's a playground, a carousel, two ponds where you can hire small wooden model sailing boats (€1.50 each), pony rides and, in summer, a large funfair with rides, stalls, flumes and a giant ferris wheel. Remember, however, that the grassy areas of the park are out of bounds (or, as the signs say, *pelouse interdite*). The gardens were laid out in the 1560s on the site of a rubbish dump and tile works (hence the name Tuileries); they were only opened to the public in the 17th century after extensive reworking by Louis XIV's great gardener, André Le Nôtre. In the 18th century, the stately gravel pathways witnessed fashionable society promenades.

Musée de l'Orangerie
Place de la Concorde, 1st
t 01 42 97 48 16
Ⓜ Concorde, **RER** Invalides
Open Closed for renovation until autumn 2004, times to be announced
Adm To be announced

Place de la Concorde

Place de la Concorde, 1st
Ⓜ Concorde

With its grand architecture, ornate fountains and great Egyptian obelisk, the Place de la Concorde is Paris' largest and most majestic square. Its charms are now rather overshadowed by six lanes of fiercely speeding traffic, but it still offers some marvellous views. To the east are the Jardin des Tuileries and the Louvre; to the west the grand sweep of the Champs Élysées and the imposing bulk of the Arc de Triomphe, while to the south you can see the neoclassical façade of the **Assemblée Nationale** (the French parliament) on the other side of the Seine. The grand colonnaded buildings on the north side of the square, both from the 1760s, are the **Hôtel de la Marine** (the French Navy department since 1792), and the **Hôtel Crillon**, one of Paris' most luxurious hotels. In the square's corners are eight statues representing the largest cities in France outside Paris: Bordeaux, Brest, Lille, Lyon, Marseille, Nantes, Rouen and Strasbourg.

The Place de la Concorde was first designed in 1753 for Louis XV as his contribution to the grandeur of Paris. Forty years later, though, the great square's history took a very different turn. Renamed 'Place de la Revolution', this was where the *guillotine*, named after its inventor Dr Guillotin, was installed to chop off the heads of aristocrats and other followers of the old regime. King Louis XVI and Marie Antoinette were both beheaded here before baying crowds. Today, the Egyptian obelisk stands more or less in the exact spot where they met their grisly ends.

The Madeleine and the Opéra

From Place de la Concorde a turn north up Rue Royale will very quickly take you to the **Madeleine**, a church built for Napoleon in the style of a classical temple in order to commemorate the glories

of ancient Rome. Today, the surrounding **Place de la Madeleine** forms the hub of one of Paris' most distinctive (and luxurious) shopping areas. Look out, in particular, for the extravagant food halls of **Hédiard** (No.21) and **Fauchon** (No.26), the poshest grocers in town. No one (especially a child) can fail to marvel at their lavish confectionery sections, piled high with ornate chocolate sculptures, boxes of sweets and sugared fruits. Everything is reassuringly expensive, and you should expect to pay in the region of €25 for six small, delicious and exquisitely wrapped chocolates.

From the Madeleine, you can take a ride on *La Météor*, Paris' most recently constructed métro line (No.14), which is electronically operated so you can sit right at the front, where the driver would normally sit, watching the tunnels rushing towards you (your kids may have to wait their turn for the prime spot). It runs down to the new Bibliothèque Nationale, via Châtelet and the

Question 4
Who did France beat to win the 1998 football World Cup and what was the score?
answer also on p.250

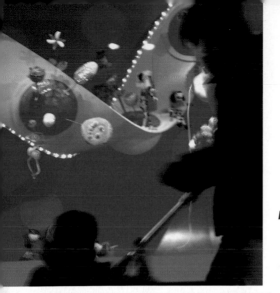

Gare de Lyon. Alternatively, a short walk up the boulevard to the right of the Madeleine will take you to the **Opéra**, also known as the Palais Garnier, perhaps the most lavish, over-the-top building in the whole of Paris (even blasé kids will have their attention grabbed by its overdose of statues). North of the Opéra, along Boulevards Haussmann and Montmartre, is the prime shopping area known as the **Grands Boulevards**, the location of several of Paris's biggest stores (see pp.172–173).

Musée Fragonard

9 Rue Scribe, 9th
t 01 47 42 93 40
Ⓜ Opéra, **RER** Auber
Open 9am–5.30pm (Mon–Sat); closed Sundays and public holidays
Adm free

In a street just behind the Opéra, this little museum fills you in on the 5,000-year-old history of perfume-making from ancient Egyptian times to the present day. Kids are allowed to sample the exclusive scents of the Fragonard Fragrance House.

Paris Story

11 bis Rue Scribe, 9th
t 01 42 66 62 06
Ⓜ Opéra, **RER** Auber
www.paris-story.com
Open Daily 9am–7pm; shows on the hour
Adm Adults €8, under-18s €8, under-6s **free**

The whole family will enjoy this multimedia show on a giant screen portraying 2,000 years of Parisian history. A virtual Victor Hugo uses the latest audiovisual technology to guide you through the event-packed centuries (English translation available). The show lasts 45 minutes.

The Champs Élysées

Av des Champs Élysées, 8th
Lower section Ⓜ Concorde, Champs Élysées–Clemenceau
Upper section Ⓜ Franklin D. Roosevelt, George V, Ⓜ/**RER** Charles de Gaulle-Étoile

The most famous street in France, and the main artery of Paris, this grand ornamental boulevard is divided into two contrasting sections. The lower section – from Place de la Concorde to the Rond

Special shops

Au Nain Bleu

406–410 Rue St Honoré, 8th (on the corner with Rue Richepance, just north of Place de la Concorde)
t 01 42 60 39 01
www.au-nain-bleu.com
Ⓜ Concorde, Madeleine
Open 9.45am–6.30pm (Mon–Sat)
Wheelchair access to ground floor only; no lifts
Suitable for all ages
Paris' greatest toy shop will cater to all your giant teddy needs. Founded in 1836, it has a great awareness of its illustrious history and can be a slightly stiff and stuffy place, but children are still enchanted by it and can happily lose themselves for a whole afternoon in among its vast vaults of toy cars, dolls' houses and board games (see p.174).

La Samaritaine

19 Rue de la Monnaie, 1st
t 01 40 41 20 20, welcome service **t** 01 40 41 22 54
www.lasamaritaine.com
Ⓜ Pont Neuf, Châtelet Les Halles
Open 9.30am–7pm (Mon–Sat), until 10pm (Thurs)
Wheelchair access
The Samaritaine, a huge two-building department store on the banks of the Seine, boasts an excellent basement toy department. There's even a carousel on hand for when your kids tire of browsing through the vast hordes of teddies, remote-controlled cars and video games. Afterwards, order a soft drink in the rooftop café of the Seine-side building and enjoy some truly spectacular views of the city (see pp.159, 172–173).

Point des Champs Élysées – is calm and serene, set in sculpted parkland and bordered on its southern side by the great fantasy constructions of the **Grand** and **Petit Palais**, built for one of Paris' world-wide exhibitions (in 1900) and which now host a range of museums and exhibitions. The upper section – from the Rond Point to the Arc de Triomphe – is bustling, lively and lined with restaurants, pavement cafés, shops, banks and cinemas.

The Champs Élysées' rise to prominence has been somewhat *ad hoc*. The lower section was laid out on parkland in the early 17th century by the royal gardener André Le Nôtre and, for over a century, remained a quiet, tree-lined alleyway. During the 18th century, the avenue was extended and began to attract the fancy of society trendsetters, who constructed well-to-do *hôtels* (town mansions) and residences along the upper section, turning it into a fashionable promenade. By the mid 19th century, it had been firmly established as Paris' most popular tourist attraction.

Its significance to the French people, however, goes much deeper than that. This, after all, is where Bismarck and Hitler made a point of marching their armies in 1870 and 1940, and where the French army led joyous national celebrations in 1945 following the Liberation. This is also where the nation came to celebrate victory in the 1998 football World Cup after France beat Brazil 3–0 in the final (an event which attracted the largest crowds since the Liberation), where the Tour de France finishes each year, and where the all-important 14 July celebrations are held.

The lower section of the Champs Élysées will probably be of most interest to kids with its park-land, fountains, buskers and marionette shows (Wednesdays, Saturdays and Sundays on the corner of Avenue Matignon and Avenue Gabriel near the Rond Point). The upper section is good for shopping (you'll find branches of the Disney Store, Virgin Megastore, Planet Hollywood and Natalys) and for having a bite to eat, sitting at a pavement café watching the Parisian world go by. The area's principal attraction for kids, the Palais de la Découverte, is just south of the Rond Point.

Palais de la Découverte

Av Franklin D. Roosevelt, 8th
t 01 40 74 00 00
www.palais-decouverte.fr
Ⓜ/RER Champs Élysées–Clemenceau, Invalides
Open 9.30am–6pm (Tues–Sat), 10am–7pm (Sundays and public holidays); closed Mondays, 1 Jan, 1 May, 14 July, 15 Aug, 25 Dec
Adm Adults €5.60, under-18s €3.70, family €12.20; €3 supplement (for the planetarium)
Wheelchair access
Suitable for all ages; allow at least 2 hours

Occupying an entire wing of the Grand Palais, the 'Palace of Discovery' tackles the problem of interesting children in science by mixing theory with as much interaction and fun as possible. It's not quite as state-of-the-art as Paris' bigger, emphatically modern, interactive science display in the Cité des Sciences et de l'Industrie at La Villette, but it has a certain special charm; on a practical level, many of the exhibits are simpler, more immediately accessible and just more enjoyable in the way they open up science than some of the more complex exhibits at La Villette. The museum is a major resource of the local education authority and, whenever you visit, you'll find yourself accompanied by at least half a dozen school parties. A special team arranges children's workshops and guided tours (age 4 upwards) on Wednesdays (normally in French but group tours can be booked in English as well).

Its galleries are full of buttons to press and levers to pull. you can charge magnets to make a metal egg spin on its end, play a note on a keyboard and watch the sound transformed into waves on an oscilloscope, control the movements of a plastic spinning solar system, or make sparks fly through the air between electrodes. Since every label, description, and video presentation is in French, it's best to whizz through the galleries pressing any button that takes your fancy rather than getting too hung up on the intricacies of scientific theory.

There are several demonstration areas: in the electrostatics gallery, you can watch a Van de Graaf generator creating 'mini' lightning, or members of the audience being charged with electricity so that their hair stands on end and sparks fly from their fingertips. A recent addition is the *Cybermetropolis*, focusing on computers and the net. The Palais has been extensively revamped in the last few years, but a few parts still have a rather old-fashioned feel with exhibits in old wooden cabinets. In contrast, however, it has an absolutely up-to-date 200-seat planetarium, which uses fibre optics to present the starscape and planetary movement in magical fashion on a celestial star-dome. The museum shop is run by **Nature et Découvertes** (*see* pp.166–167) and is filled with dinosaur models, astronomy charts, kaleidoscopes and telescopes, some of which are for serious astronomers (the most powerful ones go for a touch over €6,000).

Arc de Triomphe

Place Charles de Gaulle-Étoile, 8th
t 01 55 37 73 77
www.monum.fr
Ⓜ/**RER** Charles de Gaulle-Étoile
Open 10am–10.30pm (1 Oct–31 Mar); 9.30am–11pm (1 Apr–30 Sept); closed public holidays
Adm Adults €7, under-25s €4.50, under-18s **free**, and **free** admission for everyone on the first Sunday of each month
Carte Musées et Monuments valid
Wheelchair access
Suitable for all ages; allow at least 1 hour

One of the world's most recognizable landmarks, the arch was commissioned in 1806 by Napoleon to celebrate his own military achievements. Originally he wanted the arch to stand in the Place de la Bastille, but his advisors convinced him that its current location would be more prominent and more fashionable. The monument was only partially complete at the time of the Emperor's final defeat at Waterloo in 1815, whereupon work on it stopped. On its eventual completion in 1836, it was dedicated instead to the revolutionary armies.

The Arc de Triomphe is decorated with dramatic relief panels depicting battle scenes from the revolutionary wars, the most famous of which is Rude's *Le Départ des Voluntaires* (on the right, looking from the city) or *La Marseillaise* (as it's more commonly known) because it commemorates the volunteers from Marseille who marched into Paris to defend the Revolution, an incident which also inspired the French national anthem, *La Marseillaise*. The Arc de Triomphe stands in line along the *Grand Axe* with two of Paris' other great monuments, the **Arc du Carrousel** in front of the Louvre, and the **Grande Arche de la Défense** to the west, both of which can be easily seen from the top of the arch – some 50m (160ft) up. Looking down, 12 ornamental boulevards radiate out from Place Charles de Gaulle explaining the square's older and still popular name – *L'Étoile* (the star).

Originally there were just five, but in the 1860s, Baron Haussmann added another seven, including Avenue Foch, still the widest street in Paris.

A small museum halfway up the arch shows a film about the monument's construction and, between its two sides, is France's Tomb of the Unknown Soldier. The top of the arch can be reached by lift or a winding 300-stair staircase. Queues are often long, so get there early.

Beyond the Étoile

West of the Arc de Triomphe the *Grand Axe*, now called Avenue de la Grande Armée, continues on towards La Défense. At Porte Maillot, two métro stops along from the Étoile, it meets the northeast corner of the **Bois de Boulogne**, largest of all Paris' green spaces. Not far from this entrance is the **Jardin d'Acclimatation**, Paris's favourite kids' amusement park with a funfair, open-air circus, puppet theatre, a hands-on science museum (Exploradome), a petting zoo, boat rides and all sorts of other attractions. A special mock train, *Le Petit Train*, runs to the Jardin from Porte Maillot station at weekends, on Wednesdays, and daily in summer holidays. For further details, *see* pp.118–119.

Grande Arche de la Défense

1 Parvis de la Défense, 4th
t 01 49 07 27 57
Ⓜ/RER Grande Arche de la Défense
Open Daily 9am–8pm (April–Sep),
9am–7pm (Oct–Mar)
Adm Adults €7, under-18s €5.50
Wheelchair access and adapted toilets
Suitable for all ages; allow at least 2 hours

'Topping off' the *Grand Axe*, the La Défense business district is a strange, otherworldly place of vast sealed office blocks, enclosed walkways and indoor shopping centres. A mini-Manhattan, neatly tucked away on the far western edge of town, its landscape is almost entirely concrete and glass. There are no gardens here, and what greenery there is sits in big imported plant pots, but the area still holds some attractions, and is worth an excursion from the city centre.

Its focal point is the Grande Arche, a whole office complex in the form of an arch – vast, angular and undeniably impressive. It was completed in 1989 for the bicentennial of the Revolution and unveiled by President Mitterand on 14 July . The left side contains the entire Ministry of Transport and Public Works, the right side contains private offices. Over 100,000 people work here, and another 35,000 live in the futuristic blocks of flats on the southern edge of the Défense complex.

You can take a thrillingly fast glass lift to the top of the arch, some 110m (360ft) up. Here you'll find an art gallery (which hosts a temporary modern art exhibitions), a restaurant and some truly spectacular views towards the Arc de Triomphe (on clear days even as far as the Louvre). In front of the arch is a great concrete concourse, home to a few sweet stalls and a vintage carousel (but few buskers or street performers), while to the left is a vast shopping mall, **Les Quatre Temps**, where you'll find outlets of the Disney Store, Nature et Découverte and a huge branch of Toys 'R' Us (see **Shop**, pp.165–174 for more details).

Info-Défense

t 01 47 74 84 24
Ⓜ/RER La Défense
Open 10am–6pm Mon–Fri (April–Oct);
9.30am–5.30pm Mon–Fri (Nov–Mar)

The Info-Défense kiosk, in front of the triangular CNIT exhibition hall, has area maps and guides.

WHERE TO EAT

1 Bistro Romain
73 Av des Champs Élysées, 8th
t 01 43 59 67 85
Ⓜ Franklin D. Roosevelt
Open Daily 11.30am–1am

2 Cafés et Thés Verlet
256 Rue St Honoré, 1st
t 01 42 60 67 39
Ⓜ Palais Royal–Musée du Louvre, Tuileries
Open Daily 9am–7pm

3 Cap Vernet
82 Av Marceau, 8th
t 01 47 20 20 40
Ⓜ/RER Charles de Gaulle-Étoile
Open Daily 12 noon–2.30pm, 7pm–11pm

4 Chicago Pizza Pie Factory
5 Rue de Berri, 8th
t 01 45 62 50 23
Ⓜ George V
Open Daily 12 noon–1am

5 Hippopotamus
42 Av des Champs Élysées, 8th
t 01 53 83 94 50
Ⓜ Franklin D. Roosevelt
Open Daily 11.30am–5am

6 Planet Hollywood
78 Av des Champs Élysées, 8th
t 01 53 83 78 27
Ⓜ Franklin D. Roosevelt
Open Daily 12 noon–1am

7 Terrasse de la Samaritaine
Quai du Louvre, Terrasse Le Toupary, 1st
t 01 40 41 29 29
Ⓜ Pont Neuf, Châtelet
Open 9.30am–7pm (Mon–Sun), until 10pm (Thurs)

8 Virgin Café
Virgin Megastore
52 Av des Champs Élysées, 8th
t 01 49 53 50 00
Ⓜ Franklin D. Roosevelt, George V
Open 10am–12 midnight (Mon–Sat), 12 noon–12 midnight (Sun)

See **Eat** pp.153–164 for details on the above restaurants/sandwich shops. See map on p.41 for the locations of the restaurants numbered above.

Food on the go

9 Le Pain Quotidien
18 Place du Marché St Honoré, 1st
t 01 42 96 32 70
Ⓜ Pyramides
Open Daily 7am–8pm

10 Lina's Sandwiches
t 01 40 15 94 95
4 Rue Cambon, 1st
Ⓜ Concorde
Open 7am–8pm (Mon–Sat)

11 15 Rue de Louvre, 1st
t 01 40 41 15 00
Ⓜ/RER Châtelet Les Halles
Open 7am–8pm (Mon–Sat)

12 8 Rue Marbeuf, 8th
t 01 47 23 92 33
Ⓜ Alma Marceau
Open 7am–8pm (Mon–Sat)

13 Aux Pains Perdus
39 Rue de Berri, 8th
Ⓜ Franklin D. Roosevelt
Open Daily 8am–8pm

14 Handmade
19 Rue Jean Mermoz, 8th
t 01 45 62 50 05
Ⓜ Franklin D. Roosevelt
Open 8am–5pm (Mon–Fri)

Eiffel Tower

This is postcard Paris, the spot where every tourist must come to pay homage to (and climb) France's greatest monument. While a trip to the Eiffel Tower is usually the highlight of any trip to Paris, there are plenty of other attractions in the area worth checking out. At the foot of the tower there's the **Champ de**

Mars, a nice, grassy park with a playground and donkey rides; a short walk away, there's the **Hôtel des Invalides**, where France's favourite tyrant, Napoleon Bonaparte, is buried, and which also houses an army museum with a whole arsenal of cannons and other military relics. Just across the river, there's the **Palais de Chaillot** Arts Complex which contains a great museum of naval history. Several other world-class museums can be found nearby dealing with Asian art, modern art and the history of fashion. The **Musée Rodin** by the Invalides is also well worth a visit with a beautiful secluded garden, café and sandpit (adults with prams get in for free). On the quays beside the river are three Parisian favourites: the main departure point for the **bateaux mouches** river boats (*see* p.31); **Les Égouts de Paris** (Sewer Museum) where you can enjoy a delightfully smelly subterranean tour; and, just one métro stop away, the ultra-modern **Parc André Citroën** with its water jets and sightseeing balloon.

Highlights

Unmissable – going right to the top of the Eiffel Tower, then having lunch in the restaurant on Level 2

Taking a tour of Paris' dark and dirty sewers

Seeing a more relaxed side of Paris in the Musée Rodin's garden café

THE SIGHTS

Eiffel Tower

Champ de Mars, 7th
t 01 44 11 23 45/01 44 11 23 23 (infoline)
www.tour-eiffel.fr
Ⓜ Bir Hakeim, Trocadéro, **RER** Champ de Mars–Tour Eiffel
Open Daily 9am–12 midnight (June–Aug); 9.30am–11pm (Sept–May) (stairs close at 6.30pm)
Adm By lift. Level 1: adults €3.70, under-12s €2.30; Level 2: adults €7, under-12s €3.90; Level 3: adults €10.20, under-12s €5.50; under-3s **free**.
By stairs. First and second levels only: €3.30
Wheelchair access
Suitable for all ages; allow at least 2 hours

You can't come to Paris and not visit the Eiffel Tower; it would be like going to New York and ignoring the Statue of Liberty, or heading off to Cairo and skipping the Pyramids. Paris has plenty of other monuments with good views, yet none can match the splendour of the great iron flagpole. Even by today's skyscraper standards, it's impossibly huge, especially when seen against the low-rise Parisian skyline. Imagine how it must have seemed 100 years ago, when the 300-m (985-ft) tower was the tallest structure in the world! The first two of its three levels are accessible by lift or stairs – take heed that there are 1,710 steps on the

way up. To get to the third level, you have to take the lift. On your way up, you'll find two restaurants, a small museum, where you can see a film on the history of the tower's construction, a gift shop, several boutiques and even a post office, where your postcards can get that all-important 'Paris Tour Eiffel' postmark. From the top platform on a clear day, you can see over 65km (40 miles).

Around 16,000 people visit the tower every day, so queues for the lifts can be very long – if you come mid-afternoon expect to wait at least 1 hour. Queues are shorter first thing in the morning and at night, when the views of the illuminated city are even more magical. The tower itself is illuminated after dark for 10 minutes following the start of each hour until 2am. Thousands of lightbulbs on the tower's sides flicker and glitter in the night sky while an enormous seachlight on the summit performs great sweeping arcs of the city.

In time-honoured tradition, this now popular monument was pretty much reviled when first unveiled in 1889 as part of a 'Universal Exhibition' held to celebrate the centenary of the Revolution. Many great figures in Paris' artistic community, including Alexandre Dumas, signed a petition against it, while Guy de Maupassant moved out of Paris so he wouldn't have to look at the 'metallic carcass'. The government considered knocking the tower down in 1909 as it seemed to serve no useful purpose (being beautiful wasn't enough). Thankfully, a function was found for the Tower in 1914 when a meteorological station and wireless antennae were built on top of it, increasing its height by 20m, to over 1,000ft. It only ceased to be the world's tallest building in 1931, with the opening of the Empire State Building in New York.

Champ de Mars

7th
Ⓜ Bir Hakeim, École Militaire, **RER** Champ de Mars–Tour Eiffel

In 1889, the Champ de Mars gardens would have been covered by a huge iron pavilion (the *Galerie des Machines*) with a moving walkway that ran through its centre from the École Militaire to the Tower. Today, the Champ de Mars contains a playground (at the furthest end away from the Tower) with slides and climbing equipment, donkey rides (€2) and large green lawns that you can walk on.

Hôtel des Invalides

Question 6
At 320m (1,050ft) high, the Eiffel Tower was the tallest structure in the world until 1931. What surpassed it?
answer also on p.250

Esplanade des Invalides, 7th
t 01 44 42 37 72
www.invalides.org
Ⓜ/RER Invalides, Ⓜ La Tour–Maubourg, Varenne
Open Daily 10am–5pm (April–Sep); 10am–6pm (Oct–Mar); museum closed on public holidays and first Sunday of the month
Adm Adults €7, under-18s €5, under-12s **free** (ticket includes entry to the dome church, the Musée de l'Armée, Musée des Plans Reliefs, Musée du General de Gaulle and Second World War Église Saint Louis des Invalides, Napoleon's tomb)
Carte Musées et Monuments valid
Wheelchair access
Suitable for children aged 6 and over
Allow at least 2 hours

Topped by a gilded dome (one of Paris' most prominent landmarks), it was built in the 17th century for the wounded and retired soldiers of Louis XIV's numerous campaigns, its wards filled with 6,000-plus battle-scarred victims. Part of it is still used as a hospital today.

The Invalides' main attraction is a shrine to one of France's secular gods, Napoleon, whose body was brought here in 1840 to a hero's funeral. Exiled on the tiny British-owned South Atlantic island of St Helena after his defeat at Waterloo in 1815, he had died in 1821, apparently poisoned by the arsenic fumes emanating from the wallpaper in his house (many of Napoleon's supporters believed this was set up deliberately by the English to bump the Emperor off). When he returned to French soil 19 years later, Napoleon's reputation had grown to mythic proportions: no longer was he the power-crazed tyrant whose lust for glory had almost destroyed France; instead, he was the embodiment of France's true revolutionary spirit. His body lies beneath the dome in a red sarcophagus (within which are a further six coffins).

The Invalides complex also contains two churches, **St Louis** and the **Église du Dôme**, built back-to-back (they originally shared an altar) – one for use by soldiers and staff, the other by the Royal family. The two congregations may have worshipped the same God but did not share the same pews. The **Esplanade des Invalides**, stretching north to the river (where you can walk across the Alexander III bridge to the Grand Palais and the Champs Élysées) is another of Paris' formal parks.

Musée de l'Armée

Napoleon's tomb aside, most people come to the Invalides to visit the Musée de l'Armée, France's national army museum with its rooms full of armour, uniforms (the museum contains over

100,000 of these), weapons and paintings. There are sections devoted to the campaigns of Louis XIV, the First World War, the Second World War (housed in the new wing Musée de l'Ordre de Libération) and, of course, to Napoleon, the last containing such singular items as a lock of his hair, his death mask and his stuffed pet dog. One curiosity worth looking out for is a 360° painting of the Battle of Rosaville. You can stand in the middle and follow the course of the battle around and around.

The top floor is reserved for the **Musée des Plans Relief** which holds a fascinating collection of scale models of France's fortified towns. The collection was begun in the 17th century under Louis XIV and added to over the next 200 years, while the models give a detailed image of many famous towns as they were in the pre-industrial era.

The Cannons

The Invalides seems to have inherited more cannons than it knows what to do with. They line the entrance, the central courtyard (known as *Le Cour d'Honneur*), and the colonnaded walkways.

If you look at the 18th-century cannons in the courtyard (which bear such emotive names as *Le Maniac*), you'll see that these instruments of war are beautifully decorated with carved reliefs of

lions and suns and sport fish-shaped handles. The 19th-century cannons lining the walkways are much more austere and sombre in comparison.

The barrel of a cannon is slightly spiralled to help the cannon ball spin as it was fired, making it easier to aim. An arrow marks where it emerged.

Musée Rodin

Hôtel Biron, 77 Rue de Varenne, 7th
t 01 44 18 61 10
www.musee-rodin.fr
Ⓜ Varenne
Open 9.30am–5.45pm Tues–Sun (April–Sept); 9.30am–4.45pm Tues–Sun (Oct–Mar)
Adm Adults €5, under-25s €3, under-18s and adults with pushchair **free**; €1 (garden only)
Carte Musées et Monuments valid
Partial wheelchair access
Suitable for all ages; allow at least 2 hours

Auguste Rodin, one of France's most influential and popular sculptors, lived in the Hôtel Biron, almost alongside the Invalides, for nearly 10 years before his death in 1917. His works and his own art collection are exhibited inside this beautifully preserved 18th-century house, with sculptures scattered throughout the pretty, enclosed garden.

Rodin's sculptures often seem to appeal to the younger generation and many will already be familiar with *The Thinker* and *The Kiss*. Children are sure to enjoy seeing sculpture outdoors and, when they've had enough, there's a sandpit with a little café alongside. It's a particular favourite with Parisian mothers. In summer art-related activities are organized by the museum for kids in French.

Question 7
How did Napoleon die?
a) Shot by an Italian peasant?
b) Blown up by a Russian bomb?
c) Poisoned by the decorations in his home?
answer also on p.250

Palais de Chaillot

Place du Trocadéro, 16th
Ⓜ Trocadéro

Built for Paris' 1937 World Exhibition, this imposing, creamy-coloured complex sits atop a hill across the Seine from the Eiffel Tower – the walk over the Pont d'Iéna bridge takes in some of Paris' most impressive vistas. Sometimes referred to by locals just as **Trocadéro** (from the Place du Trocadéro alongside it), it's made up of two grand pavilions, which envelop a central terrace decorated with monumental statues. The tiered **Jardins du Trocadéro** beneath it, stretching down towards the water's edge, contain a vintage carousel and fountains, as well as a lively throng of souvenir sellers and skateboarders.

The Palais is home to two museums currently undergoing renovation and reorganization – the **Musée de la Marine** (Maritime Museum) and the soon-to-open **Cité de l'Architecture** (formerly the Musée des Monuments Historiques) in 2005. The ethnographic museum, the **Musée de l'Homme**, will soon reopen its doors at the Musée de Quai Branly across the river by the Eiffel Tower, while the **Musée du Cinéma** is moving to new premises in Bercy (within the cultural complex there).

Musée de la Marine

Place de Chaillot, 17 Place du Trocadéro, 16th
t 01 53 65 69 53
www.musee-marine.fr
Ⓜ Trocadéro
Open 10am–5.50pm (Mon, Wed–Sun); closed Tuesdays
Adm Adults €5.80, under-25s €3.80, under-5s **free**
Carte Musées et Monuments valid
Wheelchair access
Suitable for all ages; allow at least 1 hour

Dedicated to French naval history, it displays hundreds of beautifully crafted model boats ranging from ancient Egyptian barges to medieval galleys, modern destroyers, submarines and aircraft carriers. There's a model of the open-decked boat that brought the Egyptian obelisk all the way from Luxor to the Place de la Concorde (*see* p.45). You can also see the workshop where many models were created and watch craftsmen at work.

Other exhibits include Napoleon's royal barge (powered by oarsmen instead of sails to make Bonaparte look like a Roman Emperor), a collection of lighthouse light bulbs and a display on the recent construction of the *Queen Mary II*, the world's largest luxury liner.

Near the Palais de Chaillot

Musée Nationale des Arts Asiatiques – Guimet

6 Place d'Iéna, 16th
t 01 56 52 53 00
www.museeguimet.fr
Ⓜ Iéna
Open 10am–6pm (Mon, Wed–Sun); closed Tuesdays
Adm Adults €5.50, under-25s €4, under-18s **free**; **free** for everyone on first Sunday of each month
Carte Musées et Monuments valid
Wheelchair access
Suitable for children aged 8 and over
Allow at least 1 hour

Reopened in 2001 after a 3-year renovation programme, it contains one of the world's important Asian art collections (Chinese ivories, Javanese shadow puppets, Indian lacquerware, Japanese ceramics and scores of big, smiling buddhas).

Musée de la Mode et du Costume

Palais Galliéra, 10 Av Pierre I de Serbie, 16th
t 01 56 52 86 00
Ⓜ Iéna, Alma Marceau
Open 10am–6pm (Tues–Sun)
Adm Adults €7, under-25s/18s €5.50/€3.50, under-13s **free**
Carte Musées et Monuments valid
Wheelchair access
Suitable for all ages; allow at least 1 hour

This 19th-century Neo-Renaissance mansion contains a 16,000-piece museum of fashion representing the last 300 years of Parisian *couture*. The collection is shown in rotation by themes such as

---

Tell me a story: **life down below**

The building of the city's 21,000km (13,000 miles) of sewers was begun in 1825 after centuries of having the Seine serve Paris both as a means of waste disposal and the main source of drinking water. During the 19th century, they were home to poor families, who found in them the cheapest lodgings in town. Today they are a tourist attraction and a few surprise residents still turn up: in 1984 a small crocodile was found living in this huge maze of underground tunnels.

'marriage' or 'town clothes'. The entrance fee includes an audioguide in English.

Palais de Tokyo

13 Av Président Wilson, 16th
t 01 47 23 54 01
www.palaisdetokyo.com
Ⓜ Iéna, Alma Marceau
Open Musée d'Art Moderne: 10am–5.30pm (Tues–Fri), 10am–7pm (Sat–Sun); Site de Création Contempororaire: 12 noon–12 midnight (Tues–Sun)
Adm Adults €5, under-25s €3, under-18s **free** (temporary exhibitions). Permanent collection **free**.
Carte Musées et Monuments valid
Wheelchair access
Suitable for children aged 6 and over
Allow at least 1 hour

Another architectural tribute to the 1937 Exhibition, it was originally called the Electricity Pavilion because of Raoul Dufy's vast mural *La Fée Electricité*. Today half the building is given over to the Musée de la Mode et du Costume, the city's small, but impressive, modern art collection (Picasso, Braque, Modigliani and a Matisse room with two versions of his famous work, *La Danse*). The other portion has become the Site de Création Contemporaire, a state-of-the-art experimental space with stark walls and an enormous skylight for rotating contemporary art exhibitions. There's also a very good café that stays open until late.

On the riverbank

The most celebrated sections along the Left Bank are towards the Île de la Cité (*see* p.79) but, on either side of the **Pont de l'Alma**, are the embarcation points for the *bateaux mouches*, just on the west side of the Alma bridge (*see* p.31) and, on the other side of the bridge, the entrance to Paris' sewers.

Les Égouts de Paris (Sewer Museum)

Entrance opposite 93 Quai d'Orsay by Pont de l'Alma, 7th
t 01 53 68 27 81
www.paris.fr
Ⓜ Alma Marceau, **RER** Pont de l'Alma
Open 11am–5pm Mon–Wed, Sat–Sun (May–Sept); 11am–4pm Mon–Wed, Sat–Sun (Oct–Dec and Feb)
Adm Adults €3.80, under-12s €3.05, under-5s **free**

Carte Musées et Monuments valid
Wheelchair hire and assistance available
Suitable for all ages; allow at least 1 hour

The smelliest tour in town, much loved by kids. The city's sewers (*égouts*) have recently become a strangely popular tourist attraction and in high season the queues can be quite long. The sewer 'experience' consists of a short film on the history of waste disposal and a quick walk through a section of the sewer network, laid out like some subterranean city. Every sewer has a sign stating the street it serves and every pipe bears the name of the building to which it is connected.

Parc André Citroën

Entrances on Rue Balard, Rue St Charles and Quai Citroën, 15th
Ⓜ Javel–André Citroën, Balard

This Seine-side park, a métro stop south of the Eiffel Tower, occupies the site of an old Citroën car factory. Billed as a 'Park for the 21st Century' with six colour-coded, high-concept flower gardens, glass houses filled with tropical plants and a computer-controlled water garden. Be sure to pack swimsuits for the randomly erupting water jets from fountains lining the park's concrete plateau. Children love rushing around trying to predict the jets and getting soaked. You can also walk on the grass without being yelled at by a park-keeper. An appealing feature is the Fortis Balloon, which offers passengers the chance to view Paris from a height of 150m (500ft) up in the air (*Mondays to Fridays €10 for adults, €9 under-18s, €5 under-12s, under-3s free; Saturdays and Sundays €12 for adults, €10 under-18s, €6 under-12s, under-3s free*). Tours of the park are offered by the parks department.

WHERE TO EAT

1 Altitude 95
1st Level, Eiffel Tower, Champ de Mars, 7th
t 01 45 55 20 04
Ⓜ Bir Hakeim, Trocadéro
Open Daily 12 noon–2.45pm, 7pm–9.45pm

2 L' Ancien Trocadéro
2 Place du Trocadéro et du 11 Novembre, 16th
t 01 47 04 94 71
Ⓜ Trocadéro
Open Daily 11.30am–1am

3 Bistro Romain
6 Place Victor Hugo, 16th
t 01 45 00 65 03
Ⓜ Victor Hugo
Open Daily 11.30am–1am

4 Brasserie XVIème Poincaré
45 Av Raymond Poincaré, 16th
t 01 47 27 72 19
Ⓜ Trocadéro
Open Daily 12 noon–12 midnight

5 Il Conte
47 Av Raymond Poincaré, 16th
t 01 47 27 98 40
Ⓜ Trocadéro
Open 12 noon–2.30pm and 7.30pm–11.30pm

6 Café du Musée Rodin
Hôtel Biron, 77 Rue de Varenne, 7th
t 01 45 50 42 34
Ⓜ Varenne
Open 9.30am–6.30pm (April–Sep);
9.30am–4.30pm (Oct–Mar)

7 Thoumieux
79 Rue St Dominique, 7th
t 01 47 05 46 44
Ⓜ Invalides, La Tour–Maubourg
Open 12 noon–3.30pm and 6.30pm–12 midnight
(Mon–Sat), 12 noon–12 midnight (Sun)

8 Le Troquet
21 Rue François Bonvin, 15th
t 01 45 65 89 00
Ⓜ Cambronne
Open 12 noon–2.30pm, 7.30pm–11pm (Tues–Sat)

See **Eat** pp.153–164 for more details on the above restaurants. *See* map on p.55 for the locations of the restaurants numbered above.

Pompidou Centre and the Marais

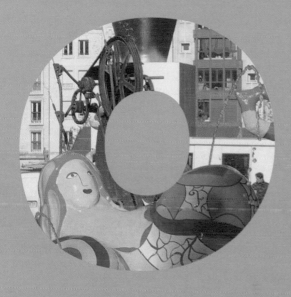

One of the most historic parts of Paris, the **Marais** is still the city's most cultured district, and one of its most attractive. Its streets are narrow and atmospheric, full of a character slowly accumulated over the centuries: traffic moves at a slower pace than in the wide boulevards, ideal for exploring and strolling. All along the Marais' streets there are elegant 17th-century mansions with intriguing little details and richly carved doorways to pick out, together with antique shops and fashion boutiques not to mention toy shops and children's clothes stores galore. The Marais also contains one of Paris' most charming squares, the **Place des Vosges**, and is home to several excellent museums, from the **Musée Carnavalet** on the city's history, to the irresistible and magical **Musée de la Curiosité**.

Closing off the Marais to one side is the **Pompidou Centre**, modern Paris' most spectacular and popular showcase for contemporary arts, and also one of its most child-friendly attractions. To the west, **Les Halles**, once the site of Paris' fruit and vegetable market, is now dominated by a vast underground shopping mall topped by a rather shabby park – not the loveliest part of Paris, but there is loads to do and all kinds of places to eat and shop are on offer. Underneath Les Halles, there's also **Châtelet Les Halles** station, the near-inescapable hub of the métro and RER systems.

Over on the eastern side of the Marais is **Place de la Bastille**, immortalized by history forever as the place where the French Revolution began and, since the 1980s, the centre of one of the liveliest, trendiest parts of Paris with quirky, individual places to shop and a great choice of restaurants. Overall it has a more international range and feel than many other parts of town.

Bonne Nouvelle Ⓜ

Strasbourg St. Denis Ⓜ

500 metres
500 yards

N

RUE RÉAUMUR **Sentier** Ⓜ

Réaumur-Sébastopol Ⓜ

RUE DE TURBIGO

République Ⓜ PLACE DE LA RÉPUBLIQUE

Temple Ⓜ

BD. DU TEMPLE

RUE DU LOUVRE

Étienne Marcel Ⓜ

❸ **St Eustache**

Arts et Métiers Ⓜ

Filles du Calvaire Ⓜ

Oberkampf Ⓜ

La Bourse

Jardin des Halles

Les Halles Ⓜ

Châtelet Les Halles ❺

Rambuteau Ⓜ

BOULEVARD DE SÉBASTOPOL

RUE BEAUBOURG

Musée de la Poupée

Musée de la Chasse et de la Nature

St. Sebastien Froissart Ⓜ

BOULEVARD BEAUMARCHAIS

Richard Lenoir Ⓜ

Forum des Halles

Châtelet Les Halles Ⓡ

RUE RAMBUTEAU

Pompidou Centre

RUE DU RENARD

Musée de l'Histoire de France

Musée Picasso

RUE DE RIVOLI

❶❶

Pont Neuf Ⓜ

Châtelet Ⓜ

Hôtel de Ville Ⓜ

Hôtel de Ville

RUE DE RIVOLI

RUE DES ROSIERS

Musée Cognacq-Jay

❾ **Musée Carnavalet**

Chemin Vert Ⓜ

Bréguet Sabin Ⓜ

❷

The Marais

RUE DES FRANCS BOURGEOIS

❽

PLACE DES VOSGES

Conciergerie

Sainte Chapelle

Cité Ⓜ

Île de la Cité

carousel

❶ **St. Paul** Ⓜ

RUE ST ANTOINE

❼ ❻

❹ PLACE DE LA BASTILLE

❿

St. Michel Nôtre-Dame Ⓡ

Nôtre Dame

Musée de la Curiosité et de la Magie

Pont Marie

RUE ST PAUL

Bastille Ⓜ

St. Michel Ⓜ

La Sorbonne Ⓜ

Île St Louis

BOULEVARD HENRI IV

Sully Morland Ⓜ

Highlights

Going up the glass tube escalators in the Pompidou Centre

Exploring the Marais streets

Learning about magic the hands-on way at the Musée de la Curiosité

Scoffing lunch amid the brasserie glitter of Bofinger

Pompidou Centre

Place Georges Pompidou, 4th

t 01 44 78 12 33

www.centrepompidou.fr

Ⓜ Hôtel de Ville, Rambuteau, Ⓜ/**RER** Châtelet Les Halles

Open Centre: 11am–10pm (Mon, Wed–Sun). Museum: 11am–9pm (Mon, Wed–Sun). Closed Tuesdays.

Adm Centre: **free**. Museum: adults €10, under-18s €8 ('Une journee au Centre' ticket gives you access to the national museum, Brancusi studio and some exhibitions); 1st Sunday of the month **free**.

Carte Musées et Monuments valid

Wheelchair access and adapted toilets

Suitable for all ages; allow at least 2 hours

Extensively revamped at the end of the 1990s, the Pompidou Centre, or Beaubourg, provides first-class entertainment for young visitors. The fun actually starts outside in the big, open square before the centre, where you'll find buskers, musicians, fire-eaters, sword-swallowers and performance artists entertaining the crowds.

The centre itself, created in the 1970s at the behest of the then French president Georges Pompidou, was designed to become a 'department store for culture': an accessible, populist museum that would act as an antidote to other more élitist institutions. The building, the work of architects Richard Rogers and Renzo Piano, was designed to be as outrageously modern as possible, and was initially pretty unpopular. All of its technical infra-structure – its wires, tubes and tunnels – is displayed prominently on the outside of the building painted in gaudy colours: electrics are lemon yellow, air conditioning vents bright blue and ventilation ducts white.

Despite the initial furore, the centre very rapidly won widespread acceptance and the majority of Parisians are now actually rather fond of it. Kids, in particular, usually respond favourably to its messy architecture and unfinished look – it's the sort of over-the-top construction they would probably come up with themselves.

A large part of the centre houses the **Musée Nationale d'Art Moderne**, where you'll find works by all the great modernists of the 20th century – Brandt, Braque, Chagall, Dalí, Kandinsky, Klee, Matisse, Modigliani, Picasso, Pollock, *et al*. The front desk provides quizzes and trails for children. Look out, too, for the **Ateliers des Enfants**, a varied programme of art workshops aimed at children aged 6–12 based around topics like 'Light and Shadows', exploring video technology, dance and art, or making improvised costumes inspired by the work of modern artists. Some workshops are short 'courses' of three or four weekly sessions and may require a fair knowledge of French, but there are shorter, more playful single afternoon sessions too. Approach reception for details of the programme.

The Pompidou also shows many films and, on the top floor, there's a great café with beautiful views of the city, best reached by the giant escalator that zigzags its way across the exterior. Come up at twilight and watch the lights of the city gradually coming into view.

The Marais

The pace of life in the Marais is somehow more relaxed than in other parts of the city. It's the neighbourhood of choice for the well-to-do with time on their hands.

A historic enclave, extending from the Hôtel de Ville to the Place de la Bastille, the Marais is famed for its graceful architecture and elegant streets, and the whole area is dotted with mansions, art galleries, clothes shops, flower sellers, cafés and museums. Saunter through its narrow streets and you can find plenty of distractions to keep both you and your kids entertained.

Once a small area of marshland (*marais* means 'marsh'), the Marais was drained and cultivated in the Middle Ages by the Knights Templar, but began its rise to prominence in 1605 when King Henri IV ordered the construction of the Place des Vosges. At a stroke, the area was turned into one of the most desirable addresses in Paris. Whole streets of mansions and luxury residences went up over the next couple of centuries as the nobility poured in. The area's fortunes, however, went the same way as the nobility's following the Revolution: its architecture went out of fashion, the monied classes moved away and the whole area became run down and dilapidated. This turned out to be something of a blessing as the Marais escaped many of the modern architectural ravages that have blighted some of the surrounding areas.

Come the early 1960s and the Marais was once again back in vogue; its historic, unspoilt landscape appealing to trendsetters searching for an alternative to high-rise modernity. Today, the area is still a great place to soak up a little old-time Parisian atmosphere and charm. In the centre of the district is the **Rue des Rosiers**, the traditional heart of Paris' Jewish community. If the whole of the Marais is superb for browsing and window-gazing, the old food shops of Rosiers with their many specialities – bakers with piles of traditional breads, bagels and pretzels, snack-packed delicatessens – are positively dazzling.

Place des Vosges

Square Louis XIII, 4th
Ⓜ **St Paul, Chemin Vert**

Paris' oldest square is a grand, formal open space lined with 36 arcaded façades of stone and brick and covered in neatly sculpted grass lawns (which you are not allowed to walk on), fountains and gravel pathways. It has long been a favourite stamping ground for school children (there's a sandpit) and *boules* players. Unlike many of Paris' squares, it hasn't (as yet) been turned into a traffic-filled roundabout, and still has a delightfully peaceful, laid-back Sunday-afternoon feel to it, even during the week.

When first laid out in the early 17th century, it was called the Place Royale. This was changed to

Shopping in the Marais

Browsing the shops of the Marais is one of the great pleasures of Paris and there's no need to leave the kids behind. In addition to antique shops, wine sellers, art galleries, cheese sellers and clothes boutiques, most streets also boast a toy shop and a children's clothes store.

As well as the shops listed here, **Catimini**, 6 Rue des Francs Bourgeois, 3rd, **Croissant**, 5 Rue St Merri, 4th, and **Jacadi**, 27 Rue Saint Antoine, 4th, are good for clothes. **Texaffaires**, 7 Rue du Temple, 4th, is good for nursery furniture and furnishings.

Cath'Art

13 Rue Ste Croix de la Bretonnerie, 4th
t 01 48 04 80 10
www.cathart.com
Marionettes, inflatables and other 'fun art' (*see* p.166).

C'est Ma Chambre

45 Rue des Archives, 3rd
t 01 48 87 26 67
Beautiful handmade bedroom furniture and toys.

La Charrue et les Étoiles

19 Rue des Francs Bourgeois, 4th
t 01 48 87 39 07
Huge collection of plastic and tin miniature figurines of the Simpsons, Spiderman, Wallace and Gromit, Tin Tin, Astérix and Obélix (*see* p.166).

Marais Plus

20 Rue des Francs Bourgeois, 3rd
t 01 48 87 01 40
Lots of educational toys and books with a tea shop on the first floor (*see* p.174).

Why!

41 Rue des Francs Bourgeois, 4th
t 01 44 61 72 75
One of a chain of stores (*see* p.167) that are temples to tackiness: furry lava lamps, humming-bird-shaped key rings and glow-in-the-dark bags.

The Marais Museums

Musée Carnavalet-Histoire de Paris

23 Rue de Sévigné, 3rd
t 01 44 59 58 58
www.paris.fr
Ⓜ St Paul, Chemin Vert
Open 10am–6pm (Tues–Sun); the 19th- and 20th-century rooms (10am–11.30am); the Louis XV period rooms (1.30pm–5.40pm)
Adm Free (charges apply to temporary exhibitions)
Carte Musées et Monuments valid
Wheelchair access via entrance at 29 Rue de Sévigné
Suitable for children aged 6 and over
Allow at least 2 hours

Set in one of the grandest mansions in the Marais, the Carnavalet reconstructs the story of Paris from pre-history to the present day through archaeological exhibits, personal effects, scale models and original house interiors – many recovered from mansions destroyed in the mid-19th century to make way for the Grands Boulevards. Kids usually like the models and house interiors best. Highlights include an incredibly detailed paper model of Paris (*c.* 1527), the glittering interior of a jeweller's shop (*c.* 1902) and the opulent salons of the Hôtels d'Uzèz, La Rivière and Wendel. There are some delightful pieces of revolutionary memorabilia such as a model *guillotine* carved in bone by French prisoners of war in England, Louis XIV's shaving kit and Napoleon's toothbrush.

Musée de la Chasse et de la Nature (Museum of Hunting and Nature)

Hôtel Guénégaud, 60 Rue des Archives, 3rd
t 01 53 01 92 40
Ⓜ Rambuteau
Open 11am–6pm (Tues–Sun), closed Mondays and public holidays
Adm Adults €4.60, under-25s €2.30, under-16s 75c, under-5s **free**
Limited wheelchair access
Suitable for children aged 8 and over
Allow at least 1 hour

This small museum in a beautiful 17th-century mansion is dedicated to the history of hunting – in France as much a proletarian pastime as an aristocratic one – and has an eclectic range of exhibits: Stone Age axes, Persian helmets, ornate crossbows, swords once owned by medieval noblemen and countless cases of stuffed animal trophies.

the catchy Place d'Indivisibilité following the French Revolution, when names with royal connotations were frowned upon. Napoleon gave it its present name in honour of the status of the Vosges as the first *département* in France to pay his new war taxes. This square was a horse market, then a site for lavish festivites before becoming a highly desirable place of residence.

Musée Cognacq-Jay

Hôtel Denon, 8 Rue Elzévir, 3rd
t 01 40 27 07 21
Ⓜ St Paul
Open 10am–6pm (Tues–Sun), closed Sundays and public holidays
Adm Free (charges apply to temporary exhibitions)
Carte Musées et Monuments valid
Limited wheelchair access
Suitable for children aged 8 and over
Allow at least 1 hour

Housed in a beautiful mansion, this collection of 18th-century European art was built up by Ernest Cognacq, founder of La Samaritaine department store, with works by Chardin, Canaletto, Fragonard, La Tour, Rembrandt, Rubens and Watteau. Children's activities and art workshops (in French) are organized by the museum in the summer.

Musée de la Curiosité et de la Magie (Museum of Curiosities and Magic)

11 Rue St Paul, 4th
t 01 42 72 13 26
www.museedelamagie.com
Ⓜ St Paul, Sully Morland
Open 2pm–7pm (Wed, Sat–Sun); daily during French school holidays
Adm Adults €7, under-12s €5, under-3s **free**
Wheelchair access
Suitable for all ages; allow at least 1 hour

Housed in a network of suitably mysterious-looking subterranean vaults, this is a performance-based museum with optical illusions, robots and interactive games which kids just love. Inside, skilled magicians are on hand to perform conjuring shows and card tricks with lots of audience participation – kids fight for the right to be the one to pick the card. Most of the magicians have some basic grasp of English and the tricks tend to self-explanatory but English-speaking guides are available and magic courses for children can be organized during the school holidays. The museum holds a permanent display of magic-related exhibits including costumes and props (such as cabinet used for sawing people in half). You can pick up equipment for your budding magicians – magic wands, trick card packs and demonstration videos – at the nearby **Magasin de Magie** on the Rue du Temple. If you've still got the magic bug, pop along to catch a matinee performance at the magic-themed café-theatre, *Double Fond*, where waiters perform magic tricks as they bring your drinks (1 Place du Marché Sainte Catherine, 4th, **t** 01 42 71 40 20, Saturday matinees 3.30pm, ages 6 and over only, **adm** €9).

Musée de l'Histoire de France

Hôtel de Soubise, 60 Rue des Francs Bourgeois, 3rd
t 01 40 27 60 96
Ⓜ Hôtel de Ville, Rambuteau, Ⓜ/**RER** Châtelet Les Halles
Open 10am–5.45pm (Mon, Wed–Fri), 1.45pm–5.45pm (Sat–Sun), closed Tuesdays
Adm Adults €3.50, under-25s €2.50, under-18s **free**

This small museum located in the elegant Hôtel de Soubise has some interesting old furniture, 18th-century paintings and a reconstruction of the private study used by the Prince and Princess de Soubise. It also hosts attractive temporary shows.

Musée Picasso

Hôtel Salé, 5 Rue De Thorigny, 3rd
t 01 42 71 25 21
Ⓜ Chemin Vert, St Paul

Open 9.30am–6pm Mon, Wed–Sun (Apr–Sept), 9.30am–5.30pm (Oct–March); closed Tuesdays
Adm Adults €5.50, under-25s €4; twin ticket (for temporary and permanent collections): adults €10, under-25s €8. First Sunday of the month, under-18s **free**
Carte Musées et Monuments valid
Wheelchair access
Suitable for children aged 10 and over
Allow at least 1 hour

Dedicated to the 20th-century's greatest artist, the museum contains the largest collection of Picasso's works, displayed in chronological order, as well as his own private collection which contains works by Braque, Cézanne, Chardin, Corot, Matisse, Renoir and Rousseau.

Musée de la Poupée (Doll Museum)

Impasse Berthaud, 3rd
t 01 42 72 73 11
Ⓜ Rambuteau
Open 10am–6pm (Tues–Sun), closed Mondays
Adm Adults €6, under-25s €4, under-18s €3, under-3s **free**

Sorry boys, but this is one for the girls. This valley of the dolls displays a century of over 500 exhibits dating from 1860 to 1200. The elaborate costumes, dolls' houses, furniture, tea sets and teddies make it a girlie wonderland. There's even a doll hospital!

Les Halles

1st
Ⓜ Châtelet Les Halles

For centuries Les Halles (pronounced *Lay Ai*) was occupied by a sprawling food market (Paris' largest) which, in the 1970s, was forced to move to the suburbs (not unlike London's Covent Garden). Now it is overrun by the **Forum des Halles** (**www**.forum-des-halles.com), a cavernous, rather shabby underground mall frequented mainly by teenage tourists and disreputable characters and, only grudgingly, by local residents. They (and anyone else visiting Paris) often find themselves passing through it at least once a day, though, because beneath it is **Châtelet Les Halles** station, the biggest junction in the whole Paris local rail network and hub of no fewer than six métro and

Can you spot?
The enormous head and hand sculpture that sits outside the Église St Eustache, the huge Gothic church overlooking the Jardin des Halles.

RER lines. It's pretty hard to avoid changing trains here, whichever direction you're coming from.

Nevertheless, there are some things that make the Forum well worth visiting with kids in tow. It has several good children's clothes and toy shops, including branches of Catamini, Complices, Du Pareil au Même, Gap, Nature et Découvertes, Petit Bateau and Why! (see pp.165–174). Alternately, take your kids for a dip in the 50m Olympic-sized underground swimming pool (**t** 01 42 36 98 44, open 11.30am–10pm Mon–Fri, 9am–7pm Sat–Sun, **adm** adults €3.80, under-16s €3); a smaller version of the **Musée Grevin** waxwork museum (*see* pp.114–115), and a multiplex cinema, the **UGC Ciné Cité**, which nearly always screens children's films, often in English (*see* p.112).

The **Jardin des Halles** (105 Rue Rambuteau, 1st), the park on top of the mall, lacks the liveliness or fun of most Parisian parks and is, in truth, rather grim, particularly at night when it attracts all sorts of undesirable characters. Its saving grace is a good supervised children's playground, the Jardin des Enfants. Although it may not look like it today, Les Halles is actually one of the oldest parts of Paris, and you can still find a few ancient monuments in amongst all the modern developments. One of the

Tell me a story: the hole at Les Halles

In 1969 the French government decided that the great food market of Les Halles had to move out of central Paris. It had been in existence for nearly 800 years and had seemed such a fundamental part of the city – as timeless as the River Seine itself – that the ease and speed with which it was sent on its way took most people by surprise, not least the traders themselves.

The government thought it had to clear the spot fast to make way for a rush of property speculation and development that would automatically arise on such a prime piece of real estate. The beautiful market buildings were sacrificed, it was argued, for the greater economic good. The rush, though, never materialized and, for over 10 years, until the Forum mall appeared, it remained unused and decrepit, the biggest urban hole in Europe.

most impressive is **St Eustache**, an almost cathedral-sized medieval church that looms above the Forum. It not only managed to escape redevelopment of the area in the 1970s but, during the revolution when many of the city's churches were closed, survived by renaming itself 'Temple of Agriculture' owing to its proximity to the market. At the far end of the Jardin des Halles is the **Bourse du Commerce**, Paris' original stock exchange.

Jardin des Enfants

105 Rue Rambuteau, 1st
t 01 45 08 07 18
Ⓜ/RER Châtelet Les Halles
Open 9am–12noon, 2pm–4pm Tues, Thurs, Fri (Sept–June), 10am–4pm (Wed, Sat), 1pm–4pm (Sun), 1pm–6pm Sundays (from April–June) 10am–7pm (Tues, Thurs, Sat–Sun), 2pm–7pm (Fri) (July–Aug), closed Mondays
Adm €0.40 for 1 hour
Suitable for ages 7–11

A well-supervised adventure playground with underground tunnels, rope swings, secret dens and pools of coloured balls. Children cannot be left here unattended, but one parent can take a rest from watching over the children while the other dives into the Forum des Halles to pick up some essential supplies.

Place de la Bastille

11th
Ⓜ Bastille

This is where the French Revolution started. Way back in 1789, this spot was occupied by the Bastille, a royal prison built around 1370, where the nation's political prisoners were held – in other words, people who had annoyed the monarch. Many were kept under the notorious *lettres de cachet*, a device that allowed the king to imprison pretty much anyone he liked for as long as he liked without having to bother going through the courts.

Over the centuries, the prison became a symbol of the corruption of royal power and was deeply hated by the Parisian lower orders. By the 1780s, however, the Bastille had been in decline for some time. It was no longer the city's main prison, the *lettres de cachet* had been abolished, and the government was actually planning to demolish it.

Indeed, when the revolution began in the summer of 1789, the Bastille held just seven prisoners.

Nonetheless, its symbolic importance was great, and, on 14 July, the revolutionary forces stormed the fortress and released the captives. Of the seven, four were swindlers, one was an English madman and another an aristocrat accused of incest, while the final prisoner, a genuine political captive who had been sent to the Bastille some 30 years before for conspiring against the king, had become so used to his surroundings that he initially refused to leave. The prison's demolition began the next day, overseen by a young entrepreneur named Palloy, who made a fortune with instant souvenirs of the event – Bastille's stones carved into models of the fortress – which he then sold to each of the 83 *départements* of France (you can see one of them in the Musée Carnavalet).

The outline of the fortress is still clearly visible on the paving stones of the square. In the centre stands a 50-m (164-ft) high column, *La Colonne de Juillet*, erected in memory of revolutionaries who died in two later upheavals, in 1830 and 1848, many of whom are buried beneath its base (Délacroix's famous painting *Liberty Leading the People*, now in the Louvre, commemorates the 1830 Revolution). The gold figure on top represents the Spirit of Liberty. The storming of the Bastille is celebrated on the square every 14 July with a lively street party (*see* p. 36).

On the southeast edge of the square is one of President Mitterand's controversial building projects, the vast, modernist **Opéra National de**

Tell me a story: the Great Revolution

If there's one thing the French love, it's a revolution. They've had four so far: in 1789, 1830, 1848 and 1871. When people refer to *the* French Revolution, though, they're talking about the first one, the peasants vs Louis XVI – the key event in France's history when ordinary people decided to take a stand against cruelty and inequality. The national anthem, *La Marseillaise*, and the flag, the *Tricoleur*, were both created at the time of the Revolution while 14 July, the day the Bastille was stormed, is France's national day, celebrated with fireworks in every town. For all the partying, however, it's worth remembering that the revolution itself was a nasty, bloodthirsty affair, its history jam-packed with violence, murder and betrayal...

A brief history of the French Revolution

1780s King Louis XVI is the absolute ruler of France; his word is law. The peasants and professionals (lawyers, doctors, magistrates) are increasingly unhappy with the situation, being particularly upset at having to pay high taxes while the king and his nobles lead lives of luxury.

1788 The year's harvest fails. The peasants are starving, but are still forced to pay their taxes.

1789 Peasants, professionals and the poor of Paris, angered by Louis' refusal to cut taxes, storm the Bastille. They set up a new parliament, the National Assembly, and insist that Louis listens to it. Louis thinks of the enormous mob ready to leap on him if he refuses and, not surprisingly, agrees.

1792 Louis tries to leave France to raise an army and defeat the revolutionaries, but he is captured and brought back to Paris.

1793 The Kings of Prussia, Austria and Spain declare war on France. They are scared that if the revolutionaries are successful their own people might revolt. Maximilien Robespierre, leader of the revolutionaries, orders that Louis XVI be executed, using a new-fangled head-chopping device, a *guillotine*. He then orders that all enemies of the revolution be wiped out. At this point, things get out of control as nobles, priests, criminals, madmen and even loyal revolutionaries who didn't happen to agree with Robespierre (plus anyone else who could possibly cause trouble) are caught in the net. People are carried to the *guillotine* through the streets in carts called *tumbrils*, usually used for taking dung and other rubbish out of the city. This period, during which some 30,000 people are killed, came to be known as 'The Terror'.

1794 The people of Paris turn on Robespierre in horror, accusing him of becoming as much of a tyrant as King Louis. He is arrested and executed.

1795 The government starts raising taxes to pay for the new wars. Some people complain that they're no better off without a king and decide they want one again. They start a revolt in Paris hoping to install Louis' brother (another Louis) as king, but they're defeated by a young general, Napoleon Bonaparte, who takes control of the government. The Revolution, he declares, is over. The time has come for Frenchmen to stop fighting one another, and start fighting everyone else.

1796 Napoleon begins the conquest of Europe.

Paris–Bastille. Although only completed in 1989, it has needed constant repairs to stop chunks of it falling on passers-by. Architectural problems aside, the complex has proved to be a tremendous success. Part of the idea behind building an opera house in what was then a run-down part of Paris was to revitalize the area. To this end, the plan was a big success, turning the Bastille into a fashionable part of town albeit in an arty, relatively low-cost way. There are good cafés and restaurants, particularly on **Rue de Lappe** and **Rue de Charonne**, east of the main square, which have become the centres of the district's café and street life.

If you walk out of Place de la Bastille to the right of the Opéra, down Rue de Lyon, you can't miss the extraordinary **Stravinsky Fountain** across the street, a fantastical construction that happily cocks a snoot at the opera house above it. Continue further down Rue de Lyon and head left up Avenue Daumesnil to the **Viaduc des Arts**, a giant old railway viaduct of over 100 arches which now houses a varied range of high-quality craft workers, artists, designers, cafés and restaurants. Only some of them are specifically oriented towards kids, but it's a fascinating place to browse. All along the top of the viaduct – where the tracks once ran – there is now the **Promenade Plantée**, a lovely, tranquil, flower-planted walkway, with unusual views of the districts alongside.

Question 8
What is a tumbril, and why would you get put into one?
answer also on p.250

1 Aux Délices d'Asie
119 Rue St Antoine, 4th
t 01 42 72 94 81
Ⓜ St Paul
Open Daily 10am–10.30pm

2 Blue Elephant
43–45 Rue de la Roquette, 11th
t 01 47 00 42 00
Ⓜ Bastille, Voltaire
Open 12 noon–2.30pm, 7pm–12 midnight
(Mon–Fri); 7–11pm (Sat–Sun)

3 Board Café
8 Rue Coquillière, 1st
t 01 40 28 97 98
Ⓜ/**RER** Châtelet Les Halles
Open Daily 11.30am–1am

4 Bofinger
5–7 Rue de la Bastille, 4th
t 01 42 72 87 82
Ⓜ Bastille
Open 12 noon–3pm, 6.30pm–1am (Mon–Fri); 12
noon–1am (Sat–Sun)

5 Le Frog & Rosbif
116 Rue St Denis, 2nd
t 01 42 36 34 73
Ⓜ Étienne Marcel, **RER** Châtelet Les Halles
Open 12 noon–3pm, 7.30–10.30pm (Mon–Fri); 12
noon–4pm, 7.30–10.30pm (Sat–Sun)

6 Indiana Café
14 Place de la Bastille, 11th
t 01 44 75 79 80
Ⓜ Bastille
Open Daily 11.30am–1.30am

7 Hippopotamus
1 Bd Beaumarchais, 4th
t 01 44 61 90 40
Ⓜ Bastille
Open Daily 11.30am–5am

8 Le Loir dans la Théière
3 Rue des Rosiers, 4th
t 01 42 72 68 12
Ⓜ St Paul
Open 11am–7pm (Mon–Fri), 10am–7pm (Sat–Sun)

9 Marais Plus
20 Rue des Francs Bourgeois, 4th
t 01 48 87 01 40
Ⓜ Rambuteau, Hôtel de Ville
Open 10am–7pm (Mon–Fri)

10 Pause Café
41 Rue de Charonne, 11th
t 01 48 06 80 33
Ⓜ Ledru-Rollin
Open Daily 7am–2am (Mon–Sat), 9am–8.30pm
(Sun)

11 Le Studio
41 Rue du Temple, 4th
t 01 42 74 10 38
Ⓜ Hôtel de Ville, **RER** Châtelet Les Halles
Open 7.30pm–11pm (Mon), 2.30pm–11pm
(Tues–Sun)

See **Eat** pp.153–164 for more details on the above restaurants. *See* map on p.65 for the locations of the restaurants numbered above.

Île de la Cité and the Left Bank

For the first 1,000 years or so of its existence, Paris was made up of small settlements on the left bank of the Seine and on the Île de la Cité. This, then, is the acorn from which the mighty sprawling oak has grown. The area's focal point is the same today as it was in the Middle Ages – the great Gothic cathedral of **Nôtre Dame**, erstwhile home of the hunchbacked bell-ringer Quasimodo. Kids are always enthralled by its bizarre gargoyles and the views from the top of the cathedral's Gothic towers. Lurking nearby is the **Conciergerie**, once a royal palace, then a prison, full of grotesque memorabilia to capture the vivid imagination of youngsters.

The **Left Bank** is Paris' traditional centre of culture and learning and its *quais* are lined with booksellers and artists. The riverbanks are among the very best places in all of Paris to go for an engrossing walk with plenty to catch the eye: the comings and goings on the Seine;

Highlights

Greeting the gargoyles of Nôtre Dame

Blinking at the rainbow light through the glass of the Sainte Chapelle

Counting bridges, boats and bookstalls on the quais of the Left Bank

Slurping up Paris' best ice creams at Berthillon on the Île St Louis

Musée du Louvre

Pont Neuf

PONT DES ARTS

SQUARE DU VERT GALANT

PONT NEUF

Passerelle Solférino

PONT ROYAL

PONT DU CARROUSEL

QUAI MALAQUAIS

Institut de France

QUAI DE CONTI

Châtelet

QUAI DES GRAND

QUAI ANATOLE FRANCE

QUAI VOLTAIRE

Hôtel de la Monnaie

R   1 Musée d'Orsay

Musée d'Orsay

RUE DES ST PÈRES

M Solférino

Odéon M

RUE DE BELLECHASSE

BOULEVARD ST GERMAIN

BOULEVARD ST GERMAIN

M Rue du Bac

M St. Germain des Prés

M Mabillon

elegant bridges (with examples from 1605 right up to the year 2000) and glorious baroque mansions. As a centrepiece on the Left Bank, there's the **Musée d'Orsay**, a wonderful museum of 19th-century art, housed in a superb, converted iron-and-glass railway station near the Pont Royal (now just a short walk away from the Louvre via a modernistic foot-bridge). Its top-floor café offers breathtaking views of the city.

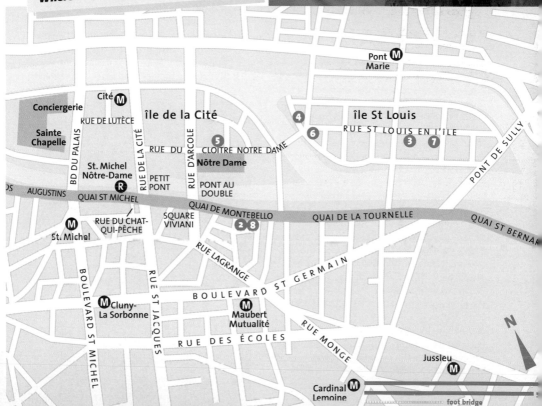

Pont Marie Ⓜ

Concergerie

Cité Ⓜ

île de la Cité

④

île St Louis

RUE DE LUTÈCE

⑥

RUE ST LOUIS EN l'île

Sainte Chapelle

BD DU PALAIS

RUE DE LA CITÉ

RUE DU

RUE D'ARCOLE

CLOÎTRE NOTRE DAME

③ ⑦

⑤

PONT DE SULLY

St. Michel Nôtre-Dame Ⓡ

Nôtre Dame

PETIT PONT

PONT AU DOUBLE

OS AUGUSTINS

QUAI ST MICHEL

QUAI DE MONTEBELLO

QUAI DE LA TOURNELLE

QUAI ST BERNA

Ⓜ St. Michel

RUE DU CHAT-QUI-PÊCHE

SQUARE VIVIANI

② ⑧

RUE LAGRANGE

BOULEVARD

ST GERMAIN

BOULEVARD ST MICHEL

RUE ST JACQUES

Ⓜ Cluny-La Sorbonne

BOULEVARD ST GERMAIN

Maubert Mutualité Ⓜ

RUE MONGE

RUE DES ÉCOLES

Jussieu Ⓜ

Cardinal Lemoine Ⓜ

foot bridge

Nôtre Dame

6 Place du Parvis de Nôtre Dame, 4th
t 01 42 34 56 10 (cathedral)
t 01 53 10 07 00 (tower)
www.monum.fr
Ⓜ Cité, **RER** St Michel Nôtre Dame
Open 8am–6.45pm (Mon–Sat), 8am–7.45pm (Sun)
(cathedral); 10am–5.30pm (1 Oct–31 March);
9.30am–7.30pm (1 Apr–30 June, 1 Sept–30 Sept);
9am–7.30pm (1 July–31 Aug), late openings until 11
pm (Sat–Sun)
Adm Tower tours Adults €5.50, under-25s €3.50,
under-18s, first Sunday of the month, 1 Oct–31 Mar
free
Adm Cathedral tours **free**, once daily, 8am–6.45pm
(Mon–Sat), 8am–7.45pm (Sun)
Carte Musées et Monuments valid
Wheelchair access to church only
Suitable for all ages; allow at least 1 hour

When Victor Hugo wrote *The Hunchback of Nôtre
Dame* in 1831, the great cathedral had already been
in existence some 700 years and its status as the
city's principal church had long since been assured.
However, Disney's more recent version will no doubt
strike a louder chord with your children, who will be
hugely excited at the prospect of visiting the home
of the movie's hunchbacked hero.

Although in an almost non-stop cycle of restoration, the cathedral still one of Paris' must-see sights.
The interior is impressive, the gloom punctured by
the glow from the beautiful stained-glass windows.
Climb to the top of the left-hand tower for dizzying
views of the Île de la Cité and the River Seine
(beware the scary gargoyles), but only 50 people are
allowed up at any one time so there is sure to be a
queue. There are 387 steps to the top and there's no
lift, so it's not suitable for very young children
(under-12s must be accompanied), or unfit adults. As
you ascend, you'll see the mighty bells once pulled
by Quasimodo, each weighing over 2 tonnes, as well
as a video presentation on the history of the cathedral. The informative guided tours (also available in
English) are run once each day around Nôtre Dame
(at noon during the week and at 2pm on weekends) .

Tell me a story:
Nôtre Dame in Quasimodo's day

In the Middle Ages churches were treated with far
less reverence than they are today. Medieval Nôtre
Dame, begun in 1163 and completed in 1345, was
used as much as a meeting place as a house of
worship. It was somewhere for people to come and
chat, strike up a deal or eat some lunch in the
company of friends. There were no seats, and the
floor was strewn with rushes and straw.
Furthermore, the statues inside the cathedral,
which today seem rather faded and dull, would
have been painted in bright, gaudy colours. Until
1785 a huge statue of St Christopher, the patron
saint of travellers, stood over the front entrance.
People used to touch it for good luck as they left.

Another feature of Nôtre Dame, right up until
Victor Hugo's time, was that it was surrounded by
houses and narrow, winding alleys. It was only in
the 1860s that Baron Haussmann, in one of his
giant 'improvement schemes' for Paris, unceremo-
niously swept away thousands of homes from the
Île de la Cité, sent their inhabitants off to eastern
Paris and created the big square or *parvis* in front
of the cathedral that we see today.

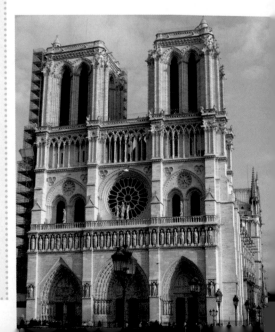

Around the Île de la Cité

The Île de la Cité was the site of the very first settlement of Paris, dating back to pre-Roman times in about 250 BC. Hence, it contains many other important buildings in addition to Nôtre Dame – not least the city's first royal palace, and later state prison, the dramatically turreted **Conciergerie**. Between the cathedral and the old palace, a good part of the island is taken up by Paris' oldest hospital the **Hôtel Dieu**, founded in AD 660, although most of the building dates from the 1860s. In the eastern corner of the Île, just to the left of Nôtre Dame, there's a little knot of medieval streets that survived Haussmann's great clean-out and provide an intriguing place to wander around. Perhaps the most attractive parts of the island, though, are the *quais* that surround it which offer great views of the Left and Right Banks, especially from the **Square du Vert Galant** by the Pont Neuf at the Île's westernmost point.

La Conciergerie

Palais de la Cité, 2 Bd du Palais, 1st
t 01 53 40 60 97
Ⓜ Cité, Châtelet

Open Daily 9.30am–6pm (April–Sept); 9am–5pm (Oct–Mar)
Adm Adults €6.10, under-25s €4.10
Combined ticket with Sainte Chapelle: adults €8, under-25s €5, under-18s and first Sunday of the month **free** (Oct–May)
Carte Musées et Monuments valid
Some wheelchair access (call ahead for assistance)
Suitable for children aged 6 and over
Allow at least 1 hour

After all the glorious architecture, magnificent vistas and beautiful bridges, it's time for a little gore. The Bastille may have achieved a more lasting fame but, in terms of lavish and unpleasant methods of incarceration and torture, the Conciergerie was where it was at. The French Revolution's most illustrious victims – including Danton, Robespierre and Marie Antoinette – all spent their final night here before mounting their *tumbrils* for the drive to the *guillotine* in the Place de la Concorde. Free special tours for children are available every Wed at 2.30pm. You can visit Marie Antoinette's reconstructed cell, where you can see her crucifix and the blade used to end her life.

Prisoners were housed in the Conciergerie according to wealth: rich nobles slept on comfortable beds and arranged for food to be brought in from outside, while the poor slept on straw and ate slops. Equality wasn't achieved until the *guillotine* blade fell. In earlier times, non-celebrity prisoners were often executed using the *oubliette*, a box lined with spikes into which the prisoner would be dropped through a trap door. Their remains would be washed away by the Seine.

The forbidding architecture of the Conciergerie – all turrets and pinnacle-roofed towers – is entirely in line with its sinister past. Long before the revolution, the fortress had played a much grander role in Parisian history as the original palace of France's kings, but was abandoned in the 1360s when the monarchy decided that the Louvre would be a more comfortable home. No longer needed as a royal residence, the Conciergerie was turned into Paris' most secure prison (which became something of a trend for unwanted French royal palaces). The Château de Vincennes suffered a similar fate.

As you walk through the huge 14th-century *Gothic Salle des Gens d'Armes*, note the corridor separated by a grill on one side. This is known as the *Rue de Paris* and was named in honour of the chief executioner, the 'Monsieur de Paris', who used it to move from one 'appointment' to another. You can be sure that no one ever willingly booked an appointment at the Conciergerie's *Salle de Toilette*, where all prisoners came for a haircut before their execution so the *guillotine* blade could be lined up properly with their necks.

Sainte Chapelle

4 Boulevard du Palais, 1st (entrance through the Palais de Justice)
t 01 53 40 60 97
Ⓜ Cité, Châtelet
Open Daily 9.30am–6pm (April–Sept); 9am–5pm (Oct–Mar)
Adm Adults €6.10, under-25s €4.10, under-12s **free** Combined ticket with the Conciergerie €8, under-25s €5, under-18s and first Sunday of the month **free**.
Carte Musées et Monuments valid
Limited wheelchair access
Suitable for children aged 6 and over
Allow at least 1 hour

It's rare for a church or chapel to be rated highly by children; unless it can offer gargoyles or views, they're usually not interested. Yet all kids seem to respond to the Sainte Chapelle despite the fact that it possesses neither – just a lot of stained glass. But these are no ordinary windows, rather vast technicolour portals which, on bright summer days, bathe the upper level of the church in a magical rainbow-like kaleidoscopic light.

The Sainte Chapelle was built in the 13th century as the royal chapel of the French kings when the

nearby Conciergerie was their main home. It was built in a very ornate, Gothic style to provide a spectacular setting for King Louis IX's collection of holy relics, which included such authentic curios as Christ's crown of thorns, Moses' staff and the front half of John the Baptist's head, all of which are now housed inside Nôtre Dame. Surrounding the chapel these days is the enormous, rambling complex of the **Palais de Justice**, the centre of royal administration before the Revolution and now the hub of France's legal system.

Square du Vert Galant

This tiny, elegant triangular park at the very end of the Île de la Cité is a favourite spot for summer picnics under the shade of its weeping willow tree – traditionally the first tree in Paris to come into leaf. One of the ideal spots in Paris for taking the air and watching the boats go by, it's also long been a favourite corner for those who come to Paris to try their hand at painting, and you'll often see artists here sitting at their easels contemplating the river. You can also embark on a Seine tour from here, with the **Vedettes du Pont Neuf** (*see* p.32).

Question 9
When was the Hôtel Dieu founded?
a) 660
b) 1660
c) 1960
answer also on p.250

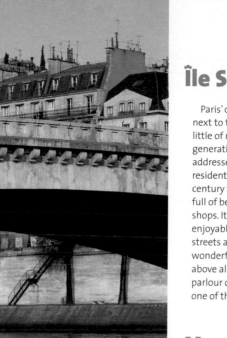

Île St Louis

Paris' other island, following on like a small boat next to the larger barge of the Île de la Cité, has little of note to fire the imagination of the younger generation. This is one of the most fashionable addresses in town, a quiet, expensive, refined residential area – scarcely touched by all the 19th-century transformations over on the Cité – that's full of beautiful historic architecture and exclusive shops. It is worth a detour, however, for the several enjoyable cafés and restaurants found along its streets and *quais* – from where you can enjoy wonderful views back towards Nôtre Dame – and, above all, for the positively legendary ice-cream parlour of **Berthillon** (*see* p. 160), where you can try one of their famed ice creams and sorbets.

Musée d'Orsay

1 Rue de Bellechasse, 7th
t 01 40 49 48 14/01 45 49 11 11 (infoline)
www.musee-orsay.fr
Ⓜ Solférino, **RER** Musée d'Orsay
Open 10am–6pm (Tues, Wed, Fri, Sat); 9am–6pm (Sun); 10am–9.45pm (Thurs); closed Mondays and 1 Jan, 1 May, 25 Dec
Adm Adults €7, under-18s/25s/Sundays €5, under-18s and first Sunday of the month **free**
Carte Musées et Monuments valid
Wheelchair access
Suitable for children aged 6 and over
Allow at least 2 hours

Cutting across the Square du Vert Galant is the superb **Pont Neuf**, the 'New Bridge' which, in spite of its name, is actually the oldest and longest surviving bridge in Paris, opened by King Henri IV in 1605. It was the first bridge across the Seine that did not have houses built along it. Carved onto its sweeping arches are some oddly smiling gargoyles, best seen by taking a boat trip along the river, which are believed to be rather uncomplimentary portraits of members of King Henri's court. In the middle of the bridge, there is a statue of Henri IV on horseback. First erected here in 1635, it was destroyed during the Revolution but, after the royals came back into favour early in the next century, a new statue of the king riding his horse was ordered to be made from a melted-down likeness of the recently defeated Napoleon. The artist who cast it, however, objected to desecrating the image of the former Emperor in this way and made a tiny statue of Napoleon which he placed inside the belly of the steed.

Animal attractions on the riverbank
Across from the Île de la Cité on the Right Bank, along the Quai de la Megisserie close to La Samaritaine department store (see p.47), there are pet shops selling puppies and an amazing variety of other animals. This nearly always fascinates kids, while afterwards, over on the Left Bank of the river, parents and children are likely to be equally engaged browsing through the fascinating variety of old books, prints, magazines and all sorts of other things on sale from the traditional bookstalls (*les bouquinistes*) beside the Seine.

A walk along the Left Bank quais

There will be many attractions that crop up along your route, but they needn't detain you; the fun of the *quais* comes from just walking about browsing through the hundreds of bookstalls (where you can pick up all your DC and Marvel favourites in French), waving at the passengers in passing *bateaux mouches*, and admiring the magnificent panoramic views. In 1992 the Paris *quais* from the Pont d'Iéna by the Eiffel Tower, all the way to the Pont de Sully at the tip of the Île St Louis, were inscribed on UNESCO's list of World Heritage sites.

On your travels, be sure to look out for the following:

▶ The **Pont au Double**, leading from the Quai de Montebello to the Île de la Cité. It's so named because travellers had to pay twice to cross it, once to get on, once to get off.

▶ The **Square Viviani**, just off the Pont au Double, where you'll find Paris' oldest tree – an acacia – which was planted by the botanist Jean Robin in 1602 and is now supported on concrete crutches.

▶ The **Petit Pont**, which spans the same stretch of river as Paris' first ever bridge, built in the 1st century BC at the time of Julius Caesar.

▶ The **Rue du Chat qui Pêche** (the 'Street of the Fishing Cat'), just off the Quai St Michel. At just 2m (6ft) wide, this is the narrowest street in Paris. It's also one of the oldest.

▶ The **Quai des Grands Augustins**, Paris' oldest *quai*, built in 1313.

▶ The **Hôtel de la Monnaie**, a vast building on the Quai de Conti. Until recently, this was France's national mint, where all the country's money was made. The new France-specific euros are now produced in Bordeaux, but the hôtel still produces the odd commemorative medal. You can take a tour of the medal workshops and find out about the history of money-making in the small **Musée de la Monnaie** museum (**t** 01 40 46 55 35, **f** 01 40 46 57 09, **www**.monnaiedeparis.fr; **open** 11am–5.30pm Tues–Fri, 12 noon–5.30pm Sat–Sun; adults €8, under-25s €6, under-16s **free**; **Carte Musées et Monuments** valid).

▶ The **Palais de l'Institut de France** on the Quai de Conti, recognizable by its distinctive dome and handsome baroque wings. It is the seat of the very grand Académie Française, which publishes France's official dictionary.

▶ The **Louvre**, which looks particularly impressive from this side of the river.

The most recently created of Paris' trilogy of great art museums, the Musée d'Orsay covers the middle period from 1848 to 1914 (the Louvre tackles what came before, the Centre Pompidou what came after). While not quite matching the standards of the Pompidou, the Musée d'Orsay is certainly more child-friendly than the Louvre. For one thing, the collection is arranged on easily accessible levels beneath the vast roof of this former train station (built back in 1900). There are excellent printed English language guides and quiz pamphlets for children (in English and French) at the information desk that will direct you to the most famous works of art. Please note that visitors cannot enter with prams and back baby carriers although you may borrow folding strollers and wheelchairs from the cloakroom.

Before you walk into the museum, be sure to point out the great clocks on its Seine-facing façade. Once inside, visit the café on the top level, where your kids can explore the huge clockwork mechanism in action behind the clock faces.

If time is short, head to the Impressionist gallery on the upper level, where you'll find Renoir's *Les Baigneuses*, Van Gogh's *La Chambre* and, every little girl's favourite, Dégas' *Petite danseuse de 14 ans*, a delicate statue of a young ballerina.

A scale model of Paris' Opéra district has been constructed underneath the ground floor, which you can tour by looking down through a glass ceiling, as if you were floating above Paris. If you and your kids start to get a little frazzled, there's a café on the upper level with an outdoor terrace and fine views and, as a surprise, even better and more intriguing views through the clock. Guided tours in English are available from Tuesday to Saturday at 11.30am, 2.30pm and 4pm.

Can you spot?
The 'Eiffel Bridge' – the Passerelle Solférino footbridge – was opened as the 36th bridge in Paris in 2000. It spans 105m (345ft) across the Seine, and permits an enjoyably traffic-free walk between the Louvre and the Quai des Tulleries and the Musée d'Orsay. Built by the same Eiffel company whose predecessors built the famous tower, this light, graceful bridge has certain resemblances to the 1889 pinnacle. Its architectural originality stems from its being built out of two giant, swooping arches: a lower arch joining both riverbanks and a higher arch linking the two embankments.

1 Café des Hauteurs (Musée d'Orsay)
1 Rue de la Légion d'Honneur, 7th
t 01 42 84 12 16
Ⓜ Solférino, **RER** Musée d'Orsay
Open 10am–5pm (Tues–Wed, Fri–Sun); 10am–9pm (Thurs)

2 Le Grenier de Nôtre Dame
18 Rue de la Bûcherie, 5th
t 01 43 29 98 29
Ⓜ St Michel Nôtre Dame, Maubert Mutualité
Open Daily 12 noon–2pm, 7.30pm–11.30pm

3 L'Îlot Vache
35 Rue St Louis en l'Île, 4th
t 01 46 33 55 16
Ⓜ Pont Marie
Open 12 noon–3pm, 7pm–12 midnight (Tues–Sun); 7pm–12 midnight (Mon)

4 La Brasserie de l'Île St Louis
55 Quai de Bourbon, 4th
t 01 43 54 02 59
Ⓜ Pont Marie
Open Daily 12 noon–3pm and 7pm–12 midnight

5 Le Vieux Bistro
14 Rue du Cloître Nôtre Dame, 4th
t 01 43 54 18 95
Ⓜ Cité, **RER** St Michel Nôtre Dame
Open Daily 12 noon–2pm, 7.30–11pm

6 Le Floré-en-l'Île
42 Quai d'Orléans, 4th
t 01 43 29 88 27
Ⓜ Cité, Sully Morland
Open 10am–10.30pm (Mon–Sat)

7 Berthillon
31 Rue St Louis en Île, 4th
t 01 43 54 31 61
Ⓜ Pont Marie
Open 10am–8pm (Wed–Sun), closed 3 weeks in August

8 Les Degrés de Nôtre Dame
10 Rue des Grands Degrés, 5th
t 01 55 42 88 88
Ⓜ Maubert Mutualité
Open 12 noon–10.30pm (Mon–Sat)

See **Eat** pp.153–164 for more details on the above restaurants. See map on pp.76–77 for the locations of the restaurants numbered above.

The Latin Quarter

South of the river on the Left Bank lie two of Paris' best parks for children – the **Jardin des Plantes**, a charming botanical garden near the Gare d'Austerlitz with hothouses, Paris' oldest zoo and a wonderful museum of natural history, and the **Jardin du Luxembourg**, one of the most elegantly traditional Parisian parks, still hugely popular with local youngsters. To get from one to the other, you have to cross Paris' famous student district, the **Latin Quarter**, with its lively bars, unusual shops and multitude of ethnic restaurants.

On its western side, beyond the Luxembourg and the Boulevard St Michel, the Latin Quarter blends into **St Germain des Prés**, renowned throughout Paris for its café life and literary gatherings, but which is also nowadays one of the city's most exclusive districts, where you'll pay upwards of €4.50 for a cola at a pavement café, and where you can browse for kids' clothes in such practical, down-to-earth stores as Baby Dior and Bonpoint. The further west towards the Invalides you go, the more exclusive it gets but, for window-shopping alone, these streets are fascinating.

Southwards from the Luxembourg is the famous district of **Montparnasse**. Hub of artistic Paris in the 1920s, it doesn't have so many obvious attractions today, except for some very good places to eat, but it does contain special points of interest that score highly with most kids: views from Paris' tallest skyscraper, an atmospheric cemetery and, for the more ghoulish, the dark, spooky underground tombs of the **Catacombs**, where bones from Paris' cemeteries were brought together and assembled.

Key

Numbers correspond to restaurants in 'Where To Eat' p.96

Highlights

Meet strange beasts in the Musêe National d'Histoire Naturelle

Run up and down between the flowers of the Luxembourg Gardens

Shop for little luxuries in St Germain

Break the number-of-crêpe-toppings record at Ty Breiz in Montparnasse

Around the Jardin des Plantes

Entrances on Rue Buffon and Rue Geoffroy St Hilaire or Rue Cuvier, 5th
t 01 40 79 30 00
ⓂJussieu, Ⓜ/**RER** Gare d'Austerlitz
Open 10am–6pm (April–Oct); 10am–5pm (Nov–Mar); daily except Mondays (museum), 1pm–5pm (Mon–Wed), 1pm–6pm 1 Apr–30 Sept (hothouses)
Adm Gardens **free**; adults €2.50, under-25s €1.50, under-4s **free** (hothouses)

Some of the flowerbeds in the Jardin des Plantes were sown as part of a royal garden in 1626 to provide Louis XIII with medicinal herbs and the Royal Garden of Medicinal Plants gave rise to the Natural History Museum in 1793. The tree-lined pathways are perfect for a good old kickabout, there's a hill-top labyrinth to whizz around and a dinosaur-skeleton climbing frame to clamber over.

Point your kids towards the 250-year-old cedar tree from Lebanon, the enormous dahlias and the weird ironbark tree from Iran. The hothouses display an impressive collection of tropical plants, including giant lillies, rubber plants and cacti.

Musée National d'Histoire Naturelle

57 Rue Cuvier, 5th
t 01 40 79 56 01

www.mnhn.fr
Ⓜ/**RER** Gare d'Austerlitz, ⓂJussieu
Open 10am–6pm (Mon, Wed–Sun), until 10pm (Thurs)
Adm Adults €7, under-25s €5, under-18s **free** (main gallery); adults €5, under-25s €3, under-18s **free** (other galleries); under-4s **free** (Mineralogy gallery)
Wheelchair access
Suitable for children aged 6 and over
Allow at least 2 hours

Paris' natural history museum, inside the Jardin des Plantes, has three galleries: the Grande Galerie de l'Évolution (Evolution Gallery), the largest and most modern; the Galerie de Minéralogie et Géologie (Mineralogy and Geology Gallery), which is more traditional; and the Galerie d'Anatomie Comparée et Paléontologie (Gallery of Comparative Anatomy and Palaeontology), which is very archaic and may leave the strongest impression for kids with its collection of 19th-century medical specimens.

La Grande Galerie de l'Évolution

Thirty years in the making, the giant 19th-century iron-frame structure of the Grande Galerie de l'Évolution has been well renovated with the addition of modern lifts, stairways and lighting. It now uses state-of-the-art technologies (audiovisual displays, interactive consoles, sound effects) to tell the story of life on earth. Marvel at the huge skeleton of the largest mammal on earth – a 13.66m- (45ft)-long blue whale, suspended from the gallery ceiling as you first enter. Other not-to-be-missed favourites include the narwhal (a horned whale, a sort of aquatic unicorn) and a

La Galerie de Paléontologie et d'Anatomie Comparée

This gallery holds a strange and bizarre collection of natural exhibits – a veritable freakshow. The walls of the ground level gallery are covered with skeletons of rhinos, hippos, giraffes, elephants, crocodiles and turtles, all mounted facing the main door through which you enter. Look out for the plastic model of a man with no skin and a fig leaf to cover his modesty. There's a ghastly collection of pickled 19th-century 'medical' and 'scientific' exhibits including a one-eyed 'cyclops' cat and chicken, Siamese twins and a child with another infant growing out of its chest feet first, a rhino heart, human brains, monkeys nailed to boards (their intestines spilling out) and a human foetus.

The heavy camphoric smell, gnarly old wooden cabinets and strange, archaic calligraphy labels in Latin add to the atmosphere. Some exhibits can leave you feeling queasy, but most kids will be fascinated and ask lots of questions. The first floor gallery with its fearsome dinosaur skeletons and giant mammoths comes as something of a relief.

range of re-created habitats (savannah, tropical jungle etc.) inhabited by a motley collection of fearsome-looking stuffed creatures. The ground floor is dedicated to aquatic creatures; on the first floor, larger mammals are mostly organized by habitat, except for special exhibits such as 'Louis XVI's rhinoceros', a stuffed specimen that was sent to the King at the height of the Revolution in 1793 and which, since then, has stayed installed in the wooden chair-like frame on which it sits.

Children will get as much enjoyment from the gallery's glass lifts, which whizz between three floors, as from the exhibits. On the second floor, the theme is man's impact on nature with a focus on demographic problems and pollution, while the third floor traces the evolution of different species. There is a strong ecological message throughout with displays on pollution and endangered or extinct species. There's a Discovery Room for under-12s where nature workshops are held, plus themed 'laboratories' for teenagers (in French).

La Galerie de Minéralogie et Géologie

This is a gawpers' paradise, full of giant crystals, meteors and cases of precious gems. Inside the Galerie de Paléobotanique you can see ancient plants: a 2m- (6ft)-wide cross-section of a 2,000-year-old sequoia and the petrified stump of a 33-million-year-old fern. Although old-fashioned compared with the Evolution Gallery, this section, too, has had a facelift in the last few years.

La Ménagerie

Jardin des Plantes, entrances on Place Valhubert, Rue Buffon and Rue Cuvier, 5th
Open Daily 9am–6pm (April–Oct); 9am–5pm (Nov–Mar)
Adm Adults €6, under-18s €3, under-4s **free**

The Ménagerie in the Jardin des Plantes, east of the rose gardens, was Paris' first zoo created at the time of the Revolution. It's rather old-fashioned with small cages and (mostly) small animals – nothing like as extensive as the zoo in the Bois de Vincennes (see p.120) – but has a tranquil charm. It's best liked by smaller children. There are llama, monkeys, deer and two bears, both called Martin.

Arènes de Lutèce

47 rue Monge, 5th
Ⓜ Cardinal Lemoine
Open Daily 9am–9.30pm (summer); 8am–5.30pm (winter)
Adm Free
Some wheelchair access
Suitable for all ages

Question 10
Which is the biggest mammal in the world?
answer also on p.250

Just northwest of the Jardin des Plantes, this is a city park with a difference. It may have the gravel paths, grassy lawns and playgrounds of other Parisian parks, but the Arènes de Lutèce has a unique feature: a well-preserved Roman arena built between the 1st and 2nd century AD for staging circus performances, theatre and gladiatorial contests. Forgotten for 1,600 years, it was rediscovered at the end of the 19th century. The authorities of the time turned the area into a park allowing you to walk around, clamber over and explore the feature to your heart's content. Take a stroll around the arena's sandy floor and sit on the surrounding stone seats imagining you're back in Roman times (even if the closest you'll get to seeing a gladiatorial contest will be watching a heated *boules* match). Although not as well equipped as some of the other local parks, the Arènes has a nice little playground and, as it's mostly patronized by locals, boasts a friendly and safe neighbourhood feel.

Jardin du Luxembourg

Entrances on Place Auguste Comte, Place Edmond Rostand and Rue de Vaugirard, 6th
t 01 45 88 55 55
Ⓜ Nôtre Dame des Champs, **RER** Luxembourg
Open Daily 10am–6pm (April–Oct); 10am–5pm (Nov–Mar)
Adm Free

A typically Parisian park with neat lawns, sculpted terraces and wooden benches, it may at first glance seem a rather unwelcoming environment for children. Whenever you visit, you'll find it

Did you know?
When Paris was under siege by the Prussians in 1870, and meat was in short supply, some strange dishes began appearing on the menus of local restaurants: consommé d'éléphant, civet de kangarou and terrine d'antilope. In a few months the Ménagerie's entire contents had been eaten (apart from the hippo, as nobody could meet the 80,000 franc asking price).

teeming with kiddies playing in the sandpit, clambering over the climbing frames in the adventure playground (*€2.40 per child, plus accompanying adult €1.50*), sailing toy boats on the hexagonal pond (*€2 each*), dashing madly around its gravel pathways, or enjoying a pony ride or a puppet show (*see p.120*). Older visitors are catered for with several *boules* pitches and tennis courts, and there are lovely apple orchards and ornamental ponds for an unusual city walk.

The park was first created as the gardens of the **Palais du Luxembourg** on its north side, built in the 1620s to be the home of Marie de Médicis, widow of King Henri IV and mother of Louis XIII. The palace now contains the French Senate. There's a very good café nearby with outdoor seating.

Centre de la Mer

195 Rue Saint Jacques, 5th
t 01 44 32 10 70
www.oceano.org
RER Luxembourg
Open 10am–12.30pm and 1.30pm–5.30pm (Tues–Fri), 10am–5.30pm (Sat–Sun); closed Mondays, 1 Jan, 1 May, 14 July, 15 Aug, 25 December
Adm Adults €4.60, under-18s €3, under-12s €2
Wheelchair access
Suitable for all ages
Allow at least 1 hour

It may not have quite the scope and range of some of the other great city aquariums in the world but the Centre de la Mer, just east of the Jardin du Luxembourg, is charming and provides a good introduction to the wonders of the deep. There are six large-ish aquarium tanks filled with all manner of sea creatures – from freshwater river fish to brightly coloured tropical coral-dwellers – surrounded by hands-on exhibits (some with

Latin primer

There are all sorts of interesting things to see if you decide to take a walk around the *Quartier Latin*, but keep an eye out especially for these:

▶ The **Old Faculty of Medicine** (13 Rue de la Bûcherie), where 19th-century students used to dissect and examine bodies stolen from local cemeteries – but only in winter, when the cold helped to preserve the corpses. It's now a college of civic administration.

▶ The **Musée de la Préfecture** (1 Rue Basse des Carmes), which relates the history of the Paris police force from its formation in 1667 to the present day. The eccentric collection features uniforms, but also bombs, weapons and devices used by the criminal fraternity over the past three centuries (**open** 9am–5pm Mon–Fri, 10am–5pm Sat; **free**).

▶ The **Musée de l'Assistance Publique** (Hôtel de Miramon, 47 Quai de la Tournelle), which focuses on the way the city has dealt with the poor over the centuries, revealing attitudes alternating between compassion and chastisement. Learn about the history of the foundling hospitals and see moving memorabilia, including bead name bracelets that parents left with their child in case they ever found the money to take them back (**t** 01 46 33 01 43; **open** 10am–4pm Tues–Sun; **adm** adults €4, under-12s free; **Carte Musées et Monuments** valid).

▶ The **Musée du Moyen Âge – Thermes de Cluny** (6 Place Paul Painlevé), which is the finest and most important of the Latin Quarter's museums and full of medieval art, tapestries, alabaster, paintings, manuscripts and weavings. Look out particularly for the heads of the kings of Judah from Nôtre Dame, which were knocked off by revolutionaries in 1792 in the mistaken belief that they represented the kings of France, and only came to light, without their noses, in 1979; it might be a good idea to pay your respects, too, to the statue of the philosopher Montaigne outside the museum, which students traditionally rub for luck before exams. The museum occupies the 15th-century mansion of the Abbots of Cluny, which in its basement contains a Roman bath complex or *Thermes*, the best-preserved Roman remains in Paris. On its north side is a newly planted 'medieval garden' containing only plants known to have existed in France during the Middle Ages (**t** 01 53 73 78 16; **open** 9.15am–5.45pm Mon and Wed–Sun; **adm** adults €5.50, under-25s €4, under-18s **free**; **Carte Musées et Monuments** valid).

▶ **La Sorbonne** (Rue de la Sorbonne), which is one of the world's most famous universities and a centre of learning since the 13th century. The present buildings date from 1885–1900.

▶ The **Panthéon** (Place du Panthéon), just south of the Sorbonne, which is a giant, Roman-looking temple modelled on the ancient Pantheon in Rome. It was first commissioned in the 1770s by King Louis XV as a church to give thanks for having shaken off an illness but, by the time it was finished in 1790, the Revolution had come around, and the building was converted into a 'Temple of Reason'. Later on, it was transformed into a collective tomb for France's great men (and a few women): Voltaire, Victor Hugo, Émile Zola and Marie Curie are all buried here. There are superb views from its famous dome (**t** 01 44 32 18 00; **open** 9.30am–6.30pm daily in summer, 10am–5.30pm daily in winter; **adm** adults €7, under-25s €4.50, under-18s **free**; **Carte Musées et Monuments** valid).

Top shopping
St Germain's children's boutiques

The Faubourg St Germain, between St Germain des Prés and the Invalides, is one of the very smartest parts of Paris, and most shops here are mid-range to expensive: they're in the business of selling elegance, not convenience, retailing mini-*haute couture* to discerning Parisian mothers. *See also* pp.165–174.

Baby Dior
252 Bd St Germain, 7th
t 01 42 22 90 90
www.dior.com
Ⓜ Solférino, Rue du Bac
Toddler essentials such as quilted fur-collared jackets, tailored sailor suits with gold buttons and a wide range of children's perfumes. The dishes of jelly beans are a nice touch.

Bonpoint
229 Bd St Germain, 7th
t 01 40 62 76 20
www.bonpoint.com
Ⓜ Solférino, Rue du Bac
Clothes that are expensive but adorable: velvet and frills for the girls, sharp suits and knicker-bockers for the boys.

Du Pareil au Même
14 Rue St Placide, 6th
t 01 45 44 04 40
www.dpam.fr
Ⓜ Sèvres Babylone
Good, sturdy dungarees, thick coats, bright T-shirts and copies of designer labels at reasonable, department store prices.

Jacadi
256 Bd St Germain, 7th
t 01 42 84 30 40
www.jacadi.fr
Ⓜ Solférino
Sweet-smelling shop with ultra-neat shop displays. Not too gaudy or controversial.

Kerstin Adolphson
157 Bd St Germain, 6th
t 01 45 48 00 14
Ⓜ St Germain des Prés

A welcoming shop, chaotically arranged, with great piles of clothes all over the place, a tile floor and wooden beams poking through the ceiling. The sort of clothes that kids would choose for themselves to wear: patterned socks, bright jackets and painted wooden clogs.

L'Oiseau de Paradis
211 Bd St Germain, 7th
t 01 45 48 97 90
Ⓜ Rue du Bac
Plastic animals, toy drum kits, dolls, wooden forts, sailing boats and Little Red Riding Hood costumes.

Petit Bateau
186 Rue de Grenelle, 7th
t 01 47 05 18 51
www.petit-bateau.com
Ⓜ La Tour Maubourg
Posh, but not over the top. If you rummage hard, you should be able to turn up something afford-able. The twirly pyjamas are very reasonable, and there are lots of nice print T-shirts to choose from.

Petit Faune
33 Rue Jacob, 6th
t 01 42 60 80 72
www.petitfaune.com
Ⓜ St German des Prés
Charming, coordinated baby and toddler knitwear, plus an attractive, eye-catching range of patterned sweaters and smocks for older children.

Six Pieds Trois Pouces
223 Bd St Germain, 7th
t 01 45 44 03 72
www.6pieds3pouces.com
Ⓜ St Germain des Prés
Exquisitely crafted children's footwear: soft leather, Italian designs and high prices.

Tartine et Chocolat
266 Bd St Germain, 7th
t 01 45 56 10 45
www.tartine-et-chocolat.com
Ⓜ Solférino
A wide range of formal, tasteful baby clothes and nursery furniture. Pastel shades predominate.

English translations) designed to show how the seas and oceans are not just one great repository of wildlife but are made up of complex ecosystems with each creature acting as an important link in the overall food chain. You can also see films (in French) of submarine voyages to the deep and puppet shows are put on during school holidays.

The Latin Quarter

Paris' celebrated student district, site of the famous **Sorbonne**, is a vibrant place. It's called the 'Latin Quarter' because, when Paris' university was first founded in 1215, the students and professors were only allowed to speak Latin, a rule enforced until the Revolution in 1790.

The old streets of the district are lined with cheap cafés, bars, academic bookstores and art house cinemas. Always lively and bustling, this is where you'll find the city's greatest concentration of restaurants. In particular, the cluster of streets immediately south of the Quai St Michel including Rue de la Huchette, Rue de la Harpe and Rue St Severin are lined almost exlusively with eateries of almost every ethnic cuisine (French, Italian, Turkish, Thai, Greek, Spanish). Many try to entice custom with elaborate seafood displays in their windows – great Busby Berkeley arrangements of crab and lobster surrounded by banks of oysters and shrimps. Make a note, too, of the Théâtre de la Huchette nearby, where Eugene Ionesco's play *The Bald Prima Donna* has been playing every night since 1957. A few minutes' walk further east on Rue de la Bûcherie is Paris' most famous English-language bookshop, **Shakespeare & Company**, with a cosy children's section (*see* p.167).

The **Boulevard St Michel** is the area's main drag, running from Place St Michel by the river, with its statue of St Michael slaying a dragon, southwards to the Luxembourg and, eventually, Montparnasse. During the 1968 student uprising at the Sorbonne, students used the cobblestones of Boulevard St

Michel as missiles to hurl at the police. **Place Maubert**, further towards the eastern side of the Latin Quarter on Boulevard St Germain, was the main square in Paris where heretics (Protestants) were hanged in the 16th century. Today it's home to a bustling food market (pastries, fish, fruit and vegetables) on Tuesdays, Thursdays and Saturdays.

St Germain des Prés

East of the Latin Quarter stands St Germain des Prés, the oldest church in Paris, parts of which date back to the 6th century. Its beautiful medieval Gothic choir has been much restored after revolutionaries knocked it about in 1792. The surrounding area has long been the capital of Parisian café society. The cafés along **Boulevard St Germain** (which are now very expensive) were once the haunt of writers, poets and artists such as Rimbaud, Sartre, Camus, Hemingway and Picasso, although its residents may now be more *au fait* with high fashion than high art. In the streets leading off from the boulevard, you can still find plenty of quirky shops and small art galleries as well as one of Paris' liveliest and classiest small food markets on **Rue de Buci** with its wonderful display of delicacies and take-away goodies.

Continue eastwards along the Boulevard St Germain and your surroundings become steadily more upmarket, especially after crossing into the 7th *arrondissement*, one of the plushest districts in the whole city, especially good for high fashion shopping. Dior, Cartier and Armani all have branches in the area and the children's shops of this side of St Germain (*see* p.92) are picture-pretty.

Around Montparnasse

South of the Luxembourg is Montparnasse, another of the Left Bank's famous districts. The favourite haunt of artists in the 1920s, it nowadays is not the most attractive part of the city (thanks to 1960s redevelopment). It does, however, retain some worthwhile attractions and popular places to sit at a table, eat and watch city life go by.

Les Catacombes

1 Place Denfert Rochereau, 14th
t 01 43 22 47 63
www.paris.fr
Ⓜ Denfert Rochereau
Open 11am–4pm (Tues), 9am–4pm (Wed–Sun)
Adm Adults €5, under-18s €2.50, under-14s **free**
No wheelchair access
Suitable for children aged 6 and over
Allow at least 1 hour

If your children want to see what 6 million skeletons look like, head south of Montparnasse cemetery towards the catacombs (the 'Empire of the Dead'). Originally Roman stone quarries, these dark and damp subterranean passageways are filled with the former residents of Paris' cemeteries, who have been moved here to prevent 'overcrowding' in the graveyards where they were first buried in the 1780s. Every year, more than 50,000 people descend the 90 steps to explore stack upon stack of ghoulish bones, and row upon row of scary skulls, many arranged in odd 'artistic' patterns. Macabre but fascinating.

Cimetière de Montparnasse

3 Bd Edgar Quinet, 14th
t 01 44 10 86 50
Ⓜ Edgar Quinet, Raspail
Open Daily 8am–6pm (April–Oct); 8am–5pm (Nov–Mar)
Adm free

Continuing the death-related theme after your trip to the Catacombs, enter this giant, rambling cementery, the largest open space in Montparnasse. Quiet, tree-lined pathways border the last resting place of French writers Sartre and Baudelaire, car manufacturer André Citroën and American actress Jean Seberg. Most engaging, though, is the monument to Mr and Mrs Pigeon at home in their bed.

Musée de la Poste

34 Boulevard de Vaugirard, 15th
t 01 42 79 24 24
www.laposte.fr/musée
Ⓜ Montparnasse Bienvenüe
Open Daily 10am–6pm; closed Sundays and public holidays
Adm Adults €4.50, under-18s €3, under-12s **free**

This renovated museum gives a lively tour of postal history on five floors. Buy your ticket at the vintage post office and explore a world of mail trivia: uniforms, pistols, carriages, bicycles, letter boxes, cartoons and fumigation tongs (used to sterilize mail from plague-ridden ships). During the 1871 Siege of Paris, people came up with ingenious methods for getting the post in and out of the blockaded city including hot-air balloons, carrier pigeons and water-tight balls (*boules de moulins*) which were floated down the Seine. This last method was not inefficient and many *boules* either never reached their destination or arrived too late (a *boule* was fished out of the river as late as 1982).

Tour Montparnasse

33 Av du Maine, 15th
t 01 45 38 52 56
www.tourmontparnasse56.com
Ⓜ Montparnasse Bienvenüe
Open Daily 9.30am–11.30pm (April–Oct); 9.30am–10.30pm (Nov–Mar)
Adm Adults €8, under-20s €6.80, under-14s €5.50, under-5s **free**
Wheelchair access
Suitable for all ages; allow at least 1 hour

The second best views in Paris and the ideal place from which to watch the 14 July Bastille Day celebrations and the spectacular firework display at Trocadéro (book tickets in advance). At 206m (676ft), it is a few hundred feet shorter than the Eiffel Tower, but has shorter queues. The Tour was Paris' first skyscraper and is still its tallest (and ugliest). Until the construction of London's Canary Wharf in the 1990s, it was also the tallest true building (as opposed to a tower like the Eiffel) in Europe. Built in the 1960s in one of the then most fashionable districts in town, it sent Parisian trend-setters packing to the districts of St Germain des Prés and the Marais. Still largely unloved, it's worth visiting for the views. You can see for over 40km (25 miles) from the 59th-floor terrace and there's old photographs showing how the city's skyline has changed over 200 years. If you want to rest in the summer, the 56th floor is windowed and air-conditioned. The small restaurant on the 56th floor has excellent views and reasonably priced food. Please note that the lift finishes on this floor and buggies have to be carried up the final flights of stairs to the roof terrace on the top floor above.

Question 11
Why is Paris' student district called the Latin Quarter?
answer also on p.250

1 Chez Léna et Mimile
32 Rue Tournefort, 5th
t 01 47 07 72 47
Ⓜ Place Monge
Open Daily 12 noon–2pm and 7.30pm–11pm

2 La Coupole
102 Boulevard du Montparnasse, 14th
t 01 42 20 14 20
Ⓜ Vavin
Open 8.30am–1am (Mon–Thurs), 8.30am–1.30am (Fri–Sat)

3 Hippopotamus
9 Rue Lagrange, 5th
t 01 43 54 13 99
Ⓜ Maubert Mutualité
Open Daily 11.30am–5am

4 Korean Barbecue
22 Rue Delambre, 14th
t 01 43 35 44 35
Ⓜ Vavin
Open Daily 11am–2pm and 7pm–11pm

5 Salon de Thé de la Mosquée de Paris
1 Place du Puits de l'Ermite, 5th
t 01 43 31 38 20
Ⓜ Censier Daubenton
Open Daily 10am–midnight

6 Le Polidor
41 Rue Monsieur le Prince, 6th
t 01 43 26 95 34
Ⓜ Odéon
Open 12 noon–2.30pm and 7pm–12.30am (Mon–Sat), 12 noon–2.30pm and 7pm–11pm (Sun)

7 Ty Breiz
52 Boulevard de Vaugirard, 15th
t 01 43 20 83 72
Ⓜ Montparnasse Bienvenüe, Pasteur
Open 12 noon–3pm and 7pm–11pm (Mon–Sat)

Crêperies
The Latin Quarter has almost as many crêperies as it does students. Try any of the following:

8 *Crêperie des Arts*
27 Rue St André des Arts, 6th
t 01 43 26 15 68
Ⓜ/**RER** St Michel Nôtre Dame
Open Daily 12 noon–1am

9 *Crêperie Cluny*
20 Rue de la Harpe, 5th
t 01 43 26 08 30
Ⓜ/**RER** St Michel Nôtre Dame
Open Daily 11am–12 midnight

10 *La Crêpe Carrée*
42 Rue Monge, 5th
t 01 43 54 31 08
Ⓜ Cardenal Lemoine
Open 12 noon–12 midnight (Tues–Sun)

See **Eat** pp.153–164 for more details on the above restaurants/crêperies. *See* map on p.87 for the locations of the restaurants/crêperies numbered above.

Montmartre

Montmartre, the old village occupying the highest hill in Paris – the *Butte Montmartre* – was once Paris' funkiest address, the haunt of artists and the site of the Moulin Rouge, where the capital's hedonists came to (quite literally) paint the town red. These days it's a rather faded belle exuding a proud, but slightly shabby, elegance. Nonetheless, the somewhat touristy atmosphere of some bits of the *butte* aside, this is still a part of Paris that's not to be missed, and one that's surprisingly child-friendly: kids will love the **Sacré Coeur**, the looming white basilica perched on the hill, almost as much as the **funicular** that takes them there. Whatever the day, jugglers, mimics and other street artists entertain the crowds in front of the basilica and up and down its steps. Children will also enjoy the vintage carousel on the **Place St Pierre**, the nearby Halle St Pierre with its children's exhibitions, and the **Place du Tertre**, where hordes of pavement artists will fight for the right to draw their portrait. All around, the winding streets of old Montmartre are full of places to catch their imagination.

To Marché aux Puces

N

5

Marcadet
Poissonniers Ⓜ

BOULEVARD BARBÈS

3

Lamarck
Caulaincourt Ⓜ

RUE CAULAINCOURT

RUE DU MONT CENIS

RUE CUSTINE

RUE DU MONT CENIS

cimetière de
Montmartre

RUE CAULAINCOURT

RUE DES SAULES

Jardin
Sauvage
St Vincent

Vineyard

Musée de
Montmartre

RUE DU MONT CENIS

Château
Rouge Ⓜ

7

RUE LEPIC

RUE DE CLIGNANCOURT

Syndicat
d'Initiative de
Montmartre

4

Sacré
Coeur

PLACE
DU TERTRE

Espace Dalí
Montmartre

RUE DES ABBESSES

RUE DES TROIS FRÈRES

Funicular

1

6

PLACE DES
ABBESSES

carousel

PLACE
ST PIERRE

Halle St Pierre/
Musée d'Art Naif

2

Moulin
Rouge

Abbesses Ⓜ

RUE YVONNE-LE-TAC

Ⓜ
Blanche

BOULEVARD DE CLICHY

BOULEVARD DE ROCHECHOUART

Ⓜ
Barbès
Rochechouart

Ⓜ Pigalle

Anvers Ⓜ

Key

**Numbers correspond to restaurants in
'Where To Eat' p.104**

Highlights

*Looking down on Paris from the Sacré
Coeur*

*Wandering through the crowds and
artists in the Place du Tertre*

*Finding out which of Montmartre's
hilly old streets has the best view*

Sacré Coeur

Parvis du Sacré Coeur, 18th
t 01 53 41 89 00
www.sacre-coeur-montmartre.com
Ⓜ Abbesses, Anvers
Open Daily. Basilica: 6am–10.45pm; dome and crypt: 9am–5.45pm
Adm Church **free**; dome and crypt, adults €4.10, under-18s €2.45, under-6s **free**
Wheelchair access to the church (call in advance for assistance)
Suitable for all ages; allow at least 1 hour

This resplendent white basilica perched high on a hill is Montmartre's dominant feature, visible from all over the city. It's a relatively modern monument by Parisian standards, commissioned in 1873 and completed in a little under 12 years. You can reach it either by clambering up a seemingly endless flight of 237 steps from Place St Pierre, where a pretty traditional carousel is permanently installed, or by taking the jaunty little funicular (*see* p.102) that runs alongside them.

The views from the steps in front of the church are pretty amazing, and from the dome they're truly spectacular: you can see the entire city spread out before you like a great 3-D patchwork.

The basilica's interior will be of limited interest to children. It's suitably dark and spooky, and the stained glass produces some magical effects, but kids won't insist on lingering for long.

Place du Tertre

Lined with cafés and bars and permanently thronged with people, the Place du Tertre, a short walk away from the Sacré Coeur, is not to

Can you spot?
The Chapelle du Martyr at 11 Rue Yvonne le Tac, just down the hill from Place St Pierre. According to legend, this chapel marks the spot where Paris' patron saint, St Denis, was beheaded by the Romans in the 3rd century. St Denis had the last laugh, however – he picked up his newly severed head and marched off to found an abbey on the other side of town. Montmartre, the 'Hill of the Martyr', was named in his honour.

Did you know?
There is always someone praying inside Sacré Coeur. Every moment of every day since 1885 there has been someone on prayer duty within the basilica (not the same person, of course).

everyone's taste. Some people cite it as an example of everything that's wrong with modern Montmartre, but, if you take it at face value, it's fun, lively, informal, and your kids will enjoy it.

Every inch of the square seems to be occupied by artists, many with original works to sell (often as not featuring a major Parisian landmark), although this is also the place to pick up cheap copies of works by the great masters. Most of the artists are portrait-painters and silhouette-cutters, who will do a flattering likeness of your child for €15–25.

Dalí Espace Montmartre

11 Rue Poulbot, 18th
t 01 42 64 40 10
Ⓜ Abbesses
Open Daily 10am–6.30pm (Sept–June); 10am–9pm (July–Aug)
Adm Adults €7, under-25s €5, under-8s **free**

Most kids enjoy this phantasmagorical, none-too-serious dive into the universe of Salvador Dalí, located just off Place du Tertre. Black-walled interiors, artistically programmed lighting and specially composed soundtracks provide the backdrop for this collection of weird and wonderful three-dimensional sculptures (mainly bronzes), which vividly bring forth some of Dalí's most famous and surrealistic images, as well as book illustrations from the *Space Elephant* and *Alice in Wonderland*.

The streets of Montmartre

Question 12
Which painter was famous for his pictures of girls performing the can-can at the Moulin Rouge?
answer also on p.250

As with the Marais, the Paris district it most resembles, Montmartre is best appreciated on foot, strolling down its narrow lanes, popping in and out of boutiques and antique shops, and stopping for rests at pavement cafés. Look out for the **Monmartrobus** (see p.102) as it potters through the old streets, for hopping on it can come as an ideal breather when the hill gets too steep to handle.

There was a village on the hill of the *Butte Montmartre* for centuries before it was absorbed into Paris in about 1860. Because of its great height and strong winds it was the site of many windmills (*moulins*), which ground corn for the city below. Later, its somewhat hidden, out-of-the-way location led to it becoming the centre of the city's risqué nightlife scene with numerous nightclubs and bars springing up at the foot of the hill around Boulevard Clichy and Pigalle. The Montmartre windmills inspired the most famous Parisian music hall of all, the **Moulin Rouge** on Place Blanche, which has now been going strong for over 110 years (and which was featured in the recent Hollywood film of the same name). It was here that showgirls first danced the can-can, and were sketched and painted by the famous artist Toulouse-Lautrec.

The streets at the top of the *butte* to the north of the Sacré Coeur are normally much quieter than those lower down and around Place du Tertre and are well worth exploring. Look out for the **Clos Montmartre** vineyard in Rue des Saules, planted in 1933 as a revival of the vineyards that had covered the hillside ever since Roman times. Grape-picking takes place on the first Saturday of October every year, and is the occasion for a great festival (the **Fête des Vendanges à Montmartre**, see p.37) that extends throughout the whole district. The celebrations include music, locals in costume, a street parade and, naturally, lots of wine sampling. By contrast, on the western side of the district, is the **Cimetière de Montmartre**, perhaps the most romantically wistful of Paris' three grand cemeteries (the others being Montparnasse, see pp.94–95, and Père Lachaise, see p.122), its leafy alleyways following the slopes of the hill. Distinguished residents include Dégas, the great dancer Nijinsky, film director François Truffaut and the can-can dancer La Goulue, who was painted many times by Toulouse-Lautrec.

Jardin Sauvage St Vincent

Entrance opposite 14 Rue St Vincent, 18th
Ⓜ Lamarck Caulaincourt
Open 2pm–6pm Sat (April–Sept); during local school terms 4pm–6pm (Mon)

A curious little 'conservation area' for the native flora (and sometimes fauna) of Montmartre, along the street from the district's vineyard. In this untended old garden, each tree, bush and plant is left to its own devices, to grow wild.

Halle St Pierre/Musée d'Art Naif

2 Rue Ronsard, 18th
t 01 42 58 72 89
www.hallesaintpierre.org
Ⓜ Anvers, Abbesses
Open 10am–6pm (Mon–Sat), workshops in French and puppet shows 3pm–4pm (Wed, Sat, Sun and weekdays in school holidays)

Did you know?
Back in the 18th century Montmartre would have been covered in windmills in which the corn was ground to make the city's daily bread.

Getting around Montmartre

Perched high up on its hill, with its narrow streets and vineyards, Montmartre has long had a sense of being a separate community within Paris. The district has its own tourist office (the *Syndicat d'Initiative*) and there are several special ways of travelling up and around the streets of the *butte*.

Syndicat d'Initiative de Montmartre
21 Place du Tertre, 18th
t 01 42 62 21 21
www.montmartrenet.com
Open Daily 10am–7pm
As well as information, the *Syndicat* offers guided tours in a variety of languages.

Funiculaire de Montmartre
Rue Tardieu–Rue St Eleuthère, 18th
Departs Daily every 5min 6.15am–12.45am
Ⓜ Anvers
Tickets As for métro and bus
One of the world's shortest 'rides', Montmartre's funicular saves you the walk from Place St Pierre up to the Sacré Coeur, with views of the city below you along the way.

Montmartrobus
Place Pigalle–Place Jules Joffrin, 18th
Departs Daily every 12min 7.50am–8pm
Ⓜ Pigalle, Abbesses, Lamarck Caulaincourt, Jules Joffrin
Tickets As for métro and bus
A minibus service for Montmartre's narrow streets, which winds its way all through the district.

Le Petit Train de Montmartre
131 rue de Clignancourt, 18th
t 01 42 62 24 00
Departs Daily every 30 min 10am–7pm (from Place Blanche)
Ⓜ Blanche
Tickets Adults €5, under-11s €3
A fun way to see Montmartre is aboard the *Petit Train* (actually pulled along the streets by a tractor disguised as a steam locomotive). The 40-minute guided tour runs all year round, 10am–7pm, and additional evening tours run on Saturdays and Sundays from May to October, and daily in July and August.

Adm Adults €6.10, under-26s €4.60, under-4s **free**, workshops €8
Wheelchair access
Suitable for all ages; allow at least 1 hour
   At the foot of the hill leading to the Sacré Coeur, to the right of the district's favourite vintage carousel, is the Halle St Pierre, a former market building, now turned into a family-friendly cultural centre, where local mothers take their charges to watch puppet shows, take part in art, dance and music workshops (in French), eat child-friendly food in the café, and wander through the museum of 'naive art'. The multivaried shows and exhibits on display in the 'museum' – high art and low art, monkeys singing in a band; giant crabs catching people in their pincers; and lions roaring their way through the jungle, often rendered in bright gaudy colours – are lively and guaranteed to please youngsters. Special events are held here at Christmas, Easter and Hallowe'en.

Musée de Montmartre
12 Rue Cortot, 18th
t 01 46 06 61 11/01 49 25 89 37
Ⓜ Anvers

Open 10am–12.30am, 1.30pm–6pm (Tues–Sun), closed Mondays
Adm Adults €4.50, under-25s €3, under-8s **free**
   This charming museum occupies a 17th-century mansion amid picturesque gardens in the centre of Montmartre, the same house where Renoir painted the *Moulin de la Galette*. The museum, which also overlooks the vineyard where Utrillo lived, contains a collection of documents and objects that bring every aspect of bohemian Montmartre to life. Separate rooms deal with the many painters who once lived and worked in the district – Renoir, Toulouse-Lautrec, Utrillo, Dufy, Modigliani. Children will probably be most interested in the scale model of the old village and the theatre of shadows.

Question 13
There's something living on Rue des Saules that you might expect to find in the countryside, not inside a big city. What is it?
answer also on p.250

Marché aux Puces de St Ouen

Around Ⓜ Porte de Clignancourt
Open 7am–6pm (Mon, Sat–Sun)

North of Montmartre, at the very top end of the 18th *arrondissement* next to the *périphérique*, you'll find the more-or-less 3,000 stalls and shops that combine to make up Paris', and indeed Europe's, largest flea market. You can come across almost anything here, from antiques and memorabilia to vintage clothing and old toys. It's one huge rummage zone, and a great place to soak up some real Parisian atmosphere. Browsers and collectors of all ages can't get enough it.

Shopping in Montmartre

As well as the flea market on the north side of the *quartier*, and any amount of souvenir outlets, Montmartre offers enough toy and sweet shops per street to keep any kids happy. The Rue des Abbesses and Rue Lepic have the most to offer window shoppers: grown-ups should check out the fabric market on Place St Pierre, but for shopping specifically for kids, head for the following:

Boudezan

24 Rue Yvonne le Tac, 18th
t 01 42 62 82 86
Reasonably priced, trendy but tasteful kids' clothes made with natural fibres (*see* p.169).

Gaspard de la Butte

10 bis Rue Yvonne le Tac, 18th
t 01 42 55 99 40
Handmade clothes for under-6s: gorgeous dungarees and sweaters in ochres and reds (*see* p.170).

Pylones

57 Rue Tardieu, 18th
t 01 46 06 37 00
www.pylones.com
Great range of toys, gadgets and gifts (*see* p.167).

Têtes en l'Air

65 Rue des Abbesses, 18th
t 01 46 06 71 19
Crazy, colourful hats for kids and adults (*see* p.173).

1 Le Chinon
49 Rue des Abbesses, 18th
t 01 42 62 07 17
Ⓜ Abbesses
Open Daily 9am–12 midnight

2 Café de la Halle St Pierre
2 Rue Ronsard, 18th
t 01 42 58 72 89
Ⓜ Anvers, Abbesses
Open 10am–6pm (Mon–Sat)

3 Le Maquis
69 Rue Caulaincourt, 18th
t 01 42 59 76 07
Ⓜ Lamarck Caulaincourt
Open 12 noon–2.30pm and 7pm–12 midnight
(Mon–Sat)

4 Patachou
9 Place du Tertre, 18th
t 01 42 51 06 06
Ⓜ Anvers
Open Daily 12 noon–12 midnight

5 Rendez-vous des Chauffeurs
11 Rue des Portes Blanches, 18th
t 01 42 64 04 17
Ⓜ Marcadet Poissoniers
Open Daily 12 noon–2.30pm and 7.30–11pm

6 Le Sancerre
35 Rue des Abbesses, 18th
t 01 42 58 08 20
Ⓜ Abbesses
Open Daily 7am–2am

7 Au Virage Lepic
61 Rue Lepic, 18th
t 01 42 52 46 79
Ⓜ Blanche
Open Daily 12 noon–3pm and 6pm–2am

See **Eat** pp.153–164 for more details on the
above restaurants. *See* map on p.99 for the
locations of the restaurants numbered above.

La Villette

The sight of French school children dragging their parents off the train at Porte de la Villette métro station should tell you all you need to know. After Disneyland® Resort Paris, the great cultural complex at La Villette is Paris' top children's attraction. It's made up of several parts: the **Cité des Sciences et de l'Industrie**, a wonderful ultramodern hands-on science museum; the **Argonaute**, a former French navy submarine, which is now a naval museum and, unofficially, an indoor climbing frame for children; the **Géode**, an enormous sci-fi globe housing an IMAX 3-D screen; a 35-acre park; a museum of music; and the **Cité des Enfants**, an enormously enjoyable, science-themed adventure playground for 3–11-year-olds. Kids will love them all.

All of these different attractions are spread around the **Parc de la Villette**, one of the most boldly modernistic of Paris' 1980s parks, with loads of (sometimes) strange but fun spaces to enjoy. Running through the park there is a much older and more placid part of the city, the waters of the **Canal de l'Ourcq**, along which you can take a boat trip down to the Seine and the centre of town (*see* pp.31–32).

CD-Rom

Highlights

Playing with lights and levers in the Cité des Sciences

Mini-engineering at the Cité des Enfants

Going on a canal cruise back to town from Parc de la Villette

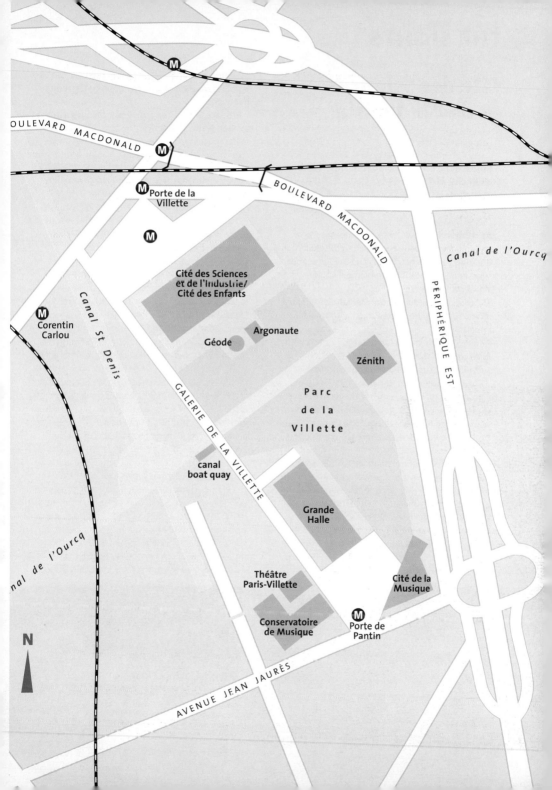

Cité des Sciences et de l'Industrie

Parc de la Villette,
30 Av Corentin Cariou, 19th
t 01 40 05 80 00 **t** 08 92 69 70 72 (reservations)
www.cite-sciences.fr
Ⓜ Porte de la Villette
Open 10am–6pm (Tues–Sat), 10am–7pm (Sun);
closed Mondays
Adm Explora pass adults €7.50, under-16s €5.50,
under-7s **free** for activities linked to the exhibitions,
the Louis Lumière 3-D cinema and the Argonaute
submarine; Planetarium supplement €2.50
Wheelchair access
The Louis Braille room at the Mediathéque library
offers translated texts for visitors with visual
impairments
Film projections in sign language for visitors with
hearing disabilities
Suitable for all ages; allow at least 2 hours

The centrepiece and hub of La Villette's grand
cultural complex, this is one of the most instructive
yet fun museums that you could ever hope to visit
with kids. Unlike the Palais de la Découverte in the
centre of town, everything here is super-modern
and hi-tech (and that includes the building itself).
Only the latest technologies are given houseroom.

Explora, the museum's permanent exhibition, is
like a vast science playground covering two floors
and over 9,000 square metres of floor space. It's
divided into 18 sections: Space, Ocean, Images,
Garden of the Future, Environment, Automobiles,
Energy, Aeronautics, Stars and Galaxies, Computer
Science, Life and Health, Expression and Behaviour,
Rocks and Volcanoes, Mathematics, Planetarium,
Medicine, Sound, and Biology and Light Games, each
boasting magisterial displays of up-to-the minute
hardware.

In **Space**, you can see a full-size reconstruction of
a moon walk, complete with space station, satellite
and a spaceman perched precariously on a tele-
scopic arm. In **Ocean**, you can examine a submarine
capable of diving 600m (1,970ft) below the ocean
waves. In **Aeronautics**, you can walk beneath the
wings and fuselage of a Mirage IV jet fighter.

Everywhere you go there are buttons to press,
videos to see (many in English), experiments to
perform and demonstrations to watch. This is
museum-going as funfair. You can test your driving
skills in a top-of-the-range driving simulator in
Automobiles, don a stethoscope and examine a
patient in **Medicine**, pretend to be a weatherman
in **Images**, examine yourself in a 'real' mirror in
Expression and Behaviour (which reverses your
image so that you can see yourself as others see
you), fire up a simple steam engine in **Energy**, or
hold a whispered conversation with someone 17m
(55ft) away in **Sound** using parabolic sound reflec-
tors (basically a couple of enormous plastic dishes
stood on their sides). **Light Games** (Jeux de Lumière)
is the museum's ultimate hands-on section, filled
with clever contraptions and devices designed to
illustrate optical illusions and tricks of the light.

You can come and go through all these areas
more or less as you please, although you will have
to queue for the space shows, held on the hour in
the **Planetarium**. The auditorium holds 300 and
seats are allocated on a first-come, first-served
basis. There are two shows – the first takes you on
a tour of the night sky, exploring stars, planets and
constellations, while the second attempts to
unravel some of the mysteries of modern
astronomy and astrophysics scientifically (it fails).

Surrounding the planetarium is an excellent astronomy gallery, **Stars and Galaxies**, where you can play with models of the solar system, weigh yourself to see how heavy you would be on Mars or Jupiter, and look through high-powered telescopes.

This is the sort of museum in which you could easily spend your whole holiday without your kids uttering so much as a single word of complaint.

In addition to the attractions listed here, the La Villette complex also contains the **Louis Lumière Cinema**, which shows nature and science documentaries including the occasional cartoon or 3-D feature; an **aquarium** with over 200 species of fish, crustaceans, molluscs and seaweed from Mediterranean coastal waters; and the **Cinaxe**, a moving movie theatre that virtually simulates a trip to the bottom of the ocean using 3-D visuals and seats mounted on hydraulic jacks.

These permanent displays are complemented by an ever-changing series of temporary exhibitions that explore the latest scientific breakthroughs.

The Géode

Open Daily hourly sessions 10am–9pm
Tickets €8.75 per film

This dazzling metal sphere is La Villette's one true architectural highlight. Inside, IMAX 3-D films are shown on a huge curved screen, which allows you to explore the beauty and wonder of the natural world while clutching a can of cola and a carton of popcorn.

The Argonaute

Open 10am–5.30pm (Tues–Fri), 10am–6.30pm (Sat–Sun)
Adm €3 (free with **Explora pass**)
No wheelchair access

Just outside the museum by the Géode, stands the Argonaute, a former French naval submarine in service from 1958 to 1982. A 'hunter-killer' submarine, it was designed to track and destroy other submarines as well as surface craft although it was never called upon to fire a torpedo in anger during its 24 years of service. Recorded audioguides, distributed at the entrance, take you on a tour of its narrow decks to see its periscope, torpedo-

launchers and the 'snug' sleeping quarters, where the sub's 50-man crew slept three to a bunk.

Cité des Enfants

t 01 40 05 12 12
Open 90-minute visits at 9.30am, 11.30am, 1.30pm and 3.30pm (Tues, Thurs, Fri), and at 10.30am, 12.30pm, 2.30pm and 4.30pm (Wed, Sat, Sun and public holidays)
Adm €5 per person per 90-minute session; children must be accompanied by an adult (max. 2 adults per family)

A science and nature museum designed specifically for younger children, the Cité des Enfants is a must. Alongside a special exhibition on electricity, there are separate areas designed for 3–5-year-olds and ages 5–12, each of which can be visited as part of a 90-minute session during which a whole host of activities is laid on. You'll find the *cité* permanently filled with hyperactive youngsters enthusiastically making badges, experimenting with pumps, gears and robots, working on a mini-construction site in plastic hard hats, arranging giant foam blocks into vaguely house-like shapes, and generally having a whale of a time – all in the name of science, of course. The nature exhibits here include an ant farm, a butterfly farm and a greenhouse. Everything is carefully supervised and many of the instructors speak English although these aren't the sort of exhibits which really require much explanation – just set them loose and watch them go.

Parc de la Villette

Plenty of non-scientific fun can be had inside La Villette's 14-hectare (35-acre) park between the Cité des Sciences et de l'Industrie and the Cité de la Musique. Designed in the 1980s by architect Bernard Tschumi to make use of a long-decrepit site that once contained stockyards and abattoirs, la Villette is ultra-modern, but still very French. A

Question 14
What was the La Villette site originally intended for?
answer also on p.250

park just wouldn't be a park to Parisians if it wasn't hugely over-designed, with more lines, paths, enclosed areas and 'special' features than are strictly necessary. La Villette is filled with extraordinary red pavilions or 'follies', which serve a range of purposes: some are climbing frames, others burger bars and first-aid points, and a few are demonstration areas where children's art workshops are held. The massive Chinese dragon slide is a nice touch.

The departure point for the **Paris Canal** boat cruises on the Canal de l'Ourcq, which runs between La Villette and the Musée d'Orsay on the Seine (*see* p.32) by the city-side of the main bridge across the canal in the middle of the park.

Cité de la Musique

The home of the Conservatoire Nationale de Musique, this 1,000-seat auditorium and excellent museum should appeal to older children.

Musée de la Musique

221 Avenue Jean Jaurès, 19th
t 01 44 84 45 00
www.cite-musique.fr
Ⓜ Porte de Pantin
Open 12 noon–6pm (Tues–Sat), 10am–6pm (Sun)
Adm Adults €6.10, under-25s €4.60, under-18s €2.30, under-6s **free**
Wheelchair access
Suitable for ages 8 and up; allow at least 1 hour

The English-language audioguide (available at the entrance) demonstrates the sounds of some of the museum's 900-plus instruments (including Beethoven's own clavichord). The interactive video screens are in French and may be of limited interest, although all youngsters will like the cut-away dolls' house-type models that beautifully re-create concert halls and opera houses down to every last detail, from the scenery to backstage mechanics. Guided tours and music classes (in French only) are also on offer.

Most of La Villette's food outlets are located within the Parc de la Villette complex itself. Each of the site's main attractions operates at least one (usually more) family-friendly eatery. For instance, the Cité des Sciences et de l'Industrie offers an ice cream parlour, a self-service restaurant, a fast food restaurant (**Croq Cité**) and a more formal Bistro (**Bistro d'Ariane**). Outside the complex, there's a number of cafés on the Avenue Corentin Cariou by Ⓜ Porte de La Villette and on the Avenue Jean Jaurès near Ⓜ Porte de Pantin to the south of the park. For something more substantial, though, you'll need to head back into town.

Kids in

08

While a great deal of the enjoyment of Paris for all ages comes from seeing the sights and exploring the bustling life of its streets and squares, there's plenty to do indoors, too, when visiting some of the world's best museums. Should you be here when the weather's grim, there are many options for catching kids' enthusiasm from cinema to circuses to theatre. Don't let the language put you off: while the pickings may be slimmer for non-French speakers, there's still lots to do in Paris and the sort of entertainment children like often requires little translation.

For **internet cafés**, *see* p.138.

Amusement arcades

La Tête dans les Nuages

5 Bd des Italiens, 2nd
t 01 53 57 31 31
Ⓜ Richelieu Drouot
Open Daily 10am–12 midnight

For 'exhibits' that will appeal, join the truants at this game mecca full of shoot 'em ups, fighting and racing games, virtual reality hook-up points, and more traditional games like table hockey and pool. You pay with pre-bought tokens (€2–5 *per game*). There's also a branch of McDonald's inside.

Cinema

America aside, no other country has such a strong cinematic tradition. Paris can justifiably call itself the cradle of cinema for it was on Rue Scribe in 1895 that the Lumière brothers held the first ever public film screening with their newly invented *cinématographe*. The film itself was just minutes long and shown to workers leaving the Lumière factory for their lunchbreak.

The French capital is full of picture houses – from huge, popcorn-filled multiplexes to Left Bank art houses. Most programmes are roughly one-third domestic titles and two-thirds international titles (generally American). Most international films are dubbed into French (advertised as VF, *Version Française*), but a growing number of cinemas show films in their original language with French subti-tles (indicated with the letters VO, *Version Originale*). Admission prices are €5.50–8.50.

Le Grand Rex

1 Bd Poissonnière, 2nd
t 01 42 36 83 93   **t** 08 36 68 05 96 (infoline)
www.legrandrex.com
Ⓜ Bonne Nouvelle
Tours 11am–5pm (Wed–Sun)
Tickets Adults €7.80, under-12s €5.95, under-3s **free**

This magnificent Art Deco building from 1932 has 2,800 seats on three levels and is a real temple of the silver screen. It offers audioguided tours, *Les Étoiles du Rex*, which take you on a magical journey into the heart of the movie backstage and let you become an actor in a famous film. Buy tickets in advance at the Paris tourist office (*see* p.144).

MK2 Sur Seine Cinema

14 Quai de la Seine, 19th
t 08 36 68 48 07
Ⓜ Stalingrad
Tickets Adults €8.10, under-12s €5.50

Children's programmes on Wednesday and weekend mornings.

UGC Ciné Cité Les Halles

Place de la Rotonde, Nouveau Forum des Halles, 1st
t 01 40 26 40 45
www.ugc.fr
Ⓜ**/RER** Châtelet Les Halles
Tickets Adults €8.80, under-12s €5.95

A 16-screen multiplex offering a big choice of movies in the Forum des Halles shopping complex.

IMAX

La Géode

30 Av Corentin Cariou, 19th
t 01 40 05 12 12
www.lageode.fr
Ⓜ Porte de la Villette
Open Daily hourly sessions 10am–9pm
Tickets €8.75

See the latest 3-D releases inside La Villette's huge metal sphere outside the Cité des Sciences et de l'Industrie (*see* pp.108–109).

Circus

A trip to the circus is a real Christmas tradition in Paris. In addition to old-fashioned sawdust and sword-swallower circuses, the city plays host to a string of modern troupes with traditional and unusual performing skills.

Cirque d'Hiver Bouglione

110 Rue Amelot, 11th
t 01 47 00 12 25
Ⓜ Filles du Calvaire
Showtime Various (call in advance)
Tickets €10–35

Probably the most famous circus venue in the world. Built in 1852 and originally called the Cirque Napoleon, today it hosts a variety of troupes and the hugely popular Christmas show which showcases young stars, some of whom go on to join celebrated groups like Cirque du Soleil.

Cirque de Paris

Parc des Chanteraines, 115 Boulevard Charles de Gaulle, Villeneuve la Garenne
t 01 47 99 40 40
Ⓜ Porte de Clignancourt, then bus 137
RER lines C1, C3 to Gennevilliers
Open Wed and Sun (Oct–June)
Showtime: 3pm–5pm; *Journée au Cirque* (a day at the circus), 10am–5pm
Tickets Show only adults €11–24, under-16s €7–15; *Journée au Cirque* adults €35, under-16s from €30
Reservations essential

The full *Journée au Cirque* at the Cirque de Paris offers an all encompassing circus experience: in the morning, kids try their hand at circus skills and train with clowns, conjurors, contortionists, trapeze artists and tightrope walkers; then they have lunch with the performers before watching the professionals do their stuff in an afternoon show. It's a hugely popular birthday treat. Villeneuve, where the circus is located, is in the curve of the Seine just west of St Denis, on the north side of Paris.

Cirque Tzigane Romanes

12 Av de Clichy, 18th
t 01 43 87 16 38
Ⓜ Place de Clichy
Showtime Daily 8.30pm (Sept–May), 3pm and 5pm (Sat)
Tickets Adults €17, under-18s €9

Wirewalkers, contortionists, gymnasts and musicians put on a beguiling show at this Gypsy Circus.

Espace Chapiteaux

Parc de la Villette, 19th
t 08 03 07 50 75
www.villette.com
Ⓜ Porte de la Villette
Showtime 8.30pm (Wed–Sat), 4pm (Sun)
Tickets Adults €17, under-25s €14, under-12s €8, under-4s **free**

The Chapiteaux hosts visiting troupes throughout the year, from the most modern experimental ensembles to traditional circus companies.

Museums

Paris has more museums than it knows what to do with. Deciding which will most appeal to your children is usually pretty straightforward: the more interactive the exhibits, the more likely they are to enjoy it. Top of the interactive list are the science museums: the **Palais de la Découverte**, the Grande Galerie d'Evolution in the **Musée National d'Histoire Naturelle** and, above all, the **Cité des Sciences et de l'Industrie**. For a list of all the museums covered in full in the main chapters of this guide, *see* opposite.

Virtually all of France's state-run museums close one day a week (usually Tuesday), although some, notably the Palais de la Découverte and La Villette, close on Monday. Some private museums, however, stay open throughout the week.

Musée de l'Air et de l'Espace

Aéroport de Paris–Le Bourget
t 01 49 92 71 99
www.mae.org
Ⓜ Gare de l'Est then bus 350
RER lines B3, B5 to Le Bourget, then bus 152
Open 10am–6pm Tues–Sun (May–Oct); 10am–5pm Tues–Sun (Nov–April)
Adm Adults €7, under-18s **free**
Carte Musées et Monuments valid

Not far outside Paris' *périphérique* ring road at the city's old airport of Le Bourget, this display, first opened in 1919, is the oldest aeronautical museum in the world. It may be the most complete overview of the conquest of the air and space you're likely to see with an exceptional collection of aircraft and other flying machines (balloons, 1900s contraptions, jets and space vehicles). If you're driving, take the A1 from Porte de la Chapelle to Le Bourget exit.

Musée des Arts d'Afrique et d'Oceanie

293 Av Daumesnil, 12th
t 01 44 74 84 80/01 43 46 51 61 (infoline)
Ⓜ Porte Dorée
Open 10am–5.30pm (Mon, Wed–Sun), closed Tuesdays
Adm Adults €4.60, under-25s €3, under-18s **free**
Carte Musées et Monuments valid

The collection of ethnographic exhibits amassed during French colonialism has been moved to the Quai Branly, soon be joined by displays from the Musée de l'Homme to form a new ethnographic museum due to open in 2006. The old location is still worth visiting for the aquarium in the basement (one of Europe's largest) with its colourful exotic fish and a pit of snapping crocodiles.

Musée des Arts Forains

Pavillons de Bercy, 53 Av des Terroirs de France, 12th
t 01 43 40 16 22
Ⓜ Bercy
Open Groups only (Sat–Sun afternoons)
Adm Adults €11.40, under-15s €3.80, under-3s **free**

A museum of 19th-century fairground art now housed in a former wine warehouse in the Bercy district south of the Gare de Lyon. Its wonderfully colourful exhibits include painted roundabouts, a tin can alley, shooting range and puppet theatre. Some kids might get a bit frustrated by all the display-only objects. There are no 'official' opening times, so it's recommended that you ring ahead.

Musée des Arts et Métiers

60 Rue Réaumur, 3rd
t 01 53 01 82 00
www.arts-et-metiers.net
Ⓜ Arts et Métiers
Open 10am–6pm (Tues–Sun), until 9.30pm (Thurs); closed Mondays and public holidays
Adm Adults €6.50, under-18s **free**

A museum in a converted 12th-century abbey dedicated to inventions and scientific discoveries. You can see examples of early televisions, robots, big clunky computers, movie cameras (including the very cameras with which the Lumière brothers produced the first-ever public film screening in Paris in 1895), cars, planes (including the fragile-looking craft that carried Louis Blériot on its maiden flight across the English Channel in 1909) plus much else besides. There are touch-screen computer displays and a few hands-on exhibits, but it is not a patch on the Cité des Sciences et de l'Industrie, Exploradome or Palais de la Découverte.

Musée Grévin

10 Bd Montmartre, 9th
t 01 47 70 85 05
www.grevin.com
Ⓜ Grands Boulevards, **RER** Auber
Open 10am–5.30pm (Mon–Fri*)*, 10am–6pm (Sat–Sun, public holidays)
Adm Adults €15, under-14s €9, under-6s **free**

Reopened in 2001 after costly refurbishment, Paris' historic wax museum has 80 new figures and presents a more modern art of display without

The museums of Paris

These museums are described in other chapters in full. If you aim to visit more than two or three, purchase a **Carte Musées et Monuments** card for unlimited entry to many of the museums and sights. You can bypass queues and this saves you time (*see* p.21).

Art

Centre Pompidou see p.66
Dalí Espace Montmartre see p.100
Musée d'Art Naïf see p.101
Musée Nat. des Arts Asiatiques – Guimet see p.60
Musée Cognacq-Jay see pp.69
Musée du Louvre see pp.42–44
Musée de la Mode et du Costume/Palais de Tokyo see pp.60 61
Musée d'Orsay see pp.81, 83
Musée Picasso see pp.69–70
Musée Rodin see p.59
Union Centrale des Arts Décoratifs see p.44

Fashion, folk arts and everyday life

Musée de la Chasse et de la Nature see p.68
Musée Fragonard see p.47
Musée de l'Homme see p.60
Musée de la Mode et du Costume see pp.60–61
Musée National des Arts et Traditions Populaires see p.119
Musée de la Poste see p.95
Musée de la Poupée (Doll Museum) see p.70

History

La Conciergerie see pp.79–80
Musée de l'Armée – Napoleon's Tomb see pp.58–59
Musée de l'Assistance Publique see p.91
Musée Carnavalet see p.68
Les Égouts de Paris (Paris Sewers) see p.61
Musée de l'Histoire de France see p.69
Musée de la Marine see p.60
Musée de la Monnaie see p.82
Musée de Montmartre see p.102
Musée National du Moyen Âge – Thermes de Cluny see p.91
Musée de la Préfecture see p.91

Music

Musée de la Musique see p.110

The Natural world

Centre de la Mer see pp.90, 93
Musée National d'Histoire Naturelle see pp.88–89

Oddities

Musée de la Curiosité et de la Magie see p.69

Science

Cité des Enfants see p.109
Cité des Sciences et de l'Industrie see p.108
Exploradome see p.119
Palais de la Découverte see p.48

Outside Paris

Musée Condé – Château de Chantilly see p.129
Château de Versailles see p.128
Château de Vincennes see p.119

having lost all of its nostalgic elegance. There are wax versions of big international celebs including Madonna, Arnold Schwarzenegger, Elvis Presley and, for domestic audiences, Gérard Depardieu and Zinédene Zidane. Kids can even have their photograph taken with their favourite star. A variety of waxwork *tableaux* depict episodes from French history – Josephine counselling Napoleon, the trial of Joan of Arc, Marie Antoinette in prison, Marat dying slumped in his bath (in the actual tub in which he died) – and everyday life, such as a *Belle Epoque* bar or a film studio. Magic and conjuring shows are held in the first-floor theatre.

Musée Jacquemart-André

158 Bd Haussmann, 8th
t 01 45 62 11 59
www.musee-jacquemart-andre.com
Ⓜ Miromesnil, Ⓜ/**RER** Charles de Gaulle-Étolle
Open Daily 10am–6pm

Adm Adults €8, under-18s €6, under-7s **free**

Restored in the 1990s, this magnificent late 19th-century town house in the Faubourg St Honoré, north of the Champs Élysées, was the home of wealthy Edouard André and his artist wife Nélie Jacquemart. It houses their private (mainly 18th-century) art collection and includes paintings by Boucher, Fragonard, Rembrandt and Botticelli. Kids will enjoy wandering around an opulent mansion from one of Paris' grandest eras and sampling the delightful tearoom beneath a Tiepolo ceiling.

Musée Nissim de Camondo

63 Rue de Monceau, 8th
t 01 53 89 06 50/01 53 89 06 50 (infoline)
www.ucad.fr
Ⓜ Monceau, Villiers
Open 10am–5pm (Wed–Sun); closed Mon, Tues, public holidays
Adm Adults €4.60, under 25s €3, under-18s **free**
Carte Musées et Monuments valid

Part of the Union Centrale des Arts Décoratifs (*see* p.44), this former house of the wealthy banker Count Moïse de Camondo is furnished and decorated with priceless 18th-century artefacts. The opulent interiors, full of elegant furniture and tapestries, will appeal to older children. The museum was named after the count's son, who died in an aerial dog fight in the First World War.

Music

Concerts du Dimanche Matin

Théâtre Musical de Paris, 1 Place du Châtelet, 1st
t 01 40 28 28 40
t 01 42 56 90 10 (children's programme)
www.chatelet-theatre.com
Ⓜ/**RER** Châtelet Les Halles, Ⓜ Châtelet
Concerts 11am on Sunday (Oct–May)
Tickets Adults €20, under-26s €10, under-14s **free**; (minimum age 4 years)
Reservations essential

Sunday morning concert programmes that allow youngsters to join in workshops (in French). They are aimed at different age groups (4–7, 8–12, 9–14) and explore different areas or strands of music while parents and older kids attend the varied classical concerts on offer at Châtelet.

Theatre and readings

Paris has a vibrant theatre scene with several family-orientated shows each year and a handful of theatres whose output is devoted to younger audiences. In recent years, there has been a significant increase in the number of English language shows held in Paris. The American Library holds storytelling sessions in English for youngsters.

The American Library

10 Rue du Général Camou, 7th
t 01 53 59 12 60
www.americanlibraryinparis.org
Ⓜ École Militaire/**RER** Pont de l'Alma
Membership €120 (family)

Storytelling sessions for 3–5-year-olds in English on Wednesdays (10.15am, 2.30pm), 3-year-olds and under (10.30am on the first and last Thursday of each month) and monthly for 6–8-year-olds.

Centre Dramatique National de Montreuil

26 Place Jean Jaurès, 93100 Montreuil
t 01 48 70 48 91
Ⓜ Mairie de Montreuil
Tickets €6–10

Plays for children with a strong moral and/or political message.

Théâtre Astral

Parc Floral de Paris, Route de la Pyramide, Bois de Vincennes, 12th
t 01 42 41 88 33/01 43 71 31 10
Ⓜ Château de Vincennes
Tickets Adults €6, child €4.20 plus admission to Parc Floral (*see* p.120)

Shows for 3–8-year-olds on epics about ogres and princesses in the bucolic setting of the Parc Floral. Reservations are necessary.

Théâtre Dunois

108 Rue du Chevaleret, 13th
t 01 45 84 72 00
www.theatredunois.org
Ⓜ Chevaleret
Tickets €5–15

Plays host to a wide range of specialist children's theatre companies.

Théâtre des Dechargeurs

3 Rue des Dechargeurs, 1st
t 01 42 36 00 02
Ⓜ/**RER** Châtelet Les Halles

A recent addition to the growing number of English language theatres in Paris.

Théâtre de Ménilmontant

15 Rue de Retrait, 20th
t 01 46 36 98 60
Ⓜ Gambetta

Hosts the occasional English-language touring company.

Théâtre du Nesle

8 Rue de Nesle, 6th
t 01 46 34 61 04
Ⓜ St Michel, Odéon

Hosts English-language productions of the classics (i.e. Shakespeare) and modern works.

Kids out

09

'Historic' Paris – within the ring of the modern *périphérique* ring road – has traditionally been a very concentrated, 'urban' city with open space of any kind at a premium. The interruptions between the streets within the city – squares, avenues, former royal gardens like the Tuileries and the Invalides – are much-cherished and much-used. The two largest areas of open space around Paris, though, are the two great *bois* or woods of Boulogne and Vincennes that flank the old city almost like a pair of ears. In former centuries, both were kept apart as royal hunting and pleasure reserves, and so escaped being built on and incorporated into the city. Since the Revolution, they have provided Parisians with essential green lungs.

More recently, Paris' local authorities have also made great efforts to create a lot more breathing spaces within the city itself, with several striking new parks opening since the 1980s. And since most Parisian children live in garden-less apartments, the city is obliged to provide them with lots of open spaces and areas to run about in. Each district has at least one playground, and most of the larger public parks and gardens boast a variety of special children's attractions – from playgrounds, boating ponds and puppet theatres to adventure playgrounds, children's zoos and even mini-funfairs in the bigger parks. Note, though, that in the more formal parks the grass is often out of bounds – look out for signs saying *pelouse interdite* (lawn forbidden); for a really big expanse of grass to run around on, head out to one or other of the Bois.

Opening times vary with the seasons, but most parks are open daily, from early morning till dusk.

Bois de Boulogne

16th
Ⓜ Les Sablons, Porte Dauphine, Porte d'Auteuil, Porte Maillot

The Bois de Boulogne on the western side of historic Paris began life in the Middle Ages as a royal hunting ground, and was only formally landscaped in the mid 19th century on the orders of Napoleon III, who wanted to create a Parisian version of London's Hyde Park. His plan was pretty successful for, since Paris' west side was also the wealthiest part of the city, the Bois soon became the most fashionable place in town to take the air.

It has many similar features to Hyde Park, too, including riding paths and a boating lake, although, as it is a much larger space, it also has room for a network of cycle paths, a couple of racecourses, a flower garden, an open-air theatre, an artificial waterfall, acres of real, leafy woodland and a whole entertainment zone for kids, the Jardin d'Acclimatation.

Jardin d'Acclimatation
Bois de Boulogne, 16th
t 01 40 67 90 82
www.jardindacclimatation.fr
Ⓜ/RER Porte Maillot, Ⓜ Les Sablons
Open Daily 10am–7pm (April–Oct); 10am–6pm (Nov–Mar)
Adm €2.50, under-4s free
Le Petit Train runs every 15 minutes 11am–6pm (Wed, Sat–Sun) and every day during the school holidays, departing from L'Orée du Bois restaurant.

The foremost reason for visiting the Bois de Boulogne with kids has to be this – Paris' favourite, most traditional amusement park, occupying 10 hectares (25 acres) within its northern confines. To reach it, you hop aboard *Le Petit Train*, a jaunty little mock-steam train that runs straight there from Porte Maillot métro station (one stop along from the Arc de Triomphe). Laid out in a circular pattern, the park also contains a small zoo (where kids can pet the long-suffering goats and sheep), a hall of mirrors, a marionette theatre, a circus, a mini-golf course, dodgems, a pony club (where kids can take rides), a couple of junior-size (but still fairly hairraising) rollercoasters, a riverboat ride, a bowling alley, an archery range, a mini-motorbike course, plus three children's museums including an inter-

Carousels
Along with circuses and fairground attractions of all kinds, the French have a great fondness for vintage carousels or *manèges*, and there are several more or less permanently installed around Paris. You can take an old-fashioned spin at the foot of the Eiffel Tower, on the other side of the Pont d'Iéna in front of the Jardins du Trocadéro, in the Parc Monceau, at the foot of the stairway in front of Sacré Coeur, by the entrance to Ⓜ St Paul, in the Place de Batignolles, in the Parc des Buttes Chaumont, and on the concourse in front of the Grande Arche de la Défense.

active science museum. Some attractions are free, others cost €2.50 each, or you can buy a book of 14 tickets for €25. There's also lots of fast food, and a babysitting service is available in summer.

Musée en Herbe
t 01 40 67 97 66
Open 10am–6pm (Mon–Fri and Sun), 2pm–6pm (Sat)
Adm €2.50, under-4s **free**
Part of the Jardin d'Acclimatation, this children's museum tries to bring art history alive through interactive exhibits and painting workshops.

Musée National des Arts et Traditions Populaires
t 01 44 17 60 00
Open 9.30am–5.30pm (Mon and Wed–Sun)
Adm €2.50, under-4s **free**
Carte Musées et Monuments valid
Located within the Bois de Boulogne just outside the Jardin d'Acclimatation, this museum is dedicated to French folk art and agricultural life and houses an all-kinds-of-everything range of exhibits, from puppet theatres and musical instruments to old toys and circus equipment.

Exploradome
t 01 53 4 90 40
Open Daily 10am–6pm
Adm €5 under-4s **free**
Hi-tech hands-on science centre filled with interactive games and experiments designed to demonstrate basic scientific principles – build a bridge, whip up your own tornado, roll a square wheel etc.

Stade Roland Garros
2 Avenue Gordon Bennett, 16th
t 01 47 43 48 48
www.rolandgarros.com
M Porte d'Auteil
Open Daily 10am–5pm, guided tours In English at 11am and 3pm
Adm Adults €7.50, under-18s €4, family €15 (to 'Tenniseum'); adults €15, under-18s €10, family €30 (with guided tour)
France's pre-eminent tennis stadium where the prestigious French Open is staged in May (*see* p.35) is located at the very southern end of the Bois de Boulogne. Previously only open during competition time, the stadium is now, following a multi-million euro revamp, open all-year-round when visitors are invited to explore the new state-of-the-art multimedia tennis museum (known as the 'tenniseum', you can watch past matches, browse a collection of historic memorabilia and play quizzes and games in the special children's workroom) and take guided tours of the stadium (in English).

Bois de Vincennes

12th
M Porte Dorée, Château de Vincennes
www.boisdevincennes.com
Paris' largest park is actually across the city from the Bois de Boulogne on the eastern, traditionally more workaday side of town. The Bois de Vincennes, another wood that served as a royal hunting estate in pre-Revolutionary times, has cycle paths, a racetrack, a baseball pitch, acres of woodland, two lakes where you can hire rowing boats and model sailing boats, a flower garden where entertainments are laid on for children each summer, Paris's zoo and a Buddhist temple that contains the largest statue of Buddha in Europe. From April to June every year the Bois also houses a great funfair, the *Foire du Trône* (*see* p.34).

Château de Vincennes
Avenue de Paris, 12th
t 01 48 08 31 20
M Château de Vincennes
Open 10am–6pm (April–Oct); 10am–5pm (Nov–Mar)
Adm Adults €5.50, under-25s €3.50, under-18s **free**
Carte Musées et Monuments valid
This palace-cum-fortress was built in the 1300s in the middle of what was then a royal hunting ground, and Henry V of England died here in 1422. By the 17th century it had fallen out of favour as a residence, especially once Louis XIV had moved the royal court to his all new grand palace of Versailles, and Vincennes was often used as an overflow prison, especially whenever Louis got into one of his 'moods' – no other French king locked up so many people. In the 1800s it was turned into a fortress, and this was the site of the Napoleonic army's last stand. From the outside it looks rather dour and militaristic, but the interior has a fairy-tale-like opulence, with gilt-covered salons.

Paris' top parks

The Paris parks, gardens and other open spaces listed here are all described in full in other chapters of this guide.

Parc Floral de Paris

Entrance on Route de la Pyramide, 12th
t 01 55 94 20 20
www.parcfloraldeparis.com
Ⓜ Château de Vincennes, then 15mins' walk
Open Daily 9.30am–8pm (April–Sept);
9.30am–5/7pm (Oct–Mar)
Adm Adults €1.50, under-18s €0.75, under-6s free

This separate park inside the Bois has an excellent adventure playground with slides, swings and climbing frames, a fascinating, walk-through butterfly house (the *Serre des Papillons*) and another miniature steam train, which wends its way through the trees. The park is also home to a children's drama company, the Théâtre Astral, which presents free concerts and children's shows every summer (*see* p.116), and the Maison de la Nature, where (French-speaking) children can learn about nature through exhibitions and workshops.

Parc Zoologique de Paris

53 Av de St Maurice, 12th
t 01 44 75 20 10
www.mnhn.fr
Ⓜ Porte Dorée
Open Daily 9am–6.30pm (April–Oct); 9am–5.30pm (Nov–Mar)
Adm Adults €6.10, under-16s €4.60, under-4s **free**

The Bois de Vincennes's biggest draw is one of the largest zoos in Europe, where you'll find hippos, rhinos, pandas, lions, tigers, kangaroo, bison and elephants. Its centrepiece is a 65m- (213ft)-high artificial mountain, the *Grand Rocher*, laid out on several lift-accessible platforms (*open Wed, Sat, Sun only, adm extra €3*). Built in the 1930s, it was renovated not long ago and is now home to herds of

Puppets in the parks

Puppetry is a great Parisian tradition, and almost every park has a marionette theatre or *guignol* (named after the leading character, a sort of Gallic version of Mr Punch), with crowds of kids regularly packed together on the ground in front of it. As ever, violence (but not domestic violence) is the mainstay of the action. Performances are usually on Wednesday afternoons and Saturday mornings.

Guignol du Jardin d'Acclimatation
Jardin d'Acclimatation, Bois de Boulogne, 16th
t 01 45 01 53 52
Ⓜ/**RER** Porte Maillot, Ⓜ Les Sablons (or with *Le Petit Train*, *see* p.102)
Showtime 3pm and 4pm (Wed, Sat and Sun)

Guignol de Paris
Parc des Buttes Chaumont, 19th
t 01 43 64 24 29
Ⓜ Buttes Chaumont
Showtime 3.30pm (Wed, Sat and Sun)

Marionettes des Champs Élysées
Jardin des Champs Élysées, Av des Champs Élysées, 8th
t 01 40 35 47 20

Ⓜ Champs Élysées–Clémenceau
Shows 3pm, 4pm and 5pm (Wed, Sat, Sun and daily during school holidays)

Marionettes du Champ de Mars
Champ de Mars, 7th
t 01 48 56 01 44
Ⓜ École Militaire
Showtime 3.15pm and 4.15pm (Wed, Sat and Sun)

Marionettes du Luxembourg
Jardin du Luxembourg, 6th
t 01 43 26 46 47
Ⓜ Vavin, Nôtre Dame des Champs
Showtime 3.15pm, 4.30pm (Wed), 11am, 3.15pm, 4.30pm (Sat and Sun)

Marionettes de Montsouris
Parc Montsouris, 14th
t 01 69 09 72 13
RER Cité Universitaire
Showtime 3.30pm and 4.30pm (Wed, Sat and Sun)

Marionettes du Parc Georges Brassens
Parc Georges Brassens, Rue des Morillons, 15th
t 01 48 42 51 80
Ⓜ Porte de Vanves
Showtime 3pm onwards (Wed, Sat and Sun)

free-ranging mountain goats. All the zoo's animal enclosures have been carefully landscaped to conceal their fences and moats, giving the complex as natural and wild a look as possible. Once a day, kids are invited to help feed the sea lions. There's also a miniature steam train which trundles around the zoo's perimeter.

Other parks

Parc de Bercy

Entrance on Rue de Bercy, Rue Jean Paul Belmondo, 12th
Ⓜ Bercy, Cour St Émilion

To the east of the Bastille, this is another of Paris' very modern parks, created in the 1990s on the north side of the river to offset the equally new Bibliothèque Nationale over on the south bank. Its striking design evokes the set geometry and formality of classic French garden design with a grid of crisscrossing paths between which there are flower, herb and vegetable gardens, some of which represent the four seasons, as well as shady pergolas and broader open spaces. The Bercy area as a whole has been at the centre of an intense flurry of regeneration in recent years with the transformation of former docks and warehouses into state-of-the-art visitor attractions including the Bercy Village shopping centre, the Palais Omnisports stadium with its brand-new public ice rink (see p.124) and, due to open in the next 2 years, the new Musée du Cinéma.

Parc des Buttes Chaumont

Entrances on Rue Botzaris, Rue Manin and Rue de Crimée, 19th
Ⓜ Buttes Chaumont, Botzaris

Situated in northeast Paris on the Buttes Chaumont hill, this area was a quarry until the 1860s, when the engineer Alphand made it into a park with a wonderfully imaginative, entirely manmade fantasy landscape. At its heart, there's an artificial lake with an equally purpose-built rocky island in the middle (reachable by two bridges), from the top of which there are great views of the city. It also contains an artificial cave complete with stalactites and stalagmites (remember, tights come down) out of which an artificial waterfall cascades, a couple of playgrounds, and donkey rides in summer.

Parc Monceau

Boulevard de Courcelles, 17th
Ⓜ Monceau

Only the Jardin du Luxembourg attracts greater numbers of well-dressed children on Sunday afternoons than this smallish park near the Grands Boulevards. The emphasis here is on elegance and formality, with neat lawns, neat children, neat gravel pathways and a tidy little pond. The park's most interesting features are its 18th- and 19th-century follies, which include a replica Egyptian pyramid and a Venetian-style bridge.

Parc Montsouris

Boulevard Jourdan, 14th
RER B2, B4 to Cité Universitaire

In the south of the city, the Parc Montsouris (literally 'Mount Mouse') has a special play area for children, a duck pond (also home to several turtles), a waterfall, a replica Moorish Palace and dozens of colourful flowerbeds.

Parc St Cloud

St Cloud
Ⓜ Pont de Sèvres, Boulogne–Pont de St Cloud

Finally, a Parisian park, where you are actually allowed to walk on the grass (or lie or run, or jump). It's just outside Paris proper (in the suburb of St Cloud, across the Seine by bridge from the end of two métro lines), but well worth a visit if you have time. Of course, being French, it's also pretty formal, with lots of landscaping, fountains and elegant shaded avenues – look out especially for the spectacular 'Grande Cascade' fountain, which is switched on every Sunday in June only at 2pm, 3pm and 4pm (to check times, call t 01 41 12 02 90). The castle that once overlooked the park was Napoleon's favourite Parisian residence, but was destroyed by fire in 1870.

Something different: Paris' cemeteries

As well as squares, woods and parks old and new, Paris also has some other, very distinctive open spaces that have been greatly appreciated for decades by lovers of atmospheric walks: its giant cemeteries. They may not seem the most obvious sightseeing destinations, especially not, perhaps, with kids, but the historic cemeteries of Paris – Montparnasse (see pp.94–95), Montmartre (see p.101) and above all Père Lachaise – are some of the

Could Jim Morrison get kicked out 'The Door'?

The lease on the grave of Père Lachaise's most famous modern 'resident' has expired and many locals would like to see him removed as his pilgrims have a tendency to deface surrounding headstones. Rumour has it, though, that the French government has designated the grave a heritage site, so he'll probably be staying put.

city's most individual, wistful and romantic places, with nothing sinister about them and plenty to inspire the imagination.

Cimetière du Père Lachaise

Boulevard de Ménilmontant, 20th
t 01 43 70 70 33
Ⓜ Père Lachaise
Open Daily 9am–5.30pm

Anyone coming to Père Lachaise looking for a little ghoulishness and gore will be sorely disappointed, and will be better off visiting the Catacombes (*see* p.94). Far from sombre, Paris' most famous cemetery is a romantic place, a beautiful, grassy, tree-lined space that has inside it, among its tombs and monuments, a real open-air sculpture museum, which kids love running around. Many of the country's most illustrious citizens are buried here, including Abelard and Héloise, Balzac, Delacroix, Proust and Edith Piaf, although it's the graves of international celebrities Oscar Wilde and Jim Morrison which nearly always attract the most attention (Chopin is also here, although fewer people take notice). Morrison's grave is covered in graffiti and has to have its own security guard. A map guiding you to all the most famous graves can be picked up at the front gates for €1.50 and guided tours are run by the Paris parks service (*see* p.34).

Sport and activities

Whether you want to take part or just watch, Paris has a sporting activity for you. At the moment, the most popular pastime with the kid-to-teen generation is rollerblading. Every Friday thousands of skaters gather at the Place d'Italie for an (officially sanctioned) 30km (18 mile) whizz through the Parisian streets. For something a little more sedate, head to the parks, many of which have public tennis courts and *boules* pitches. The most prestigious spectator sports are tennis (see the yearly star-studded French Open in May) and rugby (internationals are played at the state-of-the-art Stade de France, just north of the *périphérique*), although football has raised its profile following France's success in the 1998 World Cup and 2000 European Championship.

Allô Sports

t 01 42 76 54 54

A handy information phone line with details on all public sports facilities in Paris and upcoming sporting events. Most staff speak English.

Cycling

The world's most prestigious cycle race, the **Tour de France**, starts and finishes every July on the Champs-Élysées (*see* pp.37, 48). For places to hire bikes and bike city tours, *see* pp.32–33.

Football

Despite having won both the 1998 World Cup and 2000 European Championship, the French attitude towards football is ambivalent. It doesn't inspire the levels of fanatical support that it does in England, Germany, Spain and Italy and most of the country's top players ply their trade abroad. Still, Paris is home to one of France's most popular club sides, Paris St Germain (PSG), who play at the Parc des Princes stadium. International football (and rugby, *see* below) matches are played at the state-of-the-art Stade de France in the suburb of St Denis, north of the Paris *périphérique*, built for the 1998 World Cup and costing several billion francs.

Parc des Princes

24 Rue du Commandant Guilbaud, 16th

t 01 42 30 03 60
www.psg.fr (PSG website)
Ⓜ Port de St Cloud

The Parc des Princes is on the western edge of the city, just south of the Bois de Boulogne. Match tickets can be bought in advance through the PSG website and from the club shop at 27 Avenue des Champs Élysées.

Stade de France

Rue Francis de Pressensé, St Denis
t 01 55 93 00 00
www.stadedefrance.com
RER B3, B5 to La Plaine–Stade de France, D1 to Stade de France St Denis
Open Daily 10am–6pm (except during events)
Guided tours Daily 10am, 2pm, 4pm
Adm Adults €10, under-18s €8.50, under-12s €7, under-6s **free**

The 80,000 seat Stade de France was built in a record 31 months – just in time for French success in the 1998 World Cup. The 90-minute guided tour includes the stands, VIP box, changing rooms and entry tunnel, but be prepared to climb 200 steps.

Ice skating

There are four indoor ice rinks around Paris, one in the 19th *arrondissement,* one in Bercy, and two just outside the *périphérique* at Boulogne Billancourt and Asnières sur Seine (accessible by métro). The most picturesque (and central) place to skate is outside the Hôtel de Ville (*see* p. 38).

Patinoire Edouard Pailleron

30 Rue Edouard Pailleron, 19th
t 01 42 08 72 26
Ⓜ Bolivar
Skate rental available

Patinoire Sonja Henie

Palais Omnisports, 12th
t 01 40 02 60 60
www.bercy.fr
Ⓜ Bercy
Skate rental available

Rinks outside the *périphérique*

1 Rue Victor Griffuelhes, Boulogne Billancourt
t 01 46 94 99 74
Ⓜ Marcel Sembat

Boulevard Pierre de Coubertin
Asnières sur Seine
t 01 47 99 96 06
Ⓜ Gabriel Péri Asnières–Gennevilliers

Riding

There are miles of bridal paths in the Bois de Boulogne and Bois de Vincennes and your child will be able to go for short pony rides in many of the Parisian parks such as the Jardin d'Acclimatation and the Jardin du Luxembourg if you join a riding club. This is not much of a choice if you're only in town for a few days because memberships are usually available for a minimum of three months. However, if your stay is longer and you speak French, get in touch with one of these clubs, all of which offer tuition for all grades of riders from complete beginners or age 5 and over. A three-month course costs in the region of €200–230.

Centre Hippique du Touring
t 01 45 01 20 88

Cercle Hippique du Bois de Vincennes
t 01 48 73 01 28

Club Bayard Equitation
t 01 43 65 46 87

Rollerblading

The in-line skating craze has caught on hugely in Paris – you'll see rollerskaters and bladers on every pavement, road and in every park. Look out for the Friday night dash around Paris when up to 28,000 skaters hurtle around the streets for 3 hours in one noisy, spectacular mass. The route is arranged by Pari Roller (*see* below) and changes each week. If your kids need to 'find their feet', the Roller Squad Institut organizes tours and lessons for 7s and over.

La Main Jaune
Place de la Porte de Champerret, 17th
t 01 47 63 26 47
Ⓜ Porte de Champerret
Open Roller-skating rink: 2.30pm–7pm (Wed and Sat); rollerdisco: 10pm to dawn (Fri and Sat), 3pm–7.30pm (Sun)

Skate hire available

Ootini
73 Avenue de la République
t 01 43 38 89 63
www.ootini.com
Ⓜ Parmentier, St Maur
Open 2pm–7pm (Mon), 11am–7pm (Tues–Sat), closed Sundays
Dedicated skate shop.

Pari Roller
40 Avenue d'Italie, 13th
t 01 43 36 89 81
www.pari-roller.com
Informal organization that sets up a different mass-skating route around Paris for competent skaters every Friday evening (at 10pm from Place Raoul d'Autry). Check the website or phone for the start point and itinerary.

Rollers et Coquillages
23/25 Rue Jean Jacques Rousseau, 1st
t 01 44 54 94 42
www.rollers-coquillages.org
Organizes mass roller-trips for all levels of ability from Place de la Bastille at 2.30pm on Sundays.

Roller Squad Institut
7 Rue Jean Giono, 13th
t 01 56 61 99 61
www.rsi.asso.fr
The 'institute' runs free group trips for beginners and kids, most Saturdays at 3pm from Les Invalides.

Sport West
21 Rue des Quatre Cheminées, Boulogne–Billancourt
t 01 46 08 29 27
Ⓜ Marcel Sembat
Outside the Paris city limits in Boulogne-Billancourt, this shop hires out roller skates and protective pads (*between €4.50 and €13 a day*).

Rugby

Rugby is France's most popular team sport – the annual Six Nations matches inspire a huge level of commitment among French spectators. The matches, which pit France against England, Ireland,

Scotland, Wales and Italy, are played at the Stade de France in St Denis (*see* p.124).

Racing Club de Paris
Stade Yves de Manoir, 12 Rue François Faber, Colombes
t 01 47 86 19 61
www.racingclubdeparis.com
Ⓜ Gabriel Péri Asnières–Gennevilliers and bus 304
Paris' main rugby club.

Skateboarding

The steps, slopes and ramps of the Les Halles shopping centre, Trocadéro and La Défense attract young skateboarders, particularly at weekends. For something more structured, head out to the indoor skateboard-rollerskate park 'Rollerparc Avenue'.

Rollerparc Avenue
100 Rue Léon Geoffrey, Vitry sur Seine
t 01 47 18 19 19
www.rollerparc.com
RER Gare des Ardoines
Open School days: 4pm–12 midnight (Mon, Tues, Fri), 11am–12 midnight (Wed and Sat), 10am–8pm (Sun); school holidays: 11am–12 midnight (Mon–Wed, Fri–Sat), 11am–8pm (Thurs and Sun)
RER Adults €10, under-10s €8, board hire from €7
Indoor skate park with a 13m half-pipe, ramps, boxes and rails plus a skate shop.

Swimming

Admission to public pools generally costs around €3–5 for adults, with under-14s half-price.

Aquaboulevard
4 Rue Louis Armand, 15th
t 01 40 60 15 15
Ⓜ Balard
Open Daily 10am–8pm, until 12 midnight (Fri–Sat)
Adm Adults €20, under-11s €10, under-3s **free**; tickets are for a 4-hour session
A huge waterpark complex with a big-heated pool surrounded by an artificial beach, waterslides, a wave pool, a lagoon and a life-size hollow model of a whale. Permanently supervised by lifeguards.

Piscine des Halles
Centre Sportif Suzanne Belioux, Forum des Halles, 10 Place de la Rotonde, 1st
t 01 42 36 98 44
Ⓜ Les Halles
See pp.70–71 for more details.

Piscine Jean-Taris
16 Rue Thouin, 5th
t 01 43 25 54 03
Ⓜ Cardinal Lemoine

Piscine Armand-Massard
66 Boulevard du Montparnasse, 15th
t 01 45 38 65 19
Ⓜ Montparnasse–Bienvenüe

Piscine Émile-Anthoine
9 Rue Jean Rey, 15th
t 01 53 69 61 59
Ⓜ Bir Hakeim

Piscine Hébert
3 Rue des Fillettes, 18th
t 01 46 07 60 01
Ⓜ Marx Dormoy

Piscine Georges-Vallerey
148 Avenue Gambetta, 20th
t 01 40 31 15 20
Ⓜ Porte des Lilas

Tennis

There are over 170 municipal courts in Paris and your best chance of getting a game is just to turn up at a court and wait. Perhaps the most idyllic courts are those in the Jardin de Luxembourg. The **Allô Sports** phoneline (*see* p.124) will give you a full list of municipal courts. Rates are usually from €5.60 per hour for an outdoor court, €11 per hour for a covered court. In May, Paris holds the **French Open** at the Roland Garros stadium (*see* p.35).

Centre Sportif La Faluère
Route de la Pyramide, Bois de Vincennes, 12th
t 01 43 74 40 93
Ⓜ Chateau de Vincennes
This sports centre has 21 all-weather and asphalt tennis courts.

Days out

There's enough to do in Paris to last a lifetime, but that doesn't mean you can't pop out every so often. The 'big one' (Disneyland® Resort Paris) aside, here are some of many possible ideas for day trips from the city, all under 1 hour's drive away.

Versailles

Château de Versailles

t 01 30 83 78 00
www.chateauversailles.fr
Open Château: 9am–6pm Tues–Sun (May–Sept); 9am–5pm Tues–Sun (Oct–April); garden: daily
Adm Château: adults €7.50, under-18s **free**, after 3.30pm **free** to all; gardens **free**
Carte Musées et Monuments valid
Tourist information office (17 Rue des Réservoirs) at the north end of the château
Audioguides and guided tours in English, restaurant and snack bars in the gardens, shop
Some wheelchair access and adapted toilets
Suitable for all ages
Allow at least 2 hours

The Château of Versailles is a grand, over-the-top palace, worthy of any Disney hero. Kids will love its sheer excess, particularly the glittering Hall of Mirrors, the enormous gilt-covered Apollo Salon (or Throne Room) and the King's bedroom, where Louis XIV (the Sun King) would rise each day in full view of his entire court. The palace is too vast to be explored in a single day, so pick up an orientation map at the information booth and let it guide you to all the best bits. Once you've had your fill of sumptuous fixtures and fittings, head for the beautiful gardens to stretch your legs and have a

Versailles
Distance from Paris 20km (12.5 miles)
By car Versailles–Château exit off A13 motorway, about 14 miles west of Paris towards Rouen; traffic permitting, the drive should take about 30mins
Parking Available (for a fee) in the Place d'Armes in front of the château
By rail RER line C5 to Versailles–Rive Gauche; the station is 700m (766 yards) from the château. There are 60 trains a day (35 on Sunday); all display a four-letter code beginning with the letter 'V'.

Did you know?
In the 17th century, the 10,000-plus residents of the château, including King Louis himself, were expected to share just three toilets!

picnic overlooking the ornate fountains and flowerbeds. As with the château, the gardens, which contain two separate 'little' palaces – the **Grand Trianon** and **Petit Trianon** – are much too big to be explored on foot, and you will be better off taking a ride aboard the glass-sided sightseeing train (recorded commentary in several languages, including English). In summer you can hire rowing boats on the Grand Canal.

Some of the splendour of Royal Versailles is re-created in a firework spectacular, the **Grandes Fêtes de Nuit**, which takes place on several weekends in summer (July–Sept), and the **Grandes Eaux Musicales**, when the fountains are set in motion to musical accompaniment (April–Oct every Sunday). For more details of these events, see p.35.

The château is extremely popular and attracts over 3 million visitors a year (roughly 8,000 a day) so aim to get there early to avoid the crowds.

France Miniature

Distance from Paris 30km (18.5 miles)
By car From Paris take the A13 motorway, turn onto the A12 south and take the France Miniature exit
By rail SNCF train from La Défense or Gare Montparnasse to La Verrière, then local bus 411 Elancourt, St Quentin en Yvelines
t 01 30 16 16 30
www.franceminiature.com
Open Daily 10am–6pm (Mar–Nov); 10am–7pm (July–Aug); closed 3–7 Nov
Adm Adults €13, under-16s €9, under-4s **free**
Fast food restaurants, audioguides, souvenir shop
Wheelchair access and adapted toilets
Suitable for all ages

Around 10km (6 miles) further west, beyond Versailles, this Gallic Lilliput in relief contains some 160 exactly scaled miniature versions of France's most famous monuments, including the Eiffel Tower, Sacré Coeur and Nôtre Dame. The park took 53 architects and model-makers over 2 years to complete. Each model has been placed in its exact setting: every street, building and landmark has been painstakingly re-created; model boats, trains, cars, passengers and pedestrians complete the effect. Firework displays are held in summer.

Chantilly

Château de Chantilly

t 03 44 62 62 60
www.chateaudechantilly.com
Open 10am–6pm Mon, Wed–Sun (Mar–June,
Sept–Oct); daily 10am–6pm (July–Aug);
10.30am–12.45pm, 2pm–5pm (Mon, Wed–Fri),
10.30am–5pm Sat–Sun (Nov–Feb)
Adm Château and park: adults €7, under-18s €6,
under-11s €2, under-4s **free**; park only: adults €2.60,
under-11s €1.50, under-4s **free**
Carte Musées et Monuments valid
Gift shops, picnic areas
Wheelchair access and adapted toilets
Suitable for all ages

Standing proudly in the middle of a lake and
surrounded by landscaped gardens, the Château de
Chantilly is the fairy-tale castle of every child's

Chantilly
Distance from Paris 48km (30 miles)
By car Chantilly exit off A1 motorway, about 40km
north of Paris, or N16 highway direct
By rail SNCF from Gare du Nord to
Chantilly–Gouvieux; 40 trains daily. The château is
a short walk or taxi ride from the station.

dreams. However, in spite of its aged and romantic
appearance, the château is a (mostly) late 19th-
century construction. In fact, since the Middle Ages,
no fewer than five separate buildings have stood
on this spot and it was rebuilt twice in the 19th
century. The château now contains the **Musée
Condé**, a fine museum of Renaissance art with
works by Raphael, Botticelli and Poussin and a
repository of rare manuscripts.

The Le Nôtre-designed gardens, which contain a
lake where you can hire boats, fountains and even a
small population of wallabies, can be toured by foot,
aboard a 'petit train' or, in style, in a horse and cart.

Musée Vivant du Cheval

t 03 44 57 13 13
www.musee-vivant-du-cheval.fr
Open 10.30am–5.30pm Mon and Wed–Sun
(Mar–Oct), also 2pm–5pm Tues (July–Aug only);
2pm–5pm Mon, Wed–Sun (Nov–Feb),
10.30am–6.30pm (Sat–Sun)
Adm Adults €8, under-18s €6.50, under-12s
€5.50, under-4s **free**
Dressage demonstrations daily at 3.30pm
Wheelchair access
Suitable for all ages

Chantilly is the capital of French horse racing
and, from a child's perspective, the town may be
most worth visiting for its wonderful stables,
which have been turned into this museum. Here
you can meet and pet over 30 beautifully groomed
horses and find out all about the history of racing
in France. At 11.30am, 3.30pm, 5.15pm (3.30pm only,
Oct–April), there are dressage demonstrations.

Around Chantilly

To the south of the château lies the **Forêt de
Chantilly**, a giant wood with kilometres of pathways and nature trails that is hugely popular as a
picnic site. Further south, across on the eastern
side of the A1 *autoroute*, exit 7, there is the **Forêt
d'Ermenonville**, another of France's ancient forests
where, deep within its confines (you'll need a car),

Tell me a story:
Louis XIV shows who's who

Versailles was built in a fit of spite. In 1661 King
Louis XIV attended a party given by his finance
minister, Nicholas Fouquet, to celebrate the
completion of Fouquet's new home, the spectacular palace of Vaux le Vicomte. So majestic was
this new château, so ornate were its gardens, and
so lavish was the party (dishes were prepared by
France's foremost chef at the time, Vatel, and
served on gold and silver plates, while entertainment was laid on by Molière, France's favourite
playwright), that the young king was consumed
with jealousy, and decided there and then to build
himself something even more opulent.

A small hunting lodge southwest of Paris was
chosen as the site for Louis' grand project and
30,000 workers spent the next 20 years building
the largest and most extravagant palace France
had ever seen, capable of sleeping over 10,000
people (including 2,000 kitchen workers) and
surrounded by the most splendid gardens in
Europe. This, though, was more than just another
big palace: it was a statement of royal power. Louis
had been so stung by Fouquet's presumption that
he built Versailles in order to reaffirm his own
standing and to remind all who visited, including
upstart finance ministers, just who was top dog.

you'll find the **Mer de Sable/Jean Richard Showgrounds**. This 20-hectare (50-acre) sea of sand dunes boasts a children's entertainment complex themed loosely based on the Wild West with riding displays, Indian attacks, games and shows (open from 30 March until 29 September).

Parc Astérix

Distance from Paris 36km (22.5 miles) north
By car Exit Parc Astérix from A1 motorway
By rail RER line B3 to Aéroport Charles de Gaulle 1; from here Courriers Île de France buses run to the park every 30min 9.30am–1.30pm; buses return every 30min from 4.30pm until 30min after the park closes (adult return €5.35, child return €3.80)
t 03 44 62 34 34
www.parcasterix.fr
Open 10am–6pm Mon–Fri (April–June); 9.30am–7pm Sat–Sun (Sept–mid Oct); daily 9.30am–7pm (July–Aug)
Opening times vary: Nov–Mar (park closed) and some days in Sept–Oct, so check for details
Adm Adults (1-day ticket) €31, 3–11s €23; adults (2-day ticket) €56, 3–11s €40; under-3s **free**
Shops, restaurants, picnic areas, pushchair rental
Wheelchair access and adapted toilets
Suitable for all ages

   It may not have as many rides and attractions as Disneyland® Resort Paris, but Parc Astérix, just off the A1 *autoroute* between Paris and Chantilly, is very genuinely French. Astérix, the Roman-bashing Gaul, has long been France's most popular cartoon character and his adventures are one of its most successful exports – translated into over 40 languages. The theme park, a big hit with both locals and tourists, is divided into themed areas, including a Gaulish village, a Roman city and Ancient Greece, each inhabited by (rubber-suited)

cartoon characters. There are also lots of hair-raising rides including *Goudurix*, a terrifying looped rollercoaster. Elsewhere you can see live attractions such as swordplay demonstrations by musketeers.

Château de Thoiry

Distance from Paris 40km (25 miles)
By car exit Paris at Porte St Cloud, take the A13 west towards Versailles, then the A12 towards Saint-Quentin-en-Yvelines; exit at Bois d'Arcy, take the N12 to Pontchartrain and then the D11 to Thoiry
t 01 34 87 52 25
www.thoiry.tm.fr
Open Daily 10am–6pm (Easter–Sep); 10am–5pm (Oct–Easter)
Adm Adults €16, under-12s €12, under-3s **free**
Restaurants, picnic areas
Wheelchair access and adapted toilets
Suitable for all ages

   In the mid 16th century, Raoul Mareau, treasurer to the king of France, part-time alchemist and all-round oddball, acquired this estate at Thoiry with the intention of 'harnessing the forces of heaven and earth'. According to legend, the château de Thoiry has the same proportions as Cheops' Pyramid in Egypt and is positioned so that, on summer and winter solstices, the sun's rays form a 'bridge of light' in the central vestibule. It's an impressive sight when the sun illuminates the entire building like a lantern. Guided tours (in English) of the interiors are available. The main family attraction is the lavish 12,000 acre French and English-style gardens, a maze, a children's play-ground and a safari park with a drive-through African game reserve. There's even a walkaround section where you can see flying displays by birds of prey and wander through a tunnel leading right into the heart of the tiger enclosure. A children's menu is available in the château restaurant.

NEED TO KNOW

Accident and emergency
American Hospital in Paris
63 Bd Victor Hugo
Neuilly sur Seine
Ⓜ Anatole France/Pont de Levallois
t 01 46 41 24 24

Airport information
www.adp.fr
Orly airport
t 01 49 75 15 15
Roissy–Charles de Gaulle airport
t 01 48 62 22 80

Babysitting
Allô! Maman Poule
t 01 47 48 01 01

Children's hospitals
Hôpital Necker
149 Rue Sèvres, 15th
t 01 44 49 40 00

24-hour chemist
84 Av des Champs Élysées, 8th
t 01 45 62 02 41

24-hour dentist
Dental Emergency Service
t 01 43 37 51 00

English-speaking chemist
Pharmacy Swann
6 Rue Castiglione, 1st
t 01 42 60 72 96

Emergencies
Ambulance **t** 15
Emergency doctor **t** 01 47 07 77 77
First-aid/Ambulance (SAMU) **t** 15/**t** 01 45 67 50 50
Fire service **t** 18
Police **t** 17

Lost property office
Bureau des Objets Trouvés
36 Rue des Morillons, 7th
t 01 55 76 20 20

Police station (Préfecture de Police)
9 Bd du Palais, 4th
t 01 53 71 33 45
www.prefecture-police-paris.interieur.gouv.fr

Taxi
Taxis Bleus
t 01 49 36 10 10
www.taxis-bleus.com

Telephone information
Operator assistance
and French directory enquiries **t** 12
www.pagesjaunes.com
International Directory Enquiries
t 32 12, followed by the country code
(44 for UK, 1 for US)
Time (*horloge parlante*) **t** 36 99

Tourist information
Paris Tourist Office
t 08 92 68 31 12
www.paris-touristoffice.com

Transport information
RATP (Paris Transport Authority)
In English
t 08 36 68 41 14
In French
t 08 36 68 77 14/01 43 46 14 14
www.ratp.fr
www.parisvisite.tm.fr
SNCF (French National Railways)
t 08 36 35 35 35/01 53 90 20 20
www.sncf.fr

Weather information
t 08 36 68 02 75

Practical A–Z

New cultures can be frightening for children, who are often more deeply affected by changes to their familiar routine than adults, so it's good to know what's what: what temperatures to expect, where to buy medicines for common ailments, when you can expect to find things open, how to make a phone call, and so on. In fact, once you've been in the city a few days you'll find that, language difficulties aside, there's little about Paris that is wholly unfamiliar. And there's one very positive thing to bear in mind: despite its hustle and bustle, Paris is actually a good deal safer than most other cities of its size and stature.

Babysitters

If you fancy an evening out without the littl'uns in tow, finding a decent, reliable, trustworthy child-minder in a strange city can be a worrisome task. Thankfully, Paris has several reputable babysitting agencies. Most charge an agency fee (from around €7 to €12) in addition to the hourly rate (around €6) that goes to the sitter. If you're out after the last métro, you'll be expected to drive the sitter home or pay for a taxi.

Ababa
t 01 45 49 46 46
Good for a pinch, and usually able to get a sitter to you within an hour; many are English-speakers.

Allô! Maman Poule
t 01 47 48 01 01
One of the biggest agencies, certain to have an English speaker available (3hrs minimum).

The American Church
65 Quai d'Orsay, 7th
t 01 40 62 05 00
www.acparis.org
Ⓜ Invalides
Open 9am–10.30pm (Mon–Sat), 1pm–7pm (Sun)

> #### Good to know
> ► Small pushchairs (strollers) are allowed in most museums.
> ► High chairs are always available in chain restaurants.

There is a free notice board in the basement with lots of useful information for locating English-speaking babysitters and au pairs.

Avec Prositting
t 01 44 37 91 11
www.prositting.com
Excellent 24-hour service. Can usually get a sitter to you within 2 hours.

Babysitting Services
t 01 46 37 51 24
www.babysittingservices.com

Inter-Service Parents
t 01 44 93 44 88
www.epe-idf.com
A phone line service that provides lists of and information on babysitting agencies.

Kid Services
t 01 42 61 90 00
www.kidservices.fr

Sagad
t 01 45 42 29 29
www.sagad.com

Climate and when to go

With benefits and pitfalls turning up in each season, there is really no perfect time to visit Paris. Springtime usually brings the best of the weather, but the worst of the crowds; summer can be sweltering and sticky, and traffic fumes can reach alarming levels, but the city won't be as crowded; most Parisians continue to take their annual holiday in late July and August. The downside of this giant migration is that many shops and businesses of all sorts will also be closed (look for the congé annuel sign in the window). On the other hand, a number of children's attractions, including the fair in the Jardin des Tuileries, are only open in late spring and summer (generally April or May to September–October). Autumn, like Spring, tends to have good weather but there is extreme congestion with a multitude of trade fairs putting hotel beds at a premium. Winter can be as cold and gloomy as anywhere else in Northern Europe, but

Average temperatures		
	F	C
January	48	9
February	47	8
March	50	10
April	60	16
May	62	17
June	74	23
July	77	25
August	78	26
September	69	20
October	62	17
November	54	12
December	45	7

the city's attractions, shops and restaurants will all be open, but much less busy and, as the short days turn to night, the city takes on a special gleam with lots of extra events and entertainments around Christmas time. Take your pick.

Electricity

France's electricity supply runs on a 220-volt current. American visitors bringing 110-volt electrical appliances will need a voltage converter; visitors from the UK only need a standard European plug adaptor to cope with French round, two-pin plugs. If you need to stock up while you're in Paris, convertors and plugs are sold at BHV, 52–64 Rue de Rivoli, 1st, Ⓜ Louvre.

Embassies in Paris

Australia
4 Rue Jean Rey, 15th
t 01 40 59 33 00
www.austgov.fr
Ⓜ Bir Hakeim

Canada
35 Av Montaigne, 8th
t 01 44 43 29 00
www.dfair-maeci.gc.ca/canadaeuropa/france
Ⓜ Franklin D. Roosevelt

Ireland
4 Rue Rude, 16th
t 01 44 17 67 00
Ⓜ Charles de Gaulle-Étoile

New Zealand
7 Rue Léonard de Vinci, 16th
t 01 45 01 43 43
www.nzembassy.com/france
Ⓜ Victor Hugo

UK
36 Rue du Faubourg St Honoré, 8th
t 01 44 51 31 00
www.amb-grandesbretagne.fr
Ⓜ Concorde

USA
2 Av Gabriel, 8th
t 01 43 12 22 22
www.amb-usa.fr
Ⓜ Concorde

Families with special needs

Sadly, access to public transport for people with mobility problems is still less than ideal in Paris. Only bus routes 20, 85 and 88 and the Météor métro line (line 14) are fully accessible, although taxis are required by law to accept disabled travellers. The RATP and SNCF offer a *Compagnon de Voyage* service to help travellers needing assistance, but it isn't free: if you require someone to accompany a child (no younger than 3 years old), an adolescent or a disabled person during a trip by train, RER, métro or bus, contact the organization on t 01 45 83 67 77 and for the hardly giveaway price of €10 per hour they will provide you with a qualified helper.

National museums usually have good wheelchair access and offer free admission to disabled visitors: detailed information is available by Minitel, 3614 HANDITEL. An excellent specialized guide is also available in English, *Access in Paris*, with lots of practical, to-the-point information based on visits to Paris by a team of disabled people. Published by Quiller Press, it can be ordered for €7.50 (plus postage) from the **Access Project** (*see* p.136).

Association des Paralysés de France

22 Rue du Pere Guérain
t 01 44 16 83 83
www.apf.asso.fr
75013 Paris
    Publishes the *Guide 98*, listing cinemas,
museums and other facilities accessible to people
with limited mobility.

Association Valentin Haüy

Service des Ventes
AVH 5, Rue Duroc, 75007 Paris
t 01 44 49 27 27
www.avh.asso.fr
    Publishes a range of audio and Braille guides for
blind and partially sighted travellers.

Comité National Français de Liaison pour la Réadaptation des Handicapés (CNRH)

Service Publications
236 bis Rue de Tolbiac, 13th
t 01 53 80 66 66
    Provides information on access and facilities
throughout the city. It also publishes *Paris–Île de
France Pour Tous*, an all-purpose guide for disabled
people (€9.15 in France, €12.20 from abroad).

Disneyland® Resort Paris Guest Communications

BP 100, 77777 Paris
Marne la Vallée, Cedex 4
www.disneylandparis.com
UK Office PO Box 305, Watford
Hertfordshire, WD1 8TP
England
t 0870 503 0303
    Produces the *Disabled Guest Guide* (*see* p.247).

In the UK

Access Project

39 Bradley Gardens, London W13 3HE
t UK (0207) 250 3222
www.accessproject-phsp.org
    Distributes the excellent *Access in Paris* guide for
disabled travellers.

Council for Disabled Children

t (0207) 843 1900
www.ncb.org.uk/cdc
    Part of the National Children's Bureau, this is a
good source of information on travel health and
further resources.

Holiday Care Service

2nd Floor, Imperial Building, Victoria Road, Horley,
Surrey RH6 9HW
t (0129) 377 4535
    Provides information sheets for families with
disabilities. All sites have been visited and assessed
by Holiday Care representatives.

RADAR (Royal Association for Disability and Rehabilitation)

Unit 12 City Forum
250 City Road, London EC1V 8AF
t (0207) 250 3222
Open 8am–5pm (Mon–Fri)
    Produces excellent guide books and information
packs for disabled travellers.

Royal National Institute for the Blind

224 Great Portland Street, London W15 5TB
t (0207) 388 1266
    Advises blind people on travel matters.

In the US

American Foundation for the Blind

15 West 16th Street, New York, NY 10011
t (212) 620 2000; toll free **t** 800 232 5463

Mobility International

PO Box 3551, Eugene, Oregon 97403, USA
t (541) 343 1284

SATH (Society for the Advancement of Travel for the Handicapped)

347 Fifth Avenue, Suite 610, New York 10016
t (212) 447 7284

In Australia

ACROD (Australian Council for the Rehabilitation of the Disabled)

PO Box 60, Curtin Act 2605
t (02) 6283 3200
www.acrod.org.au

Insurance

    It's vital that you take out travel insurance before
your trip. This should cover, at a bare minimum,
cancellation due to illness, travel delays, accidents,
lost luggage, lost passports, lost or stolen belong-
ings, personal liability, legal expenses, emergency

flights and medical cover. Remember that you are not obliged to buy insurance from the same travel company that sold you your holiday, and it's always well worth shopping around. Most insurance companies offer free insurance to children under the age of 2 as part of the parents' policy. Consider also annual insurance policies, which can be especially cost-effective for families with two or more older children. When travelling, always keep the insurance company's 24-hour emergency number close to hand – if you have a mobile phone, it's worth storing it in the memory.

The most important aspect of any travel insurance policy is its medical cover. You should look for cover equivalent to around £5 million ($8 million). If a resident of the European Union, Iceland, Liechtenstein or Norway, you are entitled to the same medical treatment as French citizens (*see* **Medical Matters**, pp.138–139). In the US and Canada, you may find that your existing insurance policies give sufficient medical cover so always check these thoroughly before taking out a new one. Canadians, in particular, are usually covered by their provincial health plans. Few American or Canadian insurance companies will issue on-the-spot payments following a reported theft or loss.

Always report stolen or lost items to the police, however trivial, so that you can make a claim when you get back home. You will usually have to wait several weeks and engage in a hefty amount of correspondence with your insurance company before any money is forthcoming.

In the UK
Association of British Insurers
t (0207) 600 3333

The Insurance Ombudsman Bureau
t 0845 600 6666
The government-appointed regulator of the insurance industry, for any complaints.

ABC Holiday Extras Travel Insurance
t 0870 844 4020

Columbus Travel Insurance
t (0207) 375 0011

Endsleigh Insurance
t (0800) 028 3571

Medicover
t 0870 735 3600

World Cover Direct
toll free t 0800 365 121

North America
Access America
US and Canada t 1 866 807 3982

Carefree Travel Insurance
US and Canada t 1 800 323 3149

MEDEX Assistance Corporation
US t (410) 453 6300

Travel Assistance International
US and Canada t 1 800 921 2828

Useful websites
French Government Tourist Office
www.francetourism.com
www.franceguide.com
Paris Tourist Office
www.paris-touristoffice.com
Île de France Regional Tourist Office
www.paris-ile-de-france.com
Paris transport information
www.ratp.fr
www.parisvisite.tm.fr
Travelling with children in Paris
http://travelwithkids.miningco.com/travel/travel-withkids/msubparis.htm
http://travelwithkids.about.com
www.parisparis.com/fr/enfant
Online maps and local information
www.mappy.fr
Plan the best road routes through Europe.
www.pagesjaunes.com
Online version of the phone book plus maps.
www.paris-anglo.com
English language guide for Francophiles.
www.paridigest.com
English language guide to the city.
www.pariscope.fr
Web version of the weekly *Pariscope* entertainment guide, mostly in French.
www.paris.org
www.parisvoice.com
English Language magazine.
Disneyland® Paris
www.disneylandparis.com
The official site.

The internet

After a good deal of initial hesitation, the internet has finally caught on in France, and both *La Poste* (the post office) and the phone company France Télécom are pulling out the stops in an effort to provide access. Soon, it is promised, you will be able to check your email at any post office, but for the moment there are still, surprisingly, noticeably fewer places providing net access in Paris (net cafés, public net centres) than in other European capitals. France Télécom has set up several internet stations where people can learn how to use the internet, send email and access the web for an hourly fee (around €4.50). There's one at 35 Rue du Cherche Midi, 6th, **t** 01 40 51 96 16, Ⓜ Sèvres Babylone. It has also introduced a new public net access terminal called *Netanoo*, which accepts prepaid phone cards (50 or 120-unit Télécards). They're currently available at Inno super-market in Montparnasse, RATP Village Service (La Défense) and most *arrondissement* city halls. Some of the most useful net cafés are listed below.

There are, however, endless internet sites with information about Paris, and a few official and unofficial sites about Disneyland® Resort Paris. *See* p.137 for the address of the official site.

Café Orbital
13 Rue de Médicis, 6th
t 01 43 25 76 77
www.cafeorbital.com
Ⓜ Odéon
Snug, small-scale cybercafé.

Cyberport Forum des Images
Forum des Halles, Porte St Eustache, 1st
t 01 44 76 63 44
Ⓜ Châtelet Les Halles
One of the most pleasant internet cafes in Paris. The first 30 minutes of connection cost €4.50; there's a nice bar serving drinks and sandwiches.

Easyinternet shop
37 Boulevard Sébastopol, 1st
t 01 40 41 09 10
www.easyeverything.com
Ⓜ Châtelet Les Halles
Centrally placed branch of the international 'Easyeverything' chain, with two more in Paris and more planned. Never the cosiest of net cafés, but the rates (from €1.50 an hour) are the best in town.

Le Web Bar
32 Rue de Picardie, 3rd
t 01 42 72 66 55
www.webbar.fr
Ⓜ Temple
Located in an old silver workshop, this net bar has become one of the trendiest spots in Paris. People not only come here to get online but also for concerts, exhibitions and fashion shows.

Lost property

Bureau des Objets Trouvés
36 Rue des Morillons, 7th
t 01 55 76 20 20
Ⓜ Convention
Open 8.30am–7pm (Mon, Wed, Fri), 8.30am–8pm (Tues and Thurs)
You will need to visit in person in order to fill out a form stating when and where you lost your item.

Maps

Michelin's *Paris Plan 14* is easily the best map of the city, while their *Environs de Paris 106* is equally good for day trips into the outskirts. Most stationery shops sell the *Plan de Paris*, the equiva-lent of the *London A–Z*, which details every single street, station and monument in the French capital. You can pick up free bus, night bus and métro route maps at any métro station (especially the RATP's very useful *Petit Plan de Paris*).

WH Smith – The English Bookshop
248 Rue de Rivoli, 1st
t 01 44 77 88 99
www.whsmith.fr
Ⓜ Concorde

Medical matters

Emergency Medical Service
t 15

24-hour call-out doctor
t 01 47 07 77 77

Dental Emergency
t 01 43 37 51 00

Anti-Poison Centre
t 01 40 37 04 04

Visitors from the European Union, Iceland, Liechtenstein and Norway are entitled to the same medical treatment as French citizens so long as they carry with them the appropriate validated form (the E111 form, for EU nationals). This covers families with dependent children up to the age of 16 (or 19, if in full-time education), and is available in the UK free of charge from post offices and health centres. Medical care, dental treatment and prescriptions (*ordonnances*) must be paid for up-front in France; 75–80 per cent of costs will be reimbursed at a later date. This can be a time-consuming procedure, however, and you're well advised to take out travel insurance with 100 per cent medical cover before you go (*see* **Insurance**, p.136). Nationals of non-EU countries should take out full travel insurance with medical cover before leaving home.

English-speaking hospitals
The American Hospital in Paris
63 Boulevard Victor Hugo, Neuilly sur Seine
t 01 46 41 25 25
Ⓜ Anatole France/Pont de Levallois

The Hertford British Hospital
3 Rue Barbès Levallois Perret
t 01 46 39 22 22
Ⓜ Anatole France

Pharmacies
French pharmacists are highly trained and can prescribe a wide range of drugs and provide a good deal of medical advice. Staff can carry out basic medical services such as cleaning and bandaging wounds (for a small fee), and indicate the nearest doctor on duty or supply a list of local doctors. Pharmacies are identified by a green neon cross.

24-hour Pharmacies
84 Avenue des Champs Elysées, 8th
t 01 45 62 02 41
Ⓜ George V
13 Place de la Nation, 11th
t 01 43 73 24 03
Ⓜ Nation

First-aid kit
Whenever and wherever you're travelling, you should always carry a first-aid kit with you. In Paris, this might contain:
► antiseptic cream and wipes
► aspirin and junior aspirin
► calamine lotion and aloe vera gel (for soothing burns, bites and stings)
► decongestant
► diarrhoea remedy and oral rehydration sachets
► high factor, zinc-based sunscreen
► lip salve
► paracetamol, tylenol or equivalent
► plasters (band aids), both fabric and waterproof
► pre-sterilized, disposable syringe and needle
► scissors
► sore-throat pastilles
► sterile wound dressings and bandages
► a thermometer
► a torch
► travel sickness preparations
► tweezers

English-speaking pharmacies
Pharmacy Swann
6 Rue Castiglione, 1st
t 01 42 60 72 96
Ⓜ Tuileries
British and American Pharmacy
1 Rue Auber, 9th
t 01 47 42 49 40
Ⓜ Auber, Opéra

Money and banks

Yes, its true: France's currency is no longer the historic franc but the European single currency, the *euro*, the symbol for which is €. Euro coins and notes finally made their appearance on the streets of the continent on 1 January 2002 and, in France, the franc ceased to be accepted as legal tender on 17 February 2002. If you have any leftover francs, you can exchange them at offices of the Banque de France.

Each euro (equivalent to 6.56 French francs) is divided into 100 cents. There are eight euro coins, for 1, 2, 5, 10, 20 and 50 cents and 1 and 2 euros, and seven notes, for 5, 10, 20, 50, 100, 200 and 500 euros. The notes are entirely uniform throughout the continent, but euro coins have a common design on one side (with the amount, 5, 10 cent and so on) and a design specific to each country on the other. However, all euro coins can be used equally in any of the 12 eurozone countries.

Most shops and restaurants accept all the big name credit and debit cards – Visa, Delta, Mastercard, American Express, Barclaycard, etc. – and nearly all French automatic cash dispensers (known as DABs, *distributeurs automatiques de billets*) will dispense money on foreign credit or bank cards linked to the international cirrus and maestro network (for which there will be a handling fee). Your bank's international banking department should be able to advise you on this.

Banks are generally open 9am–5pm (Mon–Fri), although some are also open on Saturday mornings. All are closed on public holidays. Travellers cheques can be changed at any bank or *bureau de change* for a commission. The Banque de France usually gives the best rates and hotels and train stations the worst.

Carrying money around with you

For safety, use a money belt around your waist under a tucked-in shirt or T-shirt. Pickpocketing is rife in certain parts of Paris, especially in the busy shopping areas like Les Halles and around the major stations, but it's a very skilful pickpocket who is able to undress you without you noticing. Otherwise, always keep wallets in trouser pockets, and hold purses and bags close to your body.

Bureaux de change
Chèquepoint
150 Av des Champs Élysées, 8th
t 01 42 56 48 63
Open 24 hours a day

Thomas Cook
52 Av des Champs Élysées, 8th

t 01 42 89 80 32
Open 8.30am–11pm
There are also branches at all six Paris mainline railway stations.

Travelex
Roissy airport
t 01 48 64 37 26
Open 6.30am–10.30pm
Orly airport
t 01 49 75 89 25
Open 6.30am–10.30pm

Lost credit cards
American Express
t 01 47 77 72 00

Mastercard/Visa
t 08 92 70 57 05

Diner's Club
t 08 10 31 41 59

Lost travellers' cheques
American Express
t 01 47 14 50 00

National holidays
There are 12 French national holidays when banks, shops, museums and businesses close, but the métro, cinemas and most restaurants stay open.
► 1 January
► Easter Sunday
► Easter Monday
► 1 May
► 8 May (VE Day)
► May (Ascension Day)
► June (Pentecost)
► 14 July (Bastille Day)
► 15 August (Assumption)
► 1 November (All Saints' Day)
► 11 November (First World War Armistice)
► 25 December (Christmas Day)

French school holidays
► Autumn half-term: 1 week, end of Oct
► Christmas: about 2 weeks
► Spring half-term: 1 week, February
► Easter: 1–2 weeks, April
► Summer: end of June until Sept

National holidays

The French have a healthy attitude to public holidays, known as *'faire le pont'*: often when a holiday falls on a Wednesday, many people take the Thursday and/or Friday off as well, to link it to the weekend. Watch out for this as it might mean that shops are closed.

School holidays

Bear in mind that the spring holidays in France revolve around the skiing season, so they seem to last for weeks on end: the country is divided up into three zones and the holidays are staggered so that the resorts can cope with the invasion of future champions. The dates given in the box (*see* opposite) should only be used as guidelines.

Necessities

Wherever you're travelling with kids, it is always worth taking a packet of wet wipes, a full change of clothing, toys to fiddle with, drinks and snacks, plus some empty, disposable bags for unforeseen eventualities. It's also a good idea to have a multi-blade pocket knife, but if you're travelling by plane, in view of current security concerns, remember to pack it in your main luggage rather than carry it in hand baggage or a coat pocket.

Packing: the bare necessities
There are a few things that always come in handy, wherever in the world you travel:
- ► an extension cord
- ► matches
- ► moisturizing cream
- ► needle and thread
- ► a night light
- ► safety pins
- ► mild soap and baby shampoo
- ► a net shopping bag
- ► a roll of sticky tape
- ► a torch or flashlight
- ► travel plug-socket converters

Opening hours

The traditional opening hours for shops and businesses are from Monday to Saturday between 9am or 10am and 7pm or 8pm, although there are various exceptions: large department stores tend to be open 9.30am–6.30pm, Monday to Saturday, with a couple of days for late opening until 9pm–10pm. A declining number of shops are closed on Monday as well as Sunday (which used to be common practice), but quite a few shops still open later than usual on Mondays, around midday. Supermarkets (*supermarchés*) are usually open on Monday. It's still the case that very, very few shops in Paris are open on Sundays, except for bakers (*boulangeries*) and cake shops (*pâtisseries*) which, by tradition, open on Sunday mornings and all day Monday, so some essential needs are catered for. Permanent street markets are open morning and afternoon (including Sunday morning, but not Monday), while travelling food markets are usually only open during the week, and begin winding down around noon. Flea markets, meanwhile, are only morning affairs, and are always open for business on Sundays, and some mornings in the week.

The branch of the **Monoprix** supermarket at 52 Avenue des Champs Élysées, 8th, **t** 01 53 77 65 65, is open 9am–12 midnight, Monday to Saturday, and is a very useful call-in when other stores are shut.

Most national museums are closed on Tuesdays, apart from science museums, which close on Mondays. Private museums are more erratic in their closing days (generally Sunday or Monday).

Post offices

Main post office
52 Rue du Louvre, 1st
t 01 43 25 76 77
Ⓜ Louvre-Rivoli
Open 24 hours daily

Most French post offices (ask for *La Poste* or *Le bureau de poste*) are open Monday to Friday between 8am and 7pm, and on Saturday between 8am and 12 noon. Because post offices handle a whole array of tasks on top of their postal duties – including providing savings accounts, wire transfer of funds, retirement plans, investment plans and mortgages – queues are often very long, and performing a relatively simple task such as posting a parcel can sometimes take over half an hour. In fact, when you visit you may find that only a couple of windows (*guichets*) are being used for normal postal functions – and woe betide you if you join the wrong queue. Look for signs saying *Envoi de Lettres et Paquets* or *Toutes Opérations*.

There's no need to go to a post office just to send a letter or postcard as stamps can be bought from any tobacconist (*tabac*) or supermarket. To send a letter or postcard up to 20g anywhere in France or the EU costs €0.50, to America €0.70.

French postcodes are five digits long. In Paris the first two are 75, the *département* number for the Seine, while the last two correspond to the appropriate *arrondissement* or district; so that 75001 is the 1st *arrondissement*, 75019 the 19th, etc. All postcodes within Paris have been abbreviated in English to 1st, 2nd, etc. in this guide, but you will also see them written in the French equivalents, 1e, 2e, and so on.

Safety and crime

Police

t 17

Fire Service

t 18

Paris, by today's standards, is a very safe city with little violent crime, few street muggings and a strong police presence (both visible and invisible; hordes of plain-clothes policemen stalk the streets tackling everyone from drug dealers to fare dodgers). The crime you are most likely to fall victim to – if it happens, which is not at all inevitable – is petty thievery of the pickpocketing, breaking-into-cars variety, and you should always take extra care with your valuables when in busy shopping districts (especially flea markets), on the métro or wherever crowds gather to watch performances by street artists. In particular, look out for groups of ragged-looking children who may be working the streets as part of a pickpocket gang. Never leave valuables in your car.

If you are a victim of a crime, report it to the nearest police station as soon as possible in order

The golden rules

▶ Don't leave valuables in your hotel room.
▶ Keep most of your money in travellers' cheques.
▶ Keep all your valuables in a money belt fastened around your waist under a tucked shirt or T-shirt.
▶ Only keep small amounts of money in your wallet or purse. Avoid keeping your wallet in your trouser pocket and hold purses and bags close to the body with the flap facing towards you and the strap over your shoulder.
▶ When you sit down at a pavement café, never ever put your bag down where you can't see it, either on the ground or (**especially**) hanging on the back of your chair.
▶ Steer clear of unfamiliar areas of the city late at night.
▶ Avoid travelling alone on the métro late at night.

to get the form needed for your insurance claim. You will need to make a statement (*procès verbal*) at the *commissariat* in the *arrondissement* in which the crime was committed. To locate the appropriate *arrondissement*, you can phone the Préfecture Centrale, **t** 01 53 71 53 71. If your passport has been stolen, you will also need to contact your consulate, who should be able to arrange emergency travel documents to tide you over.

Always carry your passport with you, preferably in a money belt or similar secure device. According to French law, French police can demand to see the ID of anyone they don't like the look of anytime they feel like it. The more hippyish or nonconformist you look, the less likely they are to like it.

Of course, when travelling with children, you need to be extra vigilant at all times. When on the streets or in a crowded place, always keep your children in front of you and continually make a head count. In the event that you do get separated, encourage your children to remain in one place and wait for you to find them. It is a good idea to supply youngsters with a whistle to blow in case they lose sight of you in a crowd. A bright cap or jacket makes them much easier to spot. If you have more than one child, colour match their clothes so that you only have one thing to watch out for. Older children may be trusted enough to explore by themselves, within bounds. Even so, always establish a central, easy-to-find meeting place, or maybe give them a spare métro ticket to keep for emergency use so they can use it to get back to the hotel. Ensure your children carry identification on them at all times (ID bracelets are a good idea) and make sure you have an up-to-date photograph of them, too, just in case.

Smoking

Many restaurants and cafés will be smokier than you may feel is healthy for your children. The French tend to ignore laws they don't like, or consider stupid, and that includes much of the anti-smoking legislation passed in the early 1990s. Although some restaurants do have proper, sectioned off no-smoking areas, in many of the smaller eateries the no-smoking section may just be a single table located by the lavatory and (just in case) furnished with an ashtray. Eating al fresco is not just the groovier alternative, it can also be considerably healthier. Smoking is banned on public transport, in cinemas and theatres.

Telephones

Coin-operated public phones are now few and far between in Paris, which means that you need to invest in a *télécarte* (phonecard), available at any tobacco shop (*tabac*), métro station, train station or post office. A 50-unit card will cost €7.40, a 120-unit card €14.75.

French phone numbers have 10 digits – there are no area codes so you must dial all 10 from anywhere in France. Paris and Île de France numbers begin with 01. If ringing Paris from abroad, dial the international code for France, 33, and then the Paris number, but omit the initial 0.

To make an international call from Paris, dial 00 followed by the country code (UK **44**, US and Canada **1**, Ireland **353**, Australia **61**, New Zealand **64**), then the local code (minus the 0 for UK numbers) and finally the number.

France Télécom has an English-speaking free phone customer information line, **t** 08 00 36 47 75.

The minitel

France Télécom's Minitel 1980s-vintage phone-line information service is fast being superseded by the worldwide internet, but many hotels here are still Minitel-equipped, and most post offices offer use of the terminals (which are like small computers) for telephone directory enquiries (Minitel 3611). There are also Minitel numbers through which you can make hotel and travel reservations, look up local addresses and get airline and train information and weather forecasts. Minitel directory use is free for the first 3 minutes, and costs around six cents per minute thereafter. For the English directory dial 3611, wait for a beep and press Connexion, then type MGS and *Envoi* followed by *Minitel en anglais*.

Time

Paris is 1 hour ahead of London (GMT), 6 hours ahead of New York, 9 hours ahead of California but 9 hours *behind* Tokyo and Sydney. The French tend to use the 24-hour clock when writing and speaking.

Tipping

A 15 per cent service charge is usually added to the bill in restaurants and cafés, and you need only tip above this if the service or food was particularly outstanding. Taxi drivers will be happy with a 10% tip, cinema ushers with 50 cents.

Toilets

The famous holes in the ground, as featured in the nightmares of generation after generation of British schoolchildren, have now largely disappeared from French bars, railways stations and the like – although you'll probably still find the odd backstreet café and restaurant, where you can indulge in a nostalgic squat (children, of course, are always convinced they're going to fall down the hole; some even do). Most museums, shops and restaurants have decent facilities, and the public toilets beneath the Place de la Madeleine with their Art Nouveau stairway and chic interiors, are worth a visit in themselves. The centrepiece is the shoeshine chair, a very good spot for a well-deserved rest.

These days many Paris streets also boast hi-tech superloos in place of the traditional sidewalk *urinoirs*. The new electronic toilets, the creation of the Décaux Company, cost €0.30 for 15 minutes and are automatically sanitized after each visit. Before you get too settled, however, do make sure that some delinquent hasn't run off with all the toilet paper.

Tourist information

Montmartre also has its own little tourist office, the Syndicat d'Initiative (*see* p.102).

Paris Convention and Visitors' Bureau
127 Av des Champs Élysées
t 08 92 68 31 12 (€0.34/minute)
www.paris-touristoffice.com
Ⓜ Charles de Gaulle-Étoile
Open Daily 9am–8pm (May–Sept); 9am–8pm Mon–Sun (Oct–April); 11am–7pm (public holidays)

Paris' excellent main tourist office is located a short distance from the Arc de Triomphe, a little way down the Champs Élysées heading back towards the centre of town. The staff are multilingual and provide a mountain of information about events, museums, restaurants and more in the city, as well as some general information on places around Paris in the Île-de-France. The office also has a souvenir shop, a bureau de change and a hotel reservation service that can book a room for the same day, and sells métro and bus tickets, phonecards, museum cards, and tickets for theatres, museums, tours and other attractions. It's closed on only one day each year – 1 May.

Branch offices
Eiffel Tower
t 01 45 51 22 15
Open Daily 11am–6.40pm (May–Sept only)
Gare de Lyon
t 01 45 26 94 82
Open 8am–8pm (Mon–Sat)

Espace Régional du Tourisme d'Île de France
Carrousel du Louvre, 99 Rue de Rivoli, 1st
t 08 03 80 80 00
From outside France **t** 01 44 50 19 98
www.paris-ile-de-france.com
Ⓜ Palais Royal–Musée du Louvre
Open Daily 10am–7pm

The tourist authority for the Île de France (Paris and its surrounding region) is the best source of information on anywhere in the small towns and countryside around Paris, but also has city maps and sells the full range of Paris transport tickets and museum cards, and has a hotel and tour booking service. The office is also more central than the Paris city office, right next to the Louvre.

Branch office
Marne la Vallée–Chessy RER station
Open Daily 9am–7pm
By the station for Disneyland® Resort Paris.

In the UK
French Tourist Office
Maison de la France, 178 Piccadilly, London W1V 0AL
t 0906 824 4123
www.franceguide.com

In the USA
French Tourist Office
444 Madison Avenue, 16th Floor, New York, NY 10022
t (212) 838 7800
9454 Wiltshire Boulevard, Beverley Hills, CA 90212
t (310) 271 6665
www.francetourism.com

Sleep

Finding family accommodation in Paris can be difficult, especially for large families (many hotels are not insured to take more than three people in one room), but it's not the impossible task that some guidebooks make out. Many chains pride themselves on their family service and Paris contains a range of hotels that offer good deals for families, often including free accommodation for under-12s, babysitting, cots and connecting rooms.

Official star hotel ratings (1 to 4) are shown in this chapter, but the French classification system allotts stars according to a checklist of facilities (not taking into account the character or quality of service), so the number of stars is not always a good guide to the attractiveness of a hotel. The room rates shown here, as is usual in French hotels, only cover the price of the room. Breakfast is charged separately. In b & b accommodation, however (see pp.150–151), breakfast is included.

Hotel booking services

The main **tourist office** at 127 Avenue des Champs Élysées (see p.144) has all kinds of hotel brochures and can book rooms for you. Rooms in Paris can also be booked online through a growing number of websites. For hotels in and around Disneyland Paris, see pp.239–244.

www.france-hotel-guide.com
Attractive hotels throughout the country.

www.myhotelinparis.com
A site used by many of the more interesting, independent town hotels.

www.hoteldiscount.com
Good rates on hotels of 2 stars and up with a freephone line in Europe on **t** 0800 1066 1066 and in the US on **t** 1 800 364 0801.

www.parishotels-discount.com
Free hotel reservation service.

www.paris.nethotels.com
Can book nearly 800 Paris hotels with a special 'family-friendly' list. The phone line in France is **t** 01 58 64 51 90.

The big chains

Hotels that are part of large chains are nearly always a safe bet for families. They may often be standardized and a bit impersonal, but you can guarantee that the rooms will be clean and well equipped, and the staff well trained.

Holiday Inn
Central Reservations in France t 08 00 91 08 55
In UK **t** 0800 897 121
www.france.sixcontinentshotels.com
The family-friendly US-based favourite operates 12 hotels in central Paris. The Place de la République branch can offer dedicated kids' suites while at the Porte de Saint Ouen branch, just outside the city centre, kids eat for free.

Ibis
Central Reservations in France t 01 60 87 91 00
In UK **t** 020 8283 4550
www.hotel-ibis.com
Most of Paris' 40 Ibis hotels are located on the edge of the city. They're a functional, good-value standbys for business travellers in France but also cater well for families.

Novotel
Central Reservations in France t 08 25 88 00 00
In UK **t** 020 8283 4500
www.novotel.com
Novotel is perhaps the most child-friendly of all the chains, having decided to consult its younger guests on how best to improve facilities. Since then, the chain has come up with a number of new features including: welcome packs for different age groups, soft drinks in the rooms and cost-cuts for parents. Kids stay for free in their parents' room (and also get breakfast for free) and most hotels also have an outdoor play area and some even have a pool. All Novotel restaurants offer a children's menu and have a special 'children's corner' where kids can go after they've finished eating to allow their parents to enjoy their meal in peace.

There are nine Novotels in central Paris – including in Bercy, Les Halles, Tour Eiffel and Gare de Lyon – plus more on the outskirts of the city.

Les Relais de Paris
38 Boulevard Magenta, 10th
t 01 44 52 75 55
www.lesrelaisdeparis.fr

When hotel-hunting, look out for...

▶ Special family packages and other discounts
▶ Interconnecting rooms (for older children)
▶ Babysitting services
▶ Separate children's mealtimes
▶ Children's menus
▶ Availability of books, games and toys

Founded in 1999, this new but growing chain operates six 2- and 3-star hotels around central Paris, most of them located in old buildings with a bit of character, which have all been fully and comfortably refurbished with modern facilities. Room rates are in the inexpensive range at around €78–105 for doubles. Family rooms are available and the Relais provides an attractive and convenient option for anyone looking for affordable rooms in the centre of Paris.

Sofitel

t 01 53 05 05 05
www.sofitel.com

The rapidly expanding Sofitel chain has some 14 upscale hotels in Paris, divided between the already comfortable but more business-like main Sofitel hotels and the Sofitel Demeure sub-chain, which is more opulent, leisurely in style and consists mostly of long-established luxury hotels that have been renovated by the chain without losing their traditional character. All Sofitel Demeures also have restaurants supervised by one of France's grandest modern chefs, Alain Ducasse. You'll find Sofitels just off the Champs Élysées, Sofitel Paris Arc de Triomphe, **t** 01 53 89 50 50, and Sofitel Paris Champs Élysées, **t** 01 40 74 64 64, and, within walking distance of the Eiffel Tower, Sofitel Demeure Le Parc, **t** 01 44 05 66 66, and Sofitel Demeure Baltimore, **t** 01 44 34 54 54.

Hotels

These hotels are divided according to the price of a double room (usually without breakfast):
Expensive/luxury over €200 a night
Moderate €100–200 a night
Inexpensive under €100 a night

Expensive/luxury

★★★★ Four Seasons Hôtel George V

31 Avenue George V, 8th
t 01 49 52 70 00 **f** 01 49 52 70 10
www.fourseasons.com
Ⓜ George V
Double rooms €650–880
Suites €1,199–9,000

Just off the Champs Élysées (see pp.47–48), the prestigious George V is superbly located in the city's most fashionable quarter and within a short walk of all the major sites. Built in the 1920s, this oasis of calm and sophistication has staff who go out of their way to please each junior guest. In addition to a stunning pool, the child-friendly services include a room service kid's menu, a babysitting service and, in your room, game consoles with a choice of games, children's videos, cots, high chairs, pushchairs/strollers, mini-bathrobes and slippers plus your choice of Bulgari child and babycare products. Disneyland passports (aka tickets) (see pp.181, 188) are available from reception as are printed lists of all the child-friendly attractions, shops and restaurants local to the area.

★★★★ Hôtel Lancaster

7 Rue de Berri, 8th
t 01 40 76 40 76 **f** 01 40 76 40 00
www.hotel-lancaster.fr
Ⓜ George V
Double rooms €399–550
Suites €750–1,599

An exclusive but homely feel, a sumptuous setting and exceptional service characterize this classic town-house hotel. Just off the Champs Élysées (see pp.47–48), it was a one-time favourite of Grace Kelly and Marlene Dietrich. It's studded with fine paintings and antiques but the Lancaster nevertheless also dotes on its junior guests. Staff go out of their way to indulge children with toys, babysitting, movies, flexible menus and charming smiles all round.

★★★★ Hôtel Le Montalembert

3 Rue de Montalembert, 7th
t 01 45 49 68 68 **f** 01 45 49 69 49
www.montalembert.com
Ⓜ Rue du Bac
Double rooms €320–440
Suites €450–750

A pioneer of the design hotel trend in Paris, just off Boulevard St Germain in the most fashionable part of Left Bank Paris (see p.82), the Montalembert is a stunning combination of contemporary style and grand Parisian 19th-century architecture. The Louvre, Musée d'Orsay and many of the city's finest shops are within walking distance. Also, in spite of its high-style image, cots, babysitting, high chairs, videos, bottle-warming machines and baskets of children's toys are available. Plus, whenever the hotel puts a cot in a room, a plush teddy bear is included for children to sleep with or keep as a souvenir. At reception you can also pick up a list of children's activities.

★★★★ Relais Saint Germain

9 Carrefour de l'Odéon, 6th
t 01 44 27 07 97   **f** 01 46 33 45 30
www.ehi.com/travel
Ⓜ Odéon
Double rooms €250–350

One of the more intimate hotels in this price bracket, the Relais, in the heart of the Latin Quarter (see pp.93–94),offers 22 spacious rooms which have all been individually decorated with a combination of antiques and high-standard modern services. Some have kitchenettes, making them excellent for families, and prices are very reasonable.

★★★★ Terrass Hotel

12 Rue Joseph de Maistre, 18th
t 01 46 06 72 85   **f** 01 42 52 29 11
www.terrass-hotel.com
Ⓜ Place de Clichy, Abbesses
Double rooms €225–250
Suites €302

Highly recommended: ask for one of its three junior suites, decorated in delightful harlequin colours. Under-13s stay for free in their parents' room while older children can stay in an interconnecting room. The restaurant is also very family-friendly with beautiful views of the city from the seventh-floor terrace, which becomes a dining area in summer. It's in Montmartre (see pp.97–104) and prices are more reasonable than you're likely to pay for this quality of accommodation in the centre of town.

Moderate

★★★ Hôtel de Fleurie

32–34 Rue Grégoire de Tours, 6th

t 01 53 73 70 00   **f** 01 53 73 70 20
www.hotel-de-fleurie.tm.fr
Ⓜ Odéon
Double rooms €160–250

A friendly and popular family-run hotel in the Latin Quarter (see pp.93–94) with antique furniture in the rooms. It has some interconnecting rooms for families and under-12s stay for free.

★★★ Hôtel des Grands Hommes

17 Place du Panthéon, 5th
t 01 46 34 19 60   **f** 01 43 26 67 32
www.hoteldesgrandhommes.com
Ⓜ Maubert Mutualité
Double rooms €113–213

Good value mid-range hotel near the Panthéon in the Latin Quarter (see pp.93–94) with antique furnishings, exposed wood beams and a literary reputation – André Breton and other surrealists honed their ideas here in the 1920s. Nowadays, babysitting is available, and there are great views from the sixth-floor balconies.

★★★ Hôtel Lenox Montparnasse

15 Rue Delambre, 14th
t 01 43 35 34 50   **f** 01 43 20 46 64
www.paris-hotel-lenox.com
Ⓜ Vavin
Double rooms €120–142

One of the more enjoyable hotels in the Montparnasse area (see pp.94–95) with beautiful furniture and fittings (including fireplaces in some rooms) and a family-friendly atmosphere.

★★★ Hôtel de l'Université

22 Rue de l'Université, 7th
t 01 42 61 09 39   **f** 01 42 60 40 84
www.hoteluniversite.com
Ⓜ St Germain des Prés
Double rooms €155–250

The Université occupies a delightfully refurbished historic town house, although its fashionable St Germain location (see p.94) also means that its rates are slightly higher than other hotels of a similar standard. There are reduced rates for kids sharing with their parents.

★★ Hôtel du Vieux Marais

8 Rue du Plâtre, 4th
t 01 42 78 47 22   **f** 01 42 78 34 32
www.paris-hotel-vieux-marais.com
Ⓜ Hôtel de Ville
Double rooms €106–130

A popular Marais (see p.67) hotel in a lovely location on an atmospheric old street. The bright, well-kept rooms have been redecorated in the last few years and staff are helpful. It doesn't have the facilities of some newer hotels and so has only 2 official stars, but all rooms have TV, telephone and en-suite bathrooms. Cots can be provided.

★★★ Novotel Paris Gare de Lyon
2 Rue Héctor Malot, 12th
t 01 44 67 60 00 **f** 01 44 67 60 60
www.novotel.com
Ⓜ/RER Gare de Lyon
Double rooms €145–183

Next door to the Gare de Lyon RER and métro stations, close to the Bastille and the Bercy centre, this branch of the child-friendly Novotel chain is outside the busiest parts of town but still not too far from the main attractions. It has family-sized rooms, a pool (note though that it is unsupervised, and deep) and good-value children's menus.

★★★ Au Relais du Louvre
19 Rue des Prêtres St Germain l'Auxerrois, 1st
t 01 40 41 96 42 **f** 01 40 41 96 44
www.france-hotel-guide.com
Ⓜ Louvre Rivoli
Double rooms €145–180

Small, 20-room hotel within sight of the great museum (see pp.42–44). Most of the rooms are quite small although there are a couple of large penthouse apartments with fully equipped kitchens that are ideal for families.

Inexpensive
★★ Grand Hôtel Jeanne d'Arc
3 Rue de Jarente, 4th
t 01 48 87 62 11 **f** 01 48 87 37 31
Ⓜ St Paul
Double rooms €78–125

In an old side street in the Marais (see p.67), this hotel is well priced for its location but make sure you know what you're getting as some rooms are tiny and a little gloomy, while others are bright and spacious. All twin rooms have two double beds. No room service or babysitting is provided but the staff are friendly and helpful.

★★ Hôtel des Arts
7 Cité Bergère, 9th
t 01 42 46 73 30 **f** 01 48 00 94 42
www.arts-hotel-paris.com

Ⓜ Grands Boulevards
Double rooms €64–78

A family-run hotel with 30 cosy rooms just around the corner from the Musée Grévin wax museum near the Grands Boulevards (see pp.114–115). The lobby and staircase are decorated with hundreds of theatre and museum posters. Cots are available.

★★ Hôtel Prima Lepic
29 Rue Lepic, 18th
t 01 46 06 44 64 **f** 01 44 46 06 66 11
www.hotel-paris-lepic.com
Ⓜ Blanche
Double rooms €96–125

This small, clean hotel has 38 good-sized rooms and is located on a lively street in the centre of Montmartre (see pp.97–104). Staying here is a nice way for the whole family to enjoy the atmosphere of this old part of Paris with the Sacré Coeur and Place du Tertre just nearby.

★★ Hôtel Résidence Alhambra
13 Rue Malte, 11th
t 01 47 00 35 52 **f** 01 43 57 98 75
www.hotelalhambra.fr
Ⓜ Oberkampf
Double rooms €59–69

In the streets north of the Bastille and the Marais, this characterful old hotel was thoroughly done up at the end of the 1990s. Many of the 58 rooms overlook a flower-filled garden courtyard, where you can have breakfast when the weather's pleasant and the hotel has a bright, fresh feel to it. Rooms are simple but comfortable, and low rates make them a bargain; there's also a big choice of rooms with three or four beds. Transport connections are good from Oberkampf métro station with direct lines to the Grand Boulevards, the Champs Élysées and the Gare du Nord going westwards and, in the opposite direction, to Bastille and Nation, where you can change onto the RER for Disneyland® Resort Paris (see p.184).

★★ Hôtel Saint Jacques
35 Rue des Écoles, 5th
t 01 44 07 45 45 **f** 01 43 25 65 50
www.hotel-saint-jacques.com
Ⓜ Maubert Mutualité
Double rooms €80–92

The Saint Jacques has 35 well-equipped rooms in a 19th-century town house around the corner from the Sorbonne, in the Latin Quarter (*see* pp.93–94). Families are welcome and cots can be provided. Scenes in the 1960s film *Charade*, with Cary Grant and Audrey Hepburn, were filmed here.

★★ Relais de Paris Gare du Nord Trudaine

73 Rue de Dunkerque, 9th
t 01 40 16 44 88 **f** 01 40 23 96 57
www.lesrelaisdeparis.com
Ⓜ/RER Gare du Nord, Ⓜ Anvers
Double rooms €78–90

One of the hotels of the good-value Relais de Paris chain (*see* pp.146–147). It is just along the street from the Gare du Nord and so very handy for anyone arriving in Paris by Eurostar. Like others in the Relais chain, it's a 19th-century hotel that has been comprehensively renovated with modern comforts. The 48 rooms are bright and pleasant. Family rooms are available.

Hostels

Hostels are probably not the first thing you consider when looking for suitable family accommodation conjuring up, as they do, images of backpackers sleeping on mouldy old mattresses in large, chilly, cramped dormitories. Hostelling, however, has changed. Throughout Europe, many hostels now actively seek out family groups and have installed the amenities necessary to attract them. Many offer family rooms, often with en-suite facilities and operate restaurants for those looking beyond the self-catering option. True, you have to make some concessions. Some hostels still insist on guests vacating the premises during the day (usually 10am–3pm) and you may be expected to help out with general chores. But these sacrifices are easily outweighted by the prices – it's quite possible to get a family room with en-suite facilities for as little as €25 per night.

Auberge Internationale des Jeunes

10 Rue Trousseau
t 01 47 00 62 00 **f** 01 47 00 33 16
www.aijparis.com
Ⓜ Ledru Rollin

Offers a choice of two-, three-, or four-person rooms, although only the 4-person rooms have bathrooms and you will be expected to vacate the premises during 'closeout' between 10am and 3pm.

MIJE

6 Rue de Fourcy, 4th
Ⓜ St Paul
11 Rue du Fauconnier, 4th
Ⓜ St Paul
12 Rue des Barres, 4th
Ⓜ Hôtel de Ville
t 01 42 74 23 45
www.hotel-saint-jacques.com

The Mije runsa network of three hostels is housed in grand 17th century Marais town houses with double, triple and quadruple rooms available, all with en-suite showers. Each hostel also operates a café restaurant.

Young and Happy Hostel

80 Rue Mouffetard, 5th
t 01 45 35 09 53 **f** 01 47 07 22 24
www.youngandhappy.fr
Ⓜ Place Monge

This Latin Quarter hostel offers double rooms (sleeping up to four people) from €23.

Bed and breakfast

Bed and breakfast (*chambres d'hôtes*) is an increasingly popular option in France, especially for families travelling and yet wishing to keep down costs. French b & b is most common in the countryside but, even in the capital, there is a growing number of rooms available in private homes, from suburban houses to grand old Parisian apartments. Many have excellent provision for parents with children. In contrast to French hotels, breakfast is always included in the room price.

Still more than in hotels, it is essential to book ahead in b & bs. If you're looking for family rooms and similar facilities, you should naturally make this clear when booking. Below are some of the best of the local b & b agencies.

Alcove & Agapes – Bed & Breakfast à Paris

8 bis Rue Coysevox, 18th
t 01 44 85 06 05 **f** 01 44 85 06 14
Double rooms €50–115

A b & b service with rooms in over 100 homes on its books, all around Paris.

Good Morning Paris

43 Rue Lacépède, 5th
t 01 47 07 28 29 **f** 01 47 07 44 45
Rooms €40–80

A choice of around 40 low-priced b & b rooms around the city.

Paris Bed and Breakfast and Apartments

www.parisbandb.com
US **t** (619) 531 1686

The choice for anyone looking for more distinctive, *charmante* bed and breakfast rooms: part of a US-based service (European b & b), this website can book rooms at a wide variety of prices all around Paris.

Aparthotels

For families looking for a little flexibility, aparthotels – a hybrid of an apartment and a hotel – can often be a good alternative to standard hotels. You get the freedom and privacy of an apartment: each aparthotel apartment is self-contained and comes with a sitting area and a fully equipped kitchenette plus the services and facilities of a hotel such as 24-hour reception, baby equipment rental, laundry, dry cleaning, housekeeping and often babysitting and a gym. Two of the best aparthotel chains are:

Aparthotels Citadines

Central Reservations in France **t** 01 41 05 79 79
f 01 41 05 78 87
In the UK **t** 0800 376 3898
www.citadines.com
Rates from €80 per day

The most prominent exponents of the aparthotel concept in France have 17 establishments around Paris including ones at Bastille, Montmartre, Opéra, Place Vendôme and the Champs Élysées. User-friendly more than characterful, all have very good facilities and amenities.

Home Plazza Bastille

74 Rue Amelot, 11th
t 01 40 21 20 00 **f** 01 47 00 82 40
www.homeplazza.com
Ⓜ St Sebastien Froissart
Rates €155–450 per day; weekend discounts

Apartment checklist

If you are thinking of renting an apartment in Paris, here are some of the basics to bear in mind:

▶ How far will your accommodation be from the nearest shops, supermarket, launderette, restaurants, parks, public transport and (if you need it) parking space?

▶ How are electricity, gas and also breakages and similar 'unforeseen eventualities' to be paid for? A credit card guarantee will often be required against possible breakages but this needs to be made clear.

▶ How many bedrooms does the flat have? The term 'sleeps 6' does not necessarily mean that there will be three bedrooms; often a sofa in the living room converts into a bed and you may even need to rearrange the room in order to create enough sleeping space.

▶ Are cots supplied and, if so, is there an additional charge for them?

▶ Are the children's rooms fitted with bunk beds and, if so, do these have safety rails?

▶ Is the garden or pool fenced off and are there nearby ponds, streams or other potential hazards?

▶ Is it safe for children to play unsupervised in the garden?

▶ Can babysitting be arranged locally?

This carefully constructed little urban 'village' of 240 mini-apartments near the Bastille (*see* pp.71–73) with its own garden courtyard is much used by business people, but is also great for travelling families who can use a little space. The self-contained suites are large, bright and modern, and all come with well-equipped kitchenettes and spacious bathrooms.

Apartment rentals

For a stay of several weeks, or even months, in Paris you would be well advised to rent an apartment. Not only does this make sound economic sense (with a bit of hunting you should be able to get something for around €400 a week although costs will rise considerably if you want to stay right in the centre of town), but it will also give you the chance to become familiar with a local community – meeting the neighbours, buying and cooking food from local shops and so on.

Self-catering can also make good sense if you're only going to be in Paris for 1 week or so. It need not be expensive even for very short periods, and it lets you do what you like when you like – get up when it suits you, nurse your colicky newborn at 3am, and scramble eggs whenever your toddler gets peckish. Again, there are some important questions that are worth asking (see p.151). The following agencies all arrange short-term rentals in Paris at a variety of price levels.

France Appartements
97 Av des Champs Élysées, 8th
t 01 56 59 31 00 f 01 56 89 31 01
www.rentapart.com

The most upmarket of the rental agencies with high-standard properties often in the most fashionable parts of town although you may also find bargains on their lists. Rents begin at around €300 per night for a one-bedroom apartment and there's a minimum booking period of 5 days.

France Lodge Locations
2 Rue Meissoneir, 17th
t 01 556 33 85 85 f 01 556 33 85 89
www.apartments-in-paris.com

One of the best choices for anyone looking for less expensive rentals, this enterprising and popular service has properties of all sizes that are often in less chic, but still central, areas of Paris, which means that you also get much closer to the real comings and goings of city life than if you keep to the usual hotel routes. Rates are a real bargain, beginning at €380 a week for a one-bedroom apartment or €460 for a two-room flat. The flats can be as varied as those in any city and the young staff really make an effort to find you what you're looking for.

Paris Appartements Services
69 Rue d'Argout, 2nd
t 01 40 28 01 28 f 01 40 28 92 01
www.paris-appartements-services.fr

A not-quite-so-plush agency but which also has a broad range of high-quality '3-star' apartments on its lists. One-bedroom apartments start at around €134 per night. Minimum rental period is 5 days.

Rothray
10 Rue Nicholas Flamel, 4th
t 01 48 87 13 37 f 01 42 78 17 72
www.rothray.com
Ⓜ Châtelet Les Halles

Compact, functional, fully furnished one- and two-bedroom apartments at decent rates. The same company has several more buildings around central Paris. Minimum rental period is seven days.

Camping

There are precious few camping facilities within Paris itself. The Île de France (the area surrounding and containing Paris) has plenty. If you don't mind commuting into the city every day during your stay, pitching a tent or hiring a mobile home, then camping sites can make a very cheap alternative to hotel accommodation. You'll find some well-equipped ones in the villages of Crevecouer en Brie, Ollainville, Toquin, Torcy, Vellevaude, Vernuil sur Seine, Triel sur Seine as well as numerous others. For a full list, log on to www.camping-paris.com. Prices for a pitch site start at around €10 plus €6–7 for each adult and €4–5 for each child under-7 (under-2s usually stay free of charge). Many sites can also offer a selection of chalets, caravans and mobile homes to rent.

The campsite closest to the city is the Hôtellerie de Plein Air in the Bois de Boulogne Campground although this isn't a true campsite (you can't pitch a tent), but rather a collection of permanent mobile homes, each equipped with two bedrooms, a bathroom, a living room and a kitchenette. Some also have TV and air conditioning. The site itself boasts a café restaurant, a mini-supermarket and a children's games room.

Hôtellerie de Plein Air
Bois de Boulogne Campground, Allée du Bord de l'Eau, 16th
t 01 45 24 30 81 f 01 42 24 42 95
www.mobilhome-paris.com
Rates Prices for a family of four start at €52 per night in the low season rising to €62 in summer (High Season).

Eat

French cooking is synonymous with culinary sophistication. Paris certainly has more than its share of smart, high-prestige establishments but, unfortunately, the attitude of many of them towards children can be more tolerant than welcoming. Never fear, however, for there are also lots of family-friendly restaurants that serve good, relatively inexpensive fixed-price lunches; many also offer smaller-size children's menus, and most eating-places will be willing to provide children's portions. Paris has a growing number of Asian and other international restaurants and global fast-food chains are always around as a standby, but look out, too, for local chains like **Hippopotamus**, which provide toys and other 'extras' for kids (*see* below). Furthermore, there are all sorts of opportunities for picking up finger-licking snacks on the hop: *crêperies* and *frites* stands can be found all around the city, or just pop into a *patisserie-boulangerie* for warm *pains au chocolat* (chocolate-filled croissants) fresh from the oven. For essential food vocabulary, *see* pp.162–164.

Chains

All the big international fast-food chains are now well established in Paris, but the city also has some more original and very child-friendly possibilities.

Bistro Romain

73 Av des Champs Élysées, 8th
t 01 43 59 67 85
Ⓜ Franklin D. Roosevelt
6 Place Victor Hugo, 16th
t 01 45 00 65 03
Ⓜ Victor Hugo
Open Daily 11.30am–1am
Fixed price menus €8.99, €12, €15, €22
Children's menu €7.40

The Romain chain prides itself on its family service, roomy tables and a menu full of kiddies' favourites (chips, burgers and chocolate mousse), as well as a range of simple pasta dishes and desserts. For more grown-up tastes, there are plenty of classic French staples. If you're ravenous, you can always take on the all-you-can-eat beef house challenge. The Champs Élysées branch is located within the swanky Galeries Élysées shopping centre with open courtyard seating.

Hippopotamus

1 Bd Beaumarchais, 4th
t 01 44 61 90 40

Ⓜ Bastille
42 Av des Champs Élysées, 8th
t 01 53 83 94 50
Ⓜ Franklin D. Roosevelt
9 Rue Lagrange, 5th
t 01 43 54 13 99
Ⓜ Maubert Mutualité
Open Daily 11.30am–5am
Fixed price menus €21.80, €14.95
Children's menu €7.50

The top child-friendly chain in Paris. Family meals are the speciality: the menu is simple (burgers, chips, steaks, ribs, baked potatoes, ice cream sundaes) and you can ask for colouring books, balloons, games and puzzles from the super-friendly staff. They're also favourite spots for children's parties, especially around Christmas and Halloween. These branches are near the Marais (*see* p.67), on the Champs Élysées (behind a Citroën dealership) and in the Latin Quarter (*see* p.93).

Planet Hollywood

78 Av des Champs Élysées, 8th
t 01 53 83 78 27
www.planethollywood.com
Ⓜ Franklin D. Roosevelt
Open Daily 12 noon–1am
Fixed price menu €15
Children's menu €10

Despite the chain's financial problems, this branch on the Champs Élysées (*see* pp.47–48) is still doing well. There's no doubt that its mix of burgers and movie memorabilia really does appeal to children (particularly older ones), who'll almost certainly demand an overpriced baseball cap.

Bistros and restaurants

Altitude 95

1st Level, Eiffel Tower, Champ de Mars, 7th
t 01 45 55 20 04
Ⓜ Bir Hakeim, Trocadéro,
RER Champ de Mars–Tour Eiffel
Open Daily 12 noon–2.45pm and 7pm–9.45pm
Fixed price menus €18, €21, €27, €48
Children's menu €9

Situated on the first level of the Eiffel Tower (95m above sea level), the views are, as you would expect, spectacular – insist on a window table. The interior is deliberately unconventional (all struts and weird metal pieces designed to loosely resemble the inside of an airship). The food is

Eating essentials

Restaurants, bistros and brasseries

The traditional French restaurant expects to serve meals only when most French people traditionally eat (lunch from 12.30 to 2pm, dinner roughly from 8.30pm), with one sitting for each session. They nearly always offer a choice of several fixed-price *menus* and a more expensive, more varied *à la carte menu*, all of which centre around a full meal of at least three courses – although restaurants rarely ever object to anyone ordering just one or two courses, especially for lunch, as many locals do. A **bistro** is also a restaurant but suggests something more casual, everyday, local or even rough and ready, and so is usually cheaper, although some Paris bistros can be quite chic and pricey. They tend to stay open later at night.

The **brasserie** is the traditional eating alternative for those who don't keep such regular hours. They're more like a combination of bar, café and restaurant and stay open all day, often from breakfast right through until late at night, around the 2–3am mark. Most usually also have set price three-course menus, but only as part of much longer lists that also offer a big choice of one-course dishes and snacks (French onion soup, bowls of mussels, salads, omelettes, sandwiches, steak and chips) for part of the brasserie idea is that you can have what you like. In Paris, the big boom era for brasseries was at the end of the 19th century and a visit to a classic 1900s brasserie such as Bofinger in the Bastille (*see* pp.71–73), all Art Nouveau woodwork, mirrors and stained glass and permanently bustling with diners and white-aproned waiters, can be a real experience.

Nowadays, with more less classifiable and more international-style eating places opening up in Paris, these divisions are no longer nearly as clear as they once were, but they still give a handy guideline as to what to expect.

Fixed price menus

The set *menu* (sometimes called a *formule*) is a French institution and the most common way of ordering a meal in restaurants. It nearly always consists of three or four courses – an *entrée* (first course), a *plat* (main course), sometimes cheese, and dessert and coffee – for a fixed price. Wines and drinks are usually charged for separately. Most restaurants offer a range of *menus* from simple to elaborate, and this is always the best-value way to eat. Many places offer low-cost *formules* for around €10 and you can easily find excellent, sophisticated menus for €15–25.

If you want to see the full menu ask for *à la carte*, but this will be very noticeably more expensive.

Children's menus

A great many restaurants and brasseries offer a *menu d'enfant* (children's menu) in their range of set price lists. Often a scaled-down, simpler version of one of the adult *formules*, it will usually cost around €5–10.

Cafés

Food available in Paris cafés has generally been just snacks – baguette sandwiches, cheese and ham croques, croissants and pastries for breakfast – but a growing number now offer salads, quiches and similar light meals.

Crêpes and crêperies

Parisian crêperies nearly all sell two kinds of pancake: *galettes* are thick, buckwheat pancakes that come with all sorts of savoury fillings, while *crêpes* as such are thinner and lighter, sweetened and filled with sweet things. Many crêperies are little cafés with table service (especially common in student districts), but *crêpes* and *galettes* are also sold at countless street stalls. They're a big favourite with local school kids, who fold them into quarters and munch them while marching along the street. As well as offering lighter meals than the traditional French restaurant, crêperies provide a very useful alternative for vegetarians.

Frites

Chips are sold on the street in France from *frite*-stands in little paper cones. Note that you'll probably be asked if you want mayonnaise on top. The same stands often sell hot sweet waffles (*gaufres*) served with jam.

Tips and service compris

By law 15 per cent is added to all restaurant bills in France to cover service and taxes (indicated by *service compris*), so there's no obligation to tip. However, in Paris it is quite common to leave a little extra in cash (never added on to a credit card slip) as an acknowledgement if and when service has been particularly good.

reasonable and staff are very welcoming to families. A big perk of dining here is that you get to use a private lift without having to stand in the queues below. The more swanky Jules Verne restaurant is on the Tower's second floor (125m above sea level).

Cap Vernet

82 Av Marceau, 8th
t 01 47 20 20 40
Ⓜ/RER Charles de Gaulle-Étoile
Open Daily 12 noon–2.30pm and 7pm–11pm
Fixed price menu Lunch €54
Children's menu €20
Savour Discovery menu €11.40 (midday Sat–Sun)
 Near the Arc de Triomphe (see pp. 49–50), this is one for budding gourmets or junior masterchefs. Guy Savoy is one of Paris's current top chefs with several restaurants around the city; at lunchtime on Saturdays and Sundays, a special Savour Discovery menu is offered here which gives young tasters the opportunity to discover a gastronomic life far beyond McDonald's. The sea and ships provide the themed décor and the crew serve up dishes that slip down as smoothly as yachts gliding through the sea. A uniquely Parisian experience.

Chez Léna et Mimile

32 Rue Tournefort, 5th
t 01 47 07 72 47
Ⓜ Place Monge
Open Daily 12 noon–2pm and 7.30pm–11pm
Fixed price menu €15, €30
 Just south of the Panthéon (see p.91), it is worth a visit for the all-you-can-eat chocolate mousse challenge. The terrace (open in summer) sits next to a pretty fountain and a small grassy square where kids can burn off excess calories.

La Coupole

102 Boulevard du Montparnasse, 14th
t 01 42 20 14 20
Ⓜ Vavin
Open 8.30am–1am (Mon–Thu), 8.30am–1.30am (Fri–Sat)
 This huge Montparnasse bar-gastrodome is filled with movers and shakers in the evening when it can be quite difficult getting a table (despite its size). It's much more family-friendly (and emptier and cheaper) in the mornings and afternoons when it can make a pleasant pit-stop during a bout of Montparnasse sightseeing. The seafood is particularly good.

Les Degrés de Nôtre Dame

10 Rue des Grands Degrés, 5th
t 01 55 42 88 88
Ⓜ Maubert Mutualité
Open 12 noon–10.30pm (Mon–Sat)
Fixed price menu €9.60, €21, €23
 Basic, inexpensive bistro outside the Latin Quarter's hustle and bustle (see pp.93–94) with views from its terrace across to Nôtre Dame.

L'Îlot Vache

35 Rue St Louis en l'Île, 4th
t 01 46 33 55 16
Ⓜ Pont Marie
Open 12 noon–3pm and 7pm–12 midnight (Tues–Sun), 7pm–12 midnight (Mon)
Fixed price menu €33
 Popular, comfortable bistro amid the quiet, affluent streets of Île St Louis (see p.81). Superior steaks are a speciality and the décor follows a suitably bovine theme. Excellent seafood to boot.

Le Maquis

69 Rue Caulaincourt, 18th
t 01 42 59 76 07
Ⓜ Lamarck Caulaincourt
Open 12 noon–2.30pm, 7pm–12 midnight (Mon–Sat)
Fixed price menu €13, €19, €25
 The top choice in Montmartre (see pp.97–104), popular both with local families and culinary aficionados. The €25 set menu is excellent and good value (highly recommended are the steaks and chocolate fondant to finish).

Le Polidor

41 Rue Monsieur le Prince, 6th
t 01 43 26 95 34
Ⓜ Odéon
Open 12 noon–2.30pm and 7pm–12.30am (Mon–Sat), 12 noon–2.30pm and 7pm–11pm (Sun)
Fixed price menu €9, €18
 One of Paris' longest-running (est. 1890) traditional bistros, near the Luxembourg in the Latin Quarter (see pp.93–94), Polidor remains hugely popular. Enormous long tables accommodate entire families, who pack in to enjoy sturdy French staples such as boeuf bourguignon and snails with garlic. The chocolate tarts are delicious and, as a final treat for your kids, it still has old Paris-style squat toilets.

Rendez-vous des Chauffeurs

11 Rue des Portes Blanches, 18th
t 01 42 64 04 17
Ⓜ Marcadet Poissonniers
Open Daily 12 noon–2.30pm and 7.30–11pm
Fixed price menu €12

A great budget choice near Montmartre (*see* pp.97–104). The lunch menu is wonderful value – a sturdy bistro meal worth twice the price – and home-made apple pie is a speciality.

Thoumieux

79 Rue St Dominique, 7th
t 01 47 05 46 44
Ⓜ Invalides, La Tour Maubourg
Open 12 noon–3.30pm and 6.30–12 midnight (Mon–Sat), 12 noon–12 midnight (Sun)
Fixed price menu €14, €28

Traditional bistro near the Invalides (*see* p.58) that fills up with local families at weekends. Children are very welcome, but good behaviour and smart dress are expected. Bistro classics fill the menu – bean-heavy *cassoulets* and *crème caramel*.

Le Troquet

21 Rue François Bonvin, 15th
t 01 45 65 89 00
Ⓜ Cambronne
Open 12 noon–2.30pm and 7.30pm–11pm (Tues–Sat). Closed Aug
Fixed price menu €22, €24, €28, 30

Though terribly traditional-looking, this back street bistro is actually something of a modern gourmet's delight and is presided over by the celebrated chef Christian Etchebest. It's also very family-friendly with attentive service and a general air of *bonhomie*. It is, however, quite expensive, especially if you stray from the fixed price menus.

Le Vieux Bistro

14 Rue du Cloître Nôtre Dame, 4th
t 01 43 54 18 95
Ⓜ Cité, **RER** St Michel Nôtre Dame
Open Daily 12 noon–2pm and 7.30pm–11pm

Right next to Nôtre Dame (*see* pp.78–79) is this shadowy, traditional bistro, providing great, real old-style French cooking. Despite such a prime tourist location, it's also very popular with locals. The *tarte tatin* is a classic: order it with the rest of your food as it takes around 45 minutes to cook.

Au Virage Lepic

61 Rue Lepic, 18th

t 01 42 52 46 79
Ⓜ Blanche
Open Daily 12 noon–3pm and 6pm–2am
Fixed price menu €14.50

An institution in Montmartre (*see* pp.97–104), this lovely old backstreet bistro is very popular with locals and has an accordionist on hand to entertain at weekends. Set menus feature satisfying classics.

Brasseries

Bofinger

5–7 Rue de la Bastille, 4th
t 01 42 72 87 82
Ⓜ Bastille
Open 12 noon–3pm and 6.30pm–1am (Mon–Fri), 12 noon–1am (Sat–Sun)
Fixed price menu €21.50, €30.50, Petit Bofinger: €18, €27

Don't be intimidated by the grand reputation, fabulous Art Nouveau interior or even the initial starchiness of the waiters at this classic brasserie just off the Place de la Bastille (*see* pp.71–73). As long as your children behave, they'll be made to feel very welcome. It's a touch pricey but a meal here needn't break the bank even if you decide to leave the safety of the set-price menus. Luckily, the food never fails to hit the spot. A smaller, cheaper version, 'Le Petit Bofinger', is just across the road.

La Brasserie de l'Île St Louis

55 Quai de Bourbon, 4th
t 01 43 54 02 59
Ⓜ Pont Marie
Open Daily 12 noon–3pm and 7pm–12 midnight
Fixed price menu €30

Fine-quality traditional brasserie on the *quais* of the Île St Louis with views of Nôtre Dame (*see* pp.78–79). Kids appreciate the omelettes or *choucroute* with ham and frankfurters and ice creams come from nearby Berthillon. Check out, too, the stuffed stork in the dining room.

Brasserie XVIème Poincaré

45 Av Raymond Poincaré, 16th
t 01 47 27 72 19
Ⓜ Trocadéro
Open Daily 12 noon–12 midnight

Cheerful brasserie north of the Trocadéro (*see* p.60) serving tasty fare. Great omelettes, and nobody turns up their nose if you ask for ketchup.

Le Sancerre
35 Rue des Abbesses, 18th
t 01 45 58 08 20
Ⓜ Abbesses
Open Daily 7am–2am
Fixed price menu €11.50

Big, very popular and groovy with live jazz musicians at weekends, this cheerful bar-restaurant in Montmartre (see pp.97–104) is one for older kids. There are enjoyable one-course dishes and sandwiches on offer.

Cafés
L'Ancien Trocadéro
2 Place Trocadéro et 11 Novembre, 16th
t 01 47 04 94 71
Ⓜ Trocadéro
Open Daily 11.30am–1am
Children's menu €11.10

Sit at a pavement table for good views of the Palais du Chaillot (see p.60) and the Eiffel Tower (just). It is a bit touristy but the food is simple and reasonably priced with salads, hamburgers and ice cream on the children's menu.

Le Floré-en-l'Île
42 Quai d'Orléans, 4th
t 01 43 29 88 27
Ⓜ Cité, Sully Morland
Open 10am–10.30pm (Mon–Sat)

Sample French-style hot chocolate on one of the quais of the Île St Louis (see p.81). You are brought two pots (one filled with chocolate, the other with hot frothy milk) to mix according to taste.

Café de la Halle St Pierre
2 Rue Ronsard, 18th
t 01 42 58 72 89
Ⓜ Anvers, Abbesses
Open 10am–6pm (Mon–Sat)

Just inside the entrance of the Halle St Pierre, Montmartre's cultural complex (see pp.101–102), this family-friendly café tirelessly serves cola and grenadine to hordes of small children.

Café des Hauteurs (Musée d'Orsay)
1 Rue de la Légion d'Honneur, 7th
t 01 42 84 12 16
Ⓜ Solférino, **RER** Musée d'Orsay
Open 10am–5pm (Tues–Wed, Fri–Sun), 10am–9pm (Thur)

The Musée d'Orsay (see pp.81, 83) has a great café on its top floor with views of the river through one of the clocks of the old 19th-century station, or from its outdoor terrace. It's accessible only to museum visitors, so you pay admission.

Café du Musée Rodin
Hôtel Biron, 77 Rue de Varenne, 7th
t 01 45 50 42 34
Ⓜ Varenne
Open 9.30am–6.30pm (April–Sep), 9.30am–4.30pm (Oct–Mar)

The café in the secluded garden of the Musée Rodin (see p.59) is a lovely spot for a snack and a think, while your kids run around to their hearts' content. Mothers with pushchairs get in for free.

Cafés et Thés Verlet
256 Rue St Honoré, 1st
t 01 42 60 67 39
Ⓜ Palais Royal–Musée du Louvre, Tuileries
Open Daily 9am–7pm

Near the Louvre (see pp.42–44), this family friendly place for afternoon tea is filled with the aroma of freshly brewed tea and coffee. There are baskets of glacé fruits and sweets for the kids, too.

Le Chinon
49 Rue des Abbesses, 18th
t 01 42 62 07 17
Ⓜ Abbesses
Open Daily 9am–12 midnight

This small café is a good pit stop when exploring Montmartre (see pp.97–104). The omelettes are excellent and service is pleasant.

Le Loir dans la Théière
3 Rue des Rosiers, 4th
t 01 42 72 68 12
Ⓜ St Paul
Open 11am–7pm (Mon–Fri), 10am–7pm (Sat–Sun)

Charmingly cluttered, this Marais tea salon (see p. 67) serves raspberry cheesecake, chocolate fondant, lemon pie and a huge range of teas.

Marais Plus
20 Rue des Francs Bourgeois, 4th
t 01 48 87 01 40
Ⓜ Rambuteau, Hôtel de Ville
Open 10am–7pm (Mon–Fri)

A relaxing and cheap café above a kids' toy-and-book shop in the Marais (see p.67). A very tasty line in quiches and pastries.

Patachou

9 Place du Tertre, 18th
t 01 42 51 06 06
Ⓜ Anvers
Open Daily 12 noon–12 midnight

A pleasant if touristy café in the heart of things in Montmartre (see pp.97–104). It's a good vantage point from which to survey the bustle on Place du Tertre, with the Eiffel Tower far off in the distance.

Pause Café

41 Rue de Charonne, 11th
t 01 48 06 80 33
Ⓜ Ledru Rollin
Open Daily 7am–2pm (Mon–Sat), 9am–8.30pm (Sun)

The weekend is the time when locals bring their kids to this funky café near the Bastille (see pp.71–73) for savoury tarts and hot dishes.

Salon de Thé de la Mosquée de Paris

1 Place du Puits de l'Ermite, 5th
t 01 43 31 38 20
Ⓜ Censier Daubenton
Open Daily 10am–12 midnight

The Arab café attached to France's oldest and most important mosque makes for an ideal pit-stop after a morning in the Jardin des Plantes (see pp.88–89). The pink marble tea house is quite extraordinary with blue and white tiles and graceful arches for a wonderfully relaxed setting. Grown-ups can refuel on Arab coffee or mint tea, while kids can't resist the Moroccan pastries, low-slung, made-for-lounging sofas and gurgling central fountain.

Terrasse de la Samaritaine

Quai du Louvre, Terrasse Le Toupary, 1st
t 01 40 41 29 29
Ⓜ Pont Neuf, Châtelet
Open 9.30am–7pm (Mon–Sun), until 10pm (Thurs)
Fixed price menu €13, €16

This delightful café on the roof of the Samaritaine department store, next to the Louvre, (see pp.42–44) has good, well-priced food.

Virgin Café

Virgin Megastore, 52 Champs Élysées, 8th
t 01 49 53 50 00
Ⓜ Franklin D. Roosevelt, George V
Open 10am–12 midnight (Mon–Sat), 12 noon–12 midnight (Sun)
Children's menu €7

Sandwich shops

Quick-service sandwich bars are increasingly popular around Paris.

Handmade

19 Rue Jean Mermoz, 8th
t 01 45 62 50 05
Ⓜ Franklin D. Roosevelt
Open 8am–5pm (Mon–Fri)

Lina's sandwiches

t 01 40 15 94 95
4 Rue Cambon, 1st
Ⓜ Concorde
Open Daily 7am–8pm (Mon–Sat)
15 Rue de Louvre, 1st
t 01 40 41 15 00
Ⓜ/**RER** Châtelet Les Halles
8 Rue Marbeuf, 8th
t 01 47 23 92 33
Ⓜ Alma Marceau
Open Daily 7am–8pm (Mon–Sat)

Aux Pains Perdus

39 Rue de Berri, 8th
t 01 43 59 10 96
Ⓜ Franklin D. Roosevelt
Open Daily 8am–8pm

Le Pain Quotidien

18 Place du Marché St Honoré, 1st
t 01 42 96 32 70
Ⓜ Pyramides
Open Daily 7am–8pm

Watch the bustle of the Champs Élysées (see pp.47–48) from a window table in the top floor café. The food – salmon on toast, hamburgers – is good and child-friendly. Prices are not over the top.

Crêperies

The biggest concentration of crêperies in Paris is in the Latin Quarter (see pp.93–94).

Crêperie des Arts

27 Rue St André des Arts, 6th
t 01 43 26 15 68
Ⓜ/**RER** St Michel
Open Daily 12 noon–1am
Fixed price menu €7.50 (lunchtime only)

This Latin Quarter favourite deserves its reputation as the best crêperie in town. It serves a huge range of savoury and sweet snacks.

La Crêpe Carrée

42 Rue Monge, 5th

t 01 43 54 31 08

Ⓜ Cardenal Lemoine

Open 12 noon–12 midnight (Tues–Sun)

Crêperie Cluny

20 Rue de la Harpe, 5th

t 01 43 26 08 30

Ⓜ**/RER** St Michel

Open Daily 11am–midnight

Ty Breiz

52 Boulevard de Vaugirard, 15th

t 01 43 20 83 72

Ⓜ Montparnasse Bienvenüe, Pasteur

Open 12 noon–3pm and 7pm–11pm (Mon–Sat)

A bargain-priced Breton crêperie-restaurant in Montparnasse (see pp.94–95). Savoury *galettes* are the house speciality: pick from tomatoes, ham, cheese, mushrooms, egg, salmon, and artichoke fillings. The sweet *crêpe* range is just as big, too.

Ice cream

Berthillon

31 Rue St Louis en l'Île, 4th

t 01 43 54 31 61

Ⓜ Pont Marie

Open 10am–8pm (Wed–Sun), closed 3 weeks Aug

Berthillon in the Île St Louis (see p.81) is by far the best and most popular ice cream parlour in town. Over 70 flavours available.

International restaurants

Aux Délices d'Asie

119 Rue St Antoine, 4th

t 01 42 72 94 81

Ⓜ St Paul

Open Daily 10am–10.30pm

Cheap, good-quality noodle house in the Marais (see p.67), serving Chinese, Vietnamese or Thai dishes. Portions are generous: eat in or take-away.

Blue Elephant

43–45 Rue de la Roquette, 11th

t 01 47 00 42 00

Ⓜ Bastille, Voltaire

Open 12 noon–2.30pm and 7pm–midnight (Mon–Fri), 7pm–11pm (Sat–Sun)

Fixed price menus €18.90, €44

Just north of the Bastille (see pp.71–73), this is part of an international chain of Thai restaurants.

Particularly welcoming to families at weekends, kids will love the jungle-like décor.

Board Café

8 Rue Coquillière, 1st

t 01 40 28 97 98

Ⓜ**/RER** Châtelet Les Halles

Open Daily 11.30am–1am

Fixed price menu €13.60, €18.60

Children's menu €10

Formerly Chicago Meatpackers, it has been converted into a haven for snowboarders and skate boarders who flock here after an afternoon spent taming the ramps and steps of the Forum des Halles (see p.70). Older kids will love the themed sections decorated with expert-autographed snow- and skateboards. The range of menus is extensive with many regional and international dishes.

Chicago Pizza Pie Factory

5 Rue de Berri, 8th

t 01 45 62 50 23

Ⓜ George V

Open Daily 12 noon–1am

Fixed price menu €9.30, €12, €16.80

Children's menu €8.54

Good value, particularly for its location just off the Champs Élysées. Order huge deep-pan American-style pizza and a salad. The children's menu consists of a mini-pizza (or chicken and chips), a drink and ice cream. Children's entertain-ment (clowns and puppet shows) are laid on on Sunday afternoons.

Il Conte

47 Av Raymond Poincaré, 16th

t 01 47 27 98 40

Ⓜ Trocadéro

Open Daily 12 noon–2.30pm and 7.30pm–11.30pm

Cosy Italian restaurant near the Palais Chaillot (see p.60). Excellent ravioli and pesto dishes. Cramped but friendly.

Le Frog & Rosbif

116 Rue St Denis, 2nd

t 01 42 36 34 73

www.frogpubs.com

Ⓜ Étienne Marcel, **RER** Châtelet Les Halles

Open 12 noon–3pm, 7.30pm–10.30pm (Mon–Fri), 12 noon–4pm, 7.30pm–10.30pm (Sat–Sun)

One of Paris' foremost 'English pubs' just north of Les Halles (see pp.70–71). Tuck into traditional pub grub (shepherd's pie, sausage and mash, chicken tikka masala) along with real cask beers, while catching up with English football games on TV.

Indiana Café

14 Place de la Bastille, 11th
t 01 44 75 79 80
www.indiana-cafe.com
Ⓜ Bastille
Open Daily 11.30–1.30am
Children's menu €8.38

Tex-Mex diner in the heart of the Bastille (*see* pp.71–73) decorated with American Indian motifs.

Korean Barbecue

22 Rue Delambre, 14th
t 01 43 35 44 35
Ⓜ Vavin
Open Daily 11am–2pm and 7pm–11pm
Fixed price menu €9, €14, €18.90, €27

On the north side of Montparnasse (*see* pp.94–95), restless kids can cook their own meals at the grills in the middle of the tables. Try the thin beef strips soaked in special sesame seed marinade.

Le Studio

41 Rue du Temple, 4th
t 01 42 74 10 38
Ⓜ Hôtel de Ville, **RER** Châtelet Les Halles
Open 7.30pm–11pm (Mon), 12.30pm–11pm (Tues–Sun)

Large, lively Tex-Mex diner with a bar lined with tequila bottles (for parents) and a lovely cobbled courtyard to run around in (for children).

Vegetarian

The 'vegetarian option' is yet to establish itself as a fixture of Parisian menus. Meatless dishes, though, are not too hard to find with international restaurants often providing more options than French establishments. Modern cafés, salons de thé and crêperies (*see* pp.159–160) are essential standbys.

Le Grénier de Nôtre Dame

18 Rue de la Bûcherie, 5th
t 01 43 29 98 29
Ⓜ St Michel, Maubert Mutualité
Open Daily 12 noon–2pm and 7.30–11.30pm
Fixed price menu €12.20, €12.95, €16.80

An excellent and cheap vegetarian restaurant on the Left Bank, a short walk from Nôtre Dame (*see* pp.78–79). There's lots of choice for kids, and they are invited to create their own non-alcoholic cocktails.

Eating with entertainment

The following restaurants, unlike the others that are listed here, do not also feature in the guide's area chapters, but have been included in this chapter because they are family-friendly and offer child-orientated entertainment, something which is still rare in Parisian restaurants.

Pavillon des Oiseaux au Jardin d'Acclimatation

Bois de Boulogne, 16th
t 01 45 02 34 00
Ⓜ Les Sablons, Ⓜ/**RER** Porte Maillot
Open Daily 10am–7pm (April–Oct); 10am–6pm (Nov–Mar)
Children's buffet menu Under-12s €23.60, under-4s, €6.90 (including the workshop)

The café-restaurant of this dedicated children's park lays on two hearty family buffets per week. On Wednesdays at 12 noon, in between being entertained by clowns, face painters and magicians, kids can tuck in to a selection of cooked meats, cheeses and cakes before attending a theatre workshop (in French) at 1pm. On Sundays, the buffet is followed by a percussion workshop (in French).

Quai Ouest

1200 Quai Marcel Dassault, St Cloud
t 01 46 02 35 54
Ⓜ Porte de St Cloud
Open Daily 12 noon–3pm, 8pm–12 midnight

Children's entertainment (face painting, conjurers) is laid on at weekends in this stylishly converted warehouse overlooking the Seine, across the river in the smart suburb of St Cloud on the west side of Paris. The brunch menu is mainly American-based (burgers, pancakes) with a few French basics. A popular birthday party venue.

Spicy Restaurant

8 Avenue Franklin D. Roosevelt
t 01 56 59 62 59
Ⓜ Franklin D. Roosevelt
Open Daily 12 noon–12 midnight
Fixed price menu €28
Children's menu €13.50

Swish central Parisian restaurant comprising a separate bar, rotisserie restaurant and mezzanine. Special Family Lunch on Sundays from 12.30pm when cartoons play on TV screens and a clown entertains the youngsters.

WHAT TO EAT

It's a shame to visit Paris and not try a few French specialities. France has a vast food vocabulary and this glossary is designed to help out whether you're ordering a restaurant meal, relaxing in a café or buying a snack at your local *boulangerie* (bakery) or *épicerie* (grocer). Also *see* **Language**, p.249.

Miscellaneous

l'addition the bill
ail garlic
assiette plate, but also a single-course dish, intended to be ordered on its own
baguette long loaf of bread
beurre butter
brochette meat (or fish) grilled on a skewer
confiture jam
crème cream
cru raw
cuit cooked
au four baked
frais, fraîche fresh/cold (drinks)
frit, frite fried
fromage cheese
fromage de chèvre goat cheese
fumé smoked
garni with vegetables
(au) gratin topped with crisp browned cheese and breadcrumbs
grillé grilled
hachis minced
huile (d'olive) oil (olive)
libre service self-service
monsieur, madame, mademoiselle what to say to attract a waiter/waitress's attention (no one says *garçon* any more)
moutarde mustard
nouilles noodles
œufs eggs
pain bread
pâte pastry, pasta
poché poached
poivre pepper
quenelles dumplings of fish or poultry
ration d'enfant children's portion
sel salt
sucre sugar
sucré sweet
tranche slice
(à la) vapeur steamed
vinaigre vinegar

Some popular snacks

choucroute Alsatian sauerkraut with pork, different sausages, and potatoes; actually a pretty heavy meal, but a brasserie standard
crêpes thin wheat pancakes, served with sweet fillings like fruit, chocolate sauce, cream, etc.
croque-madame croque-monsieur with a fried egg on top
croque-monsieur grilled cheese and ham on toast
galettes thickish, buckwheat pancakes, eaten with mushrooms, cheese and other savoury fillings
omelette (au jambon, fromage, aux champignons) omelette with ham, cheese, mushroom or potentially many other fillings, usually served with salad
quiche savoury tart
raclette toasted cheese with potatoes, onions and pickles
salade composée mixed salad with a variety of ingredients – meats, anchovies, cheeses, fruit; very popular nowadays for light lunches, and many modern French brasserie-style restaurants offer a list of several *salades composées*, nearly always with vegetarian choices among them
sandwich yes, a sandwich, but nearly always made with half a baguette, or French stick
tartine open sandwich on flat, buttered bread, with cold meats, cheeses or other toppings

Starters and soups

bouillon broth
consommé clear soup
crudités raw vegetable platter
potage thick vegetable soup
soupe à l'oignon French onion soup
velouté very thick, smooth soup
vol-au-vent puff pastry case with savoury filling

Fish, shellfish

anchois anchovies
bar sea bass
cabillaud fresh cod
carrelet plaice
Coquilles St Jacques scallops
crabe crab
crevettes grises shrimps
crevettes roses prawns
daurade sea bream
cuisses de grenouilles frogs' legs
escargots snails
friture mixed platter of deep fried fish
fruits de mer seafood
homard lobster

huîtres oysters
limande lemon sole
lotte monkfish
loup (de mer) sea bass
maquereau mackerel
moules mussels
raie skate
rouget red mullet
saumon salmon
sole (à la meunière) sole (with butter, lemon and parsley)
thon tuna
truite trout

Meat and poultry

agneau lamb
ailerons chicken wings
andouillette chitterling (tripe) sausage
biftek beefsteak
blanc breast or white meat
bœuf beef
boudin blanc sausage of white meat
boudin noir black pudding
caille quail
canard, caneton duck
cheval horsemeat
dinde, dindon turkey
estouffade braised meat stew
foie liver
foie gras fattened duck or goose liver
fricadelle meatball
jambon ham
jambon cru air-dried, salt-cured ham
lapin rabbit
lard (lardons) bacon (diced bacon)
merguez spicy North African sausage
navarin (d'agneau) (lamb) stew with vegetables
os bone
porc pork
poulet chicken
poussin spring chicken
rillettes potted meats (of duck, pork, rabbit...)
rognons kidneys
saucisses sausages
saucisson sliced, salami-type sausage, eaten cold
tête de veau head of veal
veau veal

Meat cuts and cooking terms

Burgers and steaks will tend to come medium-rare (*à point*), unless you make sure to order them *bien cuit* (well done). If you want to have a more French-style steak, ask for your meat *saignant* (rare) or *bleu* (very rare).

carré (d'agneau) rack (of lamb)
contre-filet, faux-filet sirloin steak
côte, côtelette chop, cutlet
cuisse thigh or leg
entrecôte ribsteak
épaule shoulder
gigot leg of lamb
graisse fat
magret, maigret (de canard) breast (of duck)
noisette (d'agneau) small round cut (of lamb)
pavé thick, square fillet
rôti roast

Salad and vegetables

artichaut artichoke
asperges asparagus
aubergine aubergine (eggplant)
avocat avocado
betterave beetroot
cèpes large, brown wild mushrooms
champignons mushrooms
chou cabbage
chou-fleur cauliflower
chou-frisé kale
choux de Bruxelles Brussels sprouts
citrouille, courge pumpkin
concombre cucumber
cornichons gherkins, pickles
courgettes courgettes (zucchini)
cresson watercress
échalote shallot
endive chicory
épinards spinach
fenouil fennel
frites chips (french fries)
haricots beans
(rouges, blancs) (kidney, white)
haricots verts green (french) beans
laitue lettuce
lentilles lentils
(épi de) maïs sweetcorn (on the cob)
morilles morel mushrooms
oignons onions
persil parsley
petits pois peas
poireaux leeks
poivron sweet red or green pepper
pomme de terre potato
riz rice

salade verte green salad
tomate tomato
truffes truffles

Desserts and pastries

biscuit cake
bonbons sweets, candy
brioche light sweetbread
clafoutis black-cherry pastry tart
compôte stewed fruit
coupe ice cream cup
crème anglaise very light custard
crème chantilly sweet whipped cream
crème fleurette double cream
crème fraîche (slightly) sour cream
crème pâtissière custard filling (in cakes, pastries)
feuilleté (aux pommes) (apple) turnover
gâteau cake
glace ice cream
madeleines small sponge cakes
miel honey
oeufs à la neige soft meringues in vanilla custard
pain au chocolat chocolate-filled pastry
palmier heart-shaped flaky pastry biscuit
petits fours tiny cakes and pastries, served with coffee
sablé shortbread
tarte, tartelette tart, little tart
tarte tatin caramelized apple tart, served upside down

Fruit and nuts

abricot apricot
ananas pineapple
banane banana
cacahouètes peanuts
cassis blackcurrant
cerise cherry
citron lemon
figues figs
fraises strawberries
fraises des bois wild strawberries
framboises raspberries
marrons chestnuts
mirabelles small yellow plums
mûres mulberry, blackberry
myrtilles bilberries
noisettes hazelnuts
noix walnuts
pamplemousse grapefruit
pêche peach
poire pear

pomme apple
prune plum
raisins (sec) grapes (raisins)

Drinks

Any French restaurant will provide a jug of water from the tap (*un carafe d'eau*) for no extra charge, on request. Paris's tap water is good quality, and most locals don't bother paying the extra for labelled *eau minerale*.

bière (à pression) beer (draught)
un demi 25cl glass, the normal size in which draught beer is served in France
bière blonde standard, light lager
bière brune dark, more ale-like beer
(demi) bouteille (half) bottle
café coffee
la carte des vins the wine list
chocolat (chaud) (hot) chocolate
citron pressé freshly squeezed lemon juice
eau (minérale) (mineral) water
(*gazeuse* sparkling, *plat, non-gazeuse* still)
glaçons ice cubes
infusion (or tisane) herbal tea
jus d'orange orange juice
kir aperitif of blackcurrant liqueur and white wine (or, with champagne, a *kir royale*)
lait milk
limonade lemonade
orange pressé freshly squeezed orange juice
sirop d'orange/de citron orange/lemon squash
thé tea
verre glass
vin blanc/rouge/rosé white/red/rosé wine

Shop

Paris is a fabulous place to shop for high fashion, fine foods and antiques, but it's also a good place to shop with children. Parisians like their children to be well dressed and you can find hundreds of children's clothes shops from bargain centres to chic emporia frequented by film stars and royalty.

The district known as the **Grands Boulevards** (around Boulevard Haussmann, north of the Opéra) contains several of Paris' biggest stores and is great for browsing. If you're looking to pick up some smart, only-in-Paris children's wear, head for **St Germain**, west of the Latin Quarter with its little chic boutiques (see p.92). One of the best places for window-shopping in Paris is the historic district of the **Marais** with its mix of food, antique, clothes, toy and odds-and-all-sorts shops (see p.68). On its eastern side the Marais ends at Place de la Bastille, to the east of which along Avenue Daumesnil is the **Viaduc des Arts**, an old railway viaduct that has been taken over by around 100 art, design and craft workshops, galleries and cafés. Most items here may be more of adult interest, but it's a fascinating place for browsing and looking at how handmade toys are made and restored. Further east still is **Bercy Village**, a new shopping complex occupying former wine warehouses.

Détaxe refund scheme

If you are a non-EU resident and have spent more than €180 in any one shop, you are eligible to claim refund on any VAT (value-added tax) paid when you leave France, so long as your stay hasn't exceeded 90 days. Simply pick up a *détaxe* form at the shop where you made your purchase, fill in your details, get customs to stamp the form when you leave France and then post it back to the shop, who will refund the money direct into your bank account or credit card. This refund scheme does not apply to food, drink or antiques.

Sales

For bargains look out for the Paris sales, which usually take place twice a year, in January and July.

Opening hours

Unless stated otherwise, shops are open from 10am to 7pm, Monday to Saturday .

Arts, crafts, gifts and hobbies
Cath'Art
13 Rue Ste Croix de la Bretonnerie, 4th
t 01 48 04 80 10

www.cathart.com
Ⓜ Hôtel de Ville

Fun and funky little Marais shop (see p.68) selling marionettes, inflatables and plastic gnomes.

La Charrue et les Étoiles
19 Rue des Francs Bourgeois, 4th
t 01 48 87 39 07
Ⓜ Chemin Vert, St Paul

An intriguing Marais shop selling a vast collection of plastic and tin miniatures (see p.68).

Deyrolle
46 Rue du Bac, 7th
t 01 42 22 30 07
Ⓜ Rue du Bac

A 170-year-old taxidermy shop in St Germain. Inside, you can get near enough to a lion to touch its whiskers, but you might have to settle for a bamboo-handled butterfly net to take home instead.

Graphigro
157 Rue Lecourbe, 15th
t 01 42 50 45 49
Ⓜ Vaugirard

If you've been inspired by the views and fancy joining the artistic throng on the Left Bank, come to Graphigro in Montparnasse (see pp.94–95), Paris' largest (and cheapest) arts suppliers, for a set of watercolours and brushes.

La Maison du Cerf Volant
7 Rue de Prague, 12th
t 01 44 68 00 75
Ⓜ Ledru Rollin
Open 10am–7pm (Tues–Sat)

Every type of kite imaginable: stunt, box and racing kites, as well as novelty kites in the shape of dragons or butterflies. Near the Bastille (see pp.71–73).

Marie Papier
26 Rue Vavin, 6th
t 01 43 26 46 44
www.mariepapier.fr
Ⓜ Vavin, Nôtre Dame des Champs

Beautiful handmade writing paper in all colours. There's also a Montparnasse branch (see pp.94–95).

Nature et Découvertes
Forum des Halles, 1st
t 01 40 28 42 16
Ⓜ Châtelet Les Halles
Carrousel du Louvre, 1st

t 01 47 03 47 43
Ⓜ Palais Royal–Musée du Louvre
Palais de la Découverte, Avenue Franklin D.
Roosevelt, 8th
t 01 45 63 46 36
Ⓜ Franklin D. Roosevelt
Passage du Havre, 109 Rue St Lazare, 9th
t 01 42 82 72 80
Ⓜ St Lazare
8–10 Court St Émilion, Bercy Village, 12th
t 01 53 33 82 40
Ⓜ Bercy
61 Rue de Passy, 16th
t 01 42 30 53 87
Ⓜ Passy
www.natureetdecouvertes.com
Open Daily 10am–8pm
This popular chain showcases an eclectic range
of goods loosely themed on nature: aromatherapy
kits, South American turquoise jewellery, iron
weather vanes, pots made out of cinnamon, and so
on. Each branch has a kids' section (*see* p.44).

Pylones
52 Galerie Vivienne, 2nd
t 01 42 61 51 60
Ⓜ Pyramides
57 Rue St Louis en l'Île, 4th
t 01 46 34 05 02
Ⓜ Pont Marie
57 Rue Tardieu, 18th
t 01 46 06 37 00
Ⓜ Abbesses
www.pylones.com
Open 10.30am–7.30pm
A chain that offers a huge range of fun gadgets,
gifts and toys for children and adults: plastic aliens,
shark staplers, painted tea pots, designer toasters,
wacky toothbrushes, toy cars, electronics and more.

Why!
22 Rue du Pont Neuf, 1st
t 01 42 33 40 33
Ⓜ Pont Neuf
14–16 Rue Jean Jacques Rousseau, 1st
t 01 42 33 36 95
Ⓜ Les Halles, Étienne Marcel
41 Rue des Francs Bourgeois, 4th
t 01 44 61 72 75
Ⓜ Chemin Vert
14–16 Rue Bernard Palissy, 6th
t 01 45 48 71 98

Ⓜ St Germain des Prés, Mabillon
Open 10.30am–7.30pm (Mon–Sat)
Temples of tackiness: furry lava lamps, humming-
bird-shaped key rings, glow-in-the-dark bags and
other things in bright colours (*see* p. 68).

Books
Chantelivre
13 Rue de Sèvres, 6th
t 01 45 48 87 90
Ⓜ Sèvres Babylone
Open 1pm–7pm (Mon), 10am–7pm (Tues–Sat)
Specialist children's bookshop near St Germain
(*see* p.94) with a big English language section.

Galignani Librairie Française et Etrangère
224 Rue de Rivoli, 1st
t 01 42 60 76 07
Ⓜ Tuileries
Galignani is said to be the oldest English-
language bookshop on the European continent,
and still stocks a huge range of English, American
and French titles. Near the Louvre (*see* pp.42–44).

Shakespeare & Company
37 Rue de la Bûcherie, 5th
t 01 43 26 96 50
www.shakespeareco.org
Ⓜ Maubert Mutualité
The haunt of Joyce, Hemingway, Beckett and other
writers, this Latin Quarter (*see* pp.93–94) bookstore,
with its labyrinth of book-filled alcoves and cubby
holes, is legendary. Go up the hidden stairway to the
cosy children's classics and rare first editions corner.

WH Smith
248 Rue de Rivoli, 1st
t 01 44 77 88 99
www.whsmith.fr
email whsmith.france@wanadoo.fr
Ⓜ Concorde
Open 9am–7.30pm (Mon–Sat), 1pm–7.30pm (Sun)
Over 70,000 English language books, including
an ample children's section on the first floor. Kids
can practise their French by picking up bilingual
versions of classics such as *James and the Giant
Peach*. Near the Louvre (*see* pp.42-44)

Chocolates and cakes
Alliance Chocolat
1 Place Victor Hugo, 16th
t 01 45 00 89 68

www.godiva.be
Ⓜ Victor Hugo
Open 10.30am–7.30pm (Tues–Sat)
A confectioners north of the Trocadéro (*see* p.60). Intricate chocolate and fruit arrangements.

Brocco
180 Rue du Temple, 3rd
t 01 42 72 19 81
Ⓜ Temple
A legendary cake shop on the Marais (*see* p.67). The chocolate concoctions and cakes are made in the back of the shop, fresh every day.

Debauve et Gallais
30 Rue des Saints Peres, 7th
t 01 45 48 54 67
Ⓜ St Germain des Prés, Rue du Bac
This elegant St Germain bonbon shop was originally a pharmacy ,where chocolate was prescribed for Louis XVI as a cure for flatulence!

Le Fleuriste du Chocolat
49 Av de la Bourdonnais, 7th
t 01 45 56 13 04
www.lefleuristeduchocolat.com
Ⓜ École Militaire, Pont de l'Alma
A novelty *chocolateur*-florist near the Eiffel Tower (*see* pp.56–57) that sells edible bouquets.

Jadis et Gourmande
39 Rue des Archives, 4th
t 01 48 04 08 03
Ⓜ Hôtel de Ville
88 Bd Port Royal, 5th
t 01 43 26 17 75
RER Port Royal
49 bis Av Franklin D. Roosevelt, 8th
t 01 42 25 06 04
Ⓜ Franklin D Roosevelt
27 Rue Boissy d'Anglas, 5th
t 01 42 65 23 23
Ⓜ Madeleine
Open 1pm–7pm (Mon), 10.30am–7.30pm (Tues–Sat)
Great novelty chocolate shops where can pick up chocolate animals, Eiffel Towers and Christmas decorations. Order in advance and you can buy a box with your child's name picked out in white and dark chocolate tiles.

La Maison du Chocolat
19 Rue de Sèvres, 6th
t 01 45 44 20 40
Ⓜ Sèvres Babylone
52 Rue François 1er, 8th
t 01 47 23 38 25
Ⓜ Franklin D. Roosevelt
225 Rue du Faubourg St Honoré, 8th
t 01 42 27 39 44
Ⓜ Ternes
89 Avenue Raymong Poincaré, 16th
t 01 40 67 77 83
Ⓜ Victor Hugo
www.lamaisonduchocolat.com
Open 9.30am–7.30pm (Mon–Sat)
Hand-painted, exquisitely wrapped sweet treats.

A la Mère de Famille
35 Rue du Faubourg Montmartre
t 01 47 70 83 69
Ⓜ Grands Boulevards
Paris' oldest sweet shop (almost 250 years old). Choose from foil-wrapped classic chocolate coins or cigarettes, and candied fruits.

A la Petite Fabrique
12 Rue St Sabin, 11th
t 01 48 05 82 02
Ⓜ Bastille
Open 10.30am–7.30pm (Tues–Sat)
See the creative process behind making elegant chocolate éclairs from steaming sticky syrup at this little shop-workshop near the Bastille (*see* pp.71–73).

Clothes
Agnes B (Children's)
2 and 10 Rue du Jour, 1st
t 01 45 08 49 89
Ⓜ Châtelet Les Halles
83 Rue d'Assas, 6th
t 01 43 54 69 21
Ⓜ Port Royal
22 Rue St Sulpice, 6th
t 01 40 51 70 69
Ⓜ St Sulpice
6–12 Rue du Vieux Colombier, 6th
t 01 44 39 02 60
Ⓜ St Sulpice
www.agnesb.fr
An enduringly fashionable name, Agnès B has taken over virtually all of Rue du Jour near Les Halles (*see* pp.70–71) with her shops. Head towards numbers 2 and 10 for her designer baby and kids clothes, plus mini versions of adult lines. There are also branches around the Jardin du Luxembourg.

Baby Dior

252 Boulevard St Germain, 7th
t 01 42 22 90 90
www.dior.com
Ⓜ Solférino, Rue du Bac
A classic St Germain's kids' boutique (*see* p.92).

Baby Tuileries

326 Rue St Honoré, 1st
t 01 42 60 42 59
Ⓜ Tuileries
Mini leather jackets, tartan skirts and trousers, button-down collars, corduroy suits, hooded duffel coats and knickerbockers. Near the Louvre (*see* pp.42–44).

Bébés en Vadrouille

47 Boulevard Henri IV, 4th
t 01 48 87 19 68
www.bbenv.com
Ⓜ Bastille
Ethnic baby clothes and pre-school equipment from Africa, South America and Asia.

Bonpoint

320 Rue St Honoré, 1st
t 01 49 27 94 82
Ⓜ Tuileries
67 Rue de l'Université, 7th
t 01 45 55 63 70
Ⓜ Assemblée Nationale, Solférino
229 Boulevard St Germain, 7th
t 01 40 62 76 20
Ⓜ Solférino, Rue du Bac
12 Avenue Montaigne, 8th
t 01 47 20 42 10
Ⓜ Franklin D. Roosevelt
15 Rue Royale, 8th
t 01 47 42 52 63
Ⓜ Concorde, Madeleine
82 Rue de Grenelle, 18th
t 01 45 48 05 45
Ⓜ Bir Hakeim
64 Avenue Raymond Poincaré, 16th
t 01 47 27 60 81
Ⓜ Victor Hugo, Trocadéro
www.bonpoint.com
The most exclusive name in town for classic kids' couture (*see* p.92).

Boudezan

24 Rue Yvonne le Tac, 18th
t 01 42 62 82 86

Ⓜ Abbesses
Reasonably priced children's clothes made from natural fibres in trendy colours and designs (*see* p.103).

La Boutique de Floriane

17 Rue Tronchet, 8th
t 01 42 65 25 95
Ⓜ Madeleine
Elegant baby clothes in pastel hues, many sporting animal motifs. Near the Madeleine (*see* p.46).

Catimini

23 Boulevard Madeleine, 1st
t 01 49 27 01 78
Ⓜ Madeleine
Forum des Halles, 1st
t 01 45 08 51 34
Ⓜ Châtelet Les Halles
6 Rue des Francs Bourgeois, 3rd
t 01 42 72 72 66
Ⓜ St Paul
114 Avenue des Champs Élysées, 8th
t 01 53 76 21 51
Ⓜ George V, Charles de Gaulle-Étoile
114 Boulevard Montparnasse, 14th
t 01 43 22 05 30
Ⓜ Vavin
311 Rue de Vaugirard, 15th
t 01 48 28 36 30
Ⓜ Vaugirard, Convention
155 Avenue Victor Hugo, 16th
t 01 47 27 93 01
Ⓜ Rue de la Pompe, Victor Hugo
www.catimini.com
Printed romper suits, voile dresses and matching accessories, games, bed linen and crockery (*see* p.68).

Dipaki

20 Rue Pont Neuf, 1st
t 01 40 26 21 00
Ⓜ Pont Neuf, Châtelet
5 Rue Bréa, 6th
t 01 43 26 04 37
Ⓜ Vavin
22 Rue Cler, 7th
t 01 47 05 47 62
Ⓜ École Militaire
46 Rue Université, 7th
t 01 42 97 49 89
Ⓜ Rue du Bac, Solférino
18 Rue Vignon, 8th
t 01 42 66 24 74

Ⓜ Madeleine
Reasonably priced baby clothes and nursery equipment in bright, primary colours.

D. Porthault
370 Rue St Honoré, 1st
t 01 47 03 09 43
Ⓜ Tuileries
A little luxury shop near the Louvre (*see* pp.42–44) selling posh baby clothes with lace, frills and bows .

Du Pareil au Même
1 Rue Saint Denis, 1st
t 01 42 36 07 57
Ⓜ Châtelet
Forum des Halles, 1st
t 01 40 13 95 29
Ⓜ Châtelet Les Halles
168 Boulevard St Germain, 6th
t 01 46 33 87 85
Ⓜ St Germain des Prés, Mabillon
17 Rue Vavin, 6th
t 01 43 54 12 34
Ⓜ Vavin
15 Rue des Mathurins, 8th
t 01 42 66 93 80
Ⓜ Havre Caumartin
165 Rue Château des Rentiers, 13th
t 01 45 83 03 08
Ⓜ Place d'Italie, Nationale
10 Boulevard Brune, 14th
t 01 45 39 65 95
Ⓜ Porte de Vanves
97 Avenue Victor Hugo, 16th
t 01 47 27 06 31
Ⓜ Victor Hugo
www.dpam.fr
Du Pareil au Même branches are oases of bargain-priced common sense with good, sturdy dungarees, thick coats and bright T-shirts, as well as copies of designer labels at decent, department store prices (*see* p.92).

Gap Kids
9 Boulevard Sebastopol, 1st
t 01 44 76 95 84
Ⓜ Châtelet
102 Rue de Rivoli, 1st
t 01 44 88 28 28
Ⓜ Châtelet
14 Rue Lobineau, 6th
t 01 44 32 07 30/31

Ⓜ Mabillon
62 Rue de Rennes, 6th
t 01 53 63 00 39
Ⓜ St Sulpice
36 Avenue Champs Élysées, 8th
t 01 56 88 48 00
Ⓜ Frankin D. Roosevelt
64 Faubourg St Antoine, 1 Rue Scribe, 9th
t 01 44 51 19 26
Ⓜ Auber
36 Rue Tronchet, 9th
t 01 42 68 20 44
Ⓜ Havre Caumartin
28–32 Avenue Victor Hugo, 16th
t 01 53 64 11 00
Ⓜ Victor Hugo
www.gapkids.com
The US chain has grown in popularity in France in the last few years because its no-nonsense styles in sweatshirts, T-shirts and denims offer an alternative to the overdesigned lines of traditional Parisian boutiques. Several branches have Baby Gap sections, which stock the equally in-demand range of sturdy, practical baby clothes.

Gaspard de la Butte
10 bis Rue Yvonne le Tac, 18th
t 01 42 55 99 40
Ⓜ Abbesses
A delightful Montmartre (*see* p.97) shop that sells a handmade clothes for under-6s – look out for the dungarees and sweaters in ochres and reds.

I Pinco Pallino
Galerie Élysées, 26 Avenue Champs Élysées
t 01 42 25 32 12
www.ipincopallino.com
Ⓜ Franklin D. Roosevelt
Italian designer kids clothes with lots of oriental-type motifs and soft leather shoes at high prices.

Jacadi
9 Avenue de l'Opéra, 1st
t 01 49 27 06 29
Ⓜ Opéra
27 Rue St Antoine, 4th
t 01 42 77 74 26
Ⓜ Bastille
4 Avenue Gobelins, 5th
t 01 43 31 43 90
Ⓜ Gobelins
76 Rue Assas, 6th

t 01 45 44 60 44
Ⓜ Nôtre Dame des Champs
256 Boulevard St Germain, 7th
t 01 42 84 30 40
Ⓜ Solférino
17 Rue Tronchet, 8th
t 01 42 65 84 98
Ⓜ Madeleine
54 Boulevard du Temple, 11th
t 01 48 06 13 10
Ⓜ République
98 Rue Caulaincourt, 18th
t 01 42 36 69 91
Ⓜ Lamarck Caulaincourt
www.jacadi.fr
   Suits and formal smocks with cutesy motifs (*see* p.92).

Kerstin Adolphson
157 Boulevard St Germain, 6th
t 01 45 48 00 14
Ⓜ St Germain des Prés
   An atmospheric St Germain shop (*see* p.92) selling patterned socks, bright jackets and painted wooden clogs.

Miki House
366 Rue St Honoré, 1st
t 01 40 20 90 98
Ⓜ Concorde, Madeleine, Tuileries
1 Place des Victoires, 1st
t 01 40 26 23 00
Ⓜ Pyramides
1 Rue du Vieux Colombier, 6th
t 01 46 33 77 55
Ⓜ St Sulpice
   Red and yellow T-shirts, shirts, and corduroy dresses all bearing the Miki smiling-bear motif.

Natalys
32 Rue St Antoine, 4th
t 01 48 87 77 42
Ⓜ Bastille, St Paul
74 Rue de Rivoli, 4th
t 01 40 29 46 35
Ⓜ Hôtel de Ville
74–76 Rue de Seine, 6th
t 01 46 33 46 48
Ⓜ Mabillon
47 Rue de Sèvres, 6th
t 01 45 48 77 12
Ⓜ St Sulpice, Sèvres Babylone

92 Avenue des Champs Élysées, 8th
t 01 43 59 17 65
Ⓜ George V
42 Rue Vignon, 9th
t 01 47 42 61 83
Ⓜ Madeleine
117 bis Rue Ordener, 18th
t 01 42 23 92 91
Ⓜ Jules Joffrin
www.natalys.fr
   Well-priced children's clothes (fur-collared coats, woollen jackets, corduroy trousers and dresses), shoes, nursery equipment, baby furniture and toys.

Petit Bateau
Forum des Halles, 1st
t 01 44 76 09 17
Ⓜ Châtelet Les Halles
81 Rue de Sèvres, 6th
t 01 45 49 48 38
Ⓜ Sévres Babylone, Vaneau
26 Rue Vavin, 6th
t 01 55 42 02 63
Ⓜ Vavin
186 Rue de Grenelle, 7th
t 01 47 05 18 51
Ⓜ La Tour Maubourg
116 Avenue des Champs Élysées, 8th
t 01 40 74 02 03
Ⓜ Charles de Gaulle-Étoile
13 Rue Tronchet, 8th
t 01 42 65 26 26
Ⓜ Madeleine
64 Avenue Victor Hugo, 16th
t 01 45 00 13 95
Ⓜ Victor Hugo
www.petitbateau.fr
   Lots of nice T-shirts and pajamas (*see* p.92).

Petit Boy
26 Rue de Turenne, 3rd
t 01 40 27 96 61
Ⓜ Chemin Vert
4 Rue Vavin, 6th
t 01 45 49 39 07
Ⓜ Vavin
55 Boulevard Pasteur, 15th
t 01 40 65 92 91
Ⓜ Pasteur
www.petitboy.free.fr
   Chunky casuals for boys and girls with zip cardigans and combat trousers.

Petit Faune

33 Rue Jacob, 6th
t 01 42 60 80 72
Ⓜ St Germain des Prés
89 Rue de Rennes
t 01 42 22 63 69
Ⓜ St Sulpice
www.petitfaune.com
   Coordinated baby and toddler knitwear, and
sweaters and smocks for older children (see p.92).

Tartine et Chocolat

24 Rue de la Paix, 2nd
t 01 47 42 10 68
Ⓜ Opéra
266 Boulevard St Germain, 7th
t 01 45 56 10 45
Ⓜ Solférino
22 Rue Boissy d'Anglais, 8th
t 01 40 17 09 03
Ⓜ Madeleine, Concorde
105 Rue du Faubourg Saint Honoré, 8th
t 01 45 62 44 04
Ⓜ St Philippe du Roule
60 Av Paul Doumer, 16th
t 01 45 04 08 94
Ⓜ Trocadéro, La Muette
www.tartine-et-chocolat.com
   Tasteful, formal baby clothes and nursery furniture in pastels and natural fibres (see p.92).

Tout Compte Fait

170 Rue du Temple, 3rd
t 01 40 27 00 42
Ⓜ Temple
62 Rue Chaussée d'Antin, 9th
t 01 48 74 16 54
Ⓜ Trinité, Chaussée d'Antin La Fayette
128 Rue du Faubourg St Antoine, 12th
t 01 43 46 94 32
Ⓜ Ledru Rollin, Faidherbe Chaligny
115 Avenue Victor Hugo, 16th
t 01 47 55 63 36
Ⓜ Victor Hugo
1 Square Clignancourt, 18th
t 01 42 64 00 21
Ⓜ Jules Joffrin
www.toutcomptefait.com
   Classic French conservative wear for the 0–4s –
button-down suits, formal dresses and duffel coats.

Department stores

BHV (Bazar de l'Hôtel de Ville)

52–64 Rue de Rivoli, 4th
t 01 42 74 90 00
www.bhv.fr
Ⓜ Hôtel de Ville
Open 9.30am–7pm (Mon–Sat), until 8.30pm (Fri)
   This no-nonsense department store opposite the
Hôtel de Ville near the Marais (see p.67), has a huge
DIY and electrical goods department in the base-
ment. There's also a big children's clothes and toy
section on the first floor.

Le Bon Marché

24–38 Rue de Sèvres, 7th
t 01 44 39 80 00
www.bonmarche.fr
Ⓜ Sèvres Babylone
Open 9.30am–7pm (Mon–Sat)
   Children's clothes and toys are in the basement
of 'The Good Buy' in St Germain, Paris' first-ever
department store, which still enjoys a very high
reputation. Over 400 square metres of floor are
dedicated to toys alone.

Galeries Lafayette

40 Boulevard Haussmann, 9th
t 01 42 82 34 56
www.galerieslafayette.com
Ⓜ Chausée d'Antin
Open 9.30am–7pm (Mon–Sat), until 9pm (Thurs)
   A truly vast store with a huge children's clothes
section. Fashion shows on Tuesdays and Fridays at
11am during the summer.

Printemps

64 Boulevard Haussmann, 9th
t 01 42 82 50 00
www.printemps.com
Ⓜ Havre Caumartin
Open 9.30am–7pm (Mon–Sat), until 10pm (Sat)
   Perhaps Paris' poshest department store. It hosts
an opulent array of fashion concessions, and a free
fashion show every Tuesday morning. Free créche
for kids aged 2–9, 2pm–7pm, Wed and Sat only
(max 2hrs).

La Samaritaine

19 Rue de la Monnaie, 1st
t 01 40 41 20 20
www.lasamaritaine.com
Ⓜ Pont Neuf, Châtelet

Open 9.30am–7pm (Mon–Sat), until 10pm (Thurs)
The best toy section of any department store in Paris. There's even a carousel and other entertainment on hand for when your kids tire of browsing through all the teddies, remote-controlled cars and video games. Visit the rooftop café for its view of the city (*see* p.47).

Flea markets

Marché aux Puces de Montreuil
20th
Ⓜ Porte de Montreuil
Open 7.30am–7pm (Sat–Mon)
A rather junky market. The traders here are less clued up than their counterparts at Saint Ouen.

Marché aux Puces de Saint Ouen
Porte de Clignancourt, 18th
t 01 40 11 54 14
Ⓜ Porte de Clignancourt
Open 7am–7pm (Sat–Mon)
Paris' largest classic flea market (at the northern end of métro line 4). There are lots of antique and bric-à-brac stalls – a great place to pick up old toys.

Marché aux Puces de Vanves
14th
Ⓜ Porte de Vanves
Open 7.30am–7pm (Sat–Sun)
The best hunting-ground for old toys and books.

Shoes and hats

Petit Petons
20 Rue St Placide, 6th
t 01 42 84 00 05
Ⓜ St Placide
2 Rue Cler, 7th
t 01 47 53 81 70
Ⓜ École Militaire
135 Rue Faubourg St Antoine, 11th
t 01 40 19 07 19
Ⓜ Ledru Rollin
Reasonably priced children's shoes.

Six Pieds Trois Pouces
223 Bd St Germain, 7th
t 01 45 44 03 72
Ⓜ St Germain des Prés
85 Rue Longchamp, 16th
t 01 45 53 64 21
Ⓜ Rue de la Pompe
78 Avenue de Wagram, 17th

t 01 46 22 81 64
Ⓜ Ternes
www.6pieds3pouces.com
Exquisite Italian footwear for kids (*see* p. 92).

Têtes en l'Air
65 Rue des Abbesses, 18th
t 01 46 06 71 19
Ⓜ Abbesses
Wacky hat shop in Montmartre (*see* pp. 97–104).

Toys and games

Baby Rêve
32 Avenue Rapp, 7th
t 01 45 51 24 00
Ⓜ École Militaire
Open 9.30am–7pm (Tues–Sat)
Pre-school toys and educational games.

Le Bonhomme de Bois
141 Rue d'Alésia, 14th
t 01 40 44 58 20
Ⓜ Alésia
Rue de la Convention, 15th
t 01 45 78 66 30
Ⓜ Javel
46 Avenue Niel, 17th
t 01 40 54 79 88
Ⓜ Pereire
43 Boulevard Malesherbes, 17th
t 01 40 17 03 33
Ⓜ Malesherbes
www.lebonhommedebois.com
Classic wooden toys (cars, boats, dolls' houses).

Le Bon Marché – L'Espace Trois Hiboux
Entrance 5 Rue de Babylone, 7th
t 01 44 39 80 00
Ⓜ Sèvres Babylone
Open 9.30am–7pm (Mon–Fri), 9.30am–8pm (Sat)
This St Germain department store contains a dazzling toy department that will enthrall children of all ages.

Boutique Descartes
6 Rue Meissoneir, 17th
t 01 42 27 50 09
Ⓜ Wagram
www.descartes-editeur.com
Open 10am–7pm (Mon–Sat)
Board games, war games and magic trick sets as well as a large collection of fantasy figurines.

Butty

84 Rue Manin, 19th
t 01 42 41 01 72
Ⓜ Porte de Pantin
Open 10am–7pm (Mon–Sat)

Soft toys, puppets, dolls and dressing-up costumes south of La Villette (*see* pp.105–110). Reasonable prices.

Le Ciel est à tout le Monde

Carrousel du Louvre, 99 Rue de Rivoli, 1st
t 01 49 27 93 03
Ⓜ Palais Royal–Musée du Louvre
10 Rue Gay Lussac, 5th
t 01 46 33 53 91
Ⓜ Luxembourg
7 Avenue Trudaine, 9th
t 01 48 78 93 40
Ⓜ Anvers, Barbes Rochechouart
www.lecielesttoutlamonde.com

A chain with a big selection of traditional toys: marionettes, dolls' houses, rocking horses and kites.

Les Deux Tisserins

36 Rue des Bernardins
t 01 46 33 88 68
Ⓜ Maubert Mutualité

Rag dolls, dolls' houses, kaleidoscopes and teddy bears, plus a small selection of children's clothes.

Gault

206 Rue de Rivoli, 1st
t 01 42 60 51 17
www.gault-france.com
Ⓜ Tuileries
Open 10am–7pm (Mon–Sat), 11am–7pm (Sun)

Dedicated to miniatures: models of cartoon characters like Tin Tin and Snow White, and beautifully crafted dioramas, house interiors and paper and porcelain houses. Close to the Louvre (*see* pp.42–44).

La Grande Récré

27 Boulevard Poissonière, 2nd
t 01 40 26 12 20
Ⓜ Grand Boulevards
143 Avenue Daumesnil, 12th
t 01 43 45 95 50
Ⓜ Château de Vincennes
Centre Comercial Place d'Italie, 230 Avenue d'Italie, 13th
t 01 53 62 15 12
Ⓜ Place d'Italie
7–11 Boulevard Barbès, 18th

t 01 42 64 90 19
Ⓜ Barbès Rochechouart
Parvis de la Cité des Sciences et de l'Industrie, 19th
t 01 46 07 00 37
Ⓜ Porte de la Villette
www.la-grande-recre.com
Open 10am–7.30pm (Mon–Sat)

Large, supremely well-equipped toy store chain. Good selection of pre-school toys and games.

Jouet International du Monde

28 Rue des Trois Bornes, 11th
t 01 43 57 68 44
Ⓜ Parmentier
Open 12 noon–8pm (Mon–Sat)

Handmade toys and games (boomerangs, yo-yos, frisbees, kites). North of the Bastille (*see* pp.71–73).

Marais Plus

20 Rue des Francs Bourgeois, 3rd
t 01 48 87 01 40
Ⓜ Rambuteau, Hôtel de Ville

Educational toys and books and a very pleasant tea shop on the first floor (*see* p.68).

Au Nain Bleu

406–410 Rue St Honoré, 8th
t 01 42 60 39 01
www.au-nain-bleu.com
Ⓜ Concorde, Madeleine
Open 9.45am–6.30pm (Mon–Sat)

Toy cars, dolls' houses and board games. Magical window displays throughout the year (*see* p.47).

L'Oiseau de Paradis

86 Rue Monge, 6th
t 01 47 07 24 32
Ⓜ Place Monge
211 Boulevard St Germain, 7th
t 01 45 48 97 90
Ⓜ Rue du Bacs
Open 9.30am–7.30pm (Tues–Sat)

Plastic animals, drum kits, dolls, wooden forts and sailing boats (*see* p.92) .

Toys 'R' Us

Centre Commercial Quatre Temps, La Défense
t 01 47 76 29 78
www.toysrus.fr
Ⓜ La Défense
Open 10am–8pm (Mon–Sat)

There's a vast branch in the shopping centre next to the Grande Arche de la Défense (*see* p.51).

DISNEYLAND® RESORT PARIS

I think what I want Disneyland to be most of all is a happy place, a place where adults and children can experience together some of the wonders of life, of adventure and feel better because of it.

Walt Disney

Step through the gates of Disneyland® Paris, and you enter one man's fantasy: a cloistered place isolated from the risks, conflicts and cares of life; litter-free and pretty, with perfect flowerbeds and pastel-coloured buildings; a place where cartoon characters loom larger than life and classic tales are enacted, fizzed up by thrilling rides and healthy loads of showbiz razzmatazz.

Surrender! Whether you are 2 or 62 years old, sick with excitement, or resigned and already exhausted, to get the most out of this truly

> *Disneyland will never be finished as long as there is a little imagination left in the world.*
> **Walt Disney**

extraordinary place you have to allow yourself to explore it with, or through, the eyes of a child. Just witnessing a child's reaction to all she encounters will be an experience in itself.

This guide takes a less than jaded look at the fabulous phenomenon of Disneyland® Resort Paris, Europe's most popular tourist attraction. With the advice provided, you and your children will have the most fantastic (and economical) time possible. Survive and enjoy!

The man behind the mouse

Walter Elias Disney was born in Chicago, Illinois, in 1901. As a boy, his family moved to Marceline, Missouri, a small country town in America's midwest, and bought a farm there. This idyllic setting remained with Walt forever, and its pre-motor-age charm fostered a yearning for romance and simple values which defined and coloured his creative vision. Main Street, USA, is said to be a carefully crafted homage to Marceline.

Getting started

Walt began drawing in high school and studied cartoon creation in his spare time. By the end of the First World War, he was working for an advertising agency in Kansas, where he met Ub Iwerks, a talented young artist. In 1922, the two young men started to make short animated cartoons under the studio name Laugh-o-Gram, which marked the start of their historic creative partnership.

One year later, Walt moved to Los Angeles and re-established the studio with his elder brother, Roy, and Iwerks. They shot to fame in 1928 with *Steamboat Willie*, the first cartoon to use synchronized sound and which featured a spindly legged mouse called Mickey, whose squeaks were provided by Walt himself. Other animated hits followed. In 1937, Walt again made history, with *Snow White and the Seven Dwarfs*, the first feature-length, full-colour, animated movie. It proved an enormous commercial and critical success.

A star is born

It was on a train journey that the idea of a cartoon mouse was first discussed. To pass the time, Walt and his wife, Lillian, put together a whimsical character based on the field mice which used to come into their old studio in Kansas. Walt

---

Wicked wicked: Disney rotters

The first-ever Disney baddie was Pete, a villain who started way back in the early days of the *Alice Comedies* in 1925, and appeared in films all the way through to *A Goofy Movie* in 1995 – a span of 70 years! Also known as Peg Leg Pete and Black Pete, this gruff, cat-like character soon became better known as Mickey Mouse's, and later Donald Duck's, number-one enemy.

How many of these notorious, latter-day Disney villains do you recognize?
- The Queen (*Snow White and the Seven Dwarfs*)
- Captain Hook (*Peter Pan*)
- Kaa (*Jungle Book*)
- Cruella De Vil (*101 Dalmatians*)
- Prince John and his sidekick Sir Hiss (*Robin Hood*)
- Professor Ratigan (*The Great Mouse Detective*)
- Ursula (*The Little Mermaid*)
- Hades (*Hercules*)
- Governor Ratcliffe (*Pocahontas*)
- Jafar (*Aladdin*)
- Gaston (*Beauty and The Beast*)
- Hopper (*A Bug's Life*)
- Frollo (*The Hunchback of Notre Dame*)
- Uncle Scar (*The Lion King*)
- Sid Phillips (*Toy Story*)
- The Queen of Hearts (*Alice in Wonderland*)
- Medusa (*The Rescuers*)
- Clayton (*Tarzan*)
- Shan-Yu (*Mulan*)
- John Silver (*Treasure Planet*)
- Lyle T. Rourke (*Atlantis*)

himself originally thought of calling him 'Mortimer Mouse', and it was Walt's wife who said she thought this sounded far too pompous, and then came up with the name Mickey.

Walt's other big idea

Walt's vision was, perhaps, most famously put to use the day he sat on a park bench watching his daughter riding a merry-go-round. Growing increasingly bored, he wondered why there shouldn't be a place specially designed for the whole family to enjoy themselves, and not just the kids? The concept of the theme park was born. The first Disneyland® Park was opened in Anaheim, California, in 1955, and proved an instant success. A few years later work began on a second site, in Florida. Sadly, Walt did not live to see its completion. A lifelong smoker, he died of cancer in 1966.

A Disneyland® Resort Paris glossary

Audio-Animatronics®

A technological breakthrough pioneered by Walt Disney himself, Audio-Animatronics brings the art of animation to 3-D figures, synchronizing mechanical movement and sound effects to give life to many of the figures in the Disney Parks.

Cast members

All Disney employees are referred to as cast members. They are trained performers familiar with the rigorous standards drilled into them at The Disney University Training Center. Lesson no.1 – smile at all times!

Guests

More than mere visitors or customers, you are made to feel a little more special by being addressed as Disney's guests.

Imagineers

The imagineers turn dreams into reality. Armed with an ideology summed up in three words – imagine, design, build – they have produced such wonders as gold nuggets that really gleam and a tumbledown cowboy town right in the heart of Europe.

Passports

Your entrance tickets to the Parks; a reminder that you are entering a new, strange and exciting country.

Pre-entertainment area

Disney-speak for a queue!

The Top 10

1 Space Mountain
2 Rock 'n' Roller Coaster Starring Aerosmith
3 Big Thunder Mountain
4 Peter Pan's Flight
5 Star Tours
6 Studio Tram Tour
7 Cinemagique
8 Phantom Manor
9 Moteurs...Action! Stunt Show Spectacular
10 Pirates of the Caribbean

Disneyland® Resort Paris

Disney began looking for a European site in 1985, and finally settled on a site near Paris. Work on the mammoth new complex started in August 1988 and involved over 2,000 suppliers, designers and architects (known as 'imagineers'), and some 8,000 construction workers.

Disneyland® Paris' dominant landmark, Sleeping Beauty Castle, was unveiled to the public on 12 October 1991. The rest of the Disney Parks were opened on 12 April 1992 and, since opening their gates for the first time, they have welcomed over 100 million visitors and employ about 12,000 people.

The Disney Parks are found 32km (20 miles) to the east of Paris and cover an area one-fifth the size of the city. They employ around 11,000 cast members each year, from 500 different professions and representing around 95 different nationalities. As well as being filled with the famous Disney characters and attractions that bring to life the great Disney cartoons (Aladdin's Enchanted World in Adventureland, Flying Carpets over Agrabah at Walt Disney Studios®, Peter Pan's Flight in Fantasyland, and plenty more), they have rides based on some non-Disney movies too – Star Tours, Indiana Jones™ and the Temple of Peril: Backwards! – and others dreamed up especially for the Disney Parks, like Space Mountain, inspired by the classic stories of Jules Verne. Ambitious expansion plans culminated in the opening of a new separate park, **Walt Disney Studios®**, in Spring 2002 (*see* pp.223–226) as one of the three components (plus **Disney® Village**) of a leisure complex with the overall name of **Disneyland® Resort Paris**. The core of the whole operation, the original Disneyland® Paris theme park with Main Street, USA, and its four 'Lands', is known as **Disneyland® Park**.

The Disney Years

1923 After his first animated film business fails, Walt and brother Roy start a tiny film studio in Hollywood, where Walt directs the first Mickey Mouse cartoon, *Plane Crazy*.

1928 *Steamboat Willie* is the first cartoon with a soundtrack.

1930 Pluto makes his debut in *The Chain Gang*.

1932 *Flowers and Trees* wins Walt Disney his first Academy Award.

1933 *Three Little Pigs* wins another Academy Award.

1934 *The Wise Little Hen* introduces a brand new character – Donald Duck.

1935 *Music Land*.

1937 Disney releases *Snow White and the Seven Dwarfs*. Whereas Disney's earlier films had all been short cartoons, *Snow White* is the first-ever full-length animated colour feature film, and is a resounding success worldwide.

1940 *Fantasia*, combining animation and classical music, and *Pinocchio* are released.

1941 Acclaim grows as *Dumbo* wins an Academy Award for Best Original Score.

1942 *Bambi*.

1943 Donald Duck appears in *Der Führer's Face*, a satirical dig at Nazi Germany.

1948 *Seal Island* is the first of a string of successful Disney nature films.

1950 Disney releases *Cinderella* and *Treasure Island*, the first Disney film to use live actors.

1951 *Alice in Wonderland*.

1953 *Peter Pan*.

1954 *20,000 Leagues Under the Sea*.

1955 Launch of the *The Mickey Mouse Club* TV show which continues to draw in audiences for the next four years. Its success coincides with the opening of Disneyland® theme park in California. Disney also releases the live-action *Davy Crockett – King of the Wild Frontier* and the animated *Lady and the Tramp*.

1959 *Sleeping Beauty*.

1960 *Swiss Family Robinson*.

1961 *One Hundred and One Dalmatians*.

1963 *The Sword in the Stone*.

1964 Academy Awards for *Mary Poppins*.

1966 Death of Walt Disney.

1967 *The Jungle Book*.

1969 *The Love Bug*.

1970 *The Aristocats*.

1971 Disneyworld® opens in Florida.

1973 *Robin Hood*.

1977 *The Many Adventures of Winnie the Pooh*.

1982 Epcot Center (Experimental Prototype Community of Tomorrow) opens in Florida.

1984 Disney President, Walt's son-in-law Ron Miller, starts up Touchstone Pictures to rekindle failing audiences, and produces *Splash*. The film's success coincides with the opening of Disneyland® Tokyo.

1988 Mickey's 60th birthday is a double celebration, as *Who Framed Roger Rabbit?* wins four Academy Awards.

1989 Disney-MGM Studios Theme Park opens in Florida.

1990 Disney establishes Hollywood Records, a mainstream record label. The same year Disney returns to producing large-scale animated features with *The Little Mermaid*, which wins two Academy Awards.

1991 *Beauty and the Beast*.

1992 Disneyland® Paris opens amid (subsequently unfounded) French concern over the Park's potential bad effect on the nation's culture.

1993 *Aladdin*.

1994 Disney releases box-office sensation, *The Lion King*, which wins an Academy Award for Elton John's score.

1995 *Pocahontas* and *Toy Story* are released. *Pocahontas* brings in over $140 million and is the third-largest-grossing film of the year.

1999 *A Bug's Life* and *Tarzan*™.

2000 *Toy Story 2*, *Dinosaur* and *Fantasia 2000* released.

2001 *Emperor's New Clothes* and *Atlantis* released.

2002 Disneyland® Resort Paris is completed with the opening of Walt Disney Studios® Park, and both *Lilo & Stitch* and *Monsters Inc.* are released.

2003 *Finding Nemo* and *Brother Bear* are released.

2004 The launch of new movies *The Incredibles* and *Hidalgo*.

Disneyland®
Resort Paris
Essentials

Price differences between the major operators are negligible, and you won't save much by going it alone. If full immersion in the Disney experience is your aim, book direct with Disneyland® Resort Paris or one of the dedicated operators offering added frills. If you only want to visit the Disney Parks for part of your holiday, then plan your own trip or choose an operator offering combined holidays that include Park bookings and visits to other parts of Paris and/or the rest of France.

Booking through Disneyland® Resort Paris

t UK 0870 503 0303   t USA (407) 934 7639
t 01 60 30 60 30
(lines are open until late, 7 days a week)
www.disneylandparis.com

Packages to suit all tastes and budgets are available for stays in all seven theme Disney hotels, which range in category from 2- to 4-star. For example, the Classic package includes two overnight stays in a Disney hotel or Resort selected hotel, plus breakfast and unlimited access to the Disney Parks during your 3-day stay. For example, a 2-night/3-day package at Disney's Hotel Santa Fe® including breakfast will cost you €103.

Specialist tour operators

A handful of operators are recognized by Disneyland® Resort Paris as healthy competition. The main advantage of booking with a specialist company is that many of its staff will have visited the Resort, and will be able to answer your questions and offer advice.

Cresta Holidays
t UK 0870 333 3303
www.crestaholidays.co.uk

An established operator to the Disney Parks offering the whole range of travel options – air, Eurostar, self-drive, fly-drive and coach – plus a huge choice of on- and off-site hotel accommodation. Free child places are offered on selected air and self-drive holidays.

Eurocamp
t UK 0870 366 7558
www.eurocamp.co.uk
email enquiries@eurocamp.co.uk

Family accommodation at the Davy Crockett Ranch® or at a range of other campsites within easy reach of the Resort.

When is it open?
Disneyland® Park: open 10am–8pm (weekdays) and 9am–8pm on weekends (2 Nov–19 December) and daily from 20 Dec 2003 to 4 Jan 2004; 9am–1am (31 Dec). From 5 Jan to 2 Apr 2004, Disneyland Park® is open 10am–8pm (Monday–Friday), 9am–8pm (Sat–Sun). 10am–8pm: 1–2 April, 10–14 May, 17–19 May, 24–28 May, 7–11 June, 14–18 June; 9am–8pm: 3 April–9 May, 15–16 May, 20–23 May, 29 May–6 June, 12–13 June, 19 Jun–9 July, 30 Aug–5 Sept, 23–31 October; 9am–11pm: 10 July–29 Aug; 6 Sept–22 Oct: 10am–8pm (weekdays), 9am–8pm (weekends). Walt Disney Studios® Park: open 10am–6pm (weekdays) and 9am–6pm (weekdays and weekends from 20 Dec 2003 to 4 Jan 2004). From 5 Jan to 2 Apr 2004, Walt Disney Studios Park® is open 10am–6pm (Monday–Friday), 9am–6pm (Sat–Sun). 9am–6pm: 3 April–9 May, 15–16 May, 20–23 May, 29 May–6 June, 19 June–15 Sept, 12–13 June, 23–31 October; 10am–6pm: 1–2 April, 4–10 May, 17–19 May, 24–28 May, 7–11 June, 14–18 June, 6 Sept–22 Oct 10am–6pm (weekdays), 9am–6pm (weekends).

Theme Park Holidays
t UK 0870 247 2000
www.themeparkholidays.com

Offers a comprehensive Disneyland® Resort Paris short break programme using on-site hotels. Special offers include reduced midweek train fares.

Going Places
t UK 0870 400 1288
www.going-places.co.uk

Transport by Eurostar, or by air from the UK's main airports, with transfers to Disneyland® Resort Paris hotels. For those who drive, there is a choice of cross-channel ferry routes and Eurotunnel.

Gold Crest Holidays
t UK 0870 700 0007
www.gold-crest.com

Provides short-break, budget coach travel with over 250 pick-up points throughout the UK. Mainly 2- to 3-star, off-site hotels, and packages that include breakfast and transfers to the Parks. One optional upgrade includes Disney Parks hotel accommodation plus park entry.

Leger Coach Tours
t UK (01709) 839839
www.leger.co.uk

Transport by coach, Eurostar, air or self drive from over 400 locations. Alongside Resort hotels, Leger offer off-site hotels with transport to and from the Parks. Offers include a Single Parent Superdeal.

Leisure Directions
t UK 0870 442 8955
www.leisuredirection.co.uk
Competitive direct-sell operator with a comprehensive short-break programme and a range of special offers (i.e. three-nights-for-the-price-of-two, free hotel upgrades and Kids Go Free deals), both on- and off-site, with self-drive, Eurostar or by air.

Osprey Holidays
t UK 0870 560 5605
www.osprey-holidays.co.uk
Scheduled flights from Edinburgh and Glasgow year round and on some flights from Newcastle. The package includes coach transfers, unlimited entry to the Disney Parks and accommodation at the Disneyland® Resort Paris hotels. Also feature a Kids Go Free offer.

Paris Travel Service
t UK 0870 191 7279
www.paris-travel.co.uk
Holidays combining central Paris and Disneyland® Resort Paris. The first UK tour operator to offer holidays to the Resort with over 50,000 satisfied customers. Special offers include Free Days and Free Nights at the Resort plus discounts for kids.

Sovereign
t UK 0870 576 8373
www.sovereign.com
All the travel options, Disney Parks hotels and off-site accommodation as well as family savings, plus a free Kids' Pack with every booking.

Thomson
t UK 0870 606 1496
www.thomson-holidays.co.uk
Options include by coach with Eurolines, self-drive crossing the channel with the Eurotunnel, P&O Stena and by Eurostar, as well as by plane from 16 UK airports. Special 'Kids Go Free' options apply on certain dates.

Travelscene
t UK 0870 777 9987
www.travelscene.co.uk
Travel by Eurostar or self-drive and stay at an off site hotel within easy reach of the Disney Parks.

Two-centre holidays
These operators offer trips that combine a stay in Paris with 1 day or more at the Disney Parks.

Canvas Holidays
t UK (0138) 362 9000
www.canvasholidays.co.uk

Cities Direct
t UK 0870 442 1820
www.citiesdirect.co.uk

What will entry to the Parks cost?
Dates of seasons may vary from year to year.
1-day Disneyland® Park/Walt Disney Studios® Park tickets admit you to **either** Disneyland® Park **or** Walt Disney Studios® Park for the day. If you spend the day at Walt Disney Studios® Park, you can go on to the main Disneyland® Paris Park 3 hours before closing time (5–8pm most of the year, 8–11pm in midsummer). **Prices** *High Season* (April–Oct, 2 weeks Christmas–New Year) adult or child €39; *Low Season* (Nov–Mar, except 2 weeks Christmas–New Year) adult or child €29.
1-day Hopper tickets give you unlimited access to the **two** Parks for the day. **Prices** adult €49, child €39.
3-day Hopper tickets give you unlimited access to the **two** Parks for 3 days (not necessarily consecutive). Valid for 3 years. **Prices** adult €107; child €80.
A special combined RER (local rail)–Disneyland® Paris ticket gives you return travel from central Paris and 1 day's entry to the Parks. **Prices** adults €45, 3–11s €33.50 (*High Season*) and adults €39, 3–11s €29.50 (*Low Season*). See p.15.
By Eurostar (return) t 0870 518 6186 or visit **www. eurostar.com.**
To Paris (from £59) **To Lille** from £55. Children (4–11) (£50), under 4s **free**. An upgrade to Castle Class first class with a snack from £139 (adult) and £80 (child). Apex-7 adult fares from £95, youth fares (under 26) from £75, child fares (4–11) from £60.
By car through the Eurotunnel (return)
From c. £170 for a car and any number of people.
By ferry (return)
From c. £90 for a car and up to nine people.
By air (return)
About £65 for the cheapest adult fare (c. £40 for children aged 3–11).

Eurotunnel Motoring Holidays
t UK 0870 333 2001
www.eurotunnel.com

Eurolines
t UK 0870 514 3219
www.gobycoach.com

French Life
t UK 0870 444 8877
www.frenchlife.co.uk

Kirker
t UK (0207) 231 3333
www.kirkerholidays.com

Thomas Cook Signature
t UK 0870 443 4449
www.thomascook.com

Other booking options

Both the internet and, in the UK, Teletext are a good bet for last-minute and discount package fares. Most companies are established and respectable although there are a few exceptions. Check for the IATA and ATOL symbols, which guarantee that your money is safe should a company fold. UK-based budget companies to consider are:

Cheapflights
www.cheapflights.co.uk

Expedia
www.expedia.co.uk

Flybe
www.flybe.com

Hotel Bargain Offers
www.hotel-bargain-offers.co.uk

Last Minute
www.lastminute.com

Travelchoice
www.travelchoice.com

Webweekends
www.webweekends.co.uk

Getting Disney Parks tickets

It will take you and your kids much longer to get in if you wait to buy tickets at the Park admission ticket windows. Disneyland® Resort Paris tickets, or 'passports', are available in advance from these outlets. Combined RER local rail–Disneyland® Paris tickets (*see* p.184) can also be bought at certain RATP offices (métro and RER stations).

► Any Disney Store in the UK.

► Keith Prowse **t** UK (0289) 023 2425, and Seligo **t** UK 0870 705 5000

► Eurostar ticket desks at London Waterloo and Ashford; the Eurostar Ticket Shop at London Victoria; the UK Eurotunnel Passenger Terminal building in Folkestone; and the Thomas Cook Bureau de Change on P&O Portsmouth ferries.

► On board P&O Stena Line ferries (Dover–Calais).

► At The Thomas Cook Bureau de Change (UK Eurotunnel Passenger Terminal in Folkestome) and Portsmouth ferry terminal.

► Paris Tourist Offices at Orly, Roissy–Charles de Gaulle airports and on Champs Élysées (*see* p.144).

► By phone in France via **t** 01 60 30 60 30 (open 7 days a week) and in Parisian airports.

► In the FNAC, Carrefour stores and reputable ticketing agencies in Paris.

► Via the Ticketnet network, Auchan supermarkets and Cora boutiques, the Disney Store and Virgin Megastore (Champs Élysées, Paris).

For more details on travel, *see pp.7–16.*

By road

From central Paris

Disneyland® Resort Paris is about 32km (20 miles) east of Paris. Head southeast (take the Porte de Bercy exit from the *périphérique*) and pick up the A4 motorway (Autoroute de l'Est) eastbound toward Metz–Nancy. Follow signs for Marne-la-Vallée until you see the exit signs for 'Parc Disneyland' with a picture of Mickey (Exit 14 on the A4).

From the airport

From Roissy–Charles de Gaulle airport, follow signs for Marne la Vallée on the A104 (La Francilienne). After 27km (17 miles), exit from the A104 to the A4 in the direction of Metz–Nancy. From Orly Airport head towards Paris, following signs for Créteil on the A86. Exit on to the A4 towards Metz/Nancy, and take Exit 14.

From the Channel coast

Disneyland® Resort Paris is easily accessible by car thanks to the excellent French motorway system. The following gives an idea of how much time to allow once you disembark; driving from Calais and the Eurotunnel also costs about €16 in tolls. For more on driving and tolls, *see pp.11–12.*

Caen 2.5 hours
Calais and the Eurotunnel 3 hours
Cherbourg 4–5 hours
Dieppe 3 hours
Le Havre 2.5 hours

Airport bus transfers

Paris has two airports: Roissy–Charles de Gaulle (CDG) and Orly. Buses run every day at 45-minute intervals, from 8.30am to 7.45pm. The Friday and Sunday service from CDG also runs every 30 minutes until 10pm, and the Friday service from

Orly runs until 9.45pm. Bus pick-up points are sign-posted 'Navettes (Shuttle) VEA Disneyland Paris'.

CDG Terminal 1 Go to Departure Level Gate 30
CDG Terminals 2A and 2C Use Gate A-11 or C-1
CDG Terminals 2B and 2D Use Gate D-12
CDG Terminals 2F Use Gate E
Orly South (International) Coach Station, Platform 2
Orly West (Domestic) Use Gate C, Level 0

Tickets cost €14 per adult or €11.50 per child (aged 3–11) each way; children under 3 travel free. Tickets can only be purchased on board. The buses serve all the Resort hotels and the Chessy coach station, but not the Davy Crockett Ranch® (if you are staying here you can take a taxi from the coach station). The journey takes about 45 minutes.

Taxis from either airport will cost around €45.

VEA Buses

t 01 60 31 72 00
www.vea.fr

Automatic information service

t 01 49 64 47 08

By rail

Direct by Eurostar from the UK

t UK 0870 518 6186
www.eurostar.com

A special daily service runs direct to Disneyland® Resort Paris from London Waterloo (April–September) and also during half-term and Christmas school holidays. A weekend service operates all year round, leaving Waterloo on Friday and returning Sunday. Trains leave Waterloo at 9.27am (Monday–Saturday) and at 9.14am (Sunday); return journeys leave Disneyland® Paris daily at 7.35pm. The trip takes 3 hours. Passport control, and even check-in at your Resort hotel, can be done at Waterloo or once you are on board the train. With the same system, you can have your luggage sent to the station ahead of

---

Top tips

▶ Major roads in France now have a local Autoroute (A) number and a newer Euroroute (E) designation.
▶ The Davy Crockett Ranch® is a short way from the main complex, on the other side of the A4, so look out for signs (junction 13, Provins–Serris).
▶ A 24-hour service station is located by Hotel Sante Fe®.

Don't miss the train!

Eurostar's service adheres to strict security codes. Much the same as when taking a flight, you are expected to check in (at least 20 minutes before the train is due to depart). Otherwise the gates are closed and your ticket will be rendered useless.

Your coach and seat number are pre-assigned on your ticket. Check this first to save yourself walking the length of the platform unnecessarily.

you on your departure. Disney cast members patrol the train and kids receive a free Disney pack. On arrival, you are often greeted by Disney characters on the station platform, only minutes from the Parks. Book with Eurostar by phone or online.

Non-direct Eurostar and TGV services

When there are no direct services, take the Eurostar to Lille (2 hours) and change platforms to a TGV (high-speed train), which will deliver you to the Parks within 90 minutes. UK passengers arriving in Lille should join the TGV train for Roissy–Charles de Gaulle airport, which goes on to Disneyland® Resort Paris. Eurostar direct to Paris (3 hours) is less convenient, as it involves either a hike at Gare du Nord to the RER local train, or a more complex switch via the métro.

The TGV railway station at Disneyland® Resort Paris has direct rail connections from Lyon (1 hour 45mins), Lille (90mins) and 20 other cities across France, offering full flexibility for access to the Disney Parks. To book any TGV connections, contact Rail Europe, t UK 0870 584 8848.

RER express train from Paris

The quickest way to get to Disneyland® Resort Paris from the city is to take the RER (local rail network) A line. It takes 40 minutes and drops you at the Parks' gates. Trains run until 12.21 am.

Return tickets to the Parks from central Paris cost around €12 for adults and €6 for 4–11s (children under 4 travel free), but a combined RER–Disneyland® Paris ticket is currently available which gives you a return train trip from anywhere in central Paris and 1 day's entry to the Parks (€39 for adults, €29 for 3–11s, children under 3 years travel for free). Ask for a billet combiné Disneyland® Paris.

You can pick up the RER train from any east-bound station on the A line, but since the line branches, check that it's an A4 train heading for Marne la Vallée–Chessy and does stop there (A2 trains branch off in a different direction). Stations within central Paris are Ⓜ La Défense, Ⓜ Charles de Gaulle-Étoile (Arc de Triomphe), Ⓜ Auber (Opéra), Ⓜ Châtelet Les Halles (central Paris), Ⓜ Gare de Lyon (major TGV station) and Ⓜ Nation.

You must buy an RER ticket before you board as Paris métro tickets are invalid. For current details, phone up the English-language RER information line on t 08 92 68 41 14 (€0.34/minute) or check out www. ratp.fr.

The closer they get to Disneyland® Resort Paris, the more excited children become. Getting them to sit tight and be-have! is impossible as soon as they realize Mickey and friends are minutes away. When they finally reach the Parks and join the throng of other children passing through the main gates, the thrill of their shared anticipation is palpable.

At the station

The Marne la Vallée–Chessy train station (used by Eurostar and RER) is located between Disney® Village and the Disney Park entrances, just 2 minutes' walk from the main gates. If you have a billet combiné RER local rail–Disneyland® Paris ticket (see p. 182), head for the 'Pluto' entrance.

If you have bought a Direct Eurostar package, you can head straight for the Disney Parks or be ushered up escalators to the first floor where Disney characters will guide you toward the shuttle bus that takes you to your hotel. Your luggage will be tranferred direct to your hotel.

If you arrive under your own steam and have a Disneyland® Resort Paris hotel booked, consider heading straight for the Disney Parks, leaving the tiresome tasks of checking-in and unpacking for later. Guest Storage, to the right of the ticket booths, remains open until midnight (€2.50 per item). Many operator packages include the services of the Disney Express Counter on the first floor, where you can drop off your luggage and have it transported to your hotel ahead of you.

There are currency exchange booths on the first floor of the station, but there are more scattered throughout the Resort, so do not feel you have to exchange all your money in one go.

Turn right after leaving the station building to get to Disneyland® Park, straight on for Walt Disney Studios® Park, or left for Disney® Village and the hotel complex. If you want to freshen up first and explore later, head left and follow the station building around to the bus station from where the free shuttle service to the hotel complex leaves every few minutes.

At your Disney hotel

Check-in can be a drawn-out process. The main snag is that you cannot book in until 3pm. Cast members are well trained in apologizing and enthusiastically suggesting that you leave your luggage with them and head straight for the Parks. If you have arrived by coach or car, this may be the last

Top tips

▶ Cast members wearing an "I" on their costumes can help answer any questions.
▶ There are lockers at the station, but the ones under Main Street Station are more convenient.
▶ An excellent information office is located in the main forecourt of Marne la Vallée station which can give details of any travel arrangements you may want to make out of the Park.
▶ You can leave and re-enter the Parks as often as you like each day provided you have your hand stamped with a pass-out permit, available at the right-hand set of exit gates.
▶ Pick up a mini-map designed for your kids at City Hall or Studio Services.
▶ Head for easy-flow attractions and those with plenty of space for your kids to wander without restriction (i.e. Adventure Isle and Pocahontas Village).
▶ If you are in a Disneyland® Resort Paris hotel, get your kids to rest after lunch, especially in summer when Disneyland® Park is open until midnight.

thing you feel like doing so head instead for a snack at one of the hotel bars or restaurants, take a stroll around Lake Disney®, or make for the shops and eateries at Disney® Village, less than 5 minutes away.

All the hotels are within walking distance of the entrance gates to the Disney Parks although, to make life even easier, a fleet of yellow shuttle buses whirl around the Resort at frequent intervals, delivering guests close to the turnstiles. There are free car parks at each of the Disneyland® Resort Paris hotels. There is valet parking at the Disneyland® Hotel and Disney's Hotel New York®.

At the car park

The visitors' car park has room for 12,000 cars. Each row of spaces is named after a Disney character – Alice, Bambi, Donald, Fleur, Jiminy, Minnie, Pinocchio, Winnie and Tigger (who is reserved for coaches). Make a note of the name of the row in which you have parked, along with the number and letter of your individual parking space. Parking is free for all hotel guests and Annual Plus passport holders (see p.188).

A moving walkway links the main car park to the centre of the Resort, next to the railway station. There is a picnic area at the end of the walkway,

and an Animal Care Centre for boarding pets during your stay (see p.190).

A special car park reserved for disabled visitors is located nearer to the entrance to the Parks.

Guest parking
Motorbikes and side-cars €5 per day (€2 after 5pm)
Cars €8 per day (€2 after 5pm)
Campers and caravans €20 per day

At the main gates

The approach to Disneyland® Park leads you through Disney Square. From there, head for the magnificent floral gardens sculpted into the shape of Mickey. To reach the main entrance turnstiles, you will need to pass under the Disneyland® Hotel to enter Walt Disney Studios® Park.

If you do not already have an entry ticket (see pp.180–182), you'll have to queue at the ticket booths. A discount is available for children aged 3–11 years. Children under the age of 3 are admitted free.

A 1-day Disneyland® Park/Walt Disney Studios® Park ticket gives you unlimited access to nearly all the attractions (there are a few exceptions, such as the video games, for which you have to pay a nominal pay-to-play fee) in **either** Disneyland® Park or Walt Disney Studios® Park during 1 day; if you spend most of your day at Walt Disney Studios®, you then have 'evening access' to Disneyland® Park for 3 hours before closing time (5–8pm most of the year, 8–11pm in midsummer). You can also buy 1-day or 3-day Hopper tickets which will admit you without restriction to both Parks.

Credit cards and travellers' cheques are all accepted in the shops; you only need cash for arcade games and snack carts. Don't worry if you've forgotten to bring euros as there are several *bureaux de change* within the Disney Parks.

Question 15
How can you tour the Disneyland Park in one go, without stopping?
answer also on p.250

GETTING AROUND DISNEYLAND® RESORT PARIS

By shuttle bus

Free shuttle buses run every 12 minutes daily (6.30am–11.00pm), connecting the station at Marne la Vallée–Chessy, Disney® Village, the Disney Park gates and Disneyland® Resort Paris hotels (except the Disneyland® Hotel and Davy Crockett Ranch®). They start one hour before the Parks open and stop at least one hour after they close.

By railroad

A 20-minute round trip is a good way to acquaint yourself with Disneyland® Park's layout. Steam trains chug around the perimeter, starting at Main Street Station and stopping at Frontierland Depot, Fantasyland and Discoveryland on the way. One arrives every 10 minutes or so. Railways were one of Walt Disney's passions, so it is no surprise that these four gleaming locomotives are a highlight of the Park. Every detail is in place from whistles and smoke-stacks to cow-catchers and brass fittings.

On foot

Disneyland® Resort Paris is quite manageable for adults but ,given the sheer scale of the place, you will see plenty of quite sizeable kids in pushchairs/strollers. The whole site is wheelchair-friendly, so these, too, can be used here with ease. Wide shop doors and aisles, generous sidewalks and stroller bays at the entrance to many of the rides keep wheels from knocking too many ankles in a crowd. If you find you overestimate your children's stamina, try hiring a pushchair for the day within Town Square Terrace (by the station or near Studio Services, just inside the Studios). The fee is €6.50.

By streetcar

In playful contrast to France's high-tech public transport system, the only other modes of transport date from the same era as the railroad. Within Disneyland® Park, horse-drawn streetcars offer a trip in reproduction trams, drawn by magnificent Percheron or Shire horses. They stop at the band-stand in the centre of Town Square. There are elegant vintage vehicles, too, such as a limousine, a police paddy wagon and a red fire truck. Just queue up at the bus stop outside Ribbons & Bows Hat Shop in Town Square, to take a short ride up Main Street, USA ,and on to Central Plaza.

Get the picture?
Keep an eye out for the Point Photo Kodak signs which direct you to the best vantage points for snaps. On Space Mountain and Big Thunder Mountain, photos are taken during the ride. These are available to buy (€12).

Guided tours

Guides are on hand to take you on a walking tour and provide you with information about the Disney Parks and their creator. Group tours (25 persons maximum) last about 2 hours for Disneyland® Park and 1 hour for Walt Disney Studios® Park. Reservations can be made at City Hall in Disneyland® Park and at Studio Services in Walt Disney Studios® Park on t 01 60 45 67 76 (free for children; €10 for adults).

The surrounding area

Kickstart your adventures by visiting the la Vallée Outlet Shopping Village. This huge shopping mall, Sea Life Centre and outlet shopping village is just 5 minutes' ride away by taxi or one stop on the train from Disneyland® Paris. On-site hotels will order you a taxi. You can easily spend an afternoon depleting your credit card on chic brand names at dramatically reduced prices. At neighbouring Sea Life Val d'Europe, there is a chance to get up close and personal with scores of sea creatures, from humble seahorses and starfish, to sharks, giant skate and rays. For more details, call t 01 60 42 35 00 or check out www.value.retail.com.

By public transport

The Paris public transport system is largely safer, cleaner and more reliable than just about anywhere else in Europe (see **Travel** pp.12–16 for more details). A single adult métro ticket costs €1.30, while a carnet of 10 tickets will save you money at €10 for adults, €5 for children.

To explore in more depth, get a *Paris Visite* tourist ticket, which comes in 1-, 2-, 3- or 5-day versions (i.e. a 3-day pass for all five zones costs €42.65 for adults, €21.30 for children), sold at métro stations and tourist offices. Disneyland® Resort Paris is in zone 5. This gives you unlimited travel on public transport – métro, bus and RER, and on SNCF trains both in Paris and the Île de France, plus a range of discounts (see p.13). You will need your passport (your real one, not the Disneyland® Paris version) in order to purchase a *Paris Visite* ticket.

The first RER train for Paris leaves the Resort station of Marne la Vallée–Chessy at about 5.15am. Thereafter, trains run every 10 to 30 minutes depending on the time of day. The journey lasts 40 minutes. Make sure, before you board, that you are on the right side of the tracks. Here trains are categorized not according to the direction in which they are travelling, but by their destination station. This can be confusing if you're not used to the system. Lines are indicated by colour and a ringed number; a letter plus a number in the case of the RER lines. RER trains A1, A3 and A5 all run through central Paris. For more detailed information, call **t** 08 92 68 41 4 or check out **www**.ratp.fr.

By car

To tour the surrounding area for a few days, it is best to hire a car rather than bring your own. Hertz is the Resort's official car hire company with a rental office at the Disneyland® Resort Paris agency in the Marne la Vallée–Chessy station. You can also book rental cars by pressing a Hertz button on your hotel room telephone or alternatively through the information desk at your hotel. Guests staying at the Resort receive concessionary rates.

You will need a valid driving licence (held for at least 1 year) plus your passport (a real one, not a Disney ticket). An International Driving Permit is recommended for translation purposes, but is not essential, and can only be used in conjunction with a normal, national driver's licence. The minimum age for renting a car is 21; there is an additional charge for drivers aged 21–25. If you do not use a major credit card to pay for car hire, you will be asked to leave a very sizeable, if refundable, cash deposit.

By taxi

There is a taxi rank outside Marne la Vallée–Chessy station. You can also call or reserve taxis at any hotel reception.

Guided tours

Ask at the regional tourist office (Espace du Tourisme, Île de France, Seine et Marne) in Disney® Village, or at the Disney Park hotel receptions, for details of excursions to various places of interest. A Cityrama guided bus tour departs for Paris from the Hotel New York® at 10am daily and returns at around 6pm. Prices vary, but a Paris day trip costs around €60 for adults, €30 for older children, and under-3s are free. Contact the tourist office direct on **t** 01 44 50 19 98, or check out **www**. paris-access.com and **www**. cityramd.com.

Disneyland® Resort Paris is a triumph of commercialism and the product of one man's vision. Even if you're sceptical at first, as soon as you pass through the gates of the Theme Park, you're likely to find a world that's bigger, brighter, busier, more beautiful and better fun than you imagined.

A number of unofficial internet sites contain information and anecdotes on Disneyland® Resort Paris. The official site (**www**.disneylandparis.com) has details of opening times, hotel listings, events, sound files, music videos and clips (in English, French, German, Spanish, Italian and Dutch).

Commercialism

Disneyland® Park provides a sweet cocktail of escapism and consumerism mixed so perfectly that spending money is part of the experience.
► **Do** bring cash, credit cards and travellers' cheques – otherwise, bring blinkers.
► **Don't** charge everything to your hotel ID card without keeping a note of what you are spending.

Doing it the Disney way

Once you enter the Resort, you realize you are not really in France at all. You are in America, a kind of imitation of America, and immediately you realize that everything in this little state comes under the watchful eye of the benevolent Disney machine.

From the moment you arrive until you leave, your actions are discreetly but firmly directed by a combination of recorded voices, robots and employees. Disney use a combination of technology (hidden security cameras) and barriers in the Parks, such as pools, fountains and flower gardens, to ensure you follow a preconceived itinerary.

The Disneyland® Resort Paris ethos is to offer a complete escape, a total Disney 'experience'. Buy in to the dream, if only for 1 day.
► **Do** comply. If you are directed to do something, it's probably for a good reason.

Cast members

Cast members are trained to adhere to a system that emphasizes safety, courtesy, efficiency and show. Everything they do is governed by the order of these points. Safety comes first and everything else takes a second place if someone is in danger.
► **Do** bear in mind that the cast members' continual vigilance is paramount to the safe and efficient running of the Parks.
► **Don't** ever attempt to cross a rope barrier, especially during a parade.

Special passes and passports

Fastpass

Book ahead for popular rides at a time that suits you with the **Fastpass** system. Go to the ride entrance, slot your ticket into the machines at the designated time and you will be given priority in the queue (available for Space Mountain, Indiana Jones™ and the Temple of Peril: Backwards!, Peter Pan's Flight, Big Thunder Mountain and Star Tours; in Walt Disney Studios® Park, for Rock 'n' Roller Coaster and Flying Carpets over Agrabah).

Disney Parks Passports

If you plan to visit the Parks three times or more in 1 year, save money with an Annual Passport. To find out more about these and other 'Special Family' offers, visit the Annual Passport Bureau next to Sleeping Beauty Castle, check the Disneyland® Resort Paris website or call **t** 01 60 30 60 69.

Classic Annual Passport

Adults €149, children (aged 3–11 inclusive) €129.

This Passport lets you enjoy the attractions and shows of both Parks all year long (even in summer) with free parking at Disneyland® Park and Disney® Village. Restricted use on certain dates (around 15 days per year). There is a 5 per cent reduction for three Passports and 10 per cent for four.

Fantasia Annual Passport

Adults €229, children (aged 3–11 inclusive) €199.

The Fantasia Annual Passport offers unlimited access to the Parks all year round and gives you a great number of advantages, from discounts to entry to specially organized events. Holders benefit from free parking, discounts in all Disneyland® Resort Paris boutiques and restaurants (except Rainforest Café®), reduced entry fees to the Buffalo Bill Wild West Show dinner-show and preferential rates on rooms in Disneyland® Resort Paris hotels. There is a 5 per cent reduction for two Passports, 10 per cent for three and a 15 per cent for four.

Disneyland Passport

Adults and children €69.

This Passport permits annual entry into Disneyland® Park only. An additional option of €28 includes annual car parking.

The rides

The Parks are essentially a fairground. Disney does it better because of the intricate 'film-set' lands, each with a legendary rollercoaster at its heart, and surrounded by must-do themed rides featuring classic cartoon characters. The credo-building, high-tech attractions draw the biggest crowds and you can easily spend half your time queueing up for rides which rarely last more than 3 minutes each.

▶ **Do** combine better-known rides with the less overrun attractions, and check for **Fastpass** rides (see box).

▶ **Don't** even bother queueing until you have read the safety restrictions box (see p.192).

The parades

You should ensure you see at least the daytime extravaganza during your stay. It may seem like a waste of good riding time but your kids will never forgive you if you don't take in at least one parade. They take place almost every afternoon and, often, again later in the day, especially in High Season.

Keep an eye out for veteran Disney visitors who insist on muscling their way to the front of the crowd shoving their kids through, then following them. Unfortunately, wedging yourself in a position that blocks these pushy types out is impossible; they simply shove through in front of the rope barrier – dangerous at night when the float drivers can't see what they're doing. Be safe in the knowledge that a cast member will warn them to step back and they will be forced do so.

▶ **Do** stake out your spot and be prepared to defend it with ferocious tenacity.

▶ **Don't** give in to pushy kids.

Parent swap!

This scheme, available on major rides, enables adults to take turns holding the baby and taking a ride. Both adults queue as far as the loading area. Once there, one adult enjoys the ride while the other keeps hold of any youngsters who are too small for the attraction. As the ride collects its fresh cargo, the adults are allowed to swap places without having to rejoin the queue.

HOW THINGS WORK

The Disney Parks are better run than most military campaigns. Cast members are always on hand to help so there is little you need to know beforehand. The following should be useful for the first-time visitor.

Babies

You will find a Baby Care Centre (*Relais Bébé*) at the top of Main Street, USA, to the left of City Hall, next to the Plaza Gardens Restaurant. They provide a baby-changing area and, behind Studio Services in Walt Disney Studios® Park, baby food, drinks and nappies for sale, a microwave to heat food and milk, plus an area to feed your baby. Most toilets are equipped with a pull-down changing table. In case of necessity, basic equipment is available in all the theme hotels.

Babysitting

A babysitter (*garde d'enfant*) can be booked through any of the hotels (up to two children per sitter), giving at least 2 hours' notice. Disneyland® Resort Paris uses an outside company and the minimum qualification is that required by French summer camps. There is a minimum charge for the first 3 hours and a set rate per 30 minutes after that plus an additional fee for all babysitting ending after 11pm.

Buggy hire

The convenience a buggy affords is worth the small outlay. You can rent a sizeable vehicle to the right of the Parks' main entrances that will take two kids up to a total weight of 50kg (110lbs) or nearly 8 stone. There is a standing platform at the back for older kids and a tall pole for you to string all your bags around. Attach something easily identifiable to this and your children will be able to spot the buggy even if they lose sight of you. Hire buggies cannot be used outside the Disney Parks. Buggies are offered on a first-come, first-served basis and the queues grow quickly. The cost is €6.50 per day.

Car parks

Both the hotels and Parks have free car parks for hotel guests. Show your Disneyland® Resort Paris ID card at the entrance. There is a separate car park for disabled visitors next to Disneyland® Hotel.

Cash

The cash dispensers inside Disneyland® Park are in the Liberty Arcade and the Discovery Arcade (behind the shops on either side of Main Street, USA). Within Walt Disney Studios® Park, you can find some at the Backlot Express Restaurant and next to Studio Services. There is a cash machine in Discoveryland by Constellations and Adventureland (between Hakuna Matata Restaurant and Colonel Haithi's Pizza Outpost). In Disney® Village, the Gaumont Cineplex has automatic cash dispensers as does Disney's Newport Bay Club Hotel®.

You will find currency exchange booths at the main entrance to the Disney Parks, just inside the gates next to City Hall and at Studio Services. In Disney® Village, exchange facilities are at the post office and at the American Express agency. You can also change money 24 hours a day at the hotels and at Marne la Vallée station. During your stay, you can pay with travellers cheques in euros or eurocheques just about anywhere.

Credit cards

All the major cards are accepted (American Express, Visa, Eurocard, Mastercard, Diners Club). As the official Disneyland® Resort Paris credit card, Visa gives cardholders certain privileges, including savings on a host of resort attractions (*see* p.190).

Dress code

You can pretty much wear what you want within the Disney Parks, so long as you do not go barefoot or bare-chested. Swimwear is frowned upon and sensible walking shoes are essential as there is a fair amount of ground to cover on foot. For rainwear, always pack a lightweight pack a mac.

Electricity

The local voltage is 220V. To use any appliances with British three-pin plugs here you will need a two-pin European plug adapter.

First aid centres

These are located by the Plaza Gardens Restaurant at the far end of Main Street, USA, behind Studio Services, and at Disney® Village and Hotel Cheyenne® (**t** 01 64 74 49 60). All are staffed by fully trained nurses and a doctor.

Guest information

At City Hall, on the left-hand side of the entrance to Main Street, USA, and Studio Services, just inside the Walt Disney Studios® Park. There is also a seasonal information point at the far end of Main Street, USA, in Central Plaza. If you have any questions or concerns, head for the Visitor Relations window to the right of the main entrance as you approach Disneyland® Park, under the railway arch.

Hairdressers

There's a salon at Lucie Saint-Clair in Disney's Hotel New York® (open 10am–7pm, Mon–Sat). Dapper Dan's Hair Cuts is a traditional men's barber on Main Street.

Language

French and English are official languages here. If a cast member is fluent in another language, this is indicated by a flag on their name badge. Though visual clues are frequently used, you will find written signs in just one language (sometimes in both). Most attractions work without words. The few that depend on narration are multilingual (in English, French and German). If not, guests are supplied with headphones.

Laundry

Disney's Hotel Cheyenne® and Disney's Hotel Santa Fe® have coin-operated laundry facilities.

Lockers

Baggage can be left at the Left Luggage rooms of the hotels (for free). For big or valuable items, there is a guest storage counter to the right of the turnstiles at the main Park entrances, under the railway arch by Visitor Relations (€2.25 per item).

Lost and found

Lost children are ushered towards the Baby Centres on Central Plaza at the far end of Main Street, USA, or next to Studio Services. Missing items should be reported at City Hall on Main Street, USA or at Studio Services. Both are good places to leave a message if you become separated from your companions. There is a Lost and Found counter outside the entrance to the Parks.

Pets

Except for guide dogs, pets are not allowed inside the Parks or anywhere else within the Resort. An Animal Care Centre is located at the exit to the main car park. The animal care fees include food and water (€8 a day per animal; €12 for an overnight stay). You may have to show certificates of health, proof of vaccination and a tattoo identification mark. For more details, call t 01 64 74 28 73.

Photography and video

You can buy camera film, batteries and disposable cameras at several of the shops and any of the hotel shops. At Town Square Photography on Main Street, USA, at Sir Mickey's (Fantasyland) and Constellations (Discoveryland), films can be dropped off and collected within two hours. You can also rent cameras and video cameras here. Within Walt Disney Studios® Park, deposit films at Studio Photo in the Front Lot. You cannot take your own flash photographs or use video cameras inside any of the attractions.

Post

Mail is collected daily from post boxes throughout the Parks and the lobbies of all theme hotels. Stamps can be bought at several shops, including The Storybook Store on Main Street, USA, and the hotels. The post office is at the Marne la Vallée train station.

Smoking

Smoking is not permitted at the attractions or in the queuing areas, but it is allowed in the rest of the Parks. Most restaurants are divided into smoking and non-smoking sections. There is a tobacco shop at the Sports Bar in Disney® Village.

Telephones

There are public phones throughout the Resort. Most operate with phone cards (see p.143). France Télécom cards (télécartes) can be bought at the RER station and at shops around the Parks. Disneyland® Resort Paris hotel rooms have direct-dial phones (see p.143 for international dialling codes).

Visa card holders

As the official credit card partner of Disneyland® Resort Paris, Visa has created special privileges for Platinum Card holders who book 3-night/4-day packages on t UK 0870 503 0309. These include 15 per cent reductions on guided tours; 10 per cent reductions in Walt Disney Studios® and Disney Village® boutiques; 10 per cent discounts on lunch in hotel restaurants, Planet Hollywood®, Rainforest Café®, Café Mickey and the Steakhouse (Disney Village®); 10 per cent reduction on green fees at Disneyland® Golf (plus two driving ranges and a free golf cart); free return travel to La Vallée Outlet Shopping Village and the Sea Life Centre Val d'Europe. Full terms and conditions apply. The 'Service Magique' programme is no longer be valid for American Express card holders.

Disneyland® Resort Paris: entrance is free for under-3s and the hotels don't charge if they share your room. Yet subjecting babies and fidgety toddlers to a route march round the Parks and to long queues is sure to lead to tears and tantrums.

If your child is under the age of 4, or nervy, check the **Safety Restrictions** (see p.192) or ask a cast member for advice before queuing. Most younger children need no more than two low-key, classic rides (such as the Mad Hatter's Tea Cups or Orbitron) and they'll be surprised by the bright colours in one day. Around Every Corner and the film set constructions and costumed characters of Audio-Animatronics®.

For the under-4s

In Disneyland® Park, characters (see **Meeting the Characters**, p.230) tend to hang out by the Ribbons & Bows Hat Shop (Town Square) each morning until lunchtime. Outside the shop, you can take a horse-drawn streetcar or vintage vehicle up Main Street, USA, to Central Plaza. Close by is Le Théâtre du Château, which has character appearances and shows at set times throughout the day. You can have souvenir photos taken here. Try to catch the daytime parade, which wends it way down Main Street, USA, late afternoon and grab a kerbside spot at the Central Plaza end of Main Street.

Fantasyland

The drawbridge leading to Sleeping Beauty Castle takes you into Fantasyland, probably the most suitable for younger children. Gentle rides include Le Carrousel de Lancelot, Mad Hatter's Tea Cups, 'It's a small world' and Le Pays des Contes de Fées. Nearby, Alice's Curious Labyrinth is a topiary maze dominated by the Queen of Hearts' castle and filled with the quirky characters from Lewis Carroll's story. It's an ideal spot to take photos. Blanche Neige et les Sept Nains, Les Voyages de Pinocchio and Peter Pan's Flight are not restricted for kids under 1, but are probably best for over-4s. Dumbo the Flying Elephant and Casey Jr are sure hits for kids over 1.

Frontierland

At Fantasyland Station take the train through the Grand Canyon Diorama (with music, animated wildlife and sound effects) to Frontierland.

Critter Coral has a petting farm: lambs, goats, rabbits, chickens and piglets are always a safe bet with toddlers. Hands can be washed at the water-trough outside. Close by is Pocahontas Indian

Village, a scaled-down adventure playground with plenty of seats for worn-out adults, or enjoy a leisurely riverboat ride on the *Molly Brown* or *Mark Twain*, which board at Thunder Mesa Riverboat Landing.

Adventureland

A short walk will take you to Adventureland, where many of the attractions are more activity-based than elsewhere in Disney Parks. The central feature is Adventure Isle, a moated twin-isle connected by two suspended rope bridges. You make your way up winding stairs and down mysterious passages, into caves and past waterfalls, to

Toilets

Main Street, USA
▶ by the Cable Car Bake Shop
▶ at Main Street Station
▶ either side of Main Street Station
▶ next to the Barbershop
▶ in Discovery Arcade

Adventureland
▶ in the Adventureland Bazaar
▶ next to Indiana Jones
▶ next to Colonel Hathi's Pizza Outpost

Frontierland
▶ next to Phantom Manor
▶ opposite Big Thunder Mountain
▶ next to the Legends of the Wild West
▶ next to the Cowboy Cookout Barbecue

Fantasyland
▶ near the Toad Hall Restaurant
▶ next to Au Châlet de la Marionette
▶ near Pizzeria Bella Notte

Discoveryland
▶ in Videopolis
▶ between Orbitron and Autopia

Disney® Village
▶ mainly in the restaurants

Walt Disney® Studios
▶ next to Studio Services
▶ within Studio 1
▶ behind the Art of Disney Animation in Animation Courtyard
▶ near entrance to Moteurs...Action! in the Backlot
▶ near exit to Rock 'n' Roller Coaster in the Backlot
▶ next to Armageddon Special Effects
▶ at Backlot Express Restaurant

Captain Hook's Galley and Pirate's Beach, the outdoor play area for mini-swashbucklers, and up to La Cabine des Robinson. It's a spectacular spot for kids who like clambering and exploring, but under-4s may find there are too many steps, and will need assistance over the more precarious parts. Some attractions are a bit dark as well, and may frighten little ones. Le Passage Enchanté d'Aladdin attracts few queues and can fascinate, rather like window shopping.

Discoveryland

Leave Discoveryland for last. There isn't much for under-4s here. Most rides are too thrilling. although Autopia, Orbitron and the indoor play area at Buzz Lightyear's Pizza Planet Restaurant are probably tame enough for over-2s. Spectacular shows are staged each day at Videopolis: they're seldom scary and the high production values will keep little ones spellbound. Videopolis is a good place to rest tired legs and grab a bite. It's huge so there's usually always somewhere to sit down.

Walt Disney Studios® Park

This is an easy park to explore with little to shout about for under-4s. The chances are you won't hit a queue (except at Flying Carpets), so it's certainly worth spending 1 hour or so here. Head right as you enter the Park proper for Flying Carpets over Agrabah. Time your visit to coincide with a character-filled performance at Animagique, a sure hit for toddlers and up and aim to arrive well ahead of time. Some hands-on, push button displays at the Art of Disney Animation are worth a peek. Look out, too, for Mickey and friends at the trailer parked outside. The mid-afternoon Cinema Parade is a spectacle worth taking a kerbside seat for.

Safety restrictions

Several attractions have age, height or health limitations (relevant to pregnant women, to people who suffer from motion sickness, heart, back or neck problems or very young, nervy kids).

Phantom Manor (Frontierland)
Dark and spooky so may frighten little children.

Big Thunder Mountain (Frontierland)
Minimum age 3; minimum height 1.02 m. Health limitations apply.

Pirates of the Caribbean (Adventureland)
Cannons, lurching descents and battle scenes may frighten small children. Health limitations apply.

Indiana Jones™ and the Temple of Peril: Backwards! (Adventureland)
Minimum age 8; minimum height of driver 1.40m. Health limitations apply.

La Plage des Pirates (Adventureland)
Maximum height: 1.40 m

Dumbo the Flying Elephant (Fantasyland)
Minimum age: 12 months.

La Tanière du Dragon (Fantasyland)
May unnerve younger children.

Blanche Neige et les Sept Nains (Fantasyland)
Very dark at times, so may frighten young or nervous children.

Peter Pan's Flight (Fantasyland)
The unsteady flight and some startling scenes may frighten younger children.

Mad Hatter's Tea Cups (Fantasyland)
Health limitations apply.

Casey Jr le Petit Train du Cirque (Fantasyland)
Minimum age 12 months.

Les Voyages de Pinocchio (Fantasyland)
Some scenes may frighten younger children.

Autopia (Discoveryland)
Minimum age 12 months; minimum height of driver 1.32 m. Health limitations apply.

Honey, I Shrunk the Audience (Discoveryland)
This racy spectacle may frighten younger children.

Orbitron (Discoveryland)
Minimum age 12 months. Health limitations apply.

Star Tours (Discoveryland)
Minimum age 3; minimum height for Arcade de Jeux Vidéo, 1.02 m. Health limitations apply.

Space Mountain (Discoveryland)
Minimum age 10; minimum height 1.32 m. Health limitations apply.

Le Visionarium (Discoveryland)
Health limitations apply.

Rock 'n' Roller Coaster (Walt Disney Studios®)
Minimum height 1.20 m. Health limitations apply.

Moteurs...Action! (Walt Disney Studios®)
May unsettle youngsters. Health limitations apply.

Armageddon SE (Walt Disney Studios®)
The special effects may frighten younger children. Health limitations apply.

Television Production Tour's Cyberspace Mountain (Walt Disney Studios®)
Minimum height 1.30 m. Health limitations apply.

Studio Tram Tour (Walt Disney Studios®)
More special effects that may unnerve youngsters.

Main Street, USA

©Disney

From the quaint clapboard shop fronts and clanking, hooting automobiles to the spotless curbs and gas lamps that spread a warm glow over everything and everyone at night, nothing is left to chance in this lovingly re-created Disney version of early-1900s, small-town America. It's extraordinarily well done. And, despite the fact that it's almost entirely composed of shops, restaurants and cafés, Main Street, USA, both excites and reassures. You feel you have known this place all your life.

Best for quality shops and snacks.
Worst for budgeting.

MAIN STREET, U.S.A.

©Disney

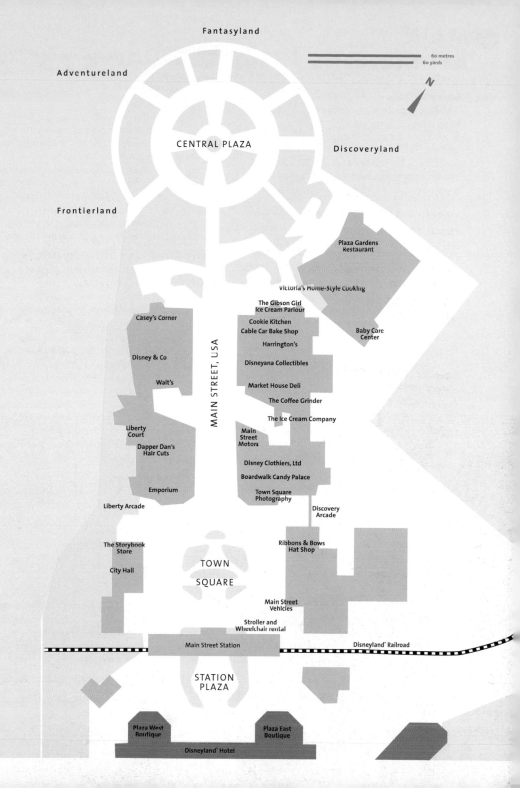

MAIN ATTRACTIONS

Disney parades

The parades which pass triumphantly down Main Street, USA, are a real focal point of any visit. The characters are on a god-given mission (and for god-read Walt) to get children involved at every opportunity. The kids lap it up, and the sound system ensures that even the most cynical of grown-ups can't help but tap a reluctant foot to the beat.

The floats are great hulking constructions of fibreglass and wood, ornately decorated in bright colours, which quiver under their own weight as they pass by. Every now and again, there is a jam and Mickey and Goofy *et al* are left dancing on the spot before they can continue. No one seems to mind and it affords an opportunity for friendly banter between audience and cast, as well as that all-important photo opportunity.

Seasonal parades operate throughout the year. For the best parade view, head for the gallery at Disneyland® Railroad Station. It offers the perfect view down Main Street to the castle. To the right of the station is City Hall, the main visitor centre for the Park and the place to go for advice, maps, dinner reservations and any other queries. There's multilingual staff here to help you.

Disneyland Railroad

Four steam-powered locomotives – W. E. Cody, C. K. Holliday, George Washington and Eureka – trundle round Disneyland® Park, stopping off at Frontierland, Fantasyland and Discoveryland.

Question 16
How are the lamps lit on Main Street?
answer also on p.250

Question 17
What are the names of the four steam-powered locomotives on the Disneyland® Railroad?
answer also on p.250

Inspired by the trains that crossed the American West in the 19th century, they skirt the entire Park, passing through the Grand Canyon Diorama and cutting through the back of Pirates of the Caribbean. The trip lasts about 20 minutes and is a good way to get a first look at Disneyland® Park, although your kids may want to jump off when they get a first glimpse of Big Thunder Mountain and hear the squeals and screams from those already on board.

Liberty Arcade and Discovery Arcade

These form the back entrances to the shops and restaurants on both sides of Main Street, USA. Their 1900s interiors have ornate lamps, wrought-iron railings and lavish window displays featuring inventions and American and French curios.

On one side, the Statue of Liberty tableau details the French origin of this symbol of New York City, which has stood at the mouth of its harbour since 1886. On the other side of Main Street, USA, follow the covered passageway to Discoveryland and stop at the Discovery Arcade to relive the age of invention. Cabinets display model flying-machines and other such 19th-century rarities. Look for the Silhouette Artist here, who will cut out and frame paper silhouettes of you to take home.

Main Street Vehicles

Vintage vehicles such as an old-fashioned police paddy wagon, a limousine and a fire truck cruise up Main Street, USA, to Central Plaza. The ride is just a bit of a giggle as you could walk the same distance in about 2 minutes. Nonetheless, a ride on a horse-drawn tram can be quite a treat for youngsters.

Central Plaza

This circular gateway to all five lands is the hub of Disneyland® Park and an ideal spot to meet up and take souvenir snaps in front of Sleeping Beauty Castle. The information point here will keep you updated on waiting times for the Disney Parks' most popular rides.

Toilets
► Close to the Disneyland® Railroad Main Street Station, opposite City Hall.
► Either side of Town Square.
► Within Liberty Arcade and Discovery Arcade.

©Disney

WHERE TO SHOP

One of the best things about Main Street, USA, is the shops. You can mooch about here searching for souvenirs while waiting for a parade to begin, get warm, get out of the rain or just do a bit of window shopping.

Plaza West and Plaza East Boutique
Your first (or last) stop for Disneyland® Paris souvenirs, T-shirts and film, set just outside Main Street Station. The kiosks are at the Park gates and normally stay open late.

Emporium
The largest store in Disneyland® Park, this is the place to find all kinds of toys and games, clothing and souvenirs. The window displays are an attraction in themselves. Inside, the old-fashioned overhead cash exchange system never fails to attract attention.

The Storybook Store
This cosy hometown bookshop is made for browsing. All kinds of books, stationery, videos, posters, CDs and cassettes are available. Tigger is there to add a personalized stamp to your child's new book.

Ribbons & Bows Hat Shop
Hats, clasps, bows and the inevitable Mickey ears. You can have your name custom-monogrammed for free on an old-fashioned sewing machine.

Lilly's Boutique
This is the place for home-lovers. Plates, glasses, cutlery, oven gloves with a picture of Minnie on them – you name it, they sell it.

Harrington's Fine China & Porcelains
Blown glass giftware is created on site, with personalization available. You will also find Chinese porcelain, crystal, and cut glass.

Dapper Dan's Hair Cuts
Real haircuts, shaves and souvenirs plus a bit of barbershop harmony and gossip from the quartet singers. Not a bad place to get away from the bustle as it is rarely busy.

Disney Clothiers, Ltd.
Plenty of fashion gear plus a sweet section of baby clothes set in a 19th-century house complete with velvet drapes and fireplace.

Did you know?
On Main Street, USA, alone there are over 225,000 light bulbs and 7,653 theme lights.

Disney & Co.
Situated in the block beyond Liberty Court. Plenty of toys, T-shirts, decorative gifts and bath accessories displayed around a large hot-air balloon.

Disneyana Collectibles
A treasure trove for serious Disney collectors – original Disney animation cels, limited-edition lithographs, rare and unusual books and unique ceramic figurines.

Town Square Photography
A replica of a photographer's studio from the 19th century. Purchase film, disposable cameras and accessories, or rent video and 35mm cameras. This is also the spot where you can pick up your professionally staged photo-encounters with the Disney characters. (7x9 inch print costs €9.90).

Boardwalk Candy Palace
Plenty of tooth decay potential with giant lollipops, chocolates and sweets at this sugar-coated paradise. Make sure you try the balls of saltwater taffy, a traditional East Coast treat. The shop is next door to Town Square Photography.

Main Street Motors
A shop originally themed on vintage cars but now entirely devoted to one of the Disney darlings – Winnie The Pooh.

Main Street, USA, is a top spot to get a bite to eat but, in keeping with its period style, you won't find anyone serving french fries.

A table and buffet service, full menu.
B counter service, full menu.
C counter service, light snacks.
V vegetarian options available.

Walt's – An American Restaurant (A, V)

A first-class eatery that celebrates the life and times of Walt Disney. Ideal spot for serious Disney fans, but kids may find the atmosphere a little formal. The menu includes traditional meat and fish dishes and meal-size salads. Walt's is THE place to breakfast with Disney characters. *Over €15.*

Plaza Gardens Restaurant (A, V)

Dine in 19th-century splendour at this stylish restaurant by the Central Plaza. The sparkling statue-filled interior and glass roof allows light to flood through even on cold days. You can even take tea with the Disney characters. *Over €15.*

Market House Deli (B, V)

Relaxed, New York-style deli serving fresh jumbo-size sandwiches and salads, including baguettes, pastrami, hot turkey and tuna. *Under €8.*

Casey's Corner (B, V)

Hot dogs, chicken nuggets, soft drinks and ragtime music, plus the chance to learn about baseball history – authentic gear and photographs of teams and players pay homage to America's national sport. *Under €8.*

Victoria's Home-Style Restaurant (B, V)

Pasta, quiches, mini-pizzas, baked potatoes and desserts in a cosy 1890s boarding house. *Under €8.*

The Coffee Grinder (C)

Midway down Main Street, USA, the smell alone will draw you to this vintage coffee house. The best spot for fresh coffee and a croissant. *Under €8.*

The Ice Cream Company (C)

Set in Discovery Arcade, the name says it all: all your favourite flavours in a cone. *Under €8.*

Cable Car Bake Shop (C)

The shop has booth seating and the décor nostal-gically evokes old San Francisco. On the way out, the Cookie Kitchen counter offers tempting bags of cookies and muffins to take away. *Under €8.*

The Gibson Girl Ice Cream Parlour (C)

All manner of colourful ice creams plus frothy milkshakes, served up in an old-fashioned milk bar. *Under €8.*

Frontierland

©Disney

©Disney

This is cowboy country – a land of wagon wheels, paddle steamers, old-timers, gloomy houses, disused mine shafts, ranches, corrals and steaks as big as hats. Snake-eyed gunfighters pace the boards beside the Lucky Nugget Saloon, ready to beat you to the draw should you step into their path, and the spooks of outlaws who met a sticky end haunt the halls of Phantom Manor, while atop Big Thunder Mountain a lone coyote cackles and howls, bending its back towards a non-existent moon.

FRONTIERLAND

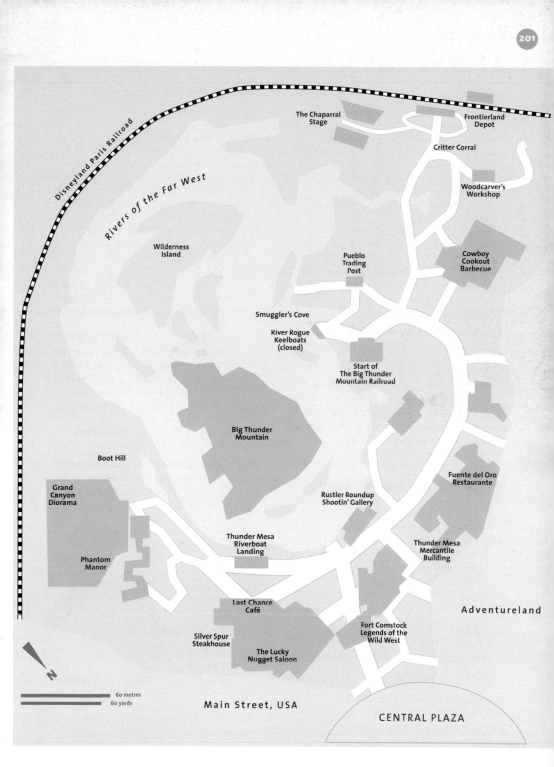

Disneyland Paris Railroad

Rivers of the Far West

The Chaparral Stage

Frontierland Depot

Critter Corral

Woodcarver's Workshop

Wilderness Island

Pueblo Trading Post

Cowboy Cookout Barbecue

Smuggler's Cove

River Rogue Keelboats (closed)

Start of The Big Thunder Mountain Railroad

Big Thunder Mountain

Boot Hill

Grand Canyon Diorama

Fuente del Oro Restaurante

Rustler Roundup Shootin' Gallery

Thunder Mesa Riverboat Landing

Thunder Mesa Mercantile Building

Phantom Manor

Last Chance Café

Adventureland

Silver Spur Steakhouse

The Lucky Nugget Saloon

Fort Comstock Legends of the Wild West

N

60 metres
60 yards

Main Street, USA

CENTRAL PLAZA

MAIN ATTRACTIONS

Question 18
How many gruesome phantoms dwell in Phantom Manor?
answer also on p.250

Phantom Manor

Just to prove it's not entirely doom and gloom, designers used 100 different shades of paint to decorate Phantom Manor, not all of them black. This once-stately house sits high on the hillside, with a shutter half off its hinges flapping lamely in the wind. It is your mission to discover the legend surrounding its past. Once you are led into a dark chamber, the doors slam shut, the lights go out and the walls move inwards and downwards, as if they're about to crush you. Ushered into 'doom buggy' carriages, you head off on a particularly spooky journey, filled with 99 cackling ghouls and phantoms. You emerge in daylight up on Boot Hill, the family graveyard. Here the racy epitaphs bring some light relief: *'Here lies Shotgun Gus, Holier now than all of us.'*

Thunder Mesa Riverboat Landing

Mississippi-style paddle boats *Mark Twain* or *Molly Brown* take you on a nostalgic boat cruise around the Rivers of the Far West (although it isn't the paddles that actually make them move; they run on underwater rails). From the top deck, you get great views of the 33m- (108ft)-high Big Thunder Mountain. It may not be all thrills and spills but it is a leisurely way to spend 15 minutes, and is especially relaxing in summer, although the boats are a little short on places to sit.

Rustler Roundup Shootin' Gallery

There is a small charge for this cartoon-style shooting gallery. Even so, it's fairly popular and is a bit of a hoot. Complete with sound effects such as ricochets and exploding dynamite, you can take aim at cacti, a windmill and, even (for a big bang), a shack filled with explosives. As many as 20 children can shoot off in all directions at once, so it's pretty difficult to tell just who has hit what. *Costs €2.*

Top tips

► Because of the weather, Frontierland does not open until 1pm during most of January and February.
► You will need a handful of €1 coins to play on the Rustler Roundup Shootin' Gallery.
► Ask about Fastpass tickets (*see* p.188) to reduce queuing time at Big Thunder Mountain.

Big Thunder Mountain

This is the centrepiece of Frontierland. All day, distant rumbles and screams emanate from its depths as the roller coaster weaves and plummets along the tracks at breakneck speed. It's extremely popular and people often jump out of the rickety looking carriages at the end and join the queue again for another go. Even queuing here is fun, as you thread your way through the Thunder Mountain mining company's HQ, growing increasingly nervous, before you reach a point where it's too late to turn back. If you want to play it safe, get into the front cart – the back few are for serious roller-coaster riders, those who are brave or simply just mad. Plunging through tunnels and hurtling around corners, even the most seasoned rider is hard-put not to scream with terror/delight when a flooding river washes away part of the track. A camera is there to record your expression. Watch out for the mine explosion, bat-filled cave, famished goat and stranded coyote. You can view your live-action mug-shot at Big Thunder Photography as you gratefully disembark. *Restrictions apply. Fastpass available.*

Disneyland Railroad – Frontierland Depot

Situated on the edge of Frontierland, the diorama is, in fact, only visible from the Disneyland® Railroad (*see* p.186). Trains pass through a 80m- (260ft)-long tunnel, taking you on a journey from dawn to dusk through a re-creation of the Grand Canyon in Arizona, one of the world's natural wonders.

The weather changes too, on your journey, with a dramatic thunderstorm closely followed by a beautiful rainbow. Look out for wild animals: grazing deer, a fox on the hunt, a rattlesnake, squirrels and raccoons.

River Rogue Keelboats

Currently closed until further notice.

Critter Corral

This small farm is entirely enclosed, allowing both barnyard animals and children to mingle freely. Lambs, ducklings, baby goats and rabbits are always a safe bet with kids who will enjoy petting and stroking the cute and cuddly animals.

There's a water trough just outside so children can wash their hands once they have finished.

The Chaparral Theatre

Superb live stage shows are hosted at this huge outdoor wooden theatre throughout the year. A highlight is *Tarzan Encounter*, which plays five times daily between 12 noon and 5.15pm and will continue to run from April to September 2004. With a nod to Edgar Rice Burroughs' original *Tarzan of the Apes* stories and a bigger one, naturally, to Disney's blockbuster animated film, it gives you a chance to discover the legend deep in the heart of the jungle, follow in Tarzan's footsteps and meet all the characters in an all-singing, all-dancing, live show There's even a chance you'll be picked out of the audience to join in the jungle action! Check your entertainment programme (available at City Hall) for performance times at the theatre.

Pocahontas Indian Village

There are strategically placed benches for adults to rest at this outdoor playground inspired by the animated film of the same name.

Toilets

▶ Opposite the entrance to Thunder Mountain in a Mexican-style pueblo.

▶ Left of the entrance to Phantom Manor, next to the undertakers, J. Nutterville.

▶ Next to the Legends of the Wild West.

Legends of the Wild West

As you enter Frontierland, you pass under the timbered stockade of Fort Comstock. If you have 10 minutes to spare, climb the wooden staircase to see a panoramic view of Frontierland and take a self-guided history tour that reveals some of the Old West's most popular legends.

You can see famous characters such as Buffalo Bill and Davy Crockett, and even an Indian chief, and there's also a chance to learn about the traditions and customs of Native Americans and to see genuine Cheyenne crafts.

Question 19

How do the paddle boats travel around the Rivers of the Far West?

answer also on p.250

WHERE TO SHOP

Thunder Mesa Mercantile Building

Three rustic stores under one roof, guarded over by the giant figures of Buffalo Bill and Kit Carson.

Tobias Norton & Sons – Frontier Traders

Leather hats, boots, belts and wallets. This is a one-stop shop for Western gear. Boys will love the pistols and holsters. If you are not keen on them having toy guns, make a sneaky detour.

Bonanza Outfitters

If you cannot be a cowboy for real, here you can at least dress like one. On sale are brand name boots, Stetsons, shirts, waistcoats, jackets, plus plenty of candy and dress-up wear for the kids.

Eureka Mining Supplies & Assay Office

In this abandoned mining shack, there is staunchly traditionally fare, such as 'Wild Western Salsa', root beer and homemade frontier toys.

Pueblo Trading Post

Here you can buy hand-crafted Indian pottery and woven rugs plus more Disney merchandise.

Woodcarver's Workshop

Watch a skilled woodworker whittle, carve and engrave your very own personalized woodcarving.

©Disney

WHERE TO EAT

A table and buffet service, full menu.
B counter service, full menu.
C counter service, light snacks.
V vegetarian option available.

Silver Spur Steakhouse (A, V)

Rather formal, old-fashioned steak house set opposite the Thunder Mesa Riverboat Landing. You can treat yourself to a top-notch meal of charcoal-grilled meat by the fireside. There is a wine menu and a choice of beers. *Over €15.*

The Lucky Nugget Saloon (A)

Old-West entertainment in the form of a 30-minute revue, showing here at set times throughout the day. For a fee, you can watch the rollicking can-can girls while you sit back and sample substantial buffet fare: for lunch there are salads and chicken wings, and pork ribs and prime rib are served at dinner, when you can eat along-side the Disney characters. *Over €15.*

Last Chance Café (B)

Overlooking Big Thunder Mountain, this is the final outpost on the way to Phantom Manor and a notorious hideout for bandits and rustlers. Enjoy the turkey drumsticks, french fries and barbecue sandwiches, but keep an eye out for the baddies posted around the walls on WANTED posters. *Under €8.*

Fuente del Oro Restaurant (B, V)

Traditional Tex-Mex dishes, including tacos, nachos, quesadillas, fajitas and chilli con carne. The outside terrace has a Mayan fountain which provides some relief for overheated kids during the summer. *Under €8.*

Cowboy Cookout Barbecue (C, V)

This huge wooden hay loft is hard to miss. Enjoy hearty cowboy grub (spare ribs, chicken, baked potato and hamburgers) and toe-tapping blue-grass band performances. However, when it is not so crowded, the vast interior can seem a little impersonal and the atmosphere becomes more school refectory than cowboy revelry. *Under €8.*

Question 20
The Tarzan Encounter show is based on a famous book. What is its title?
answer also on p.250

Adventureland

ADVENTURELAND

©Disney

Adventureland is at once more exotic and, at the same time, gentler than the other lands. The mix of African, Moorish and Aztec elements, the covered market complex in the Bazar and the wealth of natural vegetation, including a bamboo garden, make it a fascinating place through which to wander, and also one of the most relaxing areas in Disneyland® Park. In addition, many of the attractions are less sophisticated, offering the chance for kids to clamber about and explore on their own. Yet at its heart there is, of course, another roller coaster, the ever-popular Indiana Jones™ and the Temple of Peril: Backwards!, a fast and furious race through the jungle, culminating in a stomach-churning loop-the-loop.

Best for unsupervised play time, especially as the evening draws to a close.
Worst for weary legs: there's a lot of climbing.

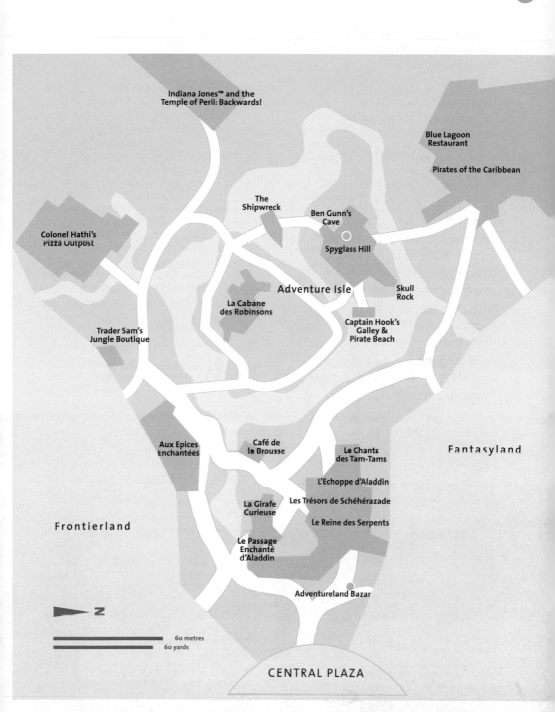

Indiana Jones™ and the
Temple of Peril: Backwards!

Blue Lagoon
Restaurant

Pirates of the Caribbean

The
Shipwreck

Ben Gunn's
Cave

Colonel Hathi's
Pizza Outpost

Spyglass Hill

Adventure Isle

Skull
Rock

La Cabane
des Robinsons

Captain Hook's
Galley &
Pirate Beach

Trader Sam's
Jungle Boutique

Aux Epices
Enchantées

Café de
la Brousse

Le Chants
des Tam-Tams

Fantasyland

L'Echoppe d'Aladdin

Les Trésors de Schéhérazade

La Girafe
Curieuse

Le Reine des Serpents

Frontierland

Le Passage
Enchanté
d'Aladdin

Adventureland Bazar

N

60 metres
60 yards

CENTRAL PLAZA

MAIN ATTRACTIONS

Pirates of the Caribbean

Housed within the confines of a grey stone fortress, the queuing area leads you towards a rocky grotto where skeletons and the remains of shipwrecks offer some odious clues about what lies ahead. You are ushered into boats by friendly pirates (who often stroll around Adventureland trying to drum up trade) and head off on an underground voyage, past scenes of pirate mayhem, roaring cannons and swashbuckling sabres. Menacing eyes peer at you from every dark corner as your boat lurches to dodge stray cannon balls. For younger children, though, the macabre atmosphere, sudden plunges, skeleton scenes, spooky fog and flames that threaten to engulf you may provoke a few nightmares. And don't forget to take your snorkel; you are likely to get splashed a little. *Restrictions apply.*

Indiana Jones™ and the Temple of Peril: Backwards!

An all too brief yet frantic roller-coaster ride which climaxes in a breathtaking 360° loop. The queuing area is in the depths of the jungle, in the abandoned camp of Indiana Jones, the so-cool archaeologist hero first seen in *Raiders of the Lost Ark*, with tents, 1940s Jeeps and upturned billy cans. To solve the mystery of what's happened to him, you enter the ruined Maya temple, watched over by huge stone cobras. Once inside, you climb into a rickety old mine cart to race through the long-buried ruins of the Temple of Peril – all at stomach-churning speed. For those with strong stomachs, make for the first carriage if you can, to appreciate fully the almost vertical drop at the ride's outset. In the flickering torchlight after dark, the attraction takes on an added dimension that's certain to spur dedicated thrill-seekers. *Restrictions apply. Fastpass available.*

Le Passage Enchanté d'Aladdin (Aladdin's Enchanted World)

This is a jewel-encrusted walk-through miniature scenes from the story of Aladdin. Clever 3-D displays, songs and special effects provide light entertainment for young fans.

Adventure Isle

Skull Rock stares with a dead and menacing expression out over the lagoon, daring kids to explore the secret caves, tunnels, waterfalls and rope bridges which cross *La Mer des Bretteurs* to reach a tropical treasure trove. There are two islets, one inspired by the Johann Wyss classic, *Swiss*

©Disney

Family Robinson, the other by Robert Louis Stevenson's *Treasure Island*. To the north, Captain Hook's pirate ship has cast anchor at Cannonball Cove. A top-deck play area draws would-be swash-bucklers, while at Teetering Rock, daredevils can really let off steam. Ben Gunn's Cave provides a series of underground tunnels that lead to a hidden chamber. It's very dark and easy to get lost as you explore, clinging to the walls until your eyes become accustomed to the gloom. With bats and skeletons, and no fewer than six entrances in and out, it is spine-chilling stuff that kids will revel in. A good place to come and burn off some pent-up energy.

Pirates' Beach

A mini training ground for junior pirates complete with a fishing-net suspension bridge, an old grounded ship and play equipment (climbing frames, walkways, and early learning games

Did you know?
The oldest visitor so far to Disneyland® Paris was 106 years old.

and toys). This outside playground is separated into two areas divided by sails: the first for children aged 3–6 and the second for children aged 7–9.

La Cabane des Robinson (The Swiss Family Robinson Treehouse)

At the Swiss Family Robinson Treehouse there are some 17,000 individual leaves on the skyscraping tree itself, each positioned by hand. This is some-thing of a literary treat as you discover how this shipwrecked Swiss family made the best of their time after surviving a shipwreck. The four levels of this 27m (88ft), spreading banyan (fig) tree are reached via makeshift stairs which spiral into the upper branches. Below the stairs, a tangled mass of roots reveals a cellar (le Ventre de la Terre), where rescued supplies are stored. The wreck itself, lying lopsided in the water, is to be found under the suspended rope bridge.

©Disney

WHERE TO SHOP

Indiana Jones™ Adventure Outpost

Everything your kids will ever need for a pioneering adventure. Clothing, bush hats, accessories, jewellery and souvenirs based on the classic Indiana Jones™ movies.

Les Trésors de Schéhérazade

Mementoes of far distant lands, left behind by Sinbad the Sailor. You will find magic lanterns, brass bells, oriental dolls and exotic clothing.

Le Coffre du Capitaine (The Captain's Coffer)

At the exit of Pirates of the Caribbean, choose from a treasure-trove of nautical novelties. The skull and crossbones gear is sure to go down well.

La Girafe Curieuse (The Curious Giraffe)

Safari clothing (some non-Disney and eco-friendly) and other gifts, all sold under the watchful gaze of a giraffe, happy nibbling away at some leaves.

WHERE TO EAT

A table and buffet service, full menu.
B counter service, full menu.
C counter service, light snacks.
V vegetarian option available.

Blue Lagoon Restaurant (A, V)

Guests can relax under a perpetual moonlit sky amid the underground tranquility of palm trees and sandy beaches. Fish and spicy Creole specialities are served on a tropical terrace as the boats from the Pirates of the Caribbean drift by. Good for kids and couples alike. *Over €15.*

Agrabah Café (B)

This atmospheric buffet-style restaurant in the bazar offers colourful, fragrant Mediterranean, Middle Eastern and African dishes including couscous, taboulleh and pastries. *Under €8.*

Colonel Hathi's Pizza Outpost (B, V)

Tucked away in a bamboo forest, talking parrots invite you in to dine on the Colonel's private veranda, and enjoy a safari snack of pizza, lasagne, spaghetti and salad. It is worth a visit just to see the authentic colonial gear. *Under €8.*

Restaurant Hakuna Matata (B, V)

The mud hut's décor is an array of masks and safari trophies. The food is less exotic with the standard fare, plus lamb kebabs. *Under €8.*

Café de la Brousse (C)

Get some shade in a native grass-thatched hut overlooking Adventure Isle, and refresh yourself with a light snack. *Under €8.*

Captain Hook's Galley (C)

You can descend into the depths of Captain Hook's galleon for drinks, cookies, sandwiches, hot dogs and doughnuts. The kids can play above deck, while you take a breather below. *Under €8.*

Question 21
To which film was Indiana Jones™ and the Temple of Doom a prequel?
answer also on p.250

©Disney

Fantasyland

FANTASYLAND

04

©Disney

Fantasyland is pink. The rides are pink, the ground is pink, the food is pink, even when it's not pink, in spirit it's pink. Younger children will enjoy the gentler rides, such as Dumbo the Flying Elephant and the Mad Hatter's Tea Cups, and race around Alice's Curious Labyrinth squealing with delight as water squirts from stone turrets. There is nothing too scary here, except for the dragon, a two-tonne beastie with bad breath and bloodshot eyes, which slumbers beneath the castle and wakes every so often to let out a deafening roar.

FANTASYLAND

©Disney

Best for infants and toddlers.
Worst for teenage thrills.

Le Pays des Contes de Fées

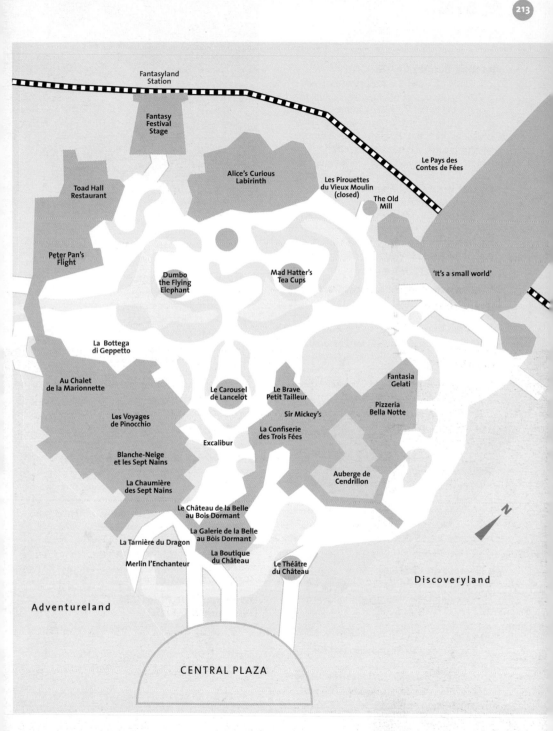

Fantasyland
Station

Fantasy
Festival
Stage

Alice's Curious
Labirinth

Les Pirouettes
du Vieux Moulin
(closed)

Le Pays des
Contes de Fées

The Old
Mill

Toad Hall
Restaurant

Peter Pan's
Flight

Dumbo
the Flying
Elephant

Mad Hatter's
Tea Cups

'It's a small world'

La Bottega
di Geppetto

Au Chalet
de la Marionnette

Fantasia
Gelati

Le Carousel
de Lancelot

Le Brave
Petit Tailleur

Pizzeria
Bella Notte

Les Voyages
de Pinocchio

Sir Mickey's

La Confiserie
des Trois Fées

Excalibur

Blanche-Neige
et les Sept Nains

La Chaumière
des Sept Nains

Auberge de
Cendrillon

Le Château de la Belle
au Bois Dormant

La Galerie de la Belle
au Bois Dormant

La Tarnière du Dragon

La Boutique
du Château

Merlin l'Enchanteur

Le Théâtre
du Château

Discoveryland

N

Adventureland

CENTRAL PLAZA

MAIN ATTRACTIONS

©Disney

Sleeping Beauty Castle

The landmark castle towers 45m (147ft) above the Disney Parks, and is the centrepiece not only of Fantasyland but of the entire complex. Its soaring design is taken from the Disney animated classic, with cubic trees, gothic spires and pink turrets faithfully reproduced to stunning effect.

Most ingenious of all is the cinematique technique of 'forced perspective', which makes the tallest tower seem even higher than it actually is. The walls themselves have been built upwards using increasingly smaller-sized bricks, deceiving the eye into believing that the battlements at the top are that much further away. Look out, too, for the central oval stained-glass 'polage' window which constantly changes scene.

La Galerie de la Belle au Bois Dormant (Sleeping Beauty Gallery)

A spiral staircase leads to an upstairs gallery where hand-painted storybooks, stained-glass windows and finely woven tapestries recall the romantic tale of the Sleeping Beauty. In the corner of the gallery, two guards are supposed to be standing watch. Both are fast asleep and their gruff snores never fail to raise a titter from children who tiptoe by.

La Tanière du Dragon (The Dragon's Dungeon)

The castle's fire-breathing dragon is Disney's largest Audio-Animatronic® figure (one of some 1,200 at Disneyland® Resort Paris), measuring an impressive 27m (88ft) in length. Weighing in at 2 tonnes, the dragon sleeps restlessly beneath the castle in a secret lair. He grumbles and snorts in his misty pool of fetid green water, before awakening with a fearsome growl.

Le Théâtre du Château

Set to the right of the castle drawbridge, this little theatre stages seasonal open-air shows (currently *Winnie the Pooh and Friends Too*). Check your entertainment programme (available from City Hall) for scheduled performances.

Fantasy Festival Stage

Colourful costumes, music and dancing bring this show to life. Magic Music Day performances take place all year except for Christmas when the Fantasy Festival Stage is home to Le Nöel de Mickey Show (Mickey's Christmas Show). You will find the theatre tucked underneath the arches of Fantasyland Station. Check your entertainment programme (available from City Hall) for scheduled performances and make sure you turn up at least 10 minutes before the show is set to begin, or you may be disappointed.

Blanche Neige et les Sept Nains (Snow White and the Seven Dwarfs)

Heigh-ho, heigh-ho, it's off on the Dwarfs' mine-train you go. From their happy cottage home, you hurtle through unforgettable scenes from the movie (alternately cute, then scary) and onwards to the bleak haunted forest where the wicked queen awaits you at every turn. A happy ending is in sight, of course, as Prince Charming arrives to save the day – still, this is one ride likely to startle impressionable youngsters.

Les Voyages de Pinocchio (Pinocchio's Travels)

Next door to the Snow White attraction, this is essentially a ghost-train ride which highlights the darker side of Carlo Collodi's classic Italian fairytale. Seated in lurching handcrafted carriages, you follow Pinocchio on his eventful journey as a wooden puppet in Geppetto's workshop, through temptation and on to his magical reincarnation as

---

Top tips

▶ La Tanière du Dragon is probably a little too terrifying for most toddlers.
▶ The queues for Peter Pan's Flight are among some of the longest. Get a Fastpass (*see* p.188), or try going during a parade

©Disney

Dumbo the Flying Elephant

Choose just how high or how low you want to fly as Dumbo takes you on this delightful aerial merry-go-round. Another fairground classic, and a perfect photo opportunity. *Restrictions apply.*

Mad Hatter's Tea Cups

Seated in one of 18 giant tea cups, you whirl out of control on the Mad Hatter's table. Your cup spins one way, while the saucer turns in the opposite direction. You control the speed using a steering wheel inside your cup. *Restrictions apply.*

Le Pays des Contes de Fées (Storybook Land)

A gentle boat cruise around miniature landscapes re-created from familiar folk stories and Disney classics. The settings are a little faded, but kids enjoy pointing out Hansel and Gretel, Aladdin, Snow White, *et al.*

Casey Jr le Petit Train du Cirque (the Little Circus Train)

Straight out of *Dumbo*, this endearing mini roller-coaster train circuits the elaborate villages of Storybook Land and is a guaranteed thumbs-up for younger kids. *Restrictions apply.*

Les Pirouettes du Vieux Moulin (Twirling Old Mill)

Closed until further notice.

'It's a small world'

A musical tribute to the cultures of the world, your canal boat drifts around the globe passing hundreds of authentically dressed, singing dolls. Despite its rather saccharine theme, the tune is catchy, the scenes captivating and the effects undeniably impressive. At the exit, an innovative display from the ride's sponsor (France Télécom) features tiny buildings with intricate synthetic video scenes playing inside. This is one you won't want to miss.

a real boy. As you might expect, rousing scenes such as Pleasure Island, Stromboli's birdcage and a ravenous Monstro the Whale will fascinate fans over 5 familiar with the movie version, but may still unnerve younger children.

Le Carrousel de Lancelot (Lancelot's Merry-Go-Round)

The manes and tails of the horses on the carousel are hand-painted in 23-carat gold leaf. Worthy of the Knights of the Round Table, these 86 graceful, galloping horses really add to the fairy-tale atmosphere. There are ornate carriages large enough for whole families to ride together.

Peter Pan's Flight

A covered wooden bridge takes you from Pinocchio's village to the opening setting for J. M. Barrie's spectacular story. Here you board a suspended pirate ship and soar over London. Starting off in the children's nursery, you are whisked out of the window and past a series of tableaux from the animated movie, culminating in Never-Never Land with Captain Hook and the Crocodile. Tinker Bell commandeers your escape with a little help from her pixie dust, and you land safe and sound in Mermaid Lagoon. *Fastpass available.*

Alice's Curious Labyrinth

In keeping with Lewis Carroll's classic children's story, *Alice in Wonderland*, this whimsical hedge-maze sets out to baffle and bemuse. You are confronted by signs pointing in every direction, dead ends, miniature doors and bizarre characters. At the heart of the maze, there is a quirky castle filled with distorting optical illusions.

Toilets
- ▶ Next to Au Châlet de la Marionette restaurant.
- ▶ Close to Pizzeria Bella Notte.
- ▶ Close to the Toad Hall Restaurant.

WHERE TO SHOP

La Boutique du Château

Deep inside Sleeping Beauty Castle, it's Christmas all year round. Shop here for Christmas cards and holiday decorations.

La Chaumière des Sept Nains

Children's clothing and costumes, character toys, and film souvenirs.

La Confiserie des Trois Fées

The sweet smell alone will draw you in. Here you'll find delectable sweets and candy in specially packaged gift boxes and tins.

Merlin L'Enchanteur

You can watch crystal being etched and buy ornate medieval figures, jewellery and glassware. It's set inside the castle, and there's a stairway leading down to the Dragon's Dungeon.

Sir Mickey's

Four stores under just one roof, fronted by a giant beanstalk.

Le Brave Petit Tailleur

Children's clothing and hats, cuddly toys, games and souvenirs.

La Bottega di Geppetto

The woodcarver's shop sells a few wooden puppets, cuckoo clocks and music boxes and hand-carved toys. It also has a good selection of babywear and souvenirs.

La Ménagerie du Royaume

Plush soft toys alongside glassware, ceramic Disney characters, jewellery, videos and other gifts.

La Petite Maison des Jouets

Under the colourful shingled roof of this olde worlde cottage you will find plush toys and other Disneyland® Resort Paris gifts.

WHERE TO EAT

A table and buffet service, full menu.
B counter service, full menu.
C counter service, light snacks.
V vegetarian option available.

Auberge de Cendrillon (A, V)

One of the few places in the whole of the Theme Park to eat French food. Cinderella's coach sits in the covered courtyard. Inside, beautiful tapestries depict scenes from the movie. The clink of grown-up cutlery and wine glasses reflects the rather formal atmosphere, but the staff are very friendly and the kids' menu is first rate. The Express Menu is good value for money, too. *Over €15.*

Pizzeria Bella Notte (B, V)

Pizza and pasta are served here in a setting inspired by the spaghetti scene from *Lady and the Tramp*. *Under €8.*

Au Châlet de la Marionette (B, V)

Basically a fast-food chicken joint, with Bavarian décor, Pinocchio theme and cosy fireplace. Choose from roast chicken, Bavarian hot dogs and omelette burgers. *Under 50F.*

Toad Hall Restaurant (B, V)

Timbered country inn, serving British fare: fish 'n' chips, chicken, sandwiches and hearty puddings. *Under €8.*

March Hare Refreshments (C)

Sickly sweet doughnuts, cookies and popcorn. *Under €8.*

The Old Mill (C)

Snack on doughnuts, french stick sandwiches (i.e. Subs) and beverages. *Under €8.*

Fantasia Gelati (C)

Delicious Italian ice cream in a cone, plus waffles and pancakes. *Under €8.*

©Disney

Question 22
How many Audio-Animatronic® figures are there in the Resort?
a) 500 or less
b) 500–2,000
c) 2,000–4,500
answer also on p.250

Discoveryland

©Disney

Discoveryland is really rather beautiful and, of the five lands, the most interesting architecturally because, being a land of tomorrow, it makes its own rules. The glistening, golden balls of Orbitron and the forbidding launch pad of Space Mountain are just as much of a draw for kids and adults as the rides themselves. Dotted around are other 'exhibits' such as a life-size X-wing fighter from *Star Wars* and a space car by Renault. Budding boffins are bound to love it.

Best for adrenaline rush.
Worst for peak-season queues.

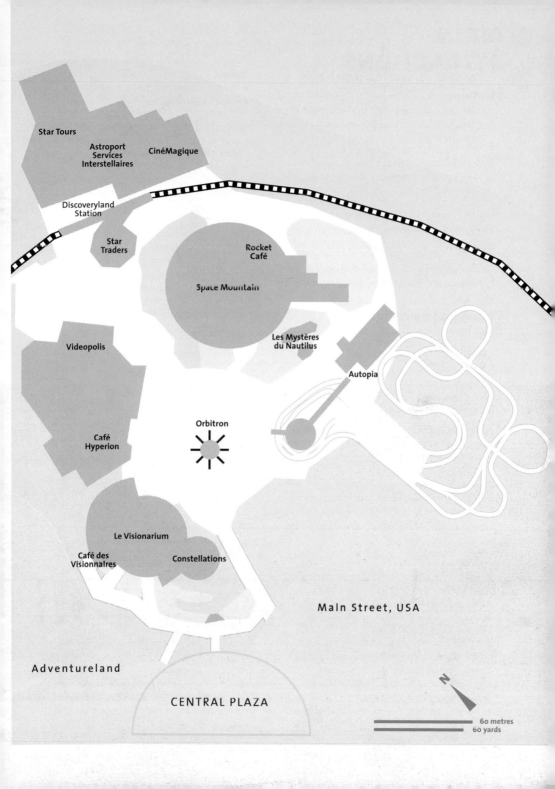

Star Tours

Astroport
Services
Interstellaires

CinéMagique

Discoveryland
Station

Star
Traders

Rocket
Café

Space Mountain

Les Mystères
du Nautilus

Videopolis

Autopia

Orbitron

Café
Hyperion

Le Visionarium

Café des
Visionnaires

Constellations

Main Street, USA

Adventureland

CENTRAL PLAZA

N

60 metres
60 yards

MAIN ATTRACTIONS

Star Tours

Anyone who climbs aboard the Starspeeder 3000 is in for an out-of-this-world space adventure. This *Star Wars*-inspired flight simulator takes you on an astonishingly realistic journey to Endor at turbulent speed, accompanied by an amateurish robot pilot, RX24. There's no real danger of course. The windscreen in front of you is, in fact, a screen projecting a 70mm showreel. Accompany this with the effects of G-force, propulsion and abrupt deceleration and you will feel as though you are really out there. George Lucas fans will be thrilled to find R2D2 and C3PO among the droids in the intergalactic loading area. They certainly help take the tedium out of queuing. *Restrictions apply. Fastpass available.*

L'Astroport Services Instellaires (Star Tours Post-Show)

At the exit to Star Tours is a state-of-the-art video arcade. As well as interactive games and simulator rides, there is a picture-morphing area which allows you to distort your own photographic image. This, as well as the 12-player Star Course game, are especially popular. *Restrictions apply.*

Space Mountain – De la Terre à la Lune (From the Earth to the Moon)

Nowhere is Disney's subtle use of dim or near nonexistent lighting put to better effect than here. Space Mountain may be the best ride in the whole park and takes place in near darkness. Inspired by Jules Verne's *From the Earth to the Moon*, this breathtaking indoor roller coaster catapults you

---

Top tips

▶ The main dialogue on Star Tours is entirely in French – the only possible drawback to an otherwise superb ride.
▶ A Fastpass (*see* p.188) cuts queuing times at Star Tours and Space Mountain.
▶ At Honey, I Shrunk the Audience, a large crowd is loaded quickly, but expect to spend up to 10 minutes before getting into the auditorium while you are herded together for a Kodak commercial.
▶ The Visionarium is highly recommended, but under-4s may get a bit distracted as it runs for a full 20 minutes.

Toilets

▶ Within Videopolis.
▶ Close to Autopia.

---

from a giant cannon into a series of pitch-black, cosmic loops and spins at a giddying 70kph around 1 kilometre of track. Thanks to a magnificent feat of engineering, a moonward-bound rocket ship carrying 24 fellow passengers is launched every 36 seconds throughout the day. A near-deafening explosion prompts your equally audible screams as the rocket embarks on a supersonic journey through the hostile wastelands of the cosmos. You're never sure when the next errant meteorite will appear as you dodge and weave your way into space on this white-knuckle ride.

For the less daring, special gangways allow you to climb the immense copper and bronze mountain and take a closer look at this high-tech, corkscrewing ride. Entrance to the viewing area is around the back, opposite Honey, I Shrunk the Audience. *Restrictions apply. Fastpass available.*

Arcade des Visionnaires

An interactive video games arcade that tempts you to part with most of your hard-earned dough.

Honey, I Shrunk the Audience

This addition to Disneyland® Park features the latest in film and digital technology. The misadventure begins as Professor Szalinski presents the invention of the year: an amazing shrinking machine. Unfortunately, it is pointed at the audience, and, what do you know? We all shrink! The combination of tactile, visual and sound effects creates a world of topsy-turvy dimensions. Special 3-D glasses bring you up close to a giant python, roaring lion and sneezing dog. Building on an age-old gag, escaping laboratory mice cause predictable panic. While this is billed as a family attraction, under-4s may be startled.

Le Visionarium (The Visionarium)

Enter into a 360° panoramic time-travel adventure hosted by the eccentric Timekeeper. This circular-vision cinema employs nine interlocking screens which completely surround you. A combination of robotics, computerized special effects and high-impact film footage takes you on a giddy voyage around Europe, as you switch between past, present and future paying tribute to the world's greatest inventions. *Restrictions apply.*

Orbitron

Inspired by Leonardo da Vinci's sketches of flying machines, this is your chance to pilot your own spaceship as you soar through a galaxy high above Discoveryland. Though it is essentially a fairground ride, it is beautifully designed and an unmistakable classic. *Restrictions apply.*

Autopia

The Autopia cars cover a distance of 730,000km each year. Junior L-drivers love the highways and byways of this retro, space-age circuit which makes its way around the futuristic city of 'Solaria'. With their cars kept steadily on track by a metal rail, all the kids have to do is press the gas pedal and steer. *Restrictions apply.*

Videopolis

Spectacular live stage shows are put on at regular intervals throughout the day in this huge, high-tech auditorium. The sheer size of the auditorium makes it a touch impersonal but there is no denying the mounting excitement as the time for the scheduled show draws closer. These are no mere fillers but quality productions on a lavish scale. Try to see one if you can.

Les Mystères du Nautilus (The Mystery of the Nautilus)

Explore the darkest depths of the ocean in Captain Nemo's legendary submarine, straight out of Disney's screen version of Jules Verne's *20,000*

Three visionaries

Leonardo da Vinci (1452–1519)

Leonardo da Vinci was a painter, sculptor, architect, musician, engineer and scientist. Far from being a jack-of-all-trades, he was a master at whatever he put his mind to. As early as the 15th century, he invented the basis for a prototype helicopter, aeroplane, tank, machine-gun, power hammer, swivel bridge and parachute. He also painted the *Mona Lisa*, which hangs in the Louvre (*see pp.42–44*).

Jules Verne (1828–1905)

Jules Verne was a French author with a fertile imagination which led him to write *Around The World in 80 Days*, *A Journey to the Centre of the Earth*, *20,000 Leagues Under The Sea* and *From the Earth to the Moon*. Many of his stories feature incredible machines (such as the submarine) which seemed fantastical to his contemporaries, but which soon became reality.

H. G. Wells (1866–1946)

H. G. Wells was a British author who, although he wrote all kinds of novels and political works, made his name writing science fiction. Among his most famous books are *The Time Machine*, *The Invisible Man* and *The War of The Worlds*.

Leagues Under the Sea. The tour holds a few spine-tingling surprises including an attack by a giant squid. Les Mystères du Nautilus can be a little disappointing if you know nothing about the story.

©Disney

Did you know?
Space Mountain cost €90 million and can accommodate 2,600 guests per hour.

WHERE TO SHOP

Constellations

This planetarium-inspired boutique offers a wide range of Disney merchandise and clothing for aspiring space cadets. Mickey fans will appreciate the wacky, flying-machine centrepiece.

Light Speed Photography

You can prove to everyone that you survived the interstellar speeds of Space Mountain by having your own photograph taken at the split second of blast-off.

Star Traders

Mainly sportswear, plus *Star Wars* souvenirs, all sorts of gadgets, gizmos, and a wide assortment of futuristic toys at this solar-panelled, intergalactic trading post.

Question 23

Which French writer's books is Space Mountain based on?

answer also on p.250

©Disney

WHERE TO EAT

B counter service, full menu.
C counter service, light snacks.
V vegetarian option available.

Café Hyperion (B, V)

Pass under the immense floating Hyperion airship (straight out of a Jules Verne novel) and you enter the futuristic Videopolis amphitheatre. Queue for a hyperburger, sandwich or salad. Multiple-screen cartoons and a live musical stage show will keep the kids engrossed. *Under* €8.

Buzz Lightyear's Pizza Planet (C, V)

Pizza Planet looks like something out of a science-fiction comic. The décor features a giant rocket-ship filled with multi-eyed mini-aliens. Choose from Mickey-shaped pizzas or the house speciality: a hamburger topped with a mini-pizza. There is a supervised theme play area with closed circuit television, so you can keep a leisurely eye on the kids. *Under* €8.

Rocket Café (C)

A selection of drinks and snacks to keep your energy levels boosted. *Under* €8.

Did you know?

There are 700 speakers strategically placed around the Disney Parks, although trying to spot just one of them is a task in itself.

Walt Disney Studios® Park

©Disney

MAIN ATTRACTIONS

Walt Disney Studios® Park opened its doors in Spring 2002 at Disneyland® Resort Paris. A Park in itself, this brand-new addition is impossible to miss thanks to a 33m-(108ft)-tall water tower with giant Mickey ears. The Park is divided up into four 'production courtyards' that give visitors the opportunity to go in front of the camera or visit film-making, television and animation behind the scenes.

There are a host of attractions with spectacular special effects – a Studio Tram Tour featuring Catastrophe Canyon, the Rock 'n' Roller Coaster starring Aerosmith, the Art of Disney® Animation and a live vehicle stunt show, Moteurs...Action! that brings you up close and personal with some of the world's best high-octane chases and crashes.

Front Lot

The main entrance to Walt Disney Studios® Park leads you into a Mediterranean courtyard full of echoes of American and European history. As you walk through the majestic Studio Gates, you'll see palm trees, a Mickey Mouse 'Sorcerer's Apprentice' water fountain and the Mickey water tower, modelled on the one near the entrance to Disney® Studios in Burbank, California since 1939.

Studio 1 is the first 'studio' you'll come across. Once inside, you find yourself on Sunset Boulevard, only to realize that the street is an elaborate film set complete with lots of movie props. If you're lucky, you might see a production in progress!

Animation Courtyard

Animation Courtyard celebrates the development of animation from its origins in Europe to the 20th century. with a range of exhibits and shows.

The **Disney Parade,** with its Disney characters and street performers, wends its way down from Backlot every afternoon and reaches its climax here. Check out the trailer opposite Animagique for a 'director' Mickey or stand by Walt Disney's statue to catch groups of improvisation artists.

The **Art of Disney® Animation** is a real hands-on experience, where children can create their own

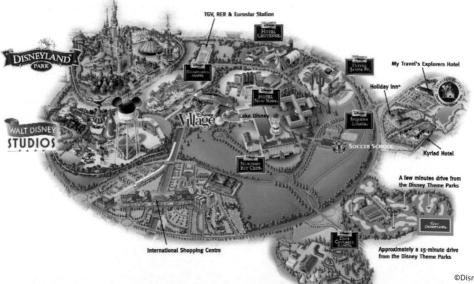

©Disney

Disney

piece of magic. Older children and adults can have a go at drawing a popular cartoon character by following step-by-step instructions under the guidance of a studio artist (who gives a demonstration first). Younger children can browse the interactive displays and use computers to colour in their favourite Disney characters and scenes.

Animagique is a colourful show in the great tradition of Czechoslovakian 'black light' theatre. Animagique brings to life famous scenes from favourite Disney animated pictures, including *The Lion King* and *Pinocchio*, in the midst of a magical and mysterious atmosphere.

Flying Carpets over Agrabah invites children on a film set by the Genie from *Aladdin*. Mayhem ensues as the actor-turned-director does his best to organize a film shoot. The climax sees guests whizzing round a giant genie's lamp on magic carpets. *Fastpass available.*

Production Courtyard

This area is the heartbeat of the studio production facilities with productions and shows taking place almost daily, offering you the opportunity to live the magic – live!

The **Television Production Tour** at Walt Disney Television Studios is home to the French Disney Channel and gives you the chance to take a rare glimpse of a busy production facility via a glass corridor. With the use of visual trickery, your image is morphed into a picture of the set to create the illusion that you are live on TV! The studio at **Disney Channel Cyberspace** allows kids and grown-ups to explore their creative talents.

Cinemagique offers a magical journey through the very best of 100 years of the moving image. Combining live performers and special effects, this tribute to European and US cinema sees real actors magically move in and out of the screen to re-create cinema's most enduring and poignant moments.

The **Studio Tram Tour** takes you on an insider's tour of the studio premises, providing a look behind the scenes at location sites, movie props, special effects, studio décor and central costuming. When the tram visits **Catastrophe Canyon**, you find out what being in the 'hot seat' means when you are plunged into the heart of an all-action film shoot!

At **CyberSpace Mountain**, you'll live a virtual reality, thrilling, simulator adventure. *Restrictions apply.*

Backlot

Home to the special effects facility, the music recording stages and the stunt workshops. Take a sneak peak behind the scenes.

Armageddon, Special Effects takes its name from the American science fiction blockbuster and sets you off on a voyage through the history of special effects and into the heart of the movie. Invited on board the film's MIR space station, you witness a meteor shower! *Restrictions apply.*

At the **Rock 'n' Roller Coaster Starring Aerosmith** you 'ride the music' in a sight and sound spectacular with hairpin turns, loops and heart-stopping drops. *Restrictions apply. Fastpass available.*

In **Moteurs...Action!**, the renowned James Bond stunt designer, Rémy Julienne, has helped to create a highly visual and dynamic show in a 3,000-seat outdoor arena. Cars leap over trucks and motorbikes come crashing through shop windows in daring stunts. The final edit is then broadcast on a giant screen, showing you how live action movie sequences are put together. *Restrictions apply.*

Walt Disney Studios® Park basics
► Entered separately from the main Disneyland® Paris Park. For ticket details, *see* pp.181, 185, 188.
► Fastpass prebooking system (*see* p.188) is available at Walt Disney Studios® Park (Rock 'n' Roller Coaster and Flying Carpets over Agrabah).

WHERE TO SHOP

Walt Disney Studios Store, Front Lot
Unique Studio souvenirs and gifts.

Studio Photo, Front Lot
For photo equipment, accessories and souvenirs.

Les Légendes d'Hollywood, Front Lot
Music and movie-themed souvenirs.

Animation Courtyard (The Disney Animation Gallery), Front Lot
Sketches of Disney characters, animation cells and must-have collectibles.

Rock Around the Shop, Backlot
Rock 'n' Roller Coaster and Aerosmith mementos.

WHERE TO EAT

B counter service, full menu.
C counter service, light snacks.
V vegetarian option available.

Restaurant en Coulisse (C, V), Front Lot
Located behind the façades of Studio 1, guests can dine behind the scenes surrounded by cinema décor. The menu serves hamburgers, chicken burgers, pizza, salads and ice cream. *Under €8.*

Studio Catering Co. (C), Animation Courtyard, Production Courtyard and Backlot
A fast-food truck serving pizzas, hot dogs, popcorn and desserts. *Under €8.*

Rendez-Vous des Stars (B, V, C), Production Courtyard
Reminiscent of the Hollywood-style refectory with better-than-average fare (mozzarella and tomatoes, baked salmon and lasagne). *Under €15.*

La Terrasse (B, V), Production Courtyard
A 264-seat capacity eatery, open on all sides, elaborately designed in Art Deco style. *Under €8.*

Backlot Express Restaurant (C, V), Backlot
Re-creating the atmosphere of a movie studio art department, its menu offers snacks, club and baguette sandwiches, quiches, salads and pastries. *Under €8.*

Café des Cascadeurs (B, V), Backlot
Every inch a 1950s American diner serving up sandwiches, hot dogs and salads. *Under €8.*

©Disney

Disneyland®
Resort Paris
Need to know

Beating the queues

Queuing can be a pretty dull affair, especially if you have to spend 1 hour waiting for a 3-minute ride. But, it's all showbusiness here, and the trick of whipping up the audience and keeping everyone excited and entertained at the very same time as you're having to wait is one Disney know very well.

Where to head first

A great help in getting round the lines at the most popular rides is the **Fastpass** prebooking system (*see* p.188). Otherwise, the attractions with the slowest-moving queues are clearly worth riding first thing, as soon as you get through the park gates. They include Big Thunder Mountain, Indiana Jones™ and the Temple of Peril: Backwards!, Dumbo the Flying Elephant, Star Tours, Peter Pan's Flight, Orbitron and Autopia in the main Disneyland® Park, and the Rock 'n' Roller Coaster and Flying Carpets in Walt Disney Studios® Park. Other attractions may appear to have long queues, but load up large groups of people very quickly, so you can leave them until later. These include Pirates of the Caribbean, Les Voyages de Pinocchio, 'It's a small world', Le Carrousel de Lancelot, the Mad Hatter's Tea Cups, Le Visionarium, Armageddon Special Effects, Cinematique and Moteurs...Action!

The early bird catches the worm

To avoid the worst of the queues, you need to arrive at Disneyland® Park early – even before the gates are open. Wait at the turnstiles until you see Mickey appear. Once you hear the train hooter give two blasts, you will know it is time to get on your starting blocks. Then, the red arrow on the front of the turnstile changes to green, giving you the all clear to enter, with your passport in hand.

Rainy days

Even Disneyland® Resort Paris loses some of its lustre on cold, bleak days – after all, this is northern Europe, not Florida. However, 80 per cent of the rides are under cover, so you can still enjoy most of them without getting your feet wet.

The Disney imagineers have considered the weather, of course, and included central heating in all the visitor areas, as well as some roaring log fires and covered queuing areas. At Disneyland® Park, you can actually get all the way from the main gate to Frontierland and then on to Adventureland and Fantasyland without ever really confronting the elements.

Even if the rain is falling, there is still no need to abandon your plans. If you are caught out unex-

---

Tips for avoiding the biggest queues

▶ Visit in Low Season. Quiet times are mid-January–February, late September, November and the first few weeks in December. The Disney Parks are also quieter during the week; on weekends and national holidays, it's more likely to be crowded.
▶ Watch the shows and parades on your first day, then use this valuable time on subsequent visits to ride the big-thrill attractions. Many of the rides are near-deserted during the Main Street parades and watching the fireworks from Dumbo the Flying Elephant or Orbitron is a real thrill.
▶ Watch the main parade from its starting point near 'It's a small world' (Fantasyland). Once the final float has gone by, head for the normally busy rides nearby (i.e. Star Tours or Peter Pan's Flight).
▶ The lines get shorter as the day draws to a close. If you can, take a break mid-afternoon and return to the Disney Parks after 5pm.

▶ If you are visiting during the shorter off-peak days, enjoy the rides during the day and leave all your shopping until you visit Disney® Village, to allow yourself to buy souvenirs after the Parks' gates have closed.
▶ On certain days during the summer season, (April–September), Disneyland® Paris hotel guests can enter the Parks 30mins before they officially open. Ask at your hotel about early entry.
▶ If you're staying at Disney's Newport Bay Club®, Sequoia Lodge®, Hotel Cheyenne® or Hotel Santa Fe® you can reserve a buffet breakfast in Fantasyland 1 hour before the official opening times and be among the first to enjoy the Parks' attractions.
▶ Walt Disney Studios® Park is generally far slower-paced and attracts fewer queueing crowds, especially mid-afternoon.

pectedly, Le Passage Enchanté d'Aladdin (Adventureland), Les Mystères du Nautilus (Discoveryland) and Legends of the Wild West (Frontierland) all offer an escape from the sudden bad weather outside. Your kids will also have fun exploring Sleeping Beauty Castle (Fantasyland). Don't forget to visit the cellar down below, for an encounter with the red-eyed, smoke-snorting (and possibly quite scary) dragon.

If the bad weather persists, head for the covered arcades either side of Main Street, USA, leading up from Town Square. Here, you can find entrances to several welcoming shops and restaurants. Liberty Arcade leads north of Dapper Dan's to Liberty Court, where you will find the Statue of Liberty Tableau. On the opposite side, Discovery Arcade has a showcase of the world's greatest inventions.

Much of Walt Disney Studios® Park has been designed with bad weather in mind. The Front Lot's Disney Studio 1 is an ideal place to come during rain showers and shop, dine or visit the behind-the-scenes movie action. Animagique, Cinemagique, Art of Disney Animation, Television Production Tour, Armageddon and Rock 'n' Roller Coaster each offer indoor entertainment

More ideas

Kids will happily spend a few hours at Videopolis, enjoying fast food, a live musical show and cartoons. Buzz Lightyear's Pizza Planet Restaurant has a supervised indoor play area and video screens so that you can keep an eye on their antics from your table. You can approach either restaurant under cover by the Discovery Arcade.

From Liberty Arcade, you can reach Frontierland without getting wet. From here, head for Adventureland Bazaar, which is a fun spot to browse in. The exotic covered courtyard has boutiques, murals, fountains and a collection of impressive movie props.

If the rain looks set to last, though, your kids may feel cheated if you do not brave it and set out to make the most of your time in the Disney Parks. Pirates of the Caribbean, Phantom Manor, Star Tours, Le Visionarium and Honey, I Shrunk the Audience all last long enough for you to enjoy their sheltered interiors and most of their queuing areas are under cover. Space Mountain, one of the fastest moving rides, doesn't last that long, but the star-studded corridor to the loading area offers a welcome breather from the rain. For the less brave,

Top tip
▶ For the most up-to-date weather reports covering the Paris area, check the net at www.met-office.gov.uk.

there are gentle rides such as the Mad Hatter's Tea Cups and Peter Pan's Flight almost entirely under cover. At Walt Disney Studios® Park, you can make the best of a bad day by 'Singing in the Rain' under a rain-filled umbrella!

Saving money

Disneyland® Resort Paris is not cheap, but it does not need to break the bank if you are sensible about how you spend your money. Once you're in, there is little to fork out on apart from food and souvenirs. Stay at one of the cheaper resort hotels and don't go mad in the shops or video arcades. If you're going to go round the Parks 'thoroughly', buying (and preferably prebuying) a 3-day ticket (see p.181), which allows you to come and go between both Parks (Disneyland® Park and Walt Disney Studios® Park), is naturally a much better idea than paying for repeat visitors and, for avid Disneyland® Resort Paris fans, annual passports (see p.188) offer significant savings. Below are a few more useful money-saving suggestions.

Money-saving tips
▶ Package prices are cheaper mid-week.
▶ Look out for special deals and promotions during the year, such as three nights-for-the-price-of-two and Kids Go Free.
▶ 1-day and 3-day Hopper tickets (see p.181) admit you to both Parks and offer the best value for money, but be sure to budget for that long a stay (including hotel bills, meals and extras).
▶ Pack a warm pullover and raincoat and visit in the winter months when both entrance ticket prices and hotel rates are cheaper.
▶ Throughout the Disney Parks, there are food carts offering filling snacks at a reasonable price. Packing your own picnic costs even less.
▶ Keep your kids away from the pay-to-play arcades. They guzzle up euro coins quicker than you can get them out of your pocket.
▶ Look out for refillable mugs which allow you to refresh your cup at no added cost.

MEETING THE CHARACTERS

Many kids come to the Disneyland® Resort Paris with a single idea – they're about to come face to face with their favourite Disney characters. During the parades they strain to catch a glimpse, then hop up and down, clapping wildly as Baloo lumbers round the corner. Elsewhere, crowds of grinning kids threaten to topple Mickey or Donald in the crush for autographs. These are not just actors dressed up as Mickey or Baloo the Bear. This *is* Mickey. This *is* Baloo. This is real.

Good guys and bad guys

All the Disney characters are briefed to act out their specific roles to their utmost and, consequently, there is the odd occasion when they can completely misjudge your child's reaction. Watch out especially for the baddies such as Hades (Hercules), Captain Hook (Peter Pan), Prince John (Robin Hood) and Stromboli and Gideon (Pinocchio). Stromboli makes a habit of snatching children's toys. Captain Hook lunges at you with his hook, and others sneer or growl menacingly. It's all done with good humour, of course, and although some children may find it confusing at first, most learn to play the game pretty quickly.

What children seem to enjoy most about the characters – apart from the excitement of being close to larger-than-life-size versions of their favourites – is the possibility that they might, just might, be singled out. It's absolutely thrilling for any child to dance with Cinderella, to be given a ticking off by Governor Ratcliffe, to be noticed by Goofy, or receive a big hug from Mickey Mouse.

Where to find them

You can pick up daily programmes with information on the best times to meet and greet the characters at the main entrances of City Hall and Studio Services.

Hotels

Mickey and his pals put in an appearance at the Disneyland® Resort Paris hotels at set times each day – the times when they are due are listed under 'Just for the kids' in **Where To Sleep** (*see* pp.239–44). Both hotel guests and day visitors are free to visit the characters at any of the hotels.

Character meals

You can dine with the characters during the day,

it is worth trying to include one of these treats in your itinerary, especially if you have younger children. Baloo, Chip 'n' Dale, Minnie or Goofy joining you at your table is sure to be an experience that will linger with youngsters for years.

At the Disneyland® Hotel's Inventions Restaurant and at Walt's Restaurant on Main Street, USA, hotel guests can book a special breakfast buffet with the Disney characters and Crockett's Tavern at the Davy Crockett Ranch® hosts a similar event. There is also a character breakfast and dinner at Café Mickey in Disney® Village. Lunch (12 noon–3pm) and dinner (6.30pm–10pm) with the Disney characters are available daily at the Lucky Nugget Saloon in Frontierland. You can also have a teatime buffet with the characters at 3pm and 4.30pm at the Plaza Gardens Restaurant on Main Street, USA. An all-you-can-eat brunch is on Sundays (12 noon–3pm) at the Steakhouse Restaurant in Disney® Village.

Disneyland Park appearances

You can get an eyeful of the gang at the Disneyland® Park entrance on Main Street, USA, each morning as you file in. Many more characters wander at leisure around the Disney Parks with set 'meet-and-greet' times throughout the day. Ask at City Hall and Studio Services for more details.

Shows

Special choreographed shows at Videopolis, Fantasy Festival Stage, Le Théâtre du Château, La Cour du Château and the Chaparral Theatre operate seasonally. Also at Animagique daily. Look out, too, for regular appearances at Studio 1.

The parades

The best opportunity to see many of the characters all together is during the daily parades which wind through Disneyland® Park, from Fantasyland down to Main Street, USA, culminating in the Town Square. During the daytime parade, children are regularly hand-plucked from the audience and invited to join in the action. Kitted out in miniature costumes, they can find themselves fighting off that nasty Captain Hook, being slipped into a sea shell to become a Little Mermaid, or clowning around at the circus with Dumbo. At Walt Disney Studios® Park, the daily Cinema Parade wends its way down from the Backlot inviting kids to play extras along the way.

As darkness falls, the nighttime parade begins its journey through Disneyland® Park, lighting the way with glittering floats filled with Disney favourites. Over a million light bulbs illuminate the way for what is, by anyone's standards, a spectacular show of lights and sound.

For the very grand finale, and that all important 'ooh!' and 'aah!' factor, a fireworks display next to Sleeping Beauty Castle is topped by the appearance of an acrobatic Tinker Bell who flits and darts, leaving angel dust in her fiery trail.

Hidden Mickeys

Ever since Disneyland® Park opened, a subculture of committed fans has steadily reported sightings of 'hidden Mickeys' dotted around the attractions. Some of the hidden Mickey claims are outrageous, others are more cryptic, but Disney do confirm these subtle touches have been built into the Disney Parks – so be sure to keep an eye out. A few of the reported sightings are listed here to get you started. If you do find one out, you can report a hidden Mickey at www.hiddenmickeys.org.

Main Street, USA
City Hall
▶ There is a hidden Mickey on the clock. The back of the minute hand and hour hand of the clock are two black circles. When they are about 15 minutes apart, they make a perfect Mickey. The hands are the ears, the centre of the clock is the head.

Main Street Station
▶ While queuing for the train you come face to face with a glass mural. On the left is a castle decorated with circular patterns. One of these circles has two Mickey ears.

Believe it or not
Now the Resort is complete, its outline makes up the biggest hidden Mickey of all. But you'll need a helicopter to spot it!

Liberty Arcade and Discovery Arcade
▶ In both arcades, there are gas lamps. If you invert the three rings, you can see a Mickey.

Frontierland
Riverboat Landing
▶ Look between the two smoke stacks on the paddle steamers and you will see an ironwork lattice with a gold star in the middle. To either side is a perfect hidden Mickey, turned sideways.

Big Thunder Mountain
▶ In the upstairs section of the queuing area is a balcony where you can look down on the queue. Directly below are three barrels. Together they form a hidden Mickey.
▶ Take a look at the out-of-order clock on the wall, facing the queue line, just to the right of the control tower. Mickey is on the hands of the clock.

Phantom Manor
▶ As you walk into the first chamber in Phantom Manor, look up at the ceiling. Above the chandelier in the middle of the room there is a design that forms a double hidden Mickey.
▶ The table setting in the ballroom scene reveals several hidden Mickeys.

Adventureland
Indiana Jones™ and the Temple of Peril: Backwards!
▶ Look at the front of any train. If you look hard, you will see an Inca-style Mickey.

Pirates of the Caribbean
▶ In the battle scene, the hole blown out of the castle wall is in the shape of a Mickey.
▶ Just before the burning town, there is a crane suspending three barrels. When the barrels turn so that you view them end-on, they form a hidden Mickey.
▶ In the treasure scene, right before the exit, are three tablets displayed on a heap of gold which make up a perfect Mickey.

Fantasyland

Sleeping Beauty Castle

▶ The lanterns at the castle's back entrance each contain three bulbs – one big one and two smaller ones, which together form a hidden Mickey.

▶ Several of the roof tiles are a different colour and form a typical Mickey head.

Auberge de Cendrillon

▶ In the third room of the restaurant, there is a raised area with a wrought-iron railing that has a full-figure Mickey as its main repeated design.

'It's a small world'

▶ To the left-hand side of the clock on the front facia of 'It's a small world', you will see a panel going from top to bottom entirely made up of hidden Mickeys.

▶ Halfway through the ride, you approach an Arabian scene (where the boat makes a sharp turn to the left). If you look towards the left of the scene as you float past, you will see Mickey on the wall, rotated 90° anti-clockwise.

Toad Hall Restaurant

▶ There are two lamp posts in front containing the restaurant's menu. Their black iron lamps have hidden Mickeys punched out all around them.

Blanche Neige et les Sept Nains

▶ In the queue area is a mural with all the characters from the film in the background. In front of Happy's right foot are three flowers that form a hidden Mickey.

▶ Inside the attraction there are three fountains. Inside each one there are three lights which make up a hidden Mickey.

Les Voyages de Pinocchio

▶ Within the attraction there is a pool table. Look closely and you will see that the eight-ball has a hidden Mickey on it.

Peter Pan's Flight

▶ Just after the nursery, you see a painted roof. On the wall, there is a hidden Mickey.

Alice's Curious Labyrinth

▶ On the taller beige castle observation stand overlooking the labyrinth (above the round opening), three stones form a perfect hidden Mickey on its side.

Discoveryland

Le Visionarium

▶ In the scene where Nine-Eye and Jules Verne are in Russia, there is a hidden Mickey on a balloon.

Orbitron

▶ The ride is topped by rotating spheres. For a brief second during the ride, three come together to form a hidden Mickey.

Les Mystères du Nautilus

▶ After the show, there are two paths to the exit. Take the left-hand one. You will see a bottle filled with fish. On one of them there is a hidden Mickey.

Space Mountain

▶ As you head towards the moon's smile, his left cheek has three 'dimple' craters. Turned the right way up, they form a perfect Mickey.

Walt Disney Studios® Park

▶ At the entrance, the pattern of metal spokes on the fence reveal Mickey's face.

▶ Look at the coloured stone floor of the waterfall featuring the Sorcerer's Apprentice.

▶ Heading towards the Armageddon attraction, on the far right side of the road opposite Cinemagique, a hidden Mickey is formed by three circles on the pavement darker than the rest. You see it best when the road is wet.

Around the hotel complex

Disneyland® Hotel

▶ If you are lucky enough to stay at the Disneyland® Hotel on the 'Castle Club' floor, you should find six golden chocolate coins on your bed every evening. They form obvious Mickey heads.

Hotel Cheyenne®

▶ At the Hotel Cheyenne® reception, in one of the windows, is a red hidden Mickey.

▶ Look closely at the coffee cups and the carpets at the Cheyenne Hotel®.

Lake Disney®

▶ Around the lake are street lamps. Every lamp has a hidden Mickey.

DISNEY® VILLAGE

Set between the Disney Parks and the hotels, this vast entertainment complex is signposted by enormous silver and red vertical columns, which seem to support nothing more than a bunch of wires. Take a closer look, though, and you'll see that the wires hold hundreds of lights, which beckon the crowds once darkness falls and the Parks close.

Disney® Village is open longer than Disneyland® Park itself, from 7.30am to 4am daily, and attempts to re-create something like the downtown atmosphere of a small American city. Inside the 'Village' there are nightclubs, bars, restaurants, shops, kiosks, a cinema and live shows. There's also a good-humoured (if unsophisticated) party spirit here, and it is a safe place to wander with your family after dark.

A car park located between Disney® Village and Disney's Newport Bay Hotel® is designated for all those free-flowing Village visitors who have no intention of using the Disney Parks.

The main attractions

Most of the attractions focus specifically on evening performances and have limited opening hours. For details of Buffalo Bill's Wild West Show and Hurricanes nightclub, see **Entertainment**, p.245.

Gaumont Cinema

A 15-screen cinema complex (including one giant screen) equipped with the latest film technology. You will find it to the right of the entrance to Disney® Village. Several films are screened in English every Monday night.

Marina Del Ray

You can rent a variety of water vehicles from the dock area for use on Lake Disney®, and even book supervised sailing tuition. Opening hours are limited during the winter months.

Disney® Village Video Arcade

All the usual video games for hi-tech children with itchy trigger fingers.

Buffalo Bill's Wild West Show

A dinner show with cowboys and Indians that captures the spirit of the gun-toting Wild West.

Minnie Train

A train (without tracks!) that rides around Lake Disney®. For the younger set.

Where to eat

In contrast to Disneyland® Park, the restaurants in Disney® Village include some familiar international favourites (and McDonald's) as well as Disney's own. Check opening times on arrival as they are subject to change without prior notice.

A table and buffet service, full menu.
B counter service, full menu.
C counter service, light snacks.
V vegetarian option available.

Annette's Diner (A, C, V)
Open All day from 11.30am

Burger and shakes, chilli, hot dogs or ice-cream sundaes. If you don't fancy a sit-down meal, there's a take-away window outside. *Between €8 and €15.*

Billy Bob's Country & Western Saloon (A, V)
Open Dinner only

There's a fun Tex-Mex buffet on the third floor of this atmospheric, mock-up saloon. A five-piece cowboy band also helps give it a properly laid-back, cowboy appeal. *Between €8 and €15.*

Café Mickey (A, V)
Open Lunch and dinner

Served breakfast (7.30am–10.30am), lunch or dinner (12.00 noon–11pm) with the Disney characters. *Over €15.*

McDonald's (B, C)
Open All day from 8am

An inventive indoor children's play area keeps kids busy while you queue. *Under €8.*

Planet Hollywood® (A, V)
Open Lunch and dinner

Burgers and American cooking in a glam, movie-memorabilia setting. Check out the gift shop and celebrity handprints on your way out. *Over €15.*

Rainforest Café® (A, V)
Open Lunch and dinner

As well as 'jungle' décor', it features a huge aquarium, an impressive menu and a shop with merchandise to rival Disney's own. Look out, too, for the shop's ecofriendly talking tree. *Over €15.*

King Ludwig's Castle (A, V)
Open Lunch and dinner

Disney® Village
Best for nightlife. It can have more appeal for adults than for young children.

WHERE TO SHOP

A menu fit for a king at this mock-up castle serving traditional Bavarian cuisine including veal, stroganoff, pork loin, strüdel and Black Forest gâteau. *Over €15.*

Sandwiches New York Style (A, C, V)
Open All day from 8am

Specialities include bagels, cookies and muffins, all served at fifties-revival formica tables. Also a take-away counter. *Under €8.*

The Steakhouse (A, V)
Open Lunch and dinner

You can order succulent prime rib or a thick T-bone steak. There is also an American brunch with the Disney characters here every Sunday. *Over €15.*

Where to shop

All shops remain open until midnight daily.

Buffalo Trading Company
Denims, boots, shirts, hats, belts, bandanas, and turquoise and silver trinkets can all be picked up at this Wild West general store.

The Disney Store
All the must-have clothes, books, toys, videos, watches and souvenirs you could ever want.

King Ludwig's Castle Store
Beer mats and schnapps glasses for adults and an assortment of dress-up, dragons and swords for the junior knight and his would-be maiden.

Hollywood Pictures
American film merchandise, books, souvenirs and postcards. Young would-be film stars can also find all their favourite dress-up costumes.

Disney Gallery
Good for stocking up on Disney collectables.

Team Mickey
The place for Disneyland® Resort Paris golf clubs, balls, polo shirts and ice-hockey shirts, US college logo sweatshirts, basketball and baseball gear.

World of Toys
Barbie is the star here surrounded by all her friends and scores of accessories. Boys tend to head straight for the huge range of model cars.

Shopping is all part of the fun at Disneyland® Resort Paris, providing it doesn't get out of hand. There are outlets aplenty throughout the Disney Parks and Disney® Village, although most sell pretty much the same range of goods – soft toys, hats, T-shirts and scarves, watches, huge lollies and souvenirs of all kinds. Some shops, however, are more specialized, and they are worth tracking down if you know what you are looking for. In all of them, prices are reasonable and the quality is good. You won't find a bargain, but neither will anything fall apart once you get it home.

Disney was the first company to successfully combine the notion of entertainment with shopping. In 1930 Walt's brother, Roy, signed the company's first international licensing contract with Borgfeldt & Co. for production and sale of Mickey Mouse merchandise. The first Mickey Mouse watch was sold by the Ingersoll Watch Company in June 1933. By 1954, 700 companies were making more than 3,000 Disney items from pyjamas and underwear to toys, games and school supplies. With Disney characters gazing out from every T-shirt and lunch box, it is no surprise that 1 in 10 guests leave the Resort with a Disneyland® Resort Paris baseball cap.

Shopping made easy
You do not have to weigh yourself down with purchases. As well as storing bulkier items in the lockers beneath Main Street Station, you can use the free Shopping Service which allows you to shop wherever you want, then collect your purchases from Disney® Village as you leave the Parks, anytime after 6pm. If you are staying on site, deliveries can be made to your hotel, allowing you to collect your shopping after 8pm. Shops will normally exchange faulty merchandise within 10

Did you know?
▶ *If Disneyland® Resort Paris placed every popcorn box sold in 1 year end-to-end, the trail would reach from Paris to Metz, a distance of some 300km (186 miles).*
▶ *60 tonnes of beef fillet are consumed here every year – three times the weight of the Eiffel Tower.*
▶ *283 tonnes of French fries are consumed at the Parks each year. Laid end to end, they would cover the distance from Paris to Moscow.*

days of purchase, so long as you can produce your receipt. You are likely to be offered a credit note rather than a refund.

Tax-free shopping

If you are normally resident outside the EU, you can obtain a *détaxe* tax refund on your purchases (this does not apply to cigarettes, alcohol, groceries and beverages). Simply present your receipts at your hotel shop or at City Hall and you will be handed the appropriate form to show to customs when you leave France. Minimum purchase is €175 per day (only on merchandise). *See also* pp.12, 166.

Unique buys

Serious collectors should head for the shops which sell items from the Walt Disney Classics Collection as well as original 'cells' (the plates used to create Disney animated movies). Find them at Harrington's Fine China and Porcelains (Main Street, USA), Galerie Mickey (Disneyland® Hotel), Hollywood Pictures and Disney Gallery (Disney® Village), the Disney Animation Gallery (Animation Courtyard) and the New York Boutique (Hotel New York®). For a lasting memory of your visit, you can pay €77 to have your name engraved on a Promenade Disney paving stone .

As well as selling clothing and gifts, the on-site hotel shops stock items you may need during your stay: sunglasses, film, toothbrushes, toothpaste, razors and a range of childcare products are available. In addition, they each feature a few one-offs in keeping with their individual theme. Hotel Cheyenne®'s General Store, for example, has Western-style souvenirs and clothing.

Top tips
▶ All receipts are headed Disneyland® Resort Paris, not by their individual shop names. You will need to make a note of which receipt relates to which gift, as each itemized receipt can be hard to decipher unless you are familiar with shorthand French (e.g. *sacados mndots* = Minnie Mouse candy-filled mini rucksack).
▶ Although there is a good deal of crossover between stores, try to remember where you saw that favoured item as you can never be sure if it will turn up at the next shop.
▶ To avoid long queues, do your shopping in the early morning and afternoon.

Did you know?
▶ If you happen to forget that all-important keepsake, you can buy it by mail order from Service Clientèle Produits on t 01 64 74 44 30.

The Planet Hollywood® restaurant and Rainforest Café®, both in Disney® Village, also have their own ranges of merchandise. And, as if the temptations of the Park boutiques aren't enough, you can complement your stay with a visit to the Val d'Europe International Shopping Mall. The 98,000-square metre mall is located a few minutes away from Disneyland® Park, and is home to over 200 boutiques in two adjoining areas, all open 10am–7pm, Monday to Saturday. The regional shopping mall features a supermarket and 140 retail, restaurant and leisure outlets, and La Vallée Shopping Village has 70 boutiques offering name brand goods at discount prices.

Barbie
World of Toys (Disney® Village)

Best for babies
La Bottega di Gepetto (Fantasyland)
Disney & Co. (Main Street, USA)
Disney Clothiers Ltd. (Main Street, USA)

Christmas goodies
La Boutique du Château (Fantasyland)

Confectionery and candy
Boardwalk Candy Palace (Main Street, USA)
La Confiserie des Trois Fées (Fantasyland)

Cowboy gear
Buffalo Trading Company (Disney® Village)
Thunder Mesa Mercantile (Frontierland)

Dress up and costume
La Chaumière des Sept Nains (Fantasyland)
Le Coffre du Capitaine (Adventureland)
Hollywood Pictures (Disney® Village)
Les Légendes d'Hollywood (Front Lot)

Sportswear
Star Traders (Discoveryland)
Team Mickey (Disney® Village)

What you can expect to pay
Disney's rigorous standards apply across the board and quality is in no way compromised when it comes to souvenirs. Clothes and toys especially are well designed and will stand the test of time.

There is little point hunting for bargains. Prices are standardized and you pay the same for a T-shirt whichever shop you visit. Some items are unique to

WHERE TO EAT

each shop, but there's a good deal of crossover. This can be helpful if you cannot find a clothing-size in one shop and want to try elsewhere.

No single item is overpriced but there are so many to choose from that a few gifts soon add up. Here are a few sample prices (subject to change):

► DVD Disney classic €35
► Mini snow globe €3.90
► Character drinking straw €3.90
► Feather-top Minnie Mouse pen €4.50
► Memo pad €3
► Mini hair grips €3
► Tinkerbell dress-up evening bag €5.90
► Mickey jelly lollipop €2
► Mickey drinking glass €2.30
► Mickey twist-top mini flask €4.45
► Pirate toy telescope €3
► Pirate bandanna €4.40
► Mini cowboy pistol €3.80
► Satin purse €4.60
► Nestlé chocolates €5.50
► Cavalry dress-up hat €9.90
► Minnie Mouse rucksack €9
► Mickey Mouse T-shirt €10.50
► Mickey baseball €4.60
► Disneyland umbrella €12
► Baseball cap €12

If as much imagination went into preparing the food as it has into making the Disney Parks, Disneyland® Resort Paris would be one of the gastronomic highlights of Europe. However, although there are over 60 places to eat, spread across the Disney Parks, Disney® Village and the hotels, what you get – with a few exceptions – is standard US fare, of a fairly high quality. There is no call to be snooty about it, of course, as it is the kind of food kids eat by the bucketful without even a murmur of complaint.

Your best bet is to find a place where the queues are not too heavy and the food is reasonable. Regardless of each restaurant's ostensible theme (be it saloon, jazz club or pirate grotto), menus tend towards standard American fast-food fare, especially at the counter-service eateries. Unfortunately, fast food is not something at which Disney excels. This is surprising, considering how well it does everything else. If you are resigned to a quick-fix, fried-food fate, you will find children's fun meals are by far the best value and should satisfy the majority of grown-ups just as readily.

What you can expect to pay

► Lucky Nugget Saloon, Frontierland, adult buffet €30, bottle of beer €6.
► Cowboy Cookout, Frontierland, two BBQ meals €19.90.
► Toad Hall, Fantasyland, adult fish and chips meal €6.70, child's meal €5.
► Studio Catering Co, Walt Disney Studios®, canned drink €2.25, potato chips €1.20.
► Rendez-vous des Stars, Walt Disney Studios®, child's meal €10, bottled water €1.85.
► Sandwiches New York Style, Disney® Village, continental breakfast €4, hot chocolate €3.

Best for breakfast

Few things can be more fun for your kids than starting their day with a gigantic buffet breakfast accompanied by some classic Disney characters. They get to meet all their favourites, cuddle, kiss, collect their autographs and have keepsake snaps taken with them. Disneyland® Hotel guests can book a character breakfast in **Inventions Restaurant** (7.30am–10.45am) and at Walt's on Main Street, USA (8am–9.30am) while guests of the Davy Crockett Ranch® can attend **Crockett's Tavern** (8am–9am or 9.30am–10.30am).

All other guests can prebook a character breakfast at **Café Mickey** in Disney® Village, though venues tend to change seasonally. Incredibly long queues build up very quickly, so arrive early. Costs adults €25, children €17, under-3s free.

Café Fantasia at the Disneyland® Hotel lives up to its name with a buffet that will set you up for the entire day. The Parkside Diner at the Hotel New York® is a relaxed Manhattan-style neighbourhood bistro offering an equally generous buffet spread. The hotel's Manhattan Restaurant is more formal but the food is just as filling.

On Main Street, USA, the Cable Car Bake Shop serves a continental breakfast.

Best for lunch

You are not permitted to take your own food into the Disney Parks, but there is a picnic site just outside the entrance, between the main car park and railway station. It's worth considering stashing a prepared picnic in one of the lockers just inside the main gate, but if you do head back outside for a picnic lunch, be sure to get your hand stamped so that you can get back in again.

When it comes to lunchtime menus, both the hotel and à la carte restaurants are somewhat variable and often rather expensive; the table service restaurants provide a budget three-course meal.

Chicken and chips at Au Chalet de la Marionette* (Fantasyland) is excellent for kids – and almost deserted at 3pm, as is the vast Cowboy Cookout* (Frontierland) which tends to be crowded at other

Top tips

▶ Some restaurants (marked in this chapter with an asterisk*) may be closed off-peak on Mon and Tues, others on Wed and Thurs.
▶ If you are set on having lunch within the Disney Parks, try to eat before midday or after 2.30pm to avoid the crush. If you have already seen the parade, eat while it is on when the restaurants are likely to be emptier.
▶ During peak holiday season, book every meal in advance to avoid disappointment.
▶ Children's menus are available in all of the Disney Parks' restaurants, as are bottle-warmers and high chairs for babies and toddlers.
▶ If you book a package you can pre-order meal coupons which allow you to enjoy mealtimes without worries about cash. These meal vouchers can be used in a selection of restaurants throughout the Parks.

Best for...

Fish & chips
Toad Hall Restaurant (Fantasyland)
Hamburger & fries
Annette's Diner (Disney® Village)
Café des Cascadeurs (Backlot)
Planet Hollywood® (Disney® Village)
Ice cream
Gibson Girl Ice Cream Parlour (Main Street, USA)
Pasta
Manhattan Restaurant (Hotel New York®)
Los Angeles Bar & Grill (Disney® Village)
Tex-Mex
Billy Bob's Country & Western Saloon (Disney® Village)
Fuente del Oro (Frontierland)
La Cantina (Hotel Santa Fe®)
Sandwiches
Market House Deli (Main Street, USA)
New York Style Sandwiches (Disney® Village)
Steaks
Silver Spur Steakhouse (Frontierland)
Hunter's Grill (Sequoia Lodge®)
Seafood
Blue Lagoon Restaurant (Adventureland)
Yacht Club (Newport Bay Club Hotel®)
The Steakhouse (Disney® Village)

times. In Discoveryland Café Hyperion* offers a popular fast-food menu plus a show, though the queues here are often far too long. Buzz Lightyear's Pizza Planet* (Discoveryland) offers your kids the chance to play safely and graze while you take a breather. At Backlot Express (Backlot), the props provide welcome diversion during a fast-food lunch.

Market House Deli on Main Street, USA, has classic American sandwiches such as hot pastrami on rye. An ice cream for dessert at neighbouring Gibson Girl Ice Cream Parlour is a fun treat. For a quick and easy snack, there are mobile food carts (chariots gourmands) dotted around serving popcorn, baked potatoes, ice creams, pretzels, pizzas, sandwiches, drinks and the like. The vendors only accept cash. Expect to pay upwards of € 2.60 for a can of fizzy drink.

Best for dinner

For full service restaurants in the Disney Parks you will pay a premium, yet the price reflects the quality both of the food and of the elaborate and imaginative décor. Their popularity means it is essential to book a table in advance if you know you want to eat at a busy time. Bookings can be made in the restaurant or at City Hall.

The experience of eating in the **Blue Lagoon***(Adventureland) is one you'll never forget. You eat on the 'shore' of a Caribbean Pirate hideaway while the boats from Pirates of the Caribbean glide past, full of drooling guests. Snapper, swordfish and Caribbean delicacies cram the menu.

Auberge de Cendrillon* in Fantasyland is hosted by cast members wearing 17th-century costumes. In keeping with its Louis XIV theme, the restaurant serves classic French cuisine (the nearest you will get to a traditional meal in this corner of France).

Walt's*, on Main Street, USA, is also a superb restaurant offering fine American fare. If you are lucky, they will seat you so that you can watch the Main Street, USA, parade in comfort from an upstairs window. The menu includes Veal Oscar, rack of lamb, crab cakes and stuffed Maine lobster.

If you choose to leave the Disney Parks to eat, you will find the hotel restaurants become less expensive the further away they are from the main entrance. All are licensed to serve alcohol. In Disney® Village itself, a clutch of good eateries provides entertainment in novel surroundings.

Annette's Diner is highly recommended, as the queues outside will confirm. You are served by fifties-style roller-skating waitresses against a chorus of memory-jerking hits. The menu is, essentially, hamburgers, shakes and fries, but the quality is great and you can order a beer. **Planet Hollywood®** has established street-cred with kids while **The Steakhouse** is excellent, if a little pricey. Towards Lake Disney, the giant **McDonald's®** has dependable prices. The Audio-Animatronics® at the **Rainforest Café®** are a guaranteed thrill for first-timers.

Birthdays

You can celebrate a birthday by ordering a Disney chocolate cake for the end of your meal. These are available from **Plaza Gardens Restaurant** on Main Street, USA, where you can even prebook a Birthday Party with the Disney characters daily at 3pm and 4.30pm. Try to give at least 2 hours' notice either at the restaurant or at the hotel information desk. It costs €18 per person.

Seasonal changes

All restaurants in the Disney Parks are open during July and August. During the winter months, several are closed all week, except during school holidays. Some may be closed on off-peak Mondays and Tuesdays, others on off-peak Wednesdays and Thursdays. You may also find that some hotel restaurants (especially those in hotels with more than one restaurant) are closed some days during the winter. None of the Disney® Village restaurants have seasonally changing opening times.

Vegetarian meals and special diets

Vegetarian food is available at most Disney® hotels and restaurants, but you may prefer to confirm this with staff before being seated. Typical vegetarian dishes include pizza, pasta, soups and salad. Kosher diets can be catered for with 48 hours' notice, as can other special dietary needs. Contact City Hall or Studio Services for details.

WHERE TO SLEEP

Top tip
Cots need to be requested at the time of booking at all the Disneyland® Resort Paris hotels.

To get the most from the Disney Parks, you should try to stay there: then you can pop back to your hotel when the kids (and you) get weary, whilst continuing to immerse yourself in the Disney experience – as much thought has gone into creating the hotels as into Parks. The attention to detail throughout is truly impressive.

Disneyland® Resort Paris reservations

t UK (0870) 503 0303 **t** USA (1) 407 934 7639
t direct 01 60 30 60 53 **f** 01 64 74 59 20
Disneyland® Resort Paris, Central Reservations, BP 105, Paris 77777, Marne la Vallée, Cedex 4, France
www.disneylandparis.com

Accommodation off site

Staying off site can work out cheaper if you are prepared to seek out budget accommodation in or around Paris (for more details of accommodation in Paris itself, see pp.145–152). You can book cheap rooms in hotels closer to the Disney Parks (see p.244) through the Seine and Marne Tourist Information Office in Disney® Village. For a small fee, they will contact the hotel on your behalf and arrange the booking.

Accommodation on site

The Resort has seven hotels, one of which is set a little way from the Disney Parks. A free shuttle bus service runs every 12 minutes between the main hotels (though not Davy Crockett Ranch®) and the Disney Parks and Disney® Village.

Staying in a Disneyland® Resort Paris hotel means you are guaranteed entrance to the Disney Parks (and are allowed in 1 hour earlier in summer). What is more, you don't have to leave the magic behind when you exit the Park gates.

While Disney would maintain that quality of service remains equal across the board, at the end of the day, you get what you pay for. Disneyland® Hotel, at the entrance of the Disneyland® Park, is the most convenient and the most expensive. The Hotel Santa Fe® is best described as cheap and cheerful. Taking into account the increasing popularity of the Resort, several new residences have opened their doors in 2003, adding a further 1,100 rooms to the Resort's existing capacity. These recent additions (billed as 'selected hotels') – the Holiday Inn (opened 28 May), My Travel's Explorer Hotel (opened 31 March) and the Kyriad Hotel (opened 31 March) – are approximately 10 minutes' free shuttle ride away from the Disney Parks. They offer the same services as the Disney hotels (left luggage, ticket sales, shuttle buses and room service).

How they work

Most rooms in the hotels accommodate up to four people, with twin double beds or one king-size bed, plus en-suite shower/bathroom. They have colour TV with satellite channels in several languages, plus a Disney® movie channel and several in-house channels about the Disney Parks.

If you book a room independently, you will be charged a one-off nightly rate: up to four guests and infants under the age of 3 can stay in one room inclusive, which can make booking direct with the hotel a good option. In peak season and at the weekends, you will often need to pay for passports to the Disney Parks at the same time as booking a room.

Hotel check in is from 3pm, check-out before 11am; all of the hotels have luggage facilities. If you require express check-out (and you are paying by credit card), your bill can be hung on your door on the morning of your departure. As long as you agree with it, your bill will be automatically charged to your credit card.

All hotel residents are issued with a personal hotel ID card, thats allows free access to its leisure facilities, car park and Hurricanes nightclub.

It is also worth using the special 'charge card' system: when you have checked in, you can give the receptionist your credit card details and then use your ID card to charge most of your purchases within the Parks and Disney® Village directly to your room account (except for bills at McDonald's®, Gaumont Cineplex, Planet Hollywood® and the Rainforest Café®). All of your shopping can even be sent straight back to your hotel, so you don't have to carry it around; a system designed to make spending money even easier.

Each hotel has currency exchange facilities plus an information and/or concierge desk, which will help you with reservations for meals, shows, golf and excursions, and other practical information.

For children

Each hotel has at least one themed restaurant featuring a children's menu, although beware long queues during peak periods (especially at the larger hotels) by booking a table in advance. They also feature a Disney shop, a daily 'meet-and-greet' the Disney characters, a pay-as-you-play video games room, and supervised activity on most days. There are plenty of activities to look forward to in the evenings and especially at weekends during school holidays and when the Parks close early in winter. While you are welcome to use other hotel restaurants, you are not entitled to use the leisure facilities at any hotels other than your own.

Staying on site

Disneyland® Hotel

t 01 60 45 65 00   **f** 01 60 45 65 33
Price €357–520 per room, per night
478 'fairytale' rooms (18 suites and 11 rooms for the disabled)
Rooms have minibar, telephone, radio, safe-deposit box, TV and air conditioning. 24hr room service. Dry cleaning service. Cots on request. Babysitting. Free valet parking. Currency exchange. Small indoor heated pool. Health club. Shop: Galerie Mickey

This award-winning hotel is the smallest on site, but by far the most luxurious. Inspired by the great hotels built on the West Coast of Florida at the turn of the 20th century, its candy pink turrets, dripping chandeliers, majestic staircases and pastel décor are fairytale-like. Even if you don't stay here, pay a visit to soak up the atmosphere.

The hotel straddles the entrance to Disneyland® Paris: guests can enjoy panoramic views of the Parks, and smile smugly at the lines of day visitors queuing up outside the gates each morning.

The hotel's 50 best (Castle Club) rooms have unforgettable views down Main Street, USA, to Sleeping Beauty Castle, and their own direct access to the Disney Parks, private lift, personalized check-in, private bar, VIP Fastpass service and complementary breakfast.

Just for the kids

▶ 'Minnie Club' corner for 4–11-year-olds, supervised at certain times: interactive CD-ROM, TV, face-painting and other organized activities.
▶ Character breakfast each morning. Disney characters appear in the main lobby every day.
▶ 'Mad Hatter's' video games room.

Dining and bars

▶ Café Fantasia: classic movie-inspired café, ovelooking the Fantasia Gardens with an evening piano bar from 7.30 pm onwards.
▶ Inventions: buffet dining and Disney mealtimes.
▶ California Grill: West Coast cuisine, with an open kitchen so you can watch your food being prepared. Views over Disneyland® Park.

Disney's Hotel New York®

t 01 60 45 73 00   **f** 01 60 45 73 33
Price €217–310 per room, per night
532 rooms (31 suites and 13 rooms for the disabled)
Rooms have Minitel terminals, minibar, telephone, radio, safe-deposit box, TV and air conditioning. 24hr room service. Dry cleaning service. Cots on request. Babysitting. Car park with valet service (fee payable). Currency exchange. Indoor and outdoor heated pools. Health club. Two floodlit tennis courts (fee payable). Open-air skating rink (Oct–Mar, fee payable). Hair salon. VIP Fastpass service (for suites). In summer, 'Velos Dingos' offers bikes and scooters for hire (April–Sept at the ice rink, fee payable). Shop: New York Boutique

After Disneyland® Hotel, this hotel on Lake Disney® is the closest to the Parks (5–10 minutes' walk) and within walking distance of Disney® Village. Based on the Manhattan skyscraper skyline, it is plush with designs from the twenties and a fountain that becomes an ice rink in winter.

The rooms are comfortable and spacious, but the hotel is quite sophisticated and probably better suited to uptown couples; the extensive adjoining convention centre attracts a lot of business. The best rooms have a lake view (supplement payable).

The best spot for families is the small children's play area adjoining the sprawling New York City Bar, where kids can play late into the evening while adults enjoy a drink. The Manhattan Restaurant is slighly more expensive than the bustling Parkside Diner, but it's well worth it (and worth reserving a table in advance to avoid the queues).

Just for the kids

▶ Roger Rabbit Corner near reception runs organized activities, interactive computers and Disney® Channel TV (daily).
▶ Goofy and friends perform a rap in reception at 8.30am, 9.30am, 10.30am and 11.30am (daily during peak season and every Sat–Sun).
▶ Disney characters in the main lobby daily.
▶ Video games arcade.

Dining and bars
- ▶ Parkside Diner: laid-back New York-style feel.
- ▶ Manhattan Restaurant: thirties-inspired club.
- ▶ New York City Bar: sprawling bar area with live evening entertainment (Thurs–Sat).

Disney's Newport Bay Club®

t 01 60 45 55 00 **f** 01 60 45 55 33
Price €194–268 per room, per night
1077 rooms (15 suites and 23 rooms for the disabled)
Rooms have minibar, telephone, radio, safe-deposit box, TV and air conditioning. Dry cleaning service. Cots on request. Babysitting. Free car park. Currency exchange. Pool. Health club. Train service for guests (€2) from Disney's Newport Bay Club® to Disney's Hotel New York® (summer period). No porters. Shop: Buy Boutique

A stylish hotel themed on the elegant 19th century resorts of New England and set on the southern shores of Lake Disney®, about 10–15 minutes' walk from Disneyland® Park. Its towering lighthouse, rocking-chair-lined verandah, awnings and pergolas re-create the atmosphere of a vast sailing club. The light and airy blue-and-white décor adds to the nautical air. Most rooms sleep four, though there are a few family rooms for up to six guests. Try to secure a room with a lake view, or even consider paying the supplement to stay on the Admiral's Floor where you can benefit from a separate check-in area, porter service, concierge and 24-hr room service.

Just for the kids
- ▶ Children's club set in the Fishermen's Wharf Bar with face painting, balloon-sculpting and colouring on selected days.
- ▶ Disney characters in the main lobby daily.
- ▶ 'Sea Horse Club' video games room.

Dining and bars
- ▶ Yacht Club: fish and shellfish.
- ▶ Cape Cod: New England cuisine.
- ▶ Fisherman's Wharf: welcoming lounge bar with views over the lake.
- ▶ Captain's Quarters: cocktail bar.

Disney's Sequoia Lodge®

t 01 60 45 51 00 **f** 01 60 45 51 33
Price €178–251 per room, per night
997 rooms (14 suites and 21 rooms for the disabled)
Rooms have minibar (Montana rooms only), telephone, radio, TV and air conditioning. Dry cleaning service. Cots on request. Babysitting. Free car park. Currency exchange. Pool. Health club. Shop: Northwest Passage

With décor based on a Rocky Mountain hunters' lodge, this hotel beside Lake Disney® is in the middle of 44,000 square metres of woodland (about 10–15 minutes' walk from the Disney Parks). There are five timber and stone-built chalets (billed as hunting lodges) surrounding the main building, but it is more convenient to stay in the main lodge. Ask for a room with a lakeside view. The Sequoia Lodge® is rather stark compared to some of the other hotels, but the roaring log fire in the lounge area is a superb focal point in winter and there's an excellent, imaginatively designed pool area.

Just for the kids
- ▶ 'Little Praire' corner with TV and activities.
- ▶ Disney characters visit daily in the main lobby and at Photo Point.
- ▶ Outdoor playground.
- ▶ 'Kit Carson' video games room.

Dining and bars
- ▶ Hunter's Grill: rôtisserie roast meats.
- ▶ Beaver Creek Tavern: international cuisine.
- ▶ Redwood Bar and Lounge: relax around the stone fireplace.

Disney's Hotel Cheyenne®

t 01 60 45 62 00 **f** 01 60 45 62 33
Price €136–205 per room, per night
1,000 rooms (21 for the disabled)
Rooms with telephone, radio, TV, central heating, fan, a double bed and two bunk beds. Launderette. Cots on request. Babysitting. Free car park. No porters. Currency exchange. Shop: General Store

Imaginatively themed as a Wild West town with its rooms spread out over 14 low-rise outbuildings on two main streets, you might easily find yourself sleeping above the bank or even the jailhouse. Covered wagons stud the way, and cast members roam Desperado Street in cowboy clobber. There's even the odd gunfight! Parents might find it a little too film-set flimsy, but it is the only hotel child-centred enough to offer rooms with bunk beds, plus free pony rides during the warmer months. The rooms are adequate, though a bit of a squeeze for a family; over half are interconnecting.

The dining area is a cavernous barn with long trestle tables. The only real drawback is that there are no leisure facilities and the hotel is some 15–20 minutes' walk from the Parks, but there's a shuttle service every 5 minutes.

Just for the kids

▶ "Little Sheriff's" corner (face painting, TV and colouring on certain days).
▶ Disney characters in reception every day.
▶ Pony rides, weather permitting every morning.
▶ Log-built 'Fort Apache' adventure playground, plus teepee-filled play area.
▶ 'Nevada' video games room.

Dining and bars

▶ Chuck Wagon Café: themed, self-service Texan market food stalls. Children's corner and Saddle Bar in the evenings.
▶ Red Garter Saloon: welcoming family atmosphere and live music.

Disney's Hotel Santa Fe®

t 01 60 45 78 00 f 01 60 45 78 33
Price €120–180 per room, per night
1000 rooms (21 rooms for the disabled)
Rooms with telephone, radio, TV and fan. Launderette. Cots on request. Babysitting. Free car park. Currency exchange. Shop: Trading Post

By far the cheapest hotel with a New Mexico desert theme complete with erupting volcano and dusty desert trails leading to 42 'pueblos'. The rooms are bright and well designed, about 15–20 minutes' walk from the Disney Parks, or take the regular shuttle bus service.

Just for the kids

▶ Restaurant kids' corner (face painting, TV and colouring on certain days).
▶ Disney characters in reception daily.
▶ 'Totem Circle' children's playground.
▶ 'Pow-Wow' video games room.

Dining and bars

▶ La Cantina: self-service, American Tex-Mex.
▶ Rio Grande Bar: Mexican cocktails, karaoke and live music with kids. Fiesta on most evenings.

Disney's Davy Crockett Ranch®

t 01 60 45 68 14 f 01 60 45 69 33
Price €156–241 per room, per night
498 double-glazed cabins for 4–6 people (four disabled cabins sleeping six people)
97 camping sites

Cabins with bath, telephone, radio, TV, heating, free car parking next to your cabin and house-keeping service on request (four-person cabins have one double bed and a foldaway bed; six-person cabins have additional twin bunk beds). Towels and linen supplied. Heated comfort stations with toilets, showers and laundry. Bicycle, roller blade and minicar rentals (fee payable). Shop: Alamo Trading Post

About 5 miles (15 mins' drive) from the Disney Parks, in the heart of a 57-hectare forest, the Ranch is billed as a wilderness hideaway and a resort in its own right. The four- or six-person trailer 'log cabins' have luxurious self-catering facilities. Each cabin is spacious and well equipped with microwave, refrigerator, hob, dishwasher and coffee-maker. At check-in, guests receive a 'welcome basket' packed with groceries. Outside there is a BBQ grill and a wooden table with connectors for electricity and water for a caravan. At the heart of the ranch is a small Western fort town with restaurant, store, pool complex, sports facilities and play areas. The Blue Springs Pool, by far the best of the Resort, is a large indoor heated pool with slides, waterfall, giant jacuzzi, and separate children's area. There are two covered tennis courts and sports fields. Outdoor activities include jogging, mountain bike trails and archery. You could easily spend a few days here without venturing out to the Parks at all.

The campsite

There are campsite facilities if you prefer to bring your own tent that, despite first-rate facilities, are quite expensive (about €60 per night for a small pitch with electrical hook-ups and its own water and drainage connections). It is better value for caravans and motorhomes.

Just for the kids

▶ Face painting and mask-making workshops, 'Little Trappers' outdoor playground, Indian teepee camp with wild animal enclosure, small farm.
▶ Disney characters appear every evening in the village square.
▶ Supervised archery, bicycle obstacle course, tennis, basketball, waterpolo and treasure hunts.
▶ Pony rides, roller skates, quad-bikes and mountain bike hire (fee payable).
▶ 'Lucky Raccoon' video games room.

Dining and bars
▶ Saloon: family lounge with country music and karaoke evenings.
▶ Crockett's Tavern: American fare. Character breakfasts available.

Disneyland Resort Paris® Selected Hotels

Direct dial and fax numbers are not available for these hotels. To book and for more information, call the Disneyland® Resort Paris booking line direct on **t** 0870 503 0303 or visit **www**. disneylandresort-paris.com ('near the Magic hotels') for listings. The following prices are Classic Package prices for a minimum 2-night stay, which includes accommodation for 2 days/3 nights, breakfast plus entry tickets for 3 days based on 2 adults and 2 children sharing a family room.

Holiday Inn
Price Adult €174, child €57 (2+2)
396 rooms (23 kid suites)
Rooms have TV with satellite channels, video games, (most with a Kids corner and bunk beds). Free car park. Concierge. Currency exchange. Indoor pool. Fitness club. Free shuttle bus service to the Disney Parks. Shopping service. Disney shop

Set in a 10-acre park with a lake and built in the style of the great French manor countryside estates, this 4-star hotel offers good family rooms with a separate sleeping area for kids designed to look like a circus tent. Inside the curtains, they've got their own TV, a shelf for drinks and a reading light on the top bunk. There's also a carousel in the spacious bar area, as well as slot-machines and ride-on cars in the lobby. The highlight for children, however, will be the leisure centre, which has a swimming pool and a kid-sized pool with slide, bubble jets and a small cascade. The room service menu is reasonably priced and offers healthy food and snacks without a hint of theme park in them.

Just for the kids
▶ Kids' corner (most rooms) with TV, video games
▶ Children's play area and outdoor play area.
▶ Indoor pool with Secret Lagoon play area.

Dining and bars
▶ Funambule Bar
▶ L'Étoile Restaurant

My Travel's Explorers Hotel
Price Adult €158, child €57 (2+2)
400 rooms
Crew rooms have TV with satellite channels, video games (fee payable) and additional 'bunk cabins' for larger families. Free car park. Concierge. Currency exchange. Indoor pool. Free shuttle bus service to the Disney Parks. Shopping service. Disney shop

The assumed home of Sir Archibald de Bacle, a lengendary explorer, this 2-star hotel offers crew rooms sleeping up to four.

Just for the kids
▶ Scally Wagg's Jungle Adventures, Harry's Action Zone and Tropical Atrium indoor play areas.
▶ Video games room.
▶ Heated indoor swimming pool with Secret Lagoon play area.

Dining and bars
▶ Three bars: Smuggler's Tavern, Traders Café Bar and Far Horizon Terrace.
▶ Three restaurants: The Captain's Library, Plantation Restaurant and Marco's Pizza Parlour.

Kyriad Hotel
Price Adult €132, child €57 (2+2)
300 rooms
Rooms have TV with satellite channels. Free car park. Concierge. Currency exchange. Two bars, one restaurant. Outdoor play area. Free shuttle bus service to the Disney Parks. Shopping service. Disney shop

With panoramic views over the surrounding woodland, this traditionally styled 2-star hotel offers rooms with a double bed and one set of bunk beds sleeping up to four.

Just for the kids
▶ Outdoor play area and garden

Dining and bars
▶ Lounge/bar

Staying off site

For ease of access, you can stay anywhere in central Paris (*see* pp.145–152 for hotel listings) that's near a métro station or the RER line. If you have a car, there are yet more options. All these hotels are located in towns around Disneyland® Resort Paris, and whilst unexceptional in terms of their surroundings, they all offer flexibility, freedom and good value for money. Most cater for children either for free or a nominal charge. For further information on hotels near Disneyland® Resort Paris contact:

French Government Tourist Office

t UK (0906) 824 4123 (calls cost 60p/minute)
f UK +44 20 4493 6594
t NY (410) 286 8310 **f** (212) 838 7855
t Chicago (312) 751 7800 **f** (312) 337 6339
t Miami (305) 373 8177 **f** (305) 373 5828
t Los Angeles (310) 271 6665 **f** (310) 276 2835
www.paris.org or **www.franceguide.com**

Locations around the Disney Parks

▶ The town of Bussy St Georges is just 12km (7.5 miles) from the Disney Parks and one stop away on the RER line. Take exit 12 from the A4 motorway, or RER station Bussy St Georges.

▶ Marne la Vallée and Collégien are just two rail stations from the Disney Parks, or 10 minutes' by car. Take exit 12 (Val Bussy) from the A4 motorway.

▶ Lesigny is 21km (13 miles) from the Parks. Take exit 18 (Lesigny Romaine) on the N104.

▶ Lognes is 15km (10 miles) away, or three stops by RER.

▶ Lagny is about 15 minutes' drive away, or 20 minutes by SNCF to Paris.

▶ Noisy le Grand, halfway between Paris and the Parks, is some 25 minutes' drive away. Take the A4 motorway, or use RER station Noisy le Grand–Mont d'Est, also on the A4 line 6 stops from the Disney Parks.

▶ For Ozoir la Ferrière, take the A4 towards Paris, exit towards Villeneuve le Comte, then follow directions for Villeneuve St Denis. Turn right in the village for Ozoir.

▶ Fontainebleau is about 32km (20 miles) from Disneyland® Resort Paris; Melun is a little closer.

Did you know?
At Buffalo Bill's Wild West Show the daily drinks consumption is 750 litres of beer and 600 litres of Coca-Cola®, whilst there are some 83,000 dishes to wash every night.

Suggested hotels

Expect to pay between anywhere between €50 and €100 for these more affordable hotels.

Golf Hotel, Bussy St Georges
t 01 64 66 30 30
Tulip Inn, Bussy St Georges from €73
t 01 64 66 11 11 **t** UK 0800 96 2720
www.goldentulip.com
Holiday Inn, Bussy St Georges from €80
t 01 64 66 35 65 or **t** UK 0800 40 5060
www.france.sixcontinentshotels.com
Hotel Formule 1, Collégien
t 08 91 70 52 94
www.hotelformule1.com
Hotel du Golfe Best Western (Hotel le Réveillon), Lesigny from €59
t 01 60 02 25 26
www.bestwestern.fr
Château de Grande Romaine, Lesigny from €75
t 01 64 43 16 00
www.grande-romaine.com
Relais Mercure (Hotel Frantour), Lognes from €80
t 01 64 80 02 50
Holiday Inn Paris Charles de Gaulle Airport
t 01 34 29 30 00 **t** UK 0800 40 5060
www.france.sixcontinentshotels.com
Express by Holiday Inn Paris, Le Bourget
t 01 45 91 10 00 **t** UK 0800 43 4040
www.france.sixcontinentshotels.com
Novotel, Marne la Vallée from €88
t 01 64 80 53 53 **t** UK 0870 609 0962
www.novotel.com
Hotel Ibis, Marne la Vallée from €57
t 01 64 68 00 83
www.accorhotels.com
Hotel Premiere Classe, Marne la Vallée
t 01 60 17 30 19
www.envergure.fr
Mercure, Noisy le Grand from €73
t 01 45 92 47 47
www.mercure.com
Novotel Atria, Noisy le Grand from €50
t 01 48 15 60 60 **t** UK 0870 609 0962
www.novotel.com
Village Hotel, Noisy le Grand
t 01 43 03 00 30
www.noisy-le-grand.villages-hotel.com
Au Pavillon Bleu, Ozoir la Ferrière
t 01 64 40 05 56

ENTERTAINMENT

While dusk signals the end of the day at the Parks, this is the green light for Disney® Village to gear up for its nocturnal guests.

Clubbing

Billy Bob's Country & Western Saloon

A country music fan's fantasy: there's a stage with live Western bands every night of the week. Nibble some nachos and do-si-do your partner to the sound of guitar, fiddle and drums. *6pm–11pm nightly.*

Hurricanes

An unpretentious late-night club for teenagers and up. Free entry for on-site hotel guests but €12 or more for anyone else! *11pm–5am nightly.*

On-screen entertainment

Gaumont Cinema

The biggest auditorium has a whacking 260-square metre screen and seating for 700 people. Film previews in English every Monday at 7.45pm and 10.30pm. Costs €8.80.

The Sports Bar

Root for your favourite team in all kinds of sports on one of 10 giant TV screens in this lively bar.

Video Games Arcade

The fastest and latest high-tech games.

Live shows

Reserve tickets in advance on **t** 01 60 45 71 00 or visit City Hall.

Buffalo Bill's Wild West Show

t 01 60 45 71 00
Shows twice nightly (6.30pm and 9.30pm)
Tickets Adults €52, children €32, including meal, drinks and a souvenir cowboy-hat

A dinner show with cowboys, Indians and real buffalo, horses and bison that relives the spirit of the Wild West through feats of acrobatic horsemanship and shooting displays. Inspired by La Legende de Buffalo Bill, it provides non-stop laughter and thrills for the entire family. Get there at least 30 minutes early to enjoy the raucous pre-show entertainment and obtain seats close to the action. The use of live animals and shifting dust in the arena means the show is not recommended for guests suffering from allergies or asthma.

SPORT AND ACTIVITIES

Plenty of thought has gone into catering for leisure time outside the Disney Parks and there are first-rate sport facilities if you have energy left at the end of the day. If spectator sports are more your style, head for the Sports Bar in Disney® Village, where uninterrupted coverage will keep you up to date with the latest scores and events. Those with twitchy fingers can test their reflexes at the wealth of video simulator games and electronic amusements in the Disney® Village arcades, or at any of the Disneyland® Resort Paris hotel games rooms.

Ball games

There's plenty of space for you and your children to kick a ball around and try out at basketball, football and volleyball on the sports fields attached to the Davy Crockett Ranch®.

Boating

At La Marina on Lake Disney® you can rent out pedaloes, canoes and motor boats (not available in winter). In the summer (April–Oct) boats can be hired from 1.30pm to nightfall, depending on the weather.

▶ Pedaloes €7 (20min)
▶ Electric boats €12 (20min)
▶ Quadri cycles two seats €8; four seats €12 (20min)
▶ Rowing boats €10 (15min)
▶ Canoes one seat €5; two seats €6 (20min)
▶ Junior jet ski €2 (20min)
▶ **Professional instructor supervision at La Marina on Lake Disney®. Sailing classes are available for €23.**

Cycling

Winding woodland trails have been laid out around Davy Crockett Ranch® for cycling and jogging. The campsite offers 24-hour bicycle rentals. Cycle rental costs vary and there is lots on offer: tandem bikes (*€7.60 for 30mins, €11.45 for 1 hour, €13.70 for 2 hours*), mountain bikes (*€5.35 for 1 hour, €6.10 for 2 hours*) and kids' bikes (*€3 for 1 hour, €5.35 for 2 hours*) There are also special family deals (*two bikes €7.60 per hour, four bikes €10.70 per hour*), plus you can hire a Rosalie bike with four places (*€10 per 30mins, €15 for 1 hour, €18 for 2 hours*) or six places (*€10.70 per hour*). Roller-skate hire is €3 per hour. During the summer months at the Hotel New York's ice rink, 'Velos Dingos' offers off beat and scooter hire for €13.70 (15 minutes).

Golf

Golf Disneyland® (in Disneyland® Park) is open all year, seven days a week, and combines the pleasure of golf with a family break. It has a 27-hole, championship-level golf course (created by architect Ronald Fream) that is broken down into flexible nine-hole sections open to golfers of all abilities, who can test their skills among the lakes, hills, waterfalls and rivers of this huge 222-acre course. There are also 25 driving ranges (10 of which are covered), a 600-square metre putting green in the shape of Mickey's head, plus a pitching green and bunker. The three nine-hole golf courses conveniently begin and end in front of the Club House and can be combined in any order, giving players three different 18-hole courses, complete with islands, lakes and bunkers. The minimum level of game required is 53.5. The first tee-off time is between 8.30am and 9am, according to the season. Before teeing off, guests can practise their swing in specially built areas, from bunker and chip shots to driving and putting.

The Golf Disneyland® Club House is home to a bar restaurant, pro shop, TV room and changing rooms. Golfing equipment is on sale at Goofy's Pro Shop and lessons are available. A few kilometres south of the main Resort and well signposted, the golf course is outside the Resort's Boulevard Circulaire between the hamlets of Magny le Hongre and Bailly–Romainvilliers (to get there, take the A4 *autoroute* in the direction of Metz–Nancy, get off at exit 14 and then follow signs for 'Disneyland Paris Golf–Magny Le Hongre'). It is open daily all year from 8.45am until sunset. For bookings, call **t** 01 60 45 68 90 or visit **www.**disneylandparis.com/uk/golf/contact/index.htm or email dlpnwy.golf@disney.com. Package rates, less expensive 'twilight green fees' and the 'Golf Passport' annual pass for unlimited access all-round Monday to Friday with discounts (€1,800 per person, €3,600 for a couple) are also available. A complete range of equipment can be hired on site.

Green fees

18 holes
WEEKEND €52 (all ages)
WEEKDAYS €32 (all ages)
9 holes
WEEKEND €37 (all ages)
WEEKDAYS €23 (all ages)

Health clubs

The Disneyland® Hotel, Disney's Hotel New York®, Disney's Newport Bay Club® and Disney's Sequoia Lodge® all have a health club with a gym. Facilities include aerobics and exercise machines, Jacuzzi, sauna, solarium and steam rooms. Membership is free during your stay but the solariums are normally extra (but free at Disney's Newport Bay Club®). A massage session costs €90 per hour and €45 per half hour.

Swimming

Both indoor and outdoor pools can be found at the Resort's hotels. There are heated indoor pools at the Disneyland® Hotel, Hotel New York®, the Newport Bay Club®, the Sequoia Lodge® and Davy Crockett Ranch®. At the Sequoia Lodge® the pool is landscaped in its own woodland chalet as part of the hotel's National Park theme. At Davy Crockett Ranch®, the Blue Springs tropical pool area is huge, complete with waterslides, a waterfall, a giant Jacuzzi inside a grotto and separate kid's pool. Both the Hotel New York® and Newport Bay Club® have good indoor pools with outdoor swimming areas. You can buy swimwear at the Bay Boutique (Newport Bay Club®), Northwest Passage (Sequoia Lodge®), Alamo Trading Post (Davy Crockett Ranch®), Galerie Mickey (Disneyland Hotel®), New York Boutique (Hotel New York®) and Team Mickey (Disney® Village).

Tennis

There are three open-air hard courts: two floodlit courts at Hotel New York, open 7am–10pm (free for hotel guests, €8 per hour for non-guests), and one at Davy Crockett Ranch®, open 9am–9pm. There is no court fee if you stay at a theme hotel. You can borrow racquets and hire a box of four balls (€8) on site, or purchase tennis gear from Team Mickey in Disney® Village. Advance reservations are essential.

Manchester United Soccer School

From Spring 2004, young footballers can participate in an unforgettable sports experience. They will be offered a two-and-a-half-hour training session with professional coaches from Manchester United using the famous teaching methods of the Old Trafford club. The school will be constructed near Disney's Sequoia Lodge®, a few minutes' walk from the Disney Parks.

VISITORS WITH SPECIAL NEEDS

Need to know

The VEA shuttle bus to the airports is unsuitable for wheelchair users but the RER train network is increasingly wheelchair-accessible.

Disneyland® Resort Paris is designed to be as user-friendly as possible for its guests. All shops, restaurants and toilet blocks are accessible by wheelchair and a *Disabled Guest Guide* is available at City Hall on Main Street, USA, Studio Services in Walt Disney Studios® Park and information booths at the hotel receptions. Special viewing areas (in the centre of Town Square, Central Square and beneath the queueing area for It's A Small World) are reserved for guests in wheelchairs along the parade route. Note that cast members are not authorized to lift disabled guests in and out of wheelchairs.

Call the special needs visitor information line on **t** 01 60 30 10 20. To order a free copy of the *Disabled Guest Guide*, call **t** 0870 503 0303 or write to:

Disneyland® Resort Paris Guest Communications

PO Box 305
Watford
Herts WD1 8TP, England
or
BP 100
Paris 77777 Marne la Vallée
Cedex 4, France
www.disneylandparis.com

Getting around

Special Services Parking is located near the entrance of the Visitors' Car Park close to the Disneyland® Hotel. All the hotel car parks have special areas reserved for guests with reduced mobility. Both wheelchair and stroller rentals are available at the Disney Parks, just inside the main entrances. Specially adapted minibuses circulate between the hotels and the Disney Parks.

Within the Parks

Disabled visitors (and up to three companions) get special access to most attractions and restaurants, and there are discounted day pass rates for

Top tips

► Despite Disney's best efforts, not all of the Parks' pathways are fully wheelchair-friendly.
► Cast members guard special viewing areas along the parade route for guests in wheelchairs.
► Avoid riding the Autopia, Star Tours or Big Thunder Mountain if you have back problems.

wheelchair users. Priority is given for prime positions in Fantasyland and on Main Street, USA, for the shows and parades. Ask a cast member for assistance at any time.

There is a free facility for wheelchair users to collect any purchases they make in the Disney Parks from one central location at the end of the day. A couple of shops feature specially designed dressing-rooms (Les Trésors de Schéhérazade and La Chaumière des Sept Nains). City Hall can issue you with a special card that entitles you to use the designated entrance for special needs guests along with three companions. Disabled guests can remain in their wheelchairs during the following attractions:

Frontierland

The Chaparral Stage
Critter Corral
Rustler Roundup Shootin' Gallery
Thunder Mesa Riverboat Landing

Adventureland

Adventure Isle
Le Passage Enchanté d'Aladdin

Fantasyland

Alice's Curious Labyrinth
Castle Courtyard
Fantasy Festival Stage
La Galerie de la Belle au Bois Dormant
La Tanière du Dragon
Le Théâtre du Château

Discoveryland

Arcade de Jeux Vidéo
Honey, I Shrunk the Audience
Les Mystères du Nautilus
Videopolis
Le Visionarium
La Voie Stellaire

More limited access

The following attractions can accommodate guests able to leave their wheelchairs and walk a short distance unassisted:

Frontierland
Big Thunder Mountain
Phantom Manor

Adventureland
Indiana Jones™ and the Temple of Peril:
Backwards!
Pirates of the Caribbean

Fantasyland
Casey Jr le Petit Train du Cirque
It's a Small World
Le Pays des Contes de Fées
Peter Pan's Flight
Les Pirouettes du Vieux Moulin (closed until
further notice)

Discoveryland
Space Mountain

Walt Disney Studios Park®, Backlot
Moteurs...Action!
Armageddon Special Effects

Walt Disney Studios Park®, Production Courtyard
Television Production Tour
Studio Tram Tour
Cinemagique

Walt Disney Studios Park®, Front Lot
Disney Studio 1

Walt Disney Studios Park®, Animation Courtyard
Art of Disney Animation
Animagique
Flying Carpets over Agrabah

Accessible with assistance
On the following rides, disabled guests will
require assistance from a companion:

Walt Disney Studios Park®, Backlot
Rock 'n' Roller Coaster Starring Aerosmith

Main Street, USA
Disneyland Railroad
Horse-drawn streetcars and motor vehicles

Frontierland
River Rogue Keelboats (closed until further notice)

Fantasyland
Blanche Neige et les Sept Nains
Le Carrousel de Lancelot
Dumbo the Flying Elephant
Mad Hatter's Tea Cups
Les Voyages de Pinocchio

Discoveryland
Autopia
Orbitron
Star Tours

Within Disney® Village
At Buffalo Bill's Wild West Show there are areas
reserved for wheelchair guests. The show is not recommended for those suffering from asthma or respiratory
allergies. At Hurricanes nightclub, an elevator is available for guests in wheelchairs. All cinemas at the
Gaumont Cineplex are wheelchair-friendly.

At the hotels
All seven theme hotels have up to 20 bedrooms
specially adapted for wheelchair guests. There are
wheelchairs for hire from the reception desk.

Catering for specific needs
Sight impaired guests
Free Braille guidebooks of the Disney Parks (in
French or English) are available at City Hall. Guide
dogs are allowed into the Parks although they are
not always permitted on attractions recommended
for sight impaired guests. French and English
Braille menus are available at Planet Hollywood®.

Hearing impaired guests
For groups of hearing impaired guests, guided
tours in sign language can be arranged (allow one
month's notice). The Gaumont Cineplex in Disney®
Village is equipped with magnetic loops.

Visitors with learning difficulties
Many of the more startling attractions not
recommended for young children may prove
equally unsettling for visitors with learning difficulties (see **Safety Restrictions**, p.192).

Language

Also, see **What to eat**, p.162, for help with French menus

Numbers

one *un*
two *deux*
three *trois*
four *quatre*
five *cinq*
six *six*
seven *sept*
eight *huit*
nine *neuf*
ten *dix*
eleven *onze*
twelve *douze*
thirteen *treize*
fourteen *quatorze*
fifteen *quinze*
sixteen *seize*
seventeen *dix-sept*
eighteen *dix-huit*
nineteen *dix-neuf*
twenty *vingt*
twenty-one *vingt-et-un*
twenty-two *vingt-deux*
thirty *trente*
forty *quarante*
fifty *cinquante*
sixty *soixante*
seventy *soixante-dix*
eighty *quatre-vingts*
ninety *quatre-vingt-dix*
one hundred *cent*
one hundred and one *cent-et-un*
one hundred and two *cent-deux*
one thousand *mille*

Days

Monday *lundi*
Tuesday *mardi*
Wednesday *mercredi*
Thursday *jeudi*
Friday *vendredi*
Saturday *samedi*
Sunday *dimanche*

Months

January *janvier*
February *février*
March *mars*
April *avril*
May *mai*
June *juin*
July *juillet*
August *août*
September *septembre*
October *octobre*
November *novembre*
December *décembre*

Time

What time is it? *Quelle heure est-il?*
month *un mois*
week *une semaine*
day *un jour/une journée*
morning *le matin*
afternoon *l'après-midi*
evening *le soir*
today *aujourd'hui*
yesterday *hier*
tomorrow *demain*
soon *bientôt*
later *plus tard*

Transport

airport *un aéroport*
bicycle *une bicyclette/un vélo*
bus stop *un arrêt d'autobus*
bus *un autobus*
railway station *la gare*
train *un train*
platform *un quai*
car *une voiture*
taxi *un taxi*
ticket office *un guichet*
ticket *un billet*
underground/subway *le métro*

Mealtime

bib *un bavoir*
bottle *un biberon*
spoon *une cuillère*
fork *une fourchette*
knife *un couteau*
glass *un verre*
beaker *un gobelet*
cup *une tasse*
plate *une assiette*
another *un/une autre*
small *petit*
hot *chaud*
cold *froid*

menu *la carte*
fixed price menu *le menu*
highchair *une chaise haute*
games *les jeux*
crayon *un crayon*
straw *une paille*

Bedtime

babysitting *le baby-sitting/la garde d'enfants*
bed *un lit*
blanket *une couverture*
bunk beds *les lits superposés*
cot *un lit d'enfant*
twin room *chambre à deux lits*
double room *chambre pour deux personnes*
single room *chambre pour une personne*
interconnecting rooms *les chambres communicantes*

General

baby *un bébé*
child *un enfant*
boy *un garçon*
girl *une fille*
doctor *un médecin*
medicine *le médicament*
nappy/diaper *une couche*
pharmacy *une pharmacie*
pushchair/stroller *une poussette*
open *ouvert*
closed *fermé*
cheap *bon marché*
expensive *cher*
bank *une banque*
entrance *entrée (f)*
exit *sortie*
hospital *un hôpital*
money *l'argent (m)*
policeman *un agent de police*
police station *un commissariat de police*
post office *la poste*
shop *un magasin*
supermarket *un supermarché*
tobacconist *un tabac*
WC *un WC/les toilettes*
men *hommes*
women *femmes*

1

The métro.

2

It's the *Mona Lisa*, the world's most famous painting, painted by Leonardo da Vinci between 1503 and 1506. It now hangs in the Louvre.

3

It was named after its inventor, Dr Joseph–Ignace Guillotin. His aim had been to create a more humane method of execution than the traditional axe, which often took several blows to sever the victim's head from their body, causing a slow-agonizing death. The good doctor's solution to this problem was to increase the force with which the blow was delivered. A razor sharp blade set between two greased wooden runners would, when released, fall with such force that it invariably severed the head at the first attempt. Not only was the guillotine more humane, it was also quicker than previous methods, so that more people could be executed per day than ever before.

4

France defeated Brazil 3–0.

5

Marseille. The National Anthem, called the *Marseillaise*, was the song sung by revolutionaries from Marseille when they marched on Paris in 1792.

6

The Empire State Building in New York, which is a massive 381m (1,250ft) tall.

7

Strange as it may seem, the answer is c. After his defeat at the battle of Waterloo in 1815, Napoleon was exiled to the island of St Helena. He became a recluse spending most of his time indoors, and he was poisoned by the arsenic used to colour the walls green.

8

It was the cart used during the French Revolution to transport condemned prisoners from their cells to the *guillotine*.

9

The answer is a. The Hôtel-Dieu is Paris' oldest hospital. Lack of medical knowledge meant that until the 19th century few patients who checked in checked out again.

10

It's the blue whale. You can see a skeleton of one of these huge beasts in the Musée National d'Histoire Naturelle. At over 30m (100ft) long and weighing over 150 tons, the blue whale is the largest creature that has ever lived, larger even than the dinosaurs.

11

It is called the Latin Quarter because until the early 19th century the university authorities insisted that everyone who lived there spoke only in Latin – and that meant everyone from the professors and students down to the kitchen staff.

12

Henri de Toulouse-Lautrec (1864–1901). You can see some of his paintings in the Musée d'Orsay.

13

A vineyard. The grape harvest is celebrated each year with a parade. The subsequent vintage is then sold for charity.

14

An abattoir. In the early 1900s, until the funding fell through, the government wanted to build a state-of-the-art carcass-cutter on this site. It's doubtful whether it would have attracted the same number of visitors as the Cité des Sciences et de l'Industrie...

15

On the steam train!

16

By gas, and so are the lamps inside the shops.

17

The names of the four steam-powered locomotives are W. E. Cody, C. K. Holliday, G. Washington and Eureka.

18

All of 99, which is a lot on each floor...

19

The paddle boats actually run on rails beneath the water, so the rigmarole of mooring them is all part of the show.

20

Tarzan of the Apes, by Edgar Rice Burroughs.

21

Raiders of the Lost Ark, which was released 3 years before *Indiana Jones™ and the Temple of Doom*.

22

The answer is b. There are approximately 1,200 Audio-Animatronic® figures in the Disney Parks.

23

Jules Verne, especially his book *From the Earth to the Moon*. He is often thought of as the man who 'invented' science fiction.

Index

Main page references are in **bold**; references to maps are in *italic*.

PICK YOUR BRAINS about ...

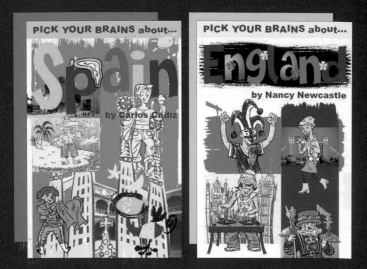

At last enquiring young minds can discover Europe in an entertaining and inventive new series.

CADOGANguides